PRIESTS,
WARRIORS,
AND
CATTLE

HERMENEUTICS
Studies in the History of Religions

GENERAL EDITOR
Kees W. Bolle
UCLA

1. Stephan Beyer, THE CULT OF TARA
2. Edward A. Armstrong, SAINT FRANCIS: NATURE MYSTIC
3. David Kinsley, THE SWORD AND THE FLUTE
4. Marija Gimbutas, THE GODS AND GODDESSES OF OLD EUROPE, 7000-3500 B.C.
5. Henry Duméry, PHENOMENOLOGY AND RELIGION
6. Wendy Doniger O'Flaherty, THE ORIGINS OF EVIL IN HINDU MYTHOLOGY
7. Åke Hultkrantz, THE RELIGIONS OF THE AMERICAN INDIANS
8. Robert D. Pelton, THE TRICKSTER IN WEST AFRICA
9. Kees Bolle, THE BHAGAVADGITA: A NEW TRANSLATION
10. Bruce Lincoln, PRIESTS, WARRIORS, AND CATTLE

PRIESTS, WARRIORS, AND CATTLE

A Study in the Ecology of Religions

Bruce Lincoln

UNIVERSITY OF CALIFORNIA PRESS
Berkeley · Los Angeles · London

Designer:	John C. W. Carroll
Compositor:	Freedmen's Organization
Printer:	Braun-Brumfield
Binder:	Braun-Brumfield
Text:	Compugraphic English (Times Roman)
Display:	Compugraphic English
Cloth:	Holliston Roxite B 53544
Paper:	50 lb P&S offset vellum, B-32

University of California Press
Berkeley and Los Angeles, California

University of California Press, Ltd.
London, England

Library of Congress Cataloging in Publication Data

Lincoln, Bruce.
    Priests, warriors, and cattle. A study in the ecology of religions.

    (Hermeneutics, studies in the history of religions; v. 10)
    Bibliography: p.
    Includes indexes.
    1. Nilotic tribes—Religion. 2. Indo-Iranians—Religion.
3. Cows (in religion, folk-lore, etc.)
4. Nilotic tribes. 5. Indo-Iranians. I. Title. II. Series.
BL2480.N46L56   299´.68   78-68826
ISBN 0-520-03880-0

1 2 3 4 5 6 7 8 9

For Louise

CONTENTS

CONTENTS

LIST OF FIGURES
AND TABLES

ACKNOWLEDGMENTS

While preparing this study it has been my privilege to benefit from the wisdom and experience of a number of outstanding scholars, to whom my debt is great. Without their generous assistance and sage advice, I doubt that my research could even have been completed, and I would like to take this opportunity to thank my teachers: J. A. B. van Buitenen, Carsten Colpe, Paul Friedrich, Eric Hamp, Charles H. Long, and Frank Reynolds. I must also thank Jaan Puhvel, William Malandra, Kees Bolle, and Edgar Polomé, who were kind enough to read and comment on sections of this work, for their invaluable assistance. Marlos Rudie and Ardis Ronnie also have my deepest gratitude for their help in preparing the manuscript for publication, as does Diane Sipes for her extremely skilled and sensitive job of copy editing, and John Feneron for his meticulous proofreading.

Special thanks are due to two people. First, I cannot begin to express my gratitude to my advisor, Mircea Eliade. His suggestions, his guidance, and his support have been of immeasurable value, and his mark is everywhere in my work. Indeed, I have profited more than I ever dared to hope from being able to study under his direction. His insight and genius are available to all in his many books, but his warmth, enthusiasm, and friendship are a particularly treasured memory for me. Second, I must conclude by thanking my wife, Louise—my sternest critic and my greatest inspiration—without whom nothing would have been possible.

ABBREVIATIONS

AB	*Aitareya Brāhmaṇa*	**OIr.**	Old Irish
Av.	Avestan	**ON**	Old Norse
AV	*Atharva Veda*	**OPers.**	Old Persian
Arm.	Armenian	**OPruss.**	Old Prussian
AS	Anglo-Saxon	**Pahl.**	Pahlavi
Bund.	*Indian or Lesser Bundahišn*	**P-I-E**	Proto-Indo-European
Dk.	*Dēnkart*	*Rām.*	*Rāmāyana*
GAv.	Gāthic Avestan	*RV*	*Ṛg Veda*
GBd.	*Greater Bundahišn*	*SB*	*Śatapatha Brāhmaṇa*
Gk.	Greek	**Skt.**	Sanskrit
Goth.	Gothic	**Toch.**	Tocharian
I-E	Indo-European	*TS*	*Taittirīya Saṃhitā*
I-I	Indo-Iranian	*Vd.*	*Vidēvdāt*
KBo	*Keilschrifttexte aus*	*Visp.*	*Vispered*
	Boghazköi	*Y.*	*Yasna*
KUB	*Keilschrifturkunden aus*	**YAv.**	Younger Avestan
	Boghazköi	*Yt.*	*Yašt*
Lat.	Latin		
Lith.	Lithuanian		
Mhb.	*Mahābhārata*		
MPers.	Middle Persian	*	Reconstructed form
OCS	Old Church Slavonic	<	Is derived from
OE	Old English	→	Is transformed to
OHG	Old High German	√	Verbal root

I

INTRODUCTION

In January of 1973, having just finished reading Stig Wikander's brilliant monograph, *Der arische Männerbund*, I had the good fortune to pick up a book by Professor Jacques Maquet entitled *Civilizations of Black Africa*.[1] In particular Maquet's chapter, "The Civilization of the Spear," in which he deals with the tribes of East Africa, was of great interest to me, and I thought that I could recognize a number of similarities between the warrior groups of the East Africans and those of the Indo-Iranians described by Wikander.

Some of these similarities are very general and might be found in any warrior group: the glorification of martial values, the existence of songs praising the valor of great heroes, and the performance of special initiatory rites for the induction of young men into the warrior order. Others, however, seemed more specific: the decoration of weapons with elaborate symbolic designs, the identification of men with beasts of prey, the cultivation of a state of furor by means of meat feasting or use of intoxicating drinks, and the aid given warriors by priests or diviners before a cattle raid, just to name a few examples.[2]

These apparent similarities appealed to my imagination, and I turned to other sources to see if I could learn more about them. It seemed an interesting exercise to lay these two cultures—the one living, the other

1. Stig Wikander, *Der arische Männerbund* (Lund, 1938); and Jacques Maquet, *Civilizations of Black Africa* (London, 1972).
2. See Wikander, *Der arische Männerbund*, pp. 24, 58-60, 74-75, 84; Maquet, pp. 113-19, 126-30, for these similarities.

1

long dead—next to one another, and to examine them for resemblances within their warrior groups.

The project was made even more intriguing by the different types of sources available for study. The East African tribes do not offer any written records but have been studied by some of the finest ethnographers of our day, such as Melville J. Herskovits, E. E. Evans-Pritchard, and Godfrey Lienhardt.[3] In contrast, the Indo-Iranians, who dispersed some time in the third or early in the second millennium b.c., left detailed texts composed in the languages of their descendants, the most important of which for our purposes are the Indian *Rg Veda* and the Iranian *Zend Avesta*.[4] Comparisons between the two sets of texts can allow reconstruction of words that belonged to the Indo-Iranian parent language,[5] and one can also reconstruct myths, rituals, divine names, common occurrences, and ideas.[6] From this evidence, one can derive a fairly clear picture of Indo-Iranian society, and such early scholars as Spiegel, Bernhard Geiger, and Güntert contributed greatly to this study.[7] Lately, as archaeological data have come to light, they have been used by such scholars as Gimbutas, Piggott, and the Allchins as an aid in reconstruction.[8]

The project, as I first conceived it, would be limited to the phenomenon of warrior groups. My hope was that by drawing from these two different

3. Melville J. Herskovits, "The Cattle Complex in East Africa," *American Anthropologist* 28 (1926): 230–72, 361–88, 494–529, 633–64 (this article was based on library research, however, not on first-hand observation); E. E. Evans-Pritchard, *The Nuer* (Oxford, 1940), and *Nuer Religion* (Oxford, 1956); Godfrey Lienhardt, *Divinity and Experience: The Religion of the Dinka* (Oxford, 1961).

4. The text used for the *Rg Veda* has been Theodor Aufrecht, *Die Hymnen des Rigveda*, 2 vols. (Bonn, 1877). Two excellent translations now exist: Karl F. Geldner, *Der Rigveda*, 4 vols. (Cambridge, Mass., 1951), and Louis Renou, *Études védiques et paninéennes*, 17 vols. (Paris, 1955–69). And the text used for the *Zend Avesta* is Karl F. Geldner, *Avesta*, 3 vols. (Stuttgart, 1896). The best complete translations to date are James Darmesteter, *Le Zend-Avesta*, 3 vols. (Paris, 1892; repr. 1960), and Fritz Wolf, *Avesta* (Berlin, 1924), but the partial works of Herman Lommel—*Die Gathas des Zarathustra* (Basel, 1971) and *Die Yašts des Awesta* (Göttingen, 1927)—are to be preferred.

5. On the linguistic relation between Indic, Iranian, and Indo-Iranian, see Romano Lazzeroni, "Per una definizione dell'unità indo-iranica," *Studi e Saggi Linguistici* 8 (1968): 131–59.

6. On linguistic paleontology in general, see the pioneer work of Otto Schrader, *Prehistoric Antiquities of the Aryan Peoples* (London, 1890). The reconstruction of myths has most recently been advanced by the work of Georges Dumézil, on which see C. Scott Littleton, *The New Comparative Mythology* (Berkeley, Calif., 1973); and "Georges Dumézil and the Rebirth of the Genetic Model," in *Myth in Indo-European Antiquity* (Berkeley, Calif., 1974), pp. 169–80.

7. Friedrich Spiegel, *Arische Periode und ihre Zustände* (Leipzig, 1887); Bernhard Geiger, *Die Aməša Spəntas* (Vienna, 1916); Hermann Güntert, *Der arische Weltkönig und Heiland* (Halle, 1923).

8. Marija Gimbutas, "The Indo-Europeans: Archaeological Problems," *American Anthropologist* 65 (1963):815–36; and "Proto-Indo-European Culture," in *Indo-European and Indo-Europeans* (Philadelphia, 1970), pp. 155–98; Stuart Piggott, *Prehistoric India to 1000 B.C.* (Baltimore, 1950), p. 248; and *Ancient Europe* (Chicago, 1965), p. 80; Bridget and Raymond Allchin, *The Birth of Indian Civilization* (Baltimore, 1968), p. 145.

societies I might be able to perceive some of the structures that are found in warrior groups in other parts of the world as well, such as North America or Melanesia. I was amazed, however, when I discovered that the similarities between the East Africans and the Indo-Iranians far transcended the matter of warrior bands. In religious matters the resemblances were overwhelming. Both groups had pantheons that focused on celestial sovereigns; both practiced animal sacrifice as the chief ritual act; both had well-established priesthoods; both had groups of martial spirits that were related to the warrior bands; both had myths telling of the creation of cattle; and both had myths of the first cattle raid.

The resemblances were not limited to matters of religion, however. Social organization was also very similar. A priestly class was well established in each case and stood at the head of the social hierarchy. Warriors were also exalted above the general lot and composed a separate social class. Some subgroups were ruled by a king, while in others the leadership was more diffuse.[9] For both East Africans and Indo-Iranians, social organization tended to be on a small scale, and the most important unit of organization was the herding party.[10] This is in keeping with the facts that the two cultures are essentially pastoral and the base of their economies is the possession of cattle.

Given the strength and number of these similarities, it seemed to me that they could not simply be fortuitous. Accordingly, I abandoned my study of warrior societies, and I began to explore in depth the broader scope of resemblances between East African and Proto-Indo-Iranian culture. The first and simplest hypothesis that sprang to mind was that of an historical connection between the groups at an early date, but the facts of the matter seem to rule this out.

As best we can piece together, the Proto-Indo-Europeans, the direct ancestors of the Indo-Iranians, flourished on the South Russian steppes during the fifth, fourth, and third millennia b.c.[11] While other theories have been advanced,[12] the South Russian thesis has been upheld by some

---

9. This is a difficult question. India clearly had kings, as attested by the I-E term *rāj-* (< P-I-E **rēg'-*, comparing Lat. *rēx* and OIr. *rī*), but the tribes of East Iran seem to have been ruled by religious leaders, termed *kavis*. In general, the Avestan terminology for leadership shows many different possibilities but no central authority: viz. lord of a house (*nmānō.paiti-*), lord of a clan (*zantu.paiti-*), and lord of a tribe (*daiŋhu.paiti-*). Similarly, some Nilotic tribes have kings (Shilluk, Lwoo), some have priestly leaders (Dinka, Masai), and some have neither (Nuer).

10. See my "Indo-Iranian **gautra-*," *Journal of Indo-European Studies* 3 (1975):161–71.

11. See Gimbutas, "Proto-Indo-European Culture."

12. The only other theory that is currently accorded any possibility posits an *Urheimat* in the Danubian plain, perhaps stretching as far north as the Ukraine. See P. Bosch-Gimpera, *Les Indo-Européens: Problèmes Archéologiques* (Paris, 1961) for the best statement of this position. See also Herman Hirt, *Indogermanica* (Halle, 1940); Hugh Hencken, "Indo-European Language and Archaeology," *Memoirs of the American Anthropological Association* 84 (1955):48–56; Robert Heine-Geldern, "Comments on Gimbutas' 'The Indo-Europeans: Archaeological Problems,' " *American Anthropologist* 66 (1964):889–93; and

of the finest of the linguists, such as Schrader and Brandenstein, and the archaeologists, such as Childe and Gimbutas, who have studied the question.[13] Most recently, Gimbutas has amassed such a persuasive body of evidence as to have convinced the majority of scholars currently active in the field.

From this home, various groups migrated westward and south-eastward, beginning in the third millennium. The westward-moving groups became the various European tribes: Greeks, Italo-Celts, Germans, and so on,[14] while the group that moved south-eastward is known as the Proto-Indo-Iranians.[15] Whether they passed into Iran via the Caucasus or by following the Oxus and Jaxaertes rivers east of the Caspian is still a matter of some debate, although the latter route seems more likely.[16] In any event, the Indians (or, more precisely, the Indo-Aryans, as these were the forerunners of the historic Indians) were the spearhead of the advance, reaching the northwest corner of India in the mid second millennium B.C.[17] The

Ward H. Goodenough, "The Evolution of Pastoralism and Indo-European Origins," *Indo-European and Indo-Europeans,* pp. 253-66. Convenient summaries of the dispute are available in James Mallory, "A Short History of the Indo-European Problem," *Journal of Indo-European Studies* 1 (1973):21-65; and Anton Scherer, "Hauptprobleme der indogermanischen Altertumskunde," *Kratylos* 1 (1956):3-21.

13. Schrader, *Prehistoric Antiquities,* pp. 437-43; Wilhelm Brandenstein, *Die erste "indogermanische" Wanderung* (Vienna, 1936), pp. 52-53. Note also George L. Trager and Henry Lee Smith, "A Chronology of Indo-Hittite," *Studies in Linguistics* 8 (1950):61-62; V. Gordon Childe, *The Aryans* (New York, 1926); Gimbutas, "The Indo-Europeans" and "Proto-Indo-European Culture." Note that most Indologists have favored this theory; see A. B. Keith, "The Home of the Indo-Europeans," *Indian Historical Quarterly* 13 (1937):4-7; R. N. Dandekar, "The Antecedents and Early Beginnings of the Vedic Period," *Proceedings of the Indian History Conference* 10 (1947):37; T. Burrow, "The Proto-Indo-Aryans," *Journal of the Royal Asiatic Society* (1973):126. The argument of the last, however, is extremely controversial and not fully convincing on all points.

14. Gimbutas, "The Indo-Europeans," pp. 829-33. The Anatolians must be regarded as a third division, separate from the Europeans and the Indo-Iranians.

15. Ibid., pp. 817, 834.

16. Gimbutas, ibid., p. 834, originally held for the Oxus-Jaxaertes route, but under pressure from Heine-Geldern, "Comments," p. 891, she reconsidered her position in "Comments on Indo-Iranians and Tokharians: A Response to R. Heine-Geldern," *American Anthropologist* 66 (1964):893-95. Entry via the Caucasus has again been championed by Bosch-Gimpera, "The Migration Route of the Indo-Aryans," *Journal of Indo-European Studies* 1 (1973):513-17, who relies heavily on Karl Jettmar, "Zur Wanderungsgeschichte der Iranier," *Die Wiener Schule der Völkerkunde* (Vienna, 1956), pp. 327-48. This is not widely accepted among Iranists, however; see Arthur Christensen, "Die Iranier," *Kulturgeschichte des alten Orients* (Munich, 1933), p. 210; Ernst Herzfeld, *Archaeological History of Iran* (London, 1935), pp. 7-8; R. Ghirshman, *Iran* (Baltimore, 1954), p. 63; Richard N. Frye, *The Heritage of Persia* (Cleveland, 1963), pp. 20 f. Jettmar himself has since reconsidered the question and now leaves it open, "Die Steppenkulturen und die Iranier des Plateaus," *Iranica Antiqua* 9 (1972):68, 88.

17. This is the most commonly accepted date; see Piggott, *Prehistoric India,* pp. 255 f.; Louis Renou, *Vedic India* (Calcutta, 1965), pp. 73, 78 f. Heine-Geldern, "The Coming of the Aryans and the End of the Harappa Civilization," *Man* 56 (1956):136-40, has argued for a date around 1200-1000 B.C., but this is not generally accepted and rests on rather scanty evidence.

Iranians occupied the land through which the Indians had passed and were well established in Iran by 1000 B.C.[18] Two other small groups of Indo-Iranians appeared in the Near East as the ruling stratum of the Kassites and the Mitanni,[19] but these groups are most probably to be regarded as small, detached bands of adventurers who penetrated through the Zagros mountains rather than any major portion of the Indo-Iranian group.[20] The final body of the Indo-Iranians were the Scyths, who remained in southern Russia until the pressure of other groups including the Huns forced them to move westward in the second century B.C.[21] Thus, the Indo-Iranians penetrated no further west than the Mitanni kingdom, which flourished in the fifteenth century B.C. and was destroyed in 1350 B.C. It is, however, far from East Africa, and while Mitanni did have relations with the ancient Egyptian empires of its time, there is no reason to suppose that contact with sub-Saharan tribes existed.

East Africa also experienced waves of migrations, but none that might have brought contact with the Indo-Iranians or other Indo-European groups. The original population seems to have been hunters and gatherers of Bushmanoid type, who were largely wiped out by later arrivals to the area, the first of whom were the Southern Cushites, who arrived around 1000 B.C. from the Ethiopian highlands.[22] They in turn were largely wiped out by two other groups who entered in the first millennium B.C., the Bantu, who entered from the south, and the Nilotes, who entered from the north and northwest, especially from the southern Sudan.[23] The Nilotes, who will play the major part in this study, remained a relatively compact

18. The most likely interpretation of the difficult archaeological evidence identifies the entry of the Iranians proper into the Zagros with the Iron I period (1300–1250 B.C.), although they were established in Eastern Iran somewhat earlier. See T. Cuyler Young, "The Iranian Migration into the Zagros," *Iran* 5 (1967):11–34; and M. M. Winn, "Thoughts on the Question of Indo-European Movements in Anatolia and Iran," *Journal of Indo-European Studies* 2 (1974):130–37, although there are points regarding this dating that are still controversial.

19. Most scholars now hold these groups to be strictly Indic, not Indo-Iranian, in origin. See Manfred Mayrhofer, *Die Indo-Arier im alten Vorderasien* (Wiesbaden, 1966), with extensive bibliography. The crucial insights were provided by Paul Thieme, "The 'Aryan' Gods of the Mitanni Treaties," *Journal of the American Oriental Society* 80 (1960):301–17. Recently Annelies Kammenhuber, *Die Arier im vorderen Orient* (Heidelberg, 1968), has sought to revive the theory of the Mitanni as Indo-Iranians, but her points have been answered by Mayrhofer, "Die vorderasiatischen Arier," *Asiatische Studien/Études Asiatiques* 23 (1969):139–54.

20. As argued by I. M. Diakonoff, "Die Arier im vorderen Orient: Ende eines Mythos," *Orientalia* 41 (1972):91–121, along lines anticipated by Georg Morgenstierne, "Indo-European K' in Kafiri," *Norsk Tidsskrift for Sprogvidenskamp* 13 (1945):234–38; and A. B. Keith, "Mitanni, India, and Iran," in *Dr. Modi Memorial Volume* (Bombay, 1930), pp. 81–94.

21. Herzfeld, p. 7.

22. George P. Murdock, *Africa: Its Peoples and their Culture History* (New York, 1959), p. 332; J. E. G. Sutton, "The Settlement of East Africa," in *Zamani: A Survey of East African History* (Nairobi, 1968), pp. 86–88.

23. Murdock, pp. 332–33; Sutton, p. 90.

INTRODUCTION

group until the fifth or sixth century A.D., although they seem to have already divided into three branches by that time: Western Nilotes (Nuer, Dinka, Lwoo), Eastern Nilotes (Masai, Turkana, and so on), and Southern Nilotes (Nandi, Kalenjin), the last of which fell under strong Cushitic influence.[24] In the period following the sixth century, however, the Nilotes exploded across East Africa, driving southward from the Sudan with the Masai leading the way.[25] In later centuries they encountered Arab traders and then the Europeans, but until that time the only non-African group with whom they had contact was the Southern Cushites, who in turn are not known to have had any dealings with the Indo-Europeans.

We can thus rule out any genetic relation or historical contact between the Nilotes and the Indo-Iranians. Similarly, there is no evidence that would support a theory of cultural diffusion. How then could one account for the similarities observed? Or were they, after all, to be considered simply fortuitous?

Another possibility presented itself at this point. Both cultures display economic systems that are based on the possession of cattle. This was one of the first features noticed by ethnographers working with the Nilotes,[26] and it is a characteristic that has long been recognized with regard to the Indo-Iranians, as well as with regard to their Indo-European ancestors and their Indian and Iranian descendants.[27] Cattle have an enormous

24. The old theories of Nilo-Hamites and "Hamitic influence" have now been discredited by Joseph Greenberg, *Studies in African Linguistic Classification* (New Haven, 1955), pp. 44-68. While Greenberg's views are now almost universally accepted, his terminology is somewhat awkward, and I have chosen to use the terms suggested by Christopher Ehret, *Southern Nilotic History* (Evanston, Ill., 1971), p. 3 and note, p. 10.

25. Murdock, p. 333.

26. See Herskovits; J. P. Crazzolara, "Die Bedeutung des Rindes bei den Nuer," *Africa* 7 (1934):300-20; and Evans-Pritchard, *The Nuer*, chap. 1, "Interest in Cattle."

27. On the Indo-Iranians, see, Spiegel, pp. 66-69. The Indo-Iranians have long been recognized as the group that best preserved Indo-European pastoralism. See Brandenstein, *Die erste "indogermanische" Wanderung*, pp. 25-29; Otto Schrader, *Die Indogermanen* (Leipzig, 1935), pp. 29-33; Peter von Bradke, *Über Methode und Ergebnisse der arischen Alterthumswissenschaft* (Giessen, 1890), pp. 190-94; R. A. Crossland, "Indo-European Origins," *Past and Present* 12 (1957):24. On their Indo-European ancestors, see Schrader, *Prehistoric Antiquities*, pp. 284-87; Albert Carnoy, *Les Indo-Européens* (Brussels, 1921), pp. 93 f. (Note, however, his misinterpretation of *pek'u-*, "livestock," as "sheep," and his consequent overestimation of the importance of this animal); Childe, p. 82; Hirt, p. 186; Giacomo Devoto, *Origini Indeuropee* (Florence, 1962), p. 262; Gimbutas, "Indo-European Culture," p. 157. On their Indian descendants, see Piggott, *Prehistoric India*, p. 266; Hem Chandra Joshi, *Recherches sur les conceptions économiques et politiques aux Indes anciennes* (Paris, 1928), pp. 42-44; Dandekar, "Antecedents of the Vedic Period," p. 36; Ludwig Alsdorf, *Beiträge zur Geschichte von Vegetarismus und Rinderverehrung in Indien* (Wiesbaden, 1961). And on their Iranian descendants, see Roland G. Kent, "Cattle Tending and Agriculture in the Avesta," *Journal of the American Oriental Society* 39 (1919):329-32; Wilhelm Geiger, *Civilization of the Eastern Iranians in Ancient Times*, 2 vols. (London, 1885):1:167-74; H. H. van der Osten, *Die Welt der Perser* (Stuttgart, 1956), p. 42; Frye, p. 22.

economic importance and constitute the measure of wealth, while supplying the basis for exchange relations.[28] This value is no doubt largely based
on their role as the chief source of food—furnishing milk, milk-products,
meat, and even blood for drinking.[29] Their value, however, goes beyond
mere food production, since their skin furnishes leather for clothing,
blankets, and thongs; their bones furnish material for tools; their dung
furnishes fuel for fires; and their urine is commonly used as a disinfectant.[30]
As is natural in such societies, cattle are generally seen as the source of all
goods.

Their importance transcends their worth in hard economic terms, however, for cattle come to play a major role in social transactions. They serve
as bridewealth[31] and wergeld,[32] in the belief that only cattle can fully make
up for the loss of a valued human member of society. Cattle are in fact an
integral part of the community, and for Nilotes and Indo-Iranians the
social order is thought to include both people *and* cattle,[33] not merely
people. Cattle are the object of intense affection, and it would seem that
the greatest desire of any herdsman is the possession of many cattle.

This longing for cattle has produced an interesting development: the
organized theft of cattle from neighboring tribes. Warfare becomes strictly
the quest for cattle, and virtually no other booty is taken.[34] The tribes
under study have become extremely efficient in their raiding, and the military groups that first prompted my interest are, in fact, specialized social
organs for the procurement of cattle; their myths, moreover, reflect this
prime interest.[35]

In addition to economic, social, and emotional importance, cattle have

---

28. Schrader, *Prehistoric Antiquities*, p. 259; Spiegel, p. 69; Herskovits, pp. 257–58, 266.

29. Spiegel, pp. 67–68; W. Geiger, p. 168; Om Prakash, *Food and Drinks in Ancient India* (Delhi, 1961), pp. 12–18; Evans-Pritchard, *The Nuer*, pp. 21, 26; R. W. E. Lewis, "The Maasai Traditional Way of Life," *Nairobi: City and Region* (London, 1967), p. 72.

30. Evans-Pritchard, *The Nuer*, pp. 29 f.; W. Geiger, pp. 167–74; von Bradke, *Über Methode*, p. 163; Schrader, *Die Indogermanen*, pp. 23–29; E. Wilhelm, *On the Use of the Urine of Oxen According to the Precepts of the Avesta* (Bombay, 1889).

31. Herskovits, pp. 361 ff.; Schrader, *Die Indogermanen*, pp. 23–24; Carnoy, p. 94.

32. Evans-Pritchard, *The Nuer*, pp. 155–56; Lienhardt, p. 25; Schrader, *Die Indoger-manen*, p. 24; Rudolf von Roth, "Wergeld im Veda," *Zeitschrift der deutschen morgen-landischen Gesellschaft* 41 (1881):672–76; Leopold von Schroeder, "Indogermanisches Wergeld," in *Festgruss an Rudolf von Roth* (Stuttgart, 1893), pp. 49–52.

33. Lienhardt, p. 20; Jakob Wackernagel, "Indoiranica: Zum Dualdvandva," *Zeitschrift für vergleichende Sprachforschung* 43 (1910):295–98; Emile Benveniste, "Sur quelques *dvandvas* avestiques," *Bulletin of the School of Oriental and African Studies* 8 (1935–37):405–408.

34. Herskovits, pp. 258, 270; Maquet, pp. 117–18; Joshi, p. 43; Geo Widengren, *Hochgottglaube im alten Iran* (Uppsala, 1938), pp. 329–30.

35. Evans-Pritchard, *The Nuer*, p. 125; A. Venkantasubbiah, "On Indra's Winning of Cows and Waters," *Zeitschrift der deutschen morgenlandischen Gesellschaft* 115 (1965):120–33 provides a convenient listing of many of the Vedic examples of cattle raiding, although his interpretation of them is unacceptable.

8

yet another role: they form the very basis of the religious system, for cattle are the sacrificial animal par excellence, and sacrifice is the central ritual in East Africa, India, and Iran.[36] The greatest honor and service men offer their gods is the presentation of an ox (cows tend not to be used), and by this action they hope to ensure their own well-being. Lesser animals may be substituted for the ox if a man is poor, but these are always thought of and referred to as cattle, for cattle are the only truly suitable victim.[37]

Given this crucial importance of cattle to both cultures, the comparison between the Nilotes and the Indo-Iranians (or even Indo-Europeans) has been suggested fairly often in the past. V. Gordon Childe was most direct: "In my opinion the state of things observed among many of the cow-keeping tribes of the Sudan and other parts of Africa approximates most closely the primitive Aryan economy."[38] H. S. Nyberg was no less direct in pointing to the Shilluk and other herding peoples of East Africa as "in sozialer Hinsicht den altiranischen Stämme sehr nahe."[39] Others, such as Widengren, Piggott, Lommel, and Duchesne-Guillemin,[40] have suggested the comparison, but as yet no systematic study has been made. Rather, these authors have preferred to make use of African materials in order to explicate specific points in Indo-European or Indo-Iranian studies. With the exception of Widengren, whose study is more broadly based, all of them have simply assumed the validity of the comparison and utilized it to shore up a weak point in an argument, or as a means of getting at an otherwise inexplicable feature of myth, ritual, or herding practice.

This kind of usage would seem to be premature, not to mention somewhat cavalier. For while all have intuited the validity of the comparison of East Africans to Indo-Iranians, no one has ever bothered to demonstrate it in any conclusive way. This may be largely because until quite recently the method for doing so was simply not available. One could explicate the social, cultural, and economic bases of religion within one unified area according to the cultural area theories developed by American anthropologists such as Kroeber and Herskovits,[41] but when one turned to the

36. Evans-Pritchard, *Nuer Religion*, pp. 248–71; Lienhardt, p. 10; R. W. E. Lewis, p. 72; Hermann Oldenberg, *Die Religion des Veda* (Berlin, 1894), p. 355; Mary Boyce, "Zoroaster the Priest," *Bulletin of the School of Oriental and African Studies* 33 (1970):22–25.
37. Evans-Pritchard, *Nuer Religion*, p. 202; Jacques Duchesne-Guillemin, "Miettes iraniennes," in *Hommages à Georges Dumézil* (Brussels, 1960), pp. 98–99.
38. Childe, p. 84.
39. H. S. Nyberg, *Die Religionen des alten Iran* (Leipzig, 1938), p. 77.
40. Widengren, *Hochgottglaube*, pp. 3–4; Piggott, *Ancient Europe*, p. 235; Herman Lommel, *Der arische Kriegsgott* (Frankfurt, 1939), pp. 62–66; J. Duchesne-Guillemin, "Autres miettes," in *Iranian Studies presented to Kaj Barr* (Copenhagen, 1966), pp. 73–74.
41. See Harold E. Driver, *The Contribution of A. L. Kroeber to Culture Area Theory and Practice* (Baltimore, 1962) for a summary. Herskovits, pp. 230 ff., places himself firmly in this tradition.

problem of comparing apparently similar culture areas, the field was almost entirely monopolized by the German and Austrian anthropologists of the *Kulturkreise* school, headed by Schmidt, Graebner, and Frobenius.[42]

Implicit in this school were two fundamental suppositions that obstructed clear analysis of the issues. One was evolutionism and the other was cultural diffusionism. The first attempted to see an almost unilinear process of development among all peoples and derived, for example, all herders from the hunters-and-gatherers who preceded them.[43] The second attempted to account for virtually all culture change and all deviations from the expected norm as the result of direct contact and transmission of cultural traits from one group to another.

The problem with these suppositions, beyond the specific test of whether they are valid for any particular case, is that they both contain a historical bias. They focus on issues of development—how things came to be as they are—rather than on describing accurately how things are at the moment of observation. Without such accurate description, accurate analysis is impossible. Often one may be led into improper comparisons, from which tainted findings can be the only result. This, unfortunately, was the case with the work of Wilhelm Koppers,[44] who vastly overemphasized the importance of the horse sacrifice for the Indo-Europeans and was thus led to compare them with the Turco-Mongols despite the fact that these are true nomads who range great distances, while the Indo-Europeans were semi-settled pastoralists who moved only relatively short distances at a time.[45]

Within the past fifteen years, however, the Swedish ethnologist and historian of religions, Ake Hultkrantz, has proposed a daring new means of attack on the problem of comparing religions rooted in similar cultures.[46]

42. See Wilhelm Schmidt, "Das System der Kulturkreise," *Wege der Kulturen* (St. Augustin, 1964), pp. 3–11; Fritz Graebner, *Das Weltbild der Primitiven* (Munich, 1924); Leo Frobenius, "Discussion of the Method of Cultural History," in *Leo Frobenius: An Anthology* (Wiesbaden, 1973), p. 14.

43. See, e.g., Wilhelm Schmidt, "Das Eigentum im Primarkulturkreis der Herdenviehzuchter Asiens und Afrikas," in *Wege der Kulturen* (St. Augustin, 1964), p. 217, for an example of the kind of errors this theory invites.

44. Wilhelm Koppers, "Die Religion der Indogermanen in ihren kulturhistorischen Beziehungen," *Anthropos* 24 (1929):1073–89; and "Pferdeopfer und Pferdekult der Indogermanen," *Wiener Beiträge zur Kulturkunde und Linguistik* 4 (1936):279–411.

45. The Turco-Mongols, in fact, own no cattle and are able to maintain their mobility only because of this fact. Even Schmidt, "Das Eigentum," p. 206, insists on the separation of horse herders and cattle herders. The I-E relationship to horses and cattle is somewhat similar to that of the North American Plains Indians to horses and buffalo: the former was highly important and much employed, but the latter was the means of subsistence. See Frank Gilbert Roe, *The Indian and the Horse* (Oklahoma, 1955), p. 196. There is, of course, the major difference that the I-E cattle were domestic, while the Indian's buffalo were not. Only the earliest Indo-Europeanists tended to see the Indo-Europeans as nomadic. Generally, since P. Giles, "The Aryans," in *The Cambridge History of India*, Vol. 1 (Cambridge, 1929), p. 60, most have recognized them as semi-settled pastoralists.

46. Ake Hultkrantz, "An Ecological Approach to Religion," *Ethnos* 31 (1966): 131–50; and "Ecology of Religion: Its Scope and Methodology," *Review of Ethnology* 4 (1974): 1–12.

Starting with the insight that religion is rooted in culture, and following J. H. Steward in seeing culture as rooted in environment,[47] Hultkrantz has argued for what he calls "an ecological approach to religion."[48] He argues that just as there are "types of culture" commonly recognized by anthropology, such as desert nomad and arctic hunting, so also are there "types of religion" that are intimately related to and in fact formed by the culture type in which they are found. He is very specific on this point and avoids any notion of historical contact or evolution in his theories: "The type of religion is in its essence timeless: in principle it should occur wherever ecological and technological conditions of a similar level and integration appear."[49] His goal is to establish these types of religion and to describe their essential features, drawing comparisons between cultures that may have no geographical or historical relation to one another but whose ecologies are similar.[50] It is just this sort of comparison that I would propose.

For Hultkrantz, the most important feature to be considered in making comparisons and in identifying cross-cultural types of religion is the means of subsistence a people employs.[51] As we have seen, cattle keeping fills this role for the Nilotes and the Indo-Iranians. Second, he feels that the usual unit of social organization that characterizes a culture must be considered.[52] Again, our two groups would seem comparable; while they have both developed such institutions as priesthood and warrior bands (kingship also appearing among the Indo-Iranians and some Nilotic groups such as the Shilluk), the fundamental unit remains the herding party. Given Hultkrantz's criteria, it would seem that we have a perfect case for study.

There is one principle on which Hultkrantz is insistent, however, and it is important to bear it in mind. Ecologically based comparisons cannot properly be used to establish single features of religions, such as the belief in a supreme being, the practice of cultic dances, and the like. These are far too fickle and may or may not appear in almost any type of environment. Rather, ecological interpretation aims at the organization of such facts into patterns and structures. It has as its goal the elucidation of whole systems of religious belief and behavior, not mere details.[53]

Thus I will focus on the separate cultures separately, respecting their individual integrity and considering them within their own contexts before venturing on conclusions of a comparative nature. In truth, I will be

47. See Julian Haynes Steward, *Theory of Culture Change* (Urbana, Ill., 1955).
48. Hultkrantz, "Ecology of Religion," p. 3.
49. Hultkrantz, "Ecological Approach to Religion," pp. 147–48.
50. Ibid., p. 131.
51. Hultkrantz, "Ecology of Religion," p. 5.
52. Ibid., p. 2.
53. Ibid., p. 2.

INTRODUCTION

undertaking not one, but three studies: the nature of the East African Nilotic religious system (Chapters 2 and 3), the nature of the Indo-Iranian religious system (Chapters 4 to 6), and the similarities between them (Chapter 7).

With regard to the first two, the differing nature of the available data will influence the means of approach. Since the Nilotes have been observed at first hand and their culture needs no reconstruction, the study can be based on ethnological reports, drawing information from several related tribes and numerous reporters, thus assuring a broad base for the investigation.

The Indo-Iranian side of the study will, of course, be somewhat more complex than the Nilotic side, since it involves the intricate work of reconstruction. As we have no Indo-Iranian texts per se from which to work, but only Indian or Iranian texts dating to later periods, I shall rely on eliciting correspondences from these two daughter cultures. Thus, the demonstration that a given feature exists in both India and Iran will be taken to prove that it was present in the Proto-Indo-Iranian period unless there is strong reason to suspect that it was transmitted directly from one group to the other at a later date.[54] Demonstration that the feature exists in other Indo-European groups will indicate that it was present even earlier, dating back to the Proto-Indo-European period.

Such reconstruction has been enormously successful in the area of linguistics, where systematic comparison has been able to reestablish not only numerous Indo-European words, but also much of the basic grammatical structure of the Proto-Indo-European language.[55] A good deal of the work in Chapters 4 to 6 will be concerned with word study. If we can, for example, establish a word for "sacrifice," then we may assume the practice of sacrifice. But reconstruction can go beyond mere word study, and I hope to be able to show the nature of Indo-Iranian deities, myths, rituals, and social organization as well, for these are crucial to any study of religion.[56] In all cases, however, I hope to preserve the rigor necessary

54. For instance, were the name of the Buddha to show up in a Middle Persian text, we could not conclude that he was a figure of Indo-Iranian origin. Clearly the age of the texts involved, the nature of later Indian and Iranian contacts, and other features will influence our judgment on whether given resemblances justify reconstruction of a proto-form and supposition of a common origin.

55. On linguistic reconstruction, see Henry M. Hoenigswald, *Language Change and Linguistic Reconstruction* (Chicago, 1960); Antoine Meillet, *La méthode comparative en linguistique historique* (Paris, 1966); and *Introduction à l'étude comparative des langues indo-européennes* (University, Alabama, 1964).

56. Briefly, there are four major theories at present on the nature of Indo-Iranian religion, all of which focus almost entirely on the nature of the pantheon, although two take account of social structure. The four are: (1) that the I-I deities are personified abstractions of a moral nature (Paul Thieme, *Mitra and Aryaman* [New Haven, Conn.: 1957]); (2) that a cosmic dualism is expressed in the pantheon (F. B. J. Kuiper, "Some Observations on Dumézil's Theory," *Numen* 8 [1961]:34–45; "The Ancient Aryan Verbal Contests," *Indo-Iranian Journal* 4 [1960]:217–81; "The Bliss of Aša," *Indo-Iranian Journal* 8 [1964]:96–129;

for linguistic reconstruction, systematically comparing Indian and Iranian evidence in the hope of reaching back to the earlier period of their common history.

It must be stressed that the studies of Nilotes and Indo-Iranians are fully separable. Each has its own data and its own methods, and material from the one will not be introduced into the other. At all costs, reasoning such as "In East Africa . . . , therefore among the Indo-Iranians . . ." will be avoided. Such a statement proves nothing and only serves to confuse the issue. Similarity between the two religious systems is that which is to be proven, and to do this we must first study each system in its own right.

Ultimately the goal in both cases will be the same: the elucidation of the religious system of a culture whose economy is based on the keeping of cattle. It is this ecological and socioeconomic similarity that allows us to move to comparison in the final chapter. For the question I am raising is in the last analysis that of the relation between culture and religion. Given similar cultures, are religions similar as well? This study is of course far too small in scope to answer a question of such magnitude. It is, rather, just one case study relevant to this major issue, and many more will have to follow before the issue is finally resolved.

---

and "The Basic Concept of Vedic Religion," *History of Religions* 15 [1975]:107-20); (3) that the pantheon is the projection of the household (H. W. Bailey, "The Second Stratum of the Indo-Iranian Gods," *Mithraic Studies* [Manchester, 1975], pp. 1-20); (4) that the pantheon is the projection of a tripartite class system (Georges Dumézil, *Naissance d'Archanges* [Paris, 1945]), this last being based on a broader theory of Indo-European religions. Each theory has its own difficulties, but they share the problem that they are all too much concerned with the gods and not enough with myth, ritual, and the other aspects of religion.

II

THE CATTLE CYCLE IN EAST AFRICA

Since Melville J. Herskovits's epoch-making work, "The Cattle Complex in East Africa,"[1] the research of many ethnologists has borne out his recognition of the crucial importance of cattle in this area. Studies focusing on the role of cattle have been conducted among the Gogo, the Karimojon, the Lwoo, the Nandi, the Pakot, the Sebei, the Dodoth, the Jie, and the Turkana[2]—all reaffirming Herskovits's central point. But among the tribes of this "cattle complex" area—the area Maquet dubbed "the civilization of the spear"[3]—those which have been subjected to the most exhaustive study have been the Nuer, Dinka, and Masai.[4]

1. Herskovits, "Cattle Complex."
2. Peter Rigby, *Cattle and Kinship Among the Gogo* (Ithaca, N.Y., 1969), and "The Symbolic Role of Cattle in Gogo Ritual," in *The Translation of Culture* (London, 1971), pp. 257–92; on the Karimojon, see K. A. Gourley, "The Ox and Identification," *Man* 7 (1972):244–54; Walter Odede, "Luo Customs with Regard to Animals," *Journal of the East Africa and Uganda Natural History Society* 72 (1942):127–35; G. W. B. Huntingford, "Some Aspects of Nandi Stock Raising," *Journal of the East Africa and Uganda Natural History Society* 50 (1933):250–62; Harold K. Schneider, "The Subsistence Role of Cattle Among the Pakot," *American Anthropologist* 59 (1957):278–300; on the Sebei, see Walter Goldschmidt, *Kambuya's Cattle* (Berkeley, Calif., 1969); on the Dodoth, see Elizabeth Marshall Thomas, *Warrior Herdsmen* (New York, 1965); on the Jie and Turkana, see P. H. Gulliver, *The Family Herds* (London, 1955).
3. Maquet, pp. 114–32.
4. The most important books on the Nuer are E. E. Evans-Pritchard, *The Nuer*, *Nuer Religion*, and *Kinship and Marriage Among the Nuer* (Oxford, 1951); J. P. Crazzolara, *Zur Gesellschaft und Religion der Nueer* (Vienna, 1953); and P. P. Howell, *A Manual of Nuer Law* (London, 1954). On the Dinka, see Lienhardt; Francis Madin Deng, *The Dinka of the Sudan* (New York, 1972), *Tradition and Modernization: A Challenge for Law Among the Dinka of the Sudan* (New Haven, Conn.: 1971), and *Africans of Two Worlds: The Dinka in Afro-Arab Sudan* (New Haven, Conn.: 1978). There are two major books on the

14

In fact, the Nuer and Dinka might almost be studied as two units of one tribe, for it now seems certain that the Nuer were originally a clan or subtribe within the Dinka.[5] Apparently they were members of a warrior clan who at some unknown date became better organized than their fellow tribesmen, broke away, and expanded to form an independent tribe.[6] Many similarities appear in the two separate peoples that can be traced to their former unity, but as the Nuer seem to have originally all been warriors, their religious system lacks some of the priestly elements found among the Dinka.[7] I will treat evidence from both tribes, but on the matter of priestly affairs I will focus primarily on the Dinka.

With regard to the Masai, supplementary evidence from the Baraguyu (who seem to be a subbranch of the Masai)[8] will also be included—because of their cattle songs, which are extremely interesting and have recently been recorded.[9]

The Importance of Cattle

In a purely practical sense, cattle are of unique importance to the tribes of East Africa. Although fish and agricultural products are eaten to a certain extent, milk and meat form the chief, and in some cases the only, elements of the diet.[10] Cattle dung is used for plaster in construction and fuel for the smudge fires that ward off mosquitoes; urine serves as the principal disinfectant. Skins go to make beds, trays, bags, tethering cords, and shields. Bones are fashioned into spoons and tools. Ultimately, almost all the objects of material culture are derived from cattle.[11]

As a partial result of this, cattle are highly valued and in fact become

Masai: A. C. Hollis, *The Masai: Their Language and Folklore* (Oxford, 1905); and M. Merker, *Die Masai* (Berlin, 1904). For a recent listing of articles, see Alan H. Jacobs, "A Bibliography of the Masai," *African Studies* 8 (1965):40-60.

5. This was the original suspicion of Howell, *Manual of Nuer Law,* p. 7; Evans-Pritchard, *The Nuer,* p. 3; and C. G. and Brenda Z. Seligman, *Pagan Tribes of the Nilotic Sudan* (London, 1932), p. 206. It has now been argued conclusively by Peter J. Newcomer, "The Nuer are Dinka," *Man* 7 (1972):5-11; and Maurice Glickman, "The Nuer and the Dinka: A Further Note," *Man* 7 (1972):586-94.

6. This is the essence of the Newcomer-Glickman thesis. The groundwork for it was laid in Marshall D. Sahlins, "The Segmentary Lineage: An Organization of Predatory Expansion," *American Anthropologist* 63 (1961):322-45.

7. This follows from the Newcomer and Sahlins articles. The type of expansion experienced by the Nuer could only be possible for a warrior clan that had gained some form of military superiority to its neighbors.

8. T. O. Beidelman, "The Baraguyu," *Tanganyika Notes and Records* 54 (1960):276.

9. T. O. Beidelman, "Some Baraguyu Cattle Songs," *Journal of African Languages* 4 (1965):1-18.

10. Crazzolara, "Bedeutung des Rindes," pp. 303-304; Evans-Pritchard, *The Nuer,* pp. 21-28; Lienhardt, pp. 4-5. Milk and meat are not only the major foods but are considered the most "noble." Masai ideology holds that one should eat nothing else and that this was done in former times. Hollis, p. 319.

11. Evans-Pritchard, *The Nuer,* pp. 28-30; Lienhardt, pp. 4-5; Deng, *The Dinka,* p. 3; Crazzolara, "Bedeutung des Rindes," pp. 301-303.

the measure of a man's wealth as well as the basic currency or means of exchange.[12] Moreover, they are the measure of prestige,[13] and, as Merker observed, the highest good fortune imaginable to a Masai is to have as many cattle as possible. His every thought and deed is directed to increasing the size of his herd, as this more than anything else will enhance his standing in the community.[14]

As a type of currency, cattle are used in all social transactions, supplying the main substance of bridewealth, blood money, inheritances, and compensation for incest or adultery.[15] Cattle do not function merely as the means of exchange, however, although that is certainly true in part. But in a certain sense cattle are also seen as equal to people, forming one half of a balanced social equation. No number of sheep or goats could suffice for bridewealth, for "only cattle can really restore to a person or group what has been lost in the value of a human member."[16] In effect, all discussions of a social exchange turn out to be discussions of cattle, and as Evans-Pritchard has put it, "their social idiom is a bovine idiom."[17]

Underlying this economic and social value of cattle is the tremendous sentimental attachment of the Nilotic peoples to their herds. Cattle are their constant companions from birth onward, and as such they are much beloved. A text recorded by Hollis reports: "The Masai love their cattle very much, and consider nothing in the world is of equal value. As with people, each cow is known by name."[18] Songs are composed to the cattle,[19]

12. Evans-Pritchard, *The Nuer*, pp. 28–30; B. Bernardi, "The Age-System of the Masai," *Annali Lateranensi* 18 (1955):261; L. James, "The Kenya Masai," *Africa* 12 (1939): 56–57. James' article is the most fascinating in this respect. As an administrator, he tried to deal with the problems that arose from the value Masai placed on cattle. Since more cattle were seen to equal more wealth, the Masai always tried to increase the size of their herds. While this merely led to expansion in precolonial days in order to accommodate the growth of the herds, the limits placed on expansion by the formation of the Masai reserve led to serious overstocking. James concluded that the only solution to this problem was reeducation of the Masai to the value of fewer but better cattle, but he realized that given the strength of Masai opinions on this subject, the task was most difficult. See especially p. 63. On the Dinka, see Hugh O'Sullivan, "Dinka Laws and Customs," *Journal of the Royal Anthropological Institute* 40 (1910):173.

13. Evans-Pritchard, *Nuer Religion*, p. 248; Crazzolara, "Bedeutung des Rindes," p. 308; Merker, p. 157; O'Sullivan, p. 173.

14. Merker, p. 157.

15. On bridewealth, see Evans-Pritchard, *The Nuer*, pp. 17, 20, 25, and passim; Deng, *The Dinka*, pp. 2–3; R. W. E. Lewis, p. 71; L. S. B. Leakey, "Some Notes on the Masai of Kenya Colony," *Journal of the Royal Anthropological Institute* 60 (1930):203; on blood money, see Evans-Pritchard, *The Nuer*, pp. 217 f.; Seligmans, p. 137; Deng, *The Dinka*, p. 3; on inheritance, see Howell, *Manual of Nuer Law*, passim; and on compensation, see ibid.; Evans-Pritchard, *Nuer Religion*, pp. 185–7.

16. Lienhardt, p. 25.

17. Evans-Pritchard, *The Nuer*, p. 19.

18. Hollis, pp. 288–89.

19. Evans-Pritchard, *The Nuer*, p. 46; Beidelman, "Some Baraguyu Cattle Songs." Now see especially Francis Mading Deng, *The Dinka and Their Songs* (Oxford, 1973).

and conversation dwells more on the animals than anything else.[20] They are decorated, paraded, and lovingly cared for, and the Dinka, who term themselves "lords of men," gladly admit that they are "slaves of cattle."[21]

It must not be thought that this affection has its roots in the economic value of cattle; rather, it is more likely to be the other way around. Cattle are valued in large measure because they are loved and not simply vice versa. This can be seen from the fact that among the Masai there are two main breeds of cattle. The cows of one variety give more milk and thus have greater economic and practical value. The other strain, however, has longer horns and is thought to be more beautiful; as a result, the latter is more highly valued.[22]

All this serves to validate Herskovits's original observation that throughout the East African area the orienting feature is the presence of cattle.[23] The structure of society itself is built on this feature, and, as we shall see, it has major consequences for the nature of the religious system. This of course is almost inevitable, for society and religion are always interdependent and ultimately inseparable. In consideration of this, I am inclined to view religion as the ideology that accounts for the structures of the social world and for man's actions within that world. For the Nilotic peoples, just as the social idiom is an idiom of cattle, the religious idiom is one of cattle also. This will be seen from an examination of the religious system of these tribes, an examination that we may begin by looking at the belief in a celestial sovereign.

The Celestial Sovereign

In the pantheon of the Nuer, Dinka, and Masai, the most important position is occupied by the god on high who created the world and who watches over it. He is known as Kwoth to the Nuer, Ngai to the Masai, and Nhialic to the Dinka.[24] The Nuer term means simply "god," "spirit,"[25] while that of the Masai is the same as their word for "rain."[26] The Dinka term is perhaps the most interesting of the three, however, in that it is a locative form of the word for "sky," literally meaning "in the sky," or "in

---

20. Evans-Pritchard, *Nuer Religion,* p. 248. In this light, many authors have pointed to the huge vocabulary possessed by Nilotic tribes to describe different types of cattle: Merker, pp. 161, 170–71; Lienhardt, p. 10; Evans-Pritchard, *Nuer Religion,* p. 248.

21. Deng, *The Dinka,* p. 2.

22. Daryll Forde, "The Masai: Cattle Herders on the East African Plateau," in *Habitat, Economy, and Society* (London, 1946), p. 295.

23. Herskovits, p. 247.

24. On the Nuer, see Crazzolara, *Zur Gesellschaft und Religion,* p. 61; Evans-Pritchard, *Nuer Religion,* p. 1; on the Masai, see Merker, p. 196; on the Dinka, see Lienhardt, p. 29.

25. Evans-Pritchard, *Nuer Religion,* p. 1.

26. Hollis, p. 264; D. Storrs Fox, "Further Notes on the Masai of Kenya Colony," *Journal of the Royal Anthropological Institute* 60 (1930):461.

the above."[27] This also sheds light on the frequent form used by the Nuer, *Kwoth a nhial,* "spirit who is in the sky."[28]

As he is located in the above, all the celestial phenomena come to be associated with him. For the Nuer, his realm takes in the heavenly bodies, their movements and actions.[29] He himself is sometimes spoken of as falling in the rain or being in the lightning and thunder.[30] In one instance the rainbow was referred to as the necklace of Kwoth.[31] Similarly, among the Masai, Ngai is associated with the sun and clouds[32] and is closely related to the rain. It would be a mistake, however, to view this god as identical with the sky. The sky is his location but not his nature.[33] The fact that he is conceived of as being "on high" serves to emphasize his transcendence but does not rule out his proximity.

In the first place, he is seen as the distant and powerful creator of the earth and everything in it.[34] At the time of his act of creation he established the world order, which he preserves and watches over in the present.[35] There is a myth among the Nuer, Dinka, and Masai telling that the god was much closer to men in the time of the beginnings and was connected to the earth by means of a rope or cord (a strip of hide in the Masai version), which broke, and this primordial event explains his present distance.[36] He is still easily accessible, however, and can be reached through prayer or sacrifice,[37] either by ordinary men[38] or by ritual specialists.[39] He

27. Lienhardt, p. 29.
28. Evans-Pritchard, *Nuer Religion,* p. 1.
29. Ibid., p. 3.
30. Ibid., p. 2.
31. Ibid.
32. Merker, p. 197.
33. Evans-Pritchard, *Nuer Religion,* pp. 1-2; Ibrahim Bedri, "More Notes on the Padang Dinka," *Sudan Notes and Records* 29 (1948):42; Lienhardt, p. 32.
34. Nhialic is also known as Acek, "he who created," Bedri, "More Notes," p. 42.
35. Merker, p. 196; Crazzolara, *Zur Gesellschaft und Religion,* p. 61; Lienhardt, p. 42.
36. Hollis, pp. 268-69; Crazzolara, *Zur Gesellschaft und Religion,* p. 68; Lienhardt, pp. 33-34; Evans-Pritchard, *Nuer Religion,* p. 10, regards this myth as Dinka in origin.
37. Crazzolara, *Zur Gesellschaft und Religion,* p. 71; Evans-Pritchard, *Nuer Religion,* p. 21; H. Fokken, "Gottesanschauungen und religiöse Überlieferungen der Masai," *Archiv für Anthropologie* 43 (1917):243.
38. Among the Nuer, technically any man can sacrifice, but in any important offering the head of a lineage or a ritual specialist (most often the *wut ghok,* "cattle expert") will preside. See Crazzolara, *Zur Gesellschaft und Religion,* p. 75; and "Bedeutung des Rindes," p. 312; Evans-Pritchard, *Nuer Religion,* p. 204. The problem is further complicated by the fact that the Nuer were originally a warrior clan of the Dinka, who have a well-established set of priestly clans who always preside at sacrifice (Lienhardt, pp. 8-9, 109, and passim). Among the Masai, the *laibon,* or priest, presides over most ceremonies (Fokken, p. 245). Thus I am inclined to believe that the less developed priestly system of the Nuer is the result of their schism from the Dinka and must be understood as a conscious reaction against the Dinka priestly organization.
39. Among the Masai the *laibons* all come from a single clan and are religious specialists valued for their ability to intercede with Ngai. They must be present and preside at all religious ceremonies (Hollis, pp. 325-26; Forde, p. 300; Fox, p. 461; Fokken, p. 245). I

is man's protector and friend, and the Nuer know him not only as *Kwoth a nhial,* "spirit who is in the sky," but also as *Kwoth me jale ka ji,* "spirit who walks with you."[40]

Some have gone so far as to describe the Nuer and Masai as "monotheistic" on the grounds of the tremendous importance accorded the celestial sovereign.[41] To do so, however, one must argue away the existence of other deities or spiritual beings. Both Crazzolara and Evans-Pritchard attempted to do this with regard to the Nuer, arguing that such figures as the Spirits of the Air or the Earth Spirits were regarded as far beneath Kwoth, who alone is *Kwoth mediid,* "the true god" or "the great god," while the others are only *kuudh* (plural of *kwoth*) *ti toana* "the small gods."[42] Both scholars felt that all sacrifice is directed to Kwoth, even when he is not the nominal recipient, and Crazzolara quotes an explanation given him by a Nuer man: "As soon as a spirit is called, he then calls to god (Kwoth), 'Grandfather, let the spirit of the children sleep.'"[43] Evans-Pritchard concludes that these other spirits are not independent of Kwoth but are "in some way hypostases of the modes and attributes of a single god."[44]

Such an argument, however, cannot be accepted. In order to see monotheism, one is forced to deny the reality of other deities. Clearly they are not the equals of the celestial sovereign, and it would appear that they are not completely independent of him. But they are real, nonetheless, and they cannot be ignored or argued away. That there is a supreme being is undeniable, but to equate the presence of a supreme being with monotheism is, as Pettazzoni saw, both cultural imperialism and the fallacy of misplaced concreteness.[45] It is almost as if Evans-Pritchard, Crazzolara, and others had learned to respect the religion of the Nuer but felt that they could not as good Christians respect a religion that was not monotheistic.[46] It seems preferable, however, to respect these peoples for what they are

---

have mentioned the Dinka priests, the "masters of the fishing spear," and the Nuer *wut ghok,* "cattle expert," in the previous note.

40. Evans-Pritchard, *Nuer Religion,* p. 8.

41. On the Nuer, see Evans-Pritchard, *Nuer Religion,* pp. 48–52; Crazzolara, *Zur Gesellschaft und Religion,* pp. 61, 71, and passim; on the Masai, see Merker, p. 196; Forde, p. 300; Fox, p. 461.

42. Crazzolara, *Zur Gesellschaft und Religion,* p. 61.

43. Ibid., p. 78. "Zunachst wird der Geist gerufen; darauf wird er zu Gott beten: 'Grossvater, lass den Geist der Kinder schlafen.'"

44. Evans-Pritchard, *Nuer Religion,* p. 49.

45. Raffaele Pettazzoni, "The Formation of Monotheism," in *Essays on the History of Religions* (Leiden, 1967), p. 5.

46. Crazzolara was a Roman Catholic priest and a well-trained anthropologist, but he was deeply influenced by and committed to the theories of Wilhelm Schmidt on the origin of religion in *Urmonotheismus.* Evans-Pritchard's late conversion to Catholicism is well-known, and while one cannot possibly suspect him of skewing his data, it is clear that he had a predisposition to seeing his own beliefs mirrored in those of others in regard to certain issues such as this.

and not try to impose categories foreign to their world upon them. Thus I am content to view both Nuer and Masai as having one sovereign god along with other, lesser deities, who are sometimes seen as his children,[47] and who often fulfill more specialized functions.[48]

It is also possible to err by undervaluing the celestial sovereign, regarding him as *deus otiosus*, a lofty figure who has withdrawn from the world following his original act of creation.[49] Certainly there is some evidence to this effect in the myth of the severed cord that was mentioned above, which can be interpreted as an explanation of the distance of a once-close deity. But the other evidence does not support such a view: Kwoth, Nhialic, and Ngai are all active gods, in the present as in the past. They preserve the world order,[50] protect their people,[51] grant them the good things in life—especially cattle and water[52]—and occasionally punish them with such calamities as sickness, drought, and cattle epidemic.[53] They receive prayers and sacrifice, and among the Masai and Dinka there is a set of priestly specialists who deal with them.[54] Certainly there is nothing otiose here. The gods are neither inaccessible nor impotent. In that the term "high god" is often used to signal a degree of otiosity, I have chosen to avoid its use. Lienhardt, for similar reasons, has called Nhialic "Divinity High."[55] For our purposes, I would prefer to denote the type of deity represented by Nhialic, Kwoth, and Ngai as the celestial sovereign. Such a designation emphasizes the literality of his location in the sky (a Dinka once asked if an airplane could see god)[56] and his function of ruling and directing earthly affairs. His sovereign role, however, has its origin in the act of creation, and it is to the myths of that act that we now turn.

The Myths of Creation

The Masai myth of *Naiteru-kop,* "the beginner of the earth," in fact begins with the world well established.[57] The first segment of the myth has

47. The Spirits of the Air are seen as Kwoth's children, although the others do not appear to be so regarded. Crazzolara, *Zur Gesellschaft und Religion,* p. 161; Evans-Pritchard, *Nuer Religion,* p. 28.
48. Most important, as we shall see, is the close relation of the Spirits of the Air to the warriors and cattle raiders. See Crazzolara, *Zur Gesellschaft und Religion,* p. 161.
49. On this concept, see Raffaele Pettazoni, *Dio: Formazione e Sviluppo del Monoteismo nella Storia delle Religioni* (Rome, 1922); and Mircea Eliade, *Patterns in Comparative Religion* (New York, 1963), pp. 38–123.
50. Merker, p. 196; Crazzolara, *Zur Gesellschaft und Religion,* p. 61; Evans-Pritchard, *Nuer Religion,* p. 6–7; Lienhardt, p. 42.
51. Evans-Pritchard, *Nuer Religion,* p. 8–9.
52. Ibid.; Lienhardt, p. 23; Fokken, pp. 242–45.
53. Merker, p. 196.
54. See n. 38, this chapter, for the absence of such specialists among the Nuer.
55. Lienhardt, passim.
56. Ibid., p. 32.
57. Text in Hollis, pp. 266–69.

to do with the Dorobo (a neighboring tribe and a traditional enemy of the Masai, usually regarded as ignorant and barbarous) and their killing of a serpent and an elephant.[58] This is effectively established as taking place in the time before creation, the chaos time before man was civilized. The Dorobo and his hunting activity designate for the Masai a savage world, in contrast to the Masai's own cattle-herding way of life. "Dorobo" is a scornful term in their usage, signifying above all one who knows nothing about cattle.[59] The myth of creation then tells of how the world came to be the civilized world of Masai and cattle through the action of the celestial sovereign, Ngai. The text reads as follows:

> God then called the Dorobo and said to him, "I wish you to come tomorrow morning for I have something to tell you."
> The Masai heard this, and in the morning he went and said to god, "I have come." God told him to take an axe, and to build a big kraal in three days. When it was ready, he was to go and search for a thin calf, which he would find in the forest. This he was to bring to the kraal and slaughter. The meat was to be tied up in the hide and not to be eaten. The hide was to be fastened outside the door of the hut, firewood was to be fetched, and a big fire lit, into which the meat was to be thrown. He was then to hide himself in the hut, and not to be startled when he heard a great noise outside resembling thunder.
> The Masai did as he was bid. He searched for a calf, which he found, and when he had slaughtered it he tied up the flesh in the hide. He fetched some firewood, lit a big fire, threw in the meat, and entered the hut, leaving the fire burning outside.
> God then caused a strip of hide to descend from heaven, which was suspended over the calf skin.
> Cattle at once commenced to descend one by one by the strip of hide until the whole of the kraal was filled— when the animals began to press against one another and to break down the hut where the Masai was.
> The Masai was startled and uttered an exclamation of astonishment. He then went outside the hut and found that the strip of hide had been cut, after which no more cattle came down from heaven.
> God asked him whether the cattle that were there were sufficient, "for," he said, "you will receive no more owing to your being surprised."
> The Masai then went away and attended to the animals that had been given him.

58. Ibid., pp. 266–68.
59. Ibid., p. 289.

The Dorobo lost the cattle and has had to shoot game for his food ever since.

Nowadays, if cattle are seen in the possession of Bantu tribes, it is presumed that they have been stolen or found, and the Masai say, "These are our animals, let us go and take them, for god in olden days gave us all the cattle upon the earth."[60]

This myth contains a number of fascinating elements. We have already discussed in brief the portion that deals with the schism between heaven and earth. We shall also have occasion to return to the segment that deals with the first sacrifice (see below, p. 33). But for the time being it should be emphasized that creation to the Masai means creation of cattle. Before cattle there was only a rude and barbaric world typified by the Dorobo. The intervention of Ngai transforms it into the world of proper civilization through the creation of cattle. Further, the cattle that are present in the world today are understood as the result of Ngai's original creative act. This becomes clear in one of Hollis's texts, where a Masai explains his reverence for grass: "Now cattle feed on grass, and the Masai love grass on this account. . . . The Masai love grass very much, for they say, 'God gave us cattle and grass, we do not separate the things which God has given us.'"[61] A similar sentiment is expressed by the Dinka: "Cattle and children are gifts from Divinity and from the clan divinity, and they always ultimately belong to Divinity."[62]

The Nuer have a creation myth similar to that of the Masai in many ways, which has been recorded in several versions.[63] The best of these is the version of Crazzolara. It is clearly a cosmogonic myth in the same sense as the Masai myth, as can be seen from the pregnant opening sentence, "There were still no cattle on the earth." Evans-Pritchard, however, has preferred to style it an "Esau and Jacob" myth.[64] The text reads as follows:

There were still no cattle on the earth. Then god collared Nuer and gave him a cow and a calf with the instructions to share them with Dinka—to give the cow to Dinka and to keep the calf himself. Then, he secretly gave Nuer the direction to come to him early in the morning in order to receive his calf. But, unobserved, Dinka had overheard this speech.

60. Ibid., pp. 268–69.
61. Hollis, pp. 289–90.
62. Lienhardt, p. 23.
63. Crazzolara, *Zur Gesellschaft und Religion*, p. 68; V. H. Fergusson, "The Nuong Nuer," *Sudan Notes and Records* 4 (1921):148–50; H. C. Jackson, "The Nuer of the Upper Nile Province," *Sudan Notes and Records* 6 (1923):70–73; Evans-Pritchard, *Nuer Religion*, p. 11.
64. Evans-Pritchard, *Nuer Religion*, p. 11.

Very early—still by night—he [Nuer] came to god's dwelling and said, "Gwah, my Father, I have come; give me my calf."

"Who are you?" asked god.

Whereupon the Nuer said, "I am Nuer."

"But now, who was it who came to me a little while ago and said he was Nuer, and to whom I consequently gave the calf?" Kwoth now asked.

The astonished Nuer replied, "I did not come. That must have been the Dinka. This was Dinka cunning; he has outwitted me."

Then god said to Nuer, "Good, now you take the cow for the present; then follow Dinka. When you have overtaken him, you may kill him and take the calf from him."

Since that time date the struggles of the Nuer against the Dinka to gain possession of their cattle.[65]

We must note that at its conclusion this myth is transformed into a model for present-day behavior. Because of the myth, the Nuer have assumed the right to raid the Dinka's stock continually.[66] Moreover, the Dinka themselves recount the same myth, although they interpret it to sanction stealing the cattle of the Nuer. As a Dinka shrine keeper told Struvé in 1907, having just completed a recitation of the myth, "And to this day the Dinka has always lived by robbery, and the Nuer by war."[67] In fact this seems to be the case, since the military inferiority of the Dinka has forced them to rely on theft and stealth to survive.[68]

The myth, then, in addition to recalling the acts of the creator, has a further function. It tells of the events of the primordial time, *illud tempus*, and establishes them as a model or charter for all subsequent action. This is the effect of any cosmogonic myth,[69] and in this case it is specifically

65. Crazzolara, *Zur Gesellschaft und Religion*, p. 68-69. "Es gab noch keine Rinder auf Erden. Da berief Gott den Nueer und gab ihm eine Kuh und eine Kälbin mit den Auftrag, sich darin mit einem Denka zu teilen: die Kuh gib dem Denka und die Kälbin behalte selbst. Er hatte dabei dem Nueer auch vertraulich die Weisung gegeben, sich in der Frühe bald bei ihm einzustellen, um so die Kälbin zu erhalten. Unbemerkt hatte jedoch der Denka das Gespräch mitangehört. In aller Frühe, noch bei Nacht, kam er nun vor die Wöhnung Gottes hin und sprach: 'Gwah, mein Vater, ich bin gekommen, gib mir mein Rind.' 'Wer bist du?' fragte Gott. Worauf der Nueer: 'Ich bin der Nueer.' 'Aber wer war es nur, der vorhin zu mir kam und sagte, er sei der Nueer, dem ich infolgedessen die Kälbin gab?' fragte nun kot. Der erstaunte Nueer erwiderte: 'Ich bin nicht gekommen, da muss es der Denka gewesen sein: es war Denka-Schlauheit; der hat mich überlistet.' Da sagte Gott zum Nueer: 'Gut, nimm dir jetzt die Kuh da; du wirst dann dem Denka folgen; wenn du ihn eingeholt hast, so magst du ihn umbringen und dir die Kälbin nehmen.' Seit jener Zeit datieren die Kämpfe der Nueer gegen die Denka, um sich in den Besitz der Rinder des anderen zu setzen.

66. Evans-Pritchard, *Nuer Religion*, p. 11.

67. Cited in Evans-Pritchard, *The Nuer*, pp. 125-26.

68. G. W. Titherington, "The Raik Dinka of Bahr el Ghazal Province," *Sudan Notes and Records* 10 (1927):198-99.

69. See Mircea Eliade, *Cosmos and History* (New York, 1954); and "Cosmogonic

cattle raiding and intertribal hostility that are thus established. It will be recalled that the Masai myth concludes on a similar note, saying, "Nowadays, if cattle are seen in the possession of Bantu tribes, it is presumed that they have been stolen or found, and the Masai say, 'These are our animals, let us go and take them, *for god in olden days* gave us all the cattle upon the earth.' "[70] Merker, making reference to this myth, observed:

> The Masai consider themselves as the chosen people of Ngai; all other tribes should be subject to them. God created the world and everything in it only for them, hence everything on earth belongs to them. Thus, when they take booty in war with another tribe, they only take what god properly gave them, what rightfully belongs to them, and what some other tribe unrightfully withholds from them. "Give us our own property freely [that is, the cattle in their possession], and we will not make war on you. If you do not do this, we will be forced to war." And this war they lead continuously against the despised, wild heathens, who do not know Ngai and do not pray to him but rather to spirits, wherefore he does not stand by them and always leads the Masai to victory for the right cause.[71]

Merker seems to be thinking like a Masai in this passage, for he uses the phrase "everything on earth" almost interchangeably with "cattle." As we have seen, god's creation of "the world and everything in it" amounts to the creation of cattle and as Merker points out here, the "everything on earth" that belongs to the Masai is really the cattle held by other tribes. In fact, the only booty that Masai ever take while raiding is their enemies' cattle.[72] And this leads to the next point, namely, the importance of warriors and the cattle raid in East African society, ideology, and religion.

Myth and Sacred History," *The Quest* (Chicago, 1969), pp. 72–87; Charles H. Long, *Alpha: The Myths of Creation* (New York, 1963), esp. pp. 18–19; and Raffaele Pettazzoni, "Myths of Beginnings and Creation Myths," *Essays on the History of Religions* (Leiden, 1967), pp. 24–36.

70. Hollis, p. 269 (emphasis mine).

71. Merker, p. 196. "Die Masai fühlen sich als das auserwählte Volk 'Ngais; ihnen sollen alle andern Völker untertan sein. Gott hat die Welt mit allem, was darin ist, nur für sie erschaffen, und ihnen gehört daher alles auf dem Erdboden. Wenn sie im Krieg gegen einen andern Volksstamm Beute machen, so nehmen sie nur das, was ihnen von Gott zu eigen gegeben ist, was ihnen rechtmässig gehört, und was ihnen jener Stamm unrechtmässig vorenthält. 'Gäben uns die es mag unser Eigentum, denn das ist das in ihrem Besitz befindliche Vieh, freiwillig, so brauchten wir sie nicht zu bekriegen. Da sie das aber nicht tun, so sind wir zum Krieg gezwungen.' Und diesen Krieg führen sie auch dauernd gegen die verachteten, wilden Heiden, die von 'Ngai nichts wissen und nicht zu ihm, sondern zu Geistern beten, weshalb er ihnen auch nicht beisteht und die Masai immer zu Siegern für die gerechte Sache macht."

72. Forde, p. 298; Leakey, p. 209; Merker, p. 95; R. W. E. Lewis, p. 69.

24

The Warrior

Among the Nilotic tribes, all men are organized into age-sets that group them with their contemporaries. A male belongs in one of three general categories: he is either a boy, a warrior, or an elder,[73] and different responsibilities accompany each of these statuses. As a boy he runs errands and helps the women with their milking, having no real status or social standing of his own.[74] But with initiation, the boy is fully transformed. He becomes a warrior,[75] a proper member of an age-set,[76] which may then begin to function as a military unit.[77] He ceases his old occupations and will never milk with the women again, for he is now charged with the protection of the tribe's herds and with the procurement of new cattle to swell their ranks.[78] Later, when he becomes too old to fight effectively, he will become an elder, giving up these duties and gaining other privileges, particularly those of advising and decision making.[79] But it is the warrior who is considered the ideal of manhood[80] and who interests us in the present section.

The warrior state is a special one, and it is not something a boy simply grows into. There is a sharp discontinuity between boyhood and warriorhood, and increasing maturity or physical growth alone are not sufficient to bridge the gap. In addition, the boy must be transformed, made over,

73. The case for the Masai is clearest. See Bernardi, "Age System of the Masai"; Leakey, pp. 187-96; R. W. E. Lewis, p. 68. For the Nuer, Evans-Pritchard contended that there was no class of elders in "The Nuer: Age-Sets," *Sudan Notes and Records* 19 (1936): 258, stressing the fact that there are no rites to mark the passage from warrior to elder. This does not seem to be a conclusive argument, however, in light of Stigand's observation that Nuer warriors could not marry until they were replaced by the next age-class; see C. H. Stigand, "Warrior Classes of the Nuer," *Sudan Notes and Records* 1 (1918):117. Deng, *The Dinka,* p. 6, and P. P. Howell, "Notes on the Ngork Dinka of Western Khordofan," *Sudan Notes and Records* 32 (1951):252 and 258, note the same type of system among the Dinka as is found among the Masai.
74. Evans-Pritchard, "The Nuer: Age-Sets," pp. 234, 254.
75. J. P. Crazzolara, "Die Gar-Zeremonie bei den Nuer," *Africa* 5 (1932):38; P. P. Howell, "The Age-Set System and the Institution of *Nak* Among the Nuer," *Sudan Notes and Records* 29 (1948):174; Stigand, p. 116; Merker, p. 63; Bernardi, "Age System of the Masai," p. 283; Leakey, p. 191; R. W. E. Lewis, p. 69; Deng, *The Dinka,* p. 6.
76. Evans-Pritchard, *The Nuer,* p. 250; Crazzolara, "Bedeutung des Rindes," p. 37; Stigand, p. 116; R. W. E. Lewis, p. 68; Bernardi, "Age System of the Masai," p. 271; Deng, *The Dinka,* p. 6.
77. Evans-Pritchard, "The Nuer: Age-Sets," p. 252; and Howell, "Age-Set System," p. 173 felt that the age-set had no military function, but Stigand, p. 117, contradicts this and tells of training in age-sets for warrior skills. Dinka evidence given by Deng, himself a Dinka, would tend to support Stigand's view (*The Dinka,* p. 73).
78. Evans-Pritchard, *Nuer Religion,* p. 238; Bernardi, "Age System of the Masai," p. 283; Merker, p. 63; R. W. E. Lewis, p. 69; Deng, *The Dinka,* pp. 73-76.
79. Among the Masai, this is marked with a ceremony. R. W. E. Lewis, p. 70, tells of warriors being forcibly deprived of their weapons. Among the Nuer and Dinka it is a more natural occurrence, coming when a man is too old to fight. Evans-Pritchard, "The Nuer: Age-Sets," p. 258.
80. James, p. 66; R. W. E. Lewis, p. 70; Evans-Pritchard, *The Nuer,* p. 254.

25

reborn, and this rebirth takes the form of an initiation. Initiation among the Nuer, Dinka, and Masai has been reported in great detail,[81] and an extended discussion of the rituals need not detain us here, but it should be noted that the basic scenario is very similar in each tribe. For our purposes, a simple outline will suffice.

The Organization of the Age-Set. When a group of boys begin to reach the proper age for initiation (anywhere from eleven to seventeen), they organize themselves in a body to pressure their elders to permit the ceremony to take place. Before the rite they are not considered an age-set proper, but in the course of events they will be bound together as a corporate body and will be given an age-set name.

Preparatory Ceremonies. These may vary widely, but they usually involve the sacrifice of an ox, known as *ol-oirupukiniek* among the Masai, "the one who causes them to be taken out of the boys' ranks."[82] These ceremonies may last for months and are more complex among the Masai than among the Nuer or Dinka.

Shaving of Head and Body. Just before the initiatory operation each candidate is completely shaved. To my knowledge, no author has commented on the significance of this action, yet it seems to me unmistakable that this is intended to represent a return to the prenatal state just before a ritual rebirth. This is even clearer in the light of other indications of rebirth symbolism—the boy is naked, is not permitted to talk, dons new clothes after the ceremony, and so on. Indeed, initiation is even referred to as "rebirth" in some instances.[83]

The Operation. The high point of the initiation, and its central act in transforming the boy into a warrior, is an operation performed on his body. Among the Masai the initiand is circumcised,[84] while among the Nuer and Dinka a series of six lateral cuts called *gar* (Nuer) or *dheeng* (Dinka) are made across each boy's forehead. The first cut among the Nuer is known as *wacdohl*, "the wiping out of boyhood."[85] This is a painful ordeal, which must be borne individually by each candidate without

81. On the Nuer, see Evans-Pritchard, "The Nuer: Age-Sets," pp. 235–44; Crazzolara, "Gar-Zeremonie," pp. 28–39; Stigand, pp. 116–18. On the Dinka, see Deng, *The Dinka,* pp. 68–73; Howell, "Notes on the Ngork Dinka," p. 258. On the Masai, see Bernardi, "Age System of the Masai," pp. 271–83; Fox, pp. 448–51; Leakey, pp. 187–91; R. W. E. Lewis, pp. 68–70; Merker, pp. 60–64. In discussing the initiatory drama, I will not attempt to fully annotate, as the summary can be confirmed by checking any of the sources listed here. Only very specific or important points will be individually noted.
82. Bernardi, "Age System of the Masai," p. 281 n.
83. After initiation, according to Merker, p. 60, the Masai regard the initiands as "reborn" (*erwachsene*).
84. This practice probably results from contact with the Cushites in the opinion of Sutton, p. 82.
85. Evans-Pritchard, "The Nuer: Age Sets," p. 239.

flinching. To show pain is shameful and bodes ill for one's career as a warrior, and one informant went so far as to state that the purpose of the ordeal is to make the boys unafraid of the spear.[86] Some idea of the courage with which the initiands face this operation may be gathered from the following Dinka initiation song:

> A knife as red as a firefly
> Stained with blood eating the veins
> He pulled it across the forehead and the skull rattled
> My head fell, a knife which leaves no veins.
>
> . . . .
>
> I said
> Do not hurry
> Arrange them [the cuts] well.
> My head lay still
> The knife was raised
> And the wounds were traced
> I hate a vein to escape.[87]

Convalescence. After their ordeal the candidates are removed to special huts, where they will rest while the wounds heal. During this time they are subject to certain ritual proscriptions; in particular, girls may not visit them in the hut. But for our purposes the most important aspect of this convalescent period is the fact that the candidates are better fed than at any other time of their lives. They are gorged on milk and meat[88] to build their strength and speed their recovery.[89]

Presentation of Ox and Spear. Toward the end of the ritual, having completed all other stages, the candidate is presented an ox and a spear by his father. These are the preeminent signs of manhood,[90] signifying that he is now able to fight and ready to assume greater responsibility for the cattle of the tribe. With the acquisition of these gifts, he becomes a warrior.

Some authors, notably Howell, Stigand, Jackson, and Merker,[91] have

---

86. Jackson, p. 145.
87. Deng, *The Dinka and Their Songs,* pp. 190–91, slightly altered.
88. Crazzolara, "Gar-Zeremonie," p. 29; Evans-Pritchard, "The Nuer: Age-Sets," pp. 242–43; Stigand, p. 116; Leakey, p. 190; Merker, p. 64; Deng, *The Dinka,* p. 73. The convalescent diet of the Masai consists only of milk and meat, taken in huge quantities, but the Nuer and Dinka initiands face the problem of having to chew without reopening the wounds on their foreheads, and thus their diet is a soft one. In particular they are given milk and some meal but especially meat, minced very fine and sometimes mixed with fat to make it easier to chew.
89. This is nowhere fully explicit, except in Leakey, p. 190, but is everywhere implied.
90. See especially Evans-Pritchard's two chapters, "Spear Symbolism" and "The Sacrificial Role of Cattle" in *Nuer Religion,* pp. 231–71.
91. Howell, "The Age-Set System," pp. 173–81; Stigand, p. 116; Jackson, p. 146; Merker, pp. 75–76.

claimed that a later "ceremony" (if so it can be called) is also involved in Nuer and Masai initiation rites. This is a giant meat feast, which occurs some weeks after the other steps when the young men retire to special camps and gorge themselves on the meat of slaughtered oxen. Evans-Pritchard, however, was not convinced that this is truly a part of the initiation proceedings,[92] and his hesitation seems justified. That these meat orgies are significant in the making of the warrior is unquestionable, but for reasons that will be discussed later, they should not be regarded as part of the initiation.

The transformation effected by the initiatory drama completely changes an individual's life. He is no longer a boy, and his boyhood task of helping the women milk becomes forbidden to him.[93] Among the Masai, this ritual prohibition against his reentering the women's world is so stringent that a warrior may not drink any milk handed to him by a woman.[94]

As his old world is closed off, however, a new world is opened up to the warrior: he is now—for the first time—permitted to raid,[95] and raiding quickly becomes the focal point of his life. It is traditionally in the raid that a man wins prestige, and colonial efforts to forbid raiding have had a terrible effect, causing demoralization and despair among the warrior class.[96] But in former times a man found glory, as well as meaning, in the raids.

The Cattle Raid

Raiding, it must be noted, is different from theft. Theft occurs by stealth, on an individual basis, and without proper sanctions. It is entirely another category in legal thought[97] and is looked on as despicable.[98] Moreover, among the Nuer and Masai it rarely occurs.[99] Raiding, on the other hand,

---

92. His position is marked by some uncertainty, however. Originally, he felt that these *nak* camps were not part of the initiation ("The Nuer: Age-Sets," p. 245-46), but in a postscript to Howell's article on "The Age-Set System," he stated that Howell may indeed be right. In *Nuer Religion*, pp. 264-65, however, he attempted—on the basis of second-hand information—to argue that the killing of cattle in these camps may be a form of sacrifice, but he is always hesitant on the point of the *nak* camps, sensing that there is some ritual significance to them but unsure of just what it is.

93. Evans-Pritchard, "The Nuer: Age-Sets," p. 253.

94. Fox, p. 453; R. W. E. Lewis, p. 70.

95. Evans-Pritchard, *The Nuer*, p. 126; Merker, p. 63.

96. On the prestige involved in raids, see Evans-Pritchard, *The Nuer*, p. 50; Merker, p. 114. T. O. Beidelman, "Beer Drinking and Cattle Theft in Ukaguru," *American Anthropologist* 63 (1961):543, tells that while large-scale raiding has been stamped out by colonial rule, petty theft of livestock still goes on. "Such thefts are not due to Baraguyu need for cattle but to the Baraguyu warriors' need for prestige." James (pp. 66-67) comments on the effects of colonialism, pointing out that the Masai, despite their martial nature, could not be converted into soldiers by the British, presumably because the King's African Rifles did not raid for cattle.

97. Howell, *Manual of Nuer Law*, p. 198-99.

98. Hollis, p. 310.

99. Ibid.; Howell, *Manual of Nuer Law*, p. 200; Evans-Pritchard, *The Nuer*, p. 165.

as we have already seen, is fully sanctioned by the myths of creation and is conducted only against enemies who are themselves perceived as thieves. Raiding is a repetition of the events that took place *in illo tempore* and is, moreover, god's will, as Kwoth announces in the Nuer myth: "Good, now you take the cow for the present; then follow Dinka. When you have overtaken him, you may kill him and take the calf from him."[100] As the Masai argue, any raid has as its purpose the recovery of what is rightfully theirs, having been given them by Ngai at the time of creation.[101] Raiding is, in a sense, a sacred activity.

On a social level, raiding is the source of prestige for the warriors, and a man earns respect by his prowess in raiding. Songs are composed and widely sung to tell of deeds in war. Consider the following Masai song:

> Ol-le Langoi, the warrior who has reddened the ground
> with the blood
> Of those whose country had not been reconnoitred.
> Who ran on ahead and returned in the evening to the van.
> I tell you he has killed—how often?—three times
> in one month.
> The cows with the crumpled horns which were shown to
> Ainsworth were in the kraal.
> We captured them because he climbed to Kimara to take
> the place of those who retired.[102]

Or this example from the Dinka:

> The Grey One [a vulture] flies in the grassy plains,
> I killed a man
> And his mother got into a mourning skirt.
> I gathered my spears.
> And I killed a man.
>
> . . . .
>
> I am a bad man
> I fly in the grassy plain
> My heart is like that of a buffalo.
> I danced around the herds I captured
> And vultures followed my spears.[103]

Sometimes the glory is not individual but is shared by the entire raiding party. For instance, in this Baraguyu song:

> They take advantage of the people of Dogom,
> They take advantage of the people of Bereko.
> The company of ole Mundoi
> Takes advantage of all the cattle camps![104]

100. Crazzolara, *Zur Gesellschaft und Religion,* p. 69.
101. Merker, p. 114.
102. Hollis, p. 354.
103. Deng, *The Dinka and Their Songs,* p. 207, slightly modified.
104. Beidelman, "Baraguyu Cattle Songs," p. 15.

Or:

> At Marek the leather hides [we wore] at our backs dried
> up and cracked.
> As we, who don't care what difficulties we must face,
> took the stolen cattle across Msere.[105]

And sometimes the songs are directed to the cattle themselves:

> Grow big my calf Leletandi!
> You of the oxen with white bellies
> Which we stole from the cement-walled enclosure of
> the English [which was said to be] impregnable.[106]

It will be noted in these songs that glory is earned by the gaining of cattle and that cattle are the only booty mentioned. In fact, cattle are the only booty desired or taken,[107] and tribes without cattle are generally left in peace.[108] Evans-Pritchard once inquired whether the Nuer could deal militarily with the powerful Shilluk and was told, "They have no cattle. If they had cattle we would raid them and take their cattle, for they do not know how to fight as we fight."[109]

Fighting is a serious business, and questions of technique are quite important. While an outside observer might attribute military prowess to the efficiency of kinship organization[110] or age-set groupings,[111] the Nilotes themselves consider a host of magico-religious preparations crucial to success. In the first place, a priest or prophet is consulted before embarking on a raid, and his advice is sought. Hollis records one such prophesy:

> The bulls that cannot move because they are so fat,
> They will be beaten by Kilepo.
> The bulls that cannot move because they are so fat,
> Half of them will be captured.[112]

Charms are obtained from the priest,[113] and while the warriors are in the field he will perform services to aid them, such as gouging the eyes or breaking the legs of animals that symbolize the enemy, or bending the points of spears that represent those of the foe.[114]

105. Ibid., p. 16.
106. Ibid., p. 11.
107. Evans-Pritchard, *The Nuer*, pp. 48–49; R. W. E. Lewis, p. 69; Merker, p. 95.
108. Evans-Pritchard, *The Nuer*, p. 127.
109. Ibid., p. 132.
110. Sahlins, pp. 338–40.
111. Forde, pp. 303–304.
112. Hollis, p. 325.
113. Forde, p. 297; Deng, *The Dinka*, p. 74; H. A. Fosbrooke, "An Administrative Survey of the Masai Social System," *Tanganyika Notes and Records* 26 (1948):15–16.
114. Evans-Pritchard, *The Nuer*, pp. 188–89; Howell, *Manual of Nuer Law*, p. 213; Lienhardt, p. 211; Seligmans, p. 217.

THE CATTLE CYCLE IN EAST AFRICA

The warriors themselves engage in many practices to increase their strength and their chances for victory. They work to bring themselves into a state of frenzy through vigorous songs and dances, or through the contemplation of secret emblems painted on their shields and weapons.[115] Often they don animal skins—particularly those of lion, civet, and leopard —in order to take on the strength and ferocity of these beasts,[116] and the origin of the many tales of lion- and leopard-men is to be found in these practices.[117]

Special decoctions are also prepared to induce a furor,[118] and the efficacy of these intoxicants is not to be doubted. Fox reports:

> Soup is made of fat and water and the bark of *il kitoloswa* or *il kiluretti* trees. The decoction of these barks makes the warrior fierce. They also ascribe to this cause the curious hysterical fits into which they frequently fall when excited. I can vouch for the *il kitoloswa*, small doses of which do, in fact, produce a fierce and unbalanced state of mind. I have never tried the *il kiluretti*.[119]

Their furor is accompanied by a state of heat, and the following song is sung by the Masai:

> The milkmen go behind us.
> We have conquered with the headdresses of the lion's mane.
> Yoa! I burn! Yoa! I burn!
> Yoa! I burn! Yoa! I burn![120]

The most important technique, however, is the consumption of raw meat,[121] a topic to which we shall return.

It should also be noted that, among the Nuer at least, the conduct of war is not watched over by the celestial sovereign but by a lesser set of deities, the Spirits of the Air.[122] These are particularly martial, bellicose

---

115. Merker, pp. 76–82.

116. Bernardi, "Age System of the Masai," p. 276; Jackson, pp. 182–83.

117. Lienhardt, p. 171 n.; see also the myth of the origin of the Nuer leopard-skin priest recorded by Crazzolara, *Zur Gesellschaft und Religion*, pp. 9–12. It seems to me that this myth of the defeat of a lion-man, Lɛd, by a leopard-man, Mɛɛm, points to the leopard-skin priest as originally having been a warrior leader whose insignia was a skin, which gave him the strength and cunning of a leopard, whereby he defeated an enemy tribe that habitually personated the lion. Such an opposition of lion-tribe and leopard-tribe is also found in the Masai-Kikuyu rivalry; see François Bugeau, "Les Wakikouyous et la guerre," *Annali Lateranensi* 7 (1943):186.

118. Fokken, p. 245.

119. Fox, pp. 453–54.

120. Hollis, p. 352.

121. Merker, pp. 83–84; Bernardi, "Age System of the Masai," pp. 298–99; Fox, pp. 453–54; Evans-Pritchard, *The Nuer*, p. 26; Howell, "The Age-Set System," p. 180; Deng, *The Dinka*, p. 72.

122. Crazzolara, *Zur Gesellschaft und Religion*, pp. 161–65; Evans-Pritchard, *The Nuer*, pp. 188–89; *Nuer Religion*, p. 45.

spirits who inspire prophets, and it is these prophets who most often organize and direct raids.[123] This would seem to indicate that the warriors have somewhat less religious prestige, a fact that is evident among the Dinka and Masai, where priests must preside over the central religious act of sacrifice.[124]

Sacrifice

Ultimately all oxen (not cows, however)[125] are intended for sacrifice.[126] They may be promised and then not given for years, but in theory, and for the most part in practice, they will ultimately be delivered up.[127] In this offering, the animal is returned to the celestial sovereign, from whom it originally came,[128] and regardless of what other spirits may be involved every sacrifice in the last analysis goes to him.[129] This is the chief form of worship among the East African tribes and their prime means of reaching their god.[130]

Animals other than cattle, however, are often sacrificed,[131] and the number of goats and sheep offered may even exceed the number of cattle.[132] This is merely a matter of economic expedience, however, for at the level of ideology all victims are regarded as cattle and are always referred to as such.[133] Even when a man tosses a pinch of tobacco into the air, he will say, "I offer you this ox."[134] Goats, sheep, or even a cucumber may be offered, as these are less expensive, but they are always thought of as substitutes for cattle. They are called cattle but are never treated with the same reverence as cattle,[135] and oxen themselves are always used for

123. Ibid.

124. See Ibrahim Bedri, "Notes on Dinka Religious Beliefs in Their Hereditary Chiefs and Rainmakers," *Sudan Notes and Records* 22 (1939):125-31; Lienhardt, pp. 8, 10, 219, 233; Fokken, p. 245.

125. Forde, p. 295; Evans-Pritchard, "Some Forms and Features of Nuer Sacrifice," *Africa* 21 (1951):112. Cows are offered at funerary ceremonies, as an exception to the general rule.

126. Evans-Pritchard, *Nuer Religion*, p. 263; Lienhardt, p. 23.

127. Evans-Pritchard, *Nuer Religion*, p. 261.

128. Crazzolara, "Bedeutung des Rindes," p. 313; R. W. E. Lewis, p. 72; Merker, p. 192; Lienhardt, p. 23.

129. Crazzolara, *Zur Gesellschaft und Religion*, p. 71; Evans-Pritchard, *Nuer Religion*, p. 200.

130. Crazzolara, *Zur Gesellschaft und Religion*, p. 71; Evans-Pritchard, *Nuer Religion*, p. 21; Lienhardt, p. 10; Stubbs, p. 248; Titherington, p. 170; Fokken, p. 245; Fosbrooke, p. 18.

131. Crazzolara, *Zur Gesellschaft und Religion*, p. 75.

132. Evans-Pritchard, "The Sacrificial Role of Cattle Among the Nuer," *Africa* 23 (1953):194.

133. Crazzolara, *Zur Gesellschaft und Religion*, p. 75; Evans-Pritchard, "Some Forms and Features," p. 112; and "Sacrificial Role of Cattle," p. 125.

134. Evans-Pritchard, "Some Forms and Features," p. 112.

135. Note the difference in practices for each type of sacrifice as described by Crazzolara, *Zur Gesellschaft und Religion*, pp. 79-81. For instance, a knife is used in the sacrifice of goats, never a spear as in cattle sacrifice.

major sacrifices, as they are the only really worthy offering.[136] As Lienhardt put it, animal sacrifice is the central religious act and cattle are the ideal victim.[137]

Sacrifice can take place on any number of occasions. There are regular seasonal sacrifices in spring at the return home and at the autumn harvest, or at the changing of the rainy and dry seasons;[138] sacrifice is performed at all rites of passage;[139] and is often offered in fulfillment of a pledge to a deity.[140] Perhaps the most frequent occasion for sacrifice is a serious illness,[141] but in truth cattle are sacrificed at every significant occasion in life.[142]

The details of sacrificial practice appear to vary somewhat with the occasion, but in general a basic pattern can be observed, and for our purposes Evans-Pritchard's description of what he calls the "piacular" sacrifice (in contrast to the "confirmatory" sacrifice) will be sufficient.[143] He discerns four moments to the ritual: presentation, consecration, invocation, and slaughter.[144] The procedures are relatively simple. An ox is brought out to the place of sacrifice and tethered there. A set of speeches is made by prominent men while libations of milk are poured out. These speeches are addressed to the spirit who is to receive the ox, and the speakers describe the reasons for which the offering is to be made, requesting certain favors from the spirit in return. In most cases, as will be seen from an examination of the texts assembled by Crazzolara, the speeches follow a simple formula: "Kwoth, take this ox, let us live."[145] Ultimately the animal is killed and eaten, its meat having been carefully divided and distributed on a hierarchical basis to those attending the ceremony.[146]

A great many complicated operations take place in this simple sacrificial scenario. On the most obvious level, a valued gift is offered to a deity by the sacrificer,[147] and on further examination we see that the gift is in

136. Crazzolara, "Bedeutung des Rindes," p. 300; and *Zur Gesellschaft und Religion,* p. 75.

137. Lienhardt, p. 10.

138. Crazzolara, *Zur Gesellschaft und Religion,* p. 81; Stubbs, p. 249; Jackson, p. 71; Fokken, p. 243.

139. Evans-Pritchard, *Nuer Religion,* p. 198; Fokken, p. 245; Lienhardt, p. 10.

140. Lienhardt, p. 106.

141. Crazzolara, "Bedeutung des Rindes," p. 312; Evans-Pritchard, *Nuer Religion,* p. 198; Merker, p. 192.

142. Evans-Pritchard, "Sacrificial Role of Cattle," p. 196.

143. Evans-Pritchard, *Nuer Religion,* p. 198.

144. Ibid., p. 272.

145. Crazzolara, *Zur Gesellschaft und Religion,* pp. 78-79.

146. Crazzolara, *Zur Gesellschaft und Religion,* p. 79, does not accept this act as part of the sacrifice, but in the light of the brilliant analysis of Lienhardt, pp. 233-34, I am forced to disagree.

147. Evans-Pritchard, *Nuer Religion,* pp. 276-82.

some sense offered as a substitute—the life of the ox standing in place of the life of the man.[148] Further, through the sacrifice men enter into relations of proximity with the deities and with the celestial sovereign, and in this sense the sacrificial animal serves as a mediator between man and god.[149] There is truth in all these views of sacrifice, and also in Lienhardt's contention that the sacrifice and the systematic division of meat constitute a recreation of the social order.[150] But the most important element in the ideology of sacrifice is that by sacrificing man returns to god what was his gift in the beginning of time and what was always rightfully his. This is confirmed among the Nuer by the language employed in the sacrificial invocations, where the sacrificer always speaks of giving Kwoth *his* beast.[151] The verb used, moreover, conveys the sense of giving that which is due, as in a debt.[152]

The effect of this gift is somewhat more complex than the simple repayment of a debt, however. In the beginning, god gave man cattle, and in sacrifice man returns those cattle to god. But just as god's gift necessitates a return, so does man's gift necessitate further reciprocation: god is expected to supply more cattle. That sacrifice calls forth such a return gift on the part of the celestial sovereign is seen most clearly in the section of the Masai creation myth that deals with the first sacrifice, where it is told that first the celestial sovereign gave a calf to Masai, requesting that Masai return it to him in sacrifice, whereupon the sovereign bestowed a wealth of cattle upon Masai. By means of the sacrifice, man completes a turn of what we may now call the "cattle cycle" and sets the process in motion once again.

The Cattle Cycle

We have thus far been describing the elements of a cycle that may be discerned in East African thought and practice. It is a cycle that traces and governs the uses of cattle—where they come from and where they go. Further, it is a sacred cycle, for its elements are described in myth and are sanctioned by the acts of the celestial sovereign and the first men *in illo tempore*. Thus the cycle begins at the beginning of time, when the celestial sovereign created this world through the creation of cattle. These cattle, moreover, were not simply created at random but were expressly given to

---

148. Crazzolara, *Zur Gesellschaft und Religion,* pp. 78–79; Evans-Pritchard, "Sacrificial Role of Cattle," p. 191; Merker, p. 192.

149. In the sense discussed by Marcel Mauss and Henri Hubert, *Sacrifice: Its Nature and Function* (Chicago, 1964). It should be noted that Evans-Pritchard commissioned the English translation of this work (see his Foreword, p. vii), and his debt to it is great. It remains the single most important theoretical work on the subject, however, and it is a debt of which he need not be ashamed.

150. Lienhardt, pp. 233–34.

151. Evans-Pritchard, "Some Forms and Features," p. 114.

152. Ibid.

the sovereign's favored tribe—Masai, Nuer, or Dinka in our accounts[153]—who are thus empowered to hold all cattle through all time.

During the events of the beginning, however, the ancestor of an enemy tribe came to steal the cattle intended for the Nuer and Masai, an event that explains the actions of his descendants today. As a result of this theft, god directed the ancestor of Nuer and Masai to retake their cattle by force and thus gave sanction to the raids carried out by Nuer and Masai warriors ever since.

The cattle procured by the warriors become, at least in one sense, part of a "national herd" belonging to the entire tribe.[154] And it is in this sense that they are offered up to the celestial sovereign in sacrifice, returning the gift that he bestowed on his tribe and creating a bond of reciprocity whereby he will again give more cattle. Such sacrifices are offered, not by the warriors who have procured the cattle for the tribe, but by priests or other ritual specialists who are particularly close to the celestial sovereign and particularly interested in cattle. Along these lines it is interesting to note that the great Masai *laibon* Mbatian, on his deathbed in 1890, promised his fellow tribesmen that after his death he would send them cattle from heaven.[155]

The movements of cattle from the divine realm through the realm of men can be schematized in a circular pattern—see Figure 1. The cycle is a sacred one, established by myth, and acted out in accordance with god's will. All the actions contained in the cycle are sacred, as they repeat primordial models and follow from divine commands. The uses and treatment of cattle are defined by this cycle, and as long as one's actions conform to it, one is assured of their religious propriety.

153. The Nuer-Dinka myth is something of a double-edged affair, and all depends on who is telling it. When Nuer relate the original gift of cattle, the myth establishes their right to own all cattle; when Dinka relate it, it establishes their right to steal.

154. This is a difficult issue. Masai warriors may not own cattle and must turn their booty over to their fathers (Bernardi, "Age System of the Masai," pp. 283-84; Merker, p. 63). Even then ownership is not complete, for the animals are marked with clan and family marks as well as individual marks of ownership (Hollis, p. 290; Forde, p. 295). Bernardi, "Age System of the Masai," pp. 267-68, has noted that cattle and water are clan possessions, although this does not preclude individual ownership as well. Moreover, as we have seen from our examination of the creation myth, there is a sense in which cattle (all cattle) belong to Masai (all Masai) from the beginning of time (Merker, pp. 114, 196). Similarly, among the Nuer, ownership of cattle is by families (Evans-Pritchard, *The Nuer,* p. 17), and there is a sense of a "national herd" that is the direct descendant of the herd of the ancestors (Evans-Pritchard, "Sacrificial Role of Cattle," p. 189).

155. Hollis, p. 327.

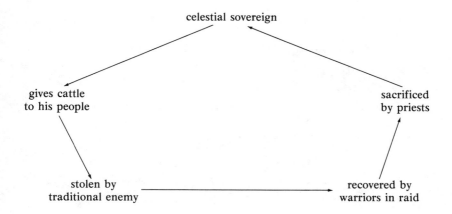

Figure 1. The East African Cattle Cycle

III

EAST AFRICA:
PRIESTLY CYCLE
AND WARRIOR CYCLE

In the preceding chapter, I have attempted to demonstrate the existence of a "cattle cycle" in East Africa—a systematic ideology that regulates and authorizes the various uses of cattle in society. This cycle is built on the myths of beginnings, which specifically tell of the creation of cattle, the first cattle raid, and the first cattle sacrifice. These myths give rise to the practices that are crucial to the East African way of life—cattle raid and cattle sacrifice. Further analysis shows, however, that what has thus far been discussed as one entity can in fact be broken down into two separate cycles, which have in some way been fused. These two cycles separate along the lines of division already noted, namely, those of priest and warrior.[1]

1. The priest is a fairly clear figure among the Masai and Dinka, although a bewildering mass of titles appear in the literature. Thus, the Masai *laibon* is called *Zauberer* (Fokken), "priest-chief" (Forde), "medicine man" (R. W. E. Lewis), and "chief priest" (Fox), among others. The Dinka *bany* is styled "chief and rainmaker" (Bedri), "chief of the spear" (Howell), "master of the fishing spear" (Lienhardt), and "diviner" (N. Nunn, "A Dinka Sacrifice," *Sudan Notes and Records* 31 [1950]:141). For the Nuer, however, the case is not nearly so simple, as there are any number of figures who may act as priests under certain circumstances. Most important of these are the *kuaar twac*, "leopard-skin priest" (Evans-Pritchard), and the *wut ghok*, the "cattle expert" (Evans-Pritchard) or "cattle chief" (Stigand), although there are others. In truth, however, the Nuer do not really have what one could call a priestly class in the same sense as the Dinka and Masai. This fact led Lienhardt, p. 219, to observe that the priestly system of the Nuer was less developed than that of the Dinka, but as we shall see, it seems more likely that the Nuer system was a warrior clan's conscious reaction against the Dinka priestly system. For this reason, it contains a number of peculiarities that are not found elsewhere in East Africa and that make the Nuer a very special example with regard to the role of priests.

Priestly and Warrior Cycles

Much of the analysis thus far has gone to show that the priest and the warrior function in very different ways within East African societies. It has seemed appropriate, however, to discuss the characteristic activities of each class as complementing those of the other and as parts of an overall pattern of organization that we have dubbed the "cattle cycle." In one sense this seems to be justified, for whatever their differences priests and warriors do share a primary concern: they both wish to secure the well-being of their tribe by procuring an abundant supply of cattle.

On a second level of concern, however, these two groups diverge sharply, for priests and warriors have differing ideas about the means of obtaining those cattle. Priests regard sacrifice as the chief means of maintaining prosperity and well-being; warriors see cattle raiding in this same light. Each group thus is inclined to view its own role as that of prime importance.

This divergence is in fact reflected in our "cattle cycle" (see Figure 1, above). The upper half of the diagram contains only elements that relate to the role of the priest. Here, sacrifice is regarded as an exchange in which gifts of cattle are given to the celestial sovereign and return gifts are received from him. Priests view this exchange as the paramount religious act, absolutely crucial for the well-being of the community and indispensable for the maintenance of continued prosperity.[2] The myth of the first sacrifice governs the practice of all sacrificial offerings, and this practice emphasizes the proximity of the priest to the celestial sovereign, who bestows all cattle.[3] The actions of the warrior are completely unrelated to the workings of this process. We can separate off the priest's role in the cattle cycle to form an independent unit that we will term the "priestly cycle" (Figure 2).

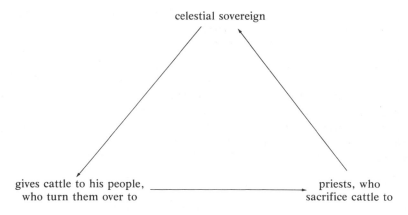

celestial sovereign

gives cattle to his people,   priests, who
who turn them over to   sacrifice cattle to

Figure 2. The East African Priestly Cycle

2. Lienhardt, p. 10; Evans-Pritchard, *Nuer Religion*, p. 197; Crazzolara, *Zur Gesellschaft und Religion*, p. 71.
3. Lienhardt, p. 23; Fokken, p. 249.

EAST AFRICA: PRIESTLY CYCLE AND WARRIOR CYCLE

In contrast, the warriors focus their attention on the raid and view military prowess as the chief means of enriching and caring for the tribe as a whole. Accordingly, they choose to emphasize the myth of the first cattle raid, and the warrior is esteemed as the ideal of manhood.[4] While priests may claim a special position or prestige by virtue of their lineage,[5] warriors can make the same type of claim by virtue of their initiation.[6]

Just as we can separate out a priestly cycle from the larger cattle cycle, so is it also possible to isolate a "warrior cycle." In large measure, priests are irrelevant to the lower half of Figure 1. The central event here is the cattle raid, whereby cattle originally lost are recovered. Even the celestial sovereign seems somehow foreign to this part of the cycle, and insofar as divine support for the warriors' endeavors is present, it seems to come from warrior-specific deities such as the Nuer Spirits of the Air,[7] rather than from on high. Thus, the workings of a separate warrior cycle can be outlined (Figure 3), and it will be noted that the warrior cycle has no point of contact with the priestly cycle, save that both share a concern for the welfare of the tribe and that obtaining cattle is understood as the means of preserving the tribe's welfare in both cases.

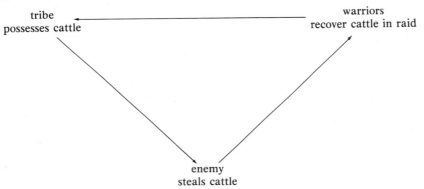

Figure 3. The East African Warrior Cycle

It is also necessary to note that the religious forms observed by the warriors are different from those of the priests. We have already seen how the chief ritual concern of the warriors is the increase of their own strength for battle by means of charms, potions, magical acts, and the eating of meat. It seems that they also have a theology somewhat different from that of the priests.

---

4. James, p. 66; R. W. E. Lewis, p. 70; Evans-Pritchard, *The Nuer*, p. 254.
5. See the literature cited below in notes 38 and 39, this chapter.
6. One must note the profound religious significance of any initiation. On this, see Mircea Eliade, *Rites and Symbols of Initiation* (New York, 1958).
7. See below, p. 39.

EAST AFRICA: PRIESTLY CYCLE AND WARRIOR CYCLE

To the priests, the celestial sovereign is the most important deity,[8] whom they invoke most often in sacrifice[9] and to whom they claim a special proximity.[10] But the warriors, especially among the Nuer, are more closely attached to other deities known as the Spirits of the Air, who are the most important spirits after the celestial sovereign.[11] These spirits are believed to inhabit the clouds or the breezes below the realm of the celestial sovereign,[12] and are sometimes regarded as his children.[13] Their chief interest is war and raiding, and they will possess a man who then becomes known as a prophet or a "man of the Spirits of the Air."[14] While possessed, he may be ordered to collect warriors and prepare for battle, and he will then embark on a raid accompanied or even led by his spirits.[15] If successful, these prophets could acquire a large following. In precolonial times they conducted cattle raids chiefly on the Dinka, but with colonization they became the chief leaders of resistance to the British.[16] In any event, the prophets were and are quite different from the priests,[17] and the Spirits of the Air are quite different from the celestial sovereign. Warriors and priests seem to have differing myths, differing rituals, differing deities, differing pursuits, differing forms of religious leadership, and indeed, differing *Weltanschauungen* in most ways. But they do hold in common a concern for the welfare of their tribe and a desire for procuring cattle, and these common elements allow them to act in cooperation.

Priests and Warriors in Cooperation

In the first place, the priests lend assistance to the warriors in their raiding, and their aid in this endeavor is considered indispensable.[18] They

---

8. The tendency to regard priestly religious forms as the only religious forms of a community is a common fallacy in the history of religions, because priests tend to be the most learned informants on religious topics. It must not be forgotten, however, that other—although perhaps less well-formulated—systems of religious thought and action do exist.

9. Crazzolara, *Zur Gesellschaft und Religion,* pp. 71, 78; Evans-Pritchard, *Nuer Religion,* pp. 200–202.

10. See below, the section, "The Supremacy of Priests."

11. Evans-Pritchard, *Nuer Religion,* p. 28.

12. Ibid.; Crazzolara, *Zur Gesellschaft und Religion,* p. 161.

13. Crazzolara, *Zur Gesellschaft und Religion,* p. 161.

14. Evans-Pritchard, *Nuer Religion,* pp. 44–45; Crazzolara, *Zur Gesellschaft und Religion,* p. 163–65.

15. Ibid.

16. Evans-Pritchard, *The Nuer,* p. 185. For specific accounts of several important prophets, see C. A. Willis, "The Cult of Deng," *Sudan Notes and Records* 11 (1928): 195–208; and Paul Coriat, "Gwek, the Witch-Doctor and the Pyramid of Dengkur," *Sudan Notes and Records* 22 (1939):221–37. For a slightly different view on the position of the prophet, see B. A. Lewis, "Nuer Spokesmen: A Note on the Institution of the *Ruic,*" *Sudan Notes and Records* 32 (1951):77–84, who argues quite convincingly that the office of prophet is not a recent development but is well-founded in Nuer institutions.

17. See the discussion in Evans-Pritchard, *Nuer Religion,* chap. 12, "Priests and Prophets," pp. 287–310.

18. Lienhardt, p. 211; Fokken, p. 245. The regular Nuer priestly authorities

must give initial permission for a raid to take place,[19] and then they may prophesy or divine its success.[20] Further, they will give charms and strengthening drinks to the warriors to aid them in battle,[21] and they will lead prayers on their behalf.[22] It is forbidden for a priest to accompany warriors into battle[23]—such would be an impossible confusion of categories—on the grounds that the sight of flowing blood would weaken the priest's vital spirit.[24] While the warriors are in the field, however, he will aid with any number of magical performances, such as bending the points of enemy spears or gouging the eyes and breaking the legs of animals that symbolize the enemy.[25] Such practices are valued highly, and some will say that they are as essential for victory as is the warriors' courage and physical prowess.[26]

The second major point of cooperation between priests and warriors appears in the performance of initiation. The priest must grant permission for initiation to take place,[27] and to a certain extent he regulates the matter of who shall be initiated through his "opening and closing" the periods of age-set formation before initiation itself.[28] He also supervises the initiation procedures, although he may not perform the operations himself.[29] But without his sanction and supervision the initiatory rituals cannot take place, and the boys cannot become warriors. Warrior status is not achieved by any process of aging or growth, but only by initiation.[30] In this the priest is indispensable, and he serves as midwife to the young men's rebirth as warriors.

Third, warriors have recourse to the priests in times of need—in sickness, drought, famine, or ill-fortune of any kind. The priests seek to find the cause of a warrior's troubles through the use of divinatory skills,[31] and

(leopard-skin priest, cattle expert, etc.) also play roles in war preparations. See Howell, *Manual of Nuer Law,* p. 213.

19. Forde, p. 297; Bedri, "Notes on Dinka Religious Beliefs," p. 131.

20. Lienhardt, p. 145; Bedri, "Notes on Dinka Religious Beliefs," p. 131; Hollis, p. 325.

21. Lienhardt, p. 145; Hollis, p. 349.

22. Lienhardt, p. 145; Bedri, "Notes on Dinka Religious Beliefs," p. 131.

23. Ibid.

24. Lienhardt, p. 145.

25. Lienhardt, p. 211; Howell, *Manual of Nuer Law,* p. 213.

26. Lienhardt, p. 211. One wonders who Dr. Lienhardt's informant was on this point—a warrior or a priest.

27. R. W. E. Lewis, p. 68; Stigand, p. 116.

28. Ibid.; Lienhardt, p. 216; Crazzolara, "Gar-Zeremonie," p. 28; Evans-Pritchard, "The Nuer: Age-Sets," pp. 235–36.

29. Among the Nuer the operation is performed by anyone who knows how (Evans-Pritchard, "The Nuer: Age-Sets," p. 238). Among the Masai the operators must be Dorobo, i.e., non-Masai, and thus clearly nonpriests (Hollis, p. 297). Priests do, however, supervise the proceedings, as they do all important ceremonial (Fox, p. 461).

30. B. Bernardi, "The Age System of the Nilo-Hamitic Peoples: A Critical Evaluation," *Africa* 22 (1952):317.

31. Lienhardt, p. 73; Forde, p. 300.

they try to remedy them by prayer or more often by sacrifice.[32] In these instances the priest determines what kind of an offering is to be made, and to what spirit or deity it should be offered.[33] The warrior provides the proper animal, and the priest presides over the ritual, securing success by means of his closer relation to the sacred realm.[34] In this respect the priest protects and looks after the warriors' welfare, and he may even undertake sacrifice on his own initiative when he foresees hardship.[35] While this is, in one sense, simply an outgrowth of the priest's role of presiding at all ceremonies[36] and of sustaining his tribe (the Dinka go so far as to say that the priests' life force sustains the life of the tribe and of the cattle),[37] it is also an important form of cooperation between priests and warriors and an important step in the cattle cycle, wherein the cattle that warriors capture on raids are handed over to the priests for sacrifice.

The Supremacy of Priests

It will be noted, however, that in all these instances of cooperation between priests and warriors, the priests invariably remain in a dominant position. They must give their permission for raids to take place or for initiation to occur; success in raids depends on their assistance; the cause of troubles can only be divined through their powers; and they alone can effectively intercede with the deities on a warrior's behalf. In all these respects warriors are totally reliant upon and subservient to priests among the Dinka and Masai, although the Nuer are a somewhat different case, as we shall see.

For the Dinka and Masai, however, the priests remain a class apart from the warriors and exalted above them. The priests are a closed group, established in hereditary fashion[38] and limited to descendants of only one subclan in the case of the Masai.[39] Furthermore, they develop long and complex myths that tell of the first priest and the origin of his powers.[40] Often he is said to have come from heaven or from the celestial sovereign

---

32. Lienhardt, p. 73; Fokken, p. 245.
33. Hollis, pp. 325–27; Forde, p. 300.
34. Ibid.
35. Fokken, p. 245.
36. Fox, p. 461; Stubbs, p. 247.
37. Lienhardt, p. 207.
38. Fokken, p. 251; Forde, p. 300; Fox, p. 461; Hollis, pp. 325–26; Bedri, "Notes on Dinka Religious Beliefs," p. 125; Lienhardt, p. 8. The Nuer priests, such as they are, are also selected on a hereditary basis. See Evans-Pritchard, *Nuer Religion,* pp. 292–93, 304.
39. They are all descendants of Kidongi, who was of the Aiser clan. See Fokken, Forde, Fox, and Hollis cited in the preceding note.
40. Fokken, pp. 250–51; Hollis, pp. 325–26; Bedri, "Notes on Dinka Religious Beliefs," pp. 125 ff.; and Lienhardt, pp. 173 ff., who gives an extremely thorough account, including many variants of the basic mythologem. See also the text in Crazzolara, *Zur Gesellschaft und Religion,* pp. 9–12 on the origin of the leopard-skin priest, which is remarkable for its warrior nature.

himself,[41] and as a result his descendants, the priests of the present day, are regarded with some awe as "descendants of a holy man or rather spirits incarnate."[42]

Accordingly, priests are given great respect. But the effects of this ideology go beyond deference: priests are also granted authority in equal measure to their prestige. Their power extends to all matters of tribal concern[43] and is largely political as well as religious in nature, although the two are not always distinguishable and the former always flows from the latter.[44] For this reason, the priests' proper role has often been misunderstood, and they were called "chiefs" in much of the early literature,[45] despite the general absence of centralized political organization in East Africa.[46]

The tribal organization of the Dinka is particularly interesting in this respect. All clans are divided into two groups. On the one hand there are the Kic clans, the warriors or commoners; on the other are the Dindyor or Bany, the priests.[47] These priests are the descendants of Aiwel Longar, the first priest, and they possess sacred spears passed down from him as emblems of their office.[48] The spears are used in sacrifice and for other rituals, such as invoking aid for victory in war,[49] but they may only be used by a proper member of a Dindyor clan, for in the hands of anyone else they will be without power.[50] The priests are truly "power-full" and are thought to support the entire tribe—people and animals—by virtue of their excess life force.[51] Accordingly they are the acknowledged masters of the tribe, while the warriors are without any right to direct or rule.[52] A hymn sung by Pagong, one of the priestly clans, is most telling in this respect:

> It was great Longar, first [priest] created by the Creator,
> And Jiel of the *awar* grass, [who] first created
> Shrines and fishing spears and the *alal* spear
> And prayer and invocation.

41. Fokken, pp. 250-51; Hollis, pp. 325-26; Bedri, "Notes on Dinka Religious Beliefs," p. 125.
42. Bedri, "Notes on Dinka Religious Beliefs," p. 125.
43. Lienhardt, pp. 210-12.
44. Forde, p. 300; Bedri, "Notes on Dinka Religious Beliefs," p. 125; Lienhardt, pp. 210-12; Stubbs, p. 247. In contrast, Fosbrooke, p. 15, undervalues the political importance of the priest, while Howell, "Notes on the Ngork Dinka," p. 264, overvalues it.
45. See note 1, this chapter.
46. See John Middleton and David Tait, eds., *Tribes Without Rulers* (London, 1958).
47. Lienhardt, p. 8; Bedri, "Notes on Dinka Religious Beliefs," p. 125.
48. Bedri, "Notes on Dinka Religious Beliefs," pp. 128-29; on the significance of the spear, see Evans-Pritchard, "Nuer Spear Symbolism," *Anthropological Quarterly* 26 (1953):1-19.
49. Lienhardt, pp. 252-54.
50. Ibid., p. 253.
51. Ibid., p. 207.
52. Bedri, "Notes on Dinka Religious Beliefs," p. 125.

> Do not cease to pray, do not cease, Longar,
> The child of the warrior clan cannot head the camp,
> You will be married into the camp . . .
> The warrior clans cannot head the camp,
> You will be married into the camp . . .
> The warrior clans cannot head the camp
> If priests and Nhialic do not help the land.
> Yet the Creator will listen, he who created Longar
>   in the past.
> If it be war, then we shall ask Pagong, all Pagong,
> Pagong of the Awan tribe, Pagong of the Wau tribe.
> In the subtribe Biong, do not Pagong lead there?
> Great master of the *alal* spear,
> If Pagong pray, the great one [Nhialic] is brought to
>   the country.[53]

All the points we have noted are contained in this hymn: the hierarchical superiority of priests to warriors, the unfitness of warriors to rule, the importance of priests for success in battle, the priests' descent from the first priest and their possession of his spear, and the special proximity of the priests to the celestial sovereign. It is clear that the price of cooperation between priests and warriors is the supremacy of priests and that the priestly cycle and warrior cycle can be fused only if priests are placed in the ascendant position.

The Eating of Meat

A particularly fascinating example of the supremacy of priests is to be seen in the ideology that surrounds meat eating, most particularly the eating of beef. Beef is much valued and constitutes the major part of the East African diet along with cow's milk.[54] Ideally, one should eat nothing but milk and meat, and in the past this may actually have been the case with the Masai,[55] although it is less clear among the Nuer and Dinka, who tend to include other items in their diet despite their primary emphasis on cattle products. Although meat is much desired, no cattle are killed for their meat alone[56] with one important exception, to which we shall return. When cattle are sacrificed or die a natural death they are consumed,[57] and in this way every animal is ultimately headed for the pot;[58] but in general

---

53. Lienhardt, p. 211, slightly altered.
54. Hollis, pp. 317, 319; Merker, p. 85; Evans-Pritchard, *The Nuer*, pp. 18, 26, 82–83; Deng, *The Dinka*, p. 2; Lienhardt, p. 4.
55. R. W. E. Lewis, p. 72; Hollis, p. 319.
56. R. W. E. Lewis, p. 72; Hollis, p. 317; Evans-Pritchard, *Nuer Religion*, p. 265; Crazzolara, "Bedeutung des Rindes," p. 304; Deng, *The Dinka*, p. 2; Lienhardt, p. 21; Titherington, p. 191.
57. Ibid.
58. Deng, *The Dinka*, p. 21.

no man will take it upon himself to kill so valuable and beloved an animal as an ox or cow simply because he is hungry. As the Masai put it, any person who would do such a thing is looked upon as a Dorobo—a barbarian who knows nothing about cattle.[59]

There are, moreover, religious sanctions against wanton slaughter. According to the Nuer and Dinka, an ox killed for meat is killed *bang lora* ("just for nothing") and may return to haunt its killer.[60] A Masai myth tells that slaughter for food violates a commandment of Ngai given when he first created cattle.[61] It is not so much that cattle are sacred and thus inviolate; rather, there is a proper way to kill them and that way is sacrifice, a process whereby the animal's life is offered up to the celestial sovereign and the meat remains as man's portion.[62] To kill an ox outside of sacrifice is to do it an injustice, to treat it disrespectfully, and more importantly, to do god an injustice as well, robbing him of the life that is properly his. Finally, it is an injustice to the entire tribe, for it deprives them of a valuable resource that might be properly used at some time. The killing of an ox is an important matter, and it must be done correctly. Regardless of one's desire for meat, one does not slaughter cattle "just for nothing."

There is, however, one exception to this rule, namely, the warriors' use of meat as a strengthening food, a highly significant practice, and the one point at which cattle are diverted from the normal flow of the cattle cycle. Warriors of the Nuer, Dinka, and Masai kill vast numbers of cattle to build up their physical strength, and in no way is this consecrated by sacrifice.

The use of strengthening food first appears during the period of convalescence following a warrior's initiatory operation.[63] After their recovery, the young Nuer men—who are now warriors—are taken to specially prepared camps, known as *nak* ("killing") camps. Each one must bring an ox, although nowadays two may share an ox.[64] The camp is separated from the village; girls are forbidden to enter; and only a few elders are present.[65] Every two or three days an ox is killed, and the novices gorge themselves on the meat, remaining in camp until every animal has been

59. Hollis, pp. 289, 317.
60. Evans-Pritchard, *Nuer Religion,* p. 265; Lienhardt, p. 21.
61. Fokken, pp. 249–50.
62. Evans-Pritchard, "Some Forms and Features," p. 115.
63. Merker, p. 64; Leakey, p. 190; Crazzolara, "Gar-Zeremonie," p. 32: Evans-Pritchard, "The Nuer: Age-Sets," p. 242; Deng, *The Dinka,* p. 72.
64. Howell, "Age-Set System," p. 175; Jackson, p. 146.
65. Howell, "Age-Set System," p. 177. Howell rightly perceived that this separation was related to the young warriors' state of spiritual peril, but he oversimplified matters by being content with categorizing this spiritual peril as related only to their liminal state in the initiation process.

killed and eaten.[66] In no way can this slaughter be understood as sacrifice;[67] its sole purpose is the strengthening of the young warriors.[68]

Among the Nuer the use of strengthening foods seems to end here, but the Masai continue to hold regular meat feasts among their warriors for years after they have been initiated.[69] Further, the warriors arrange meat feasts just before battle in order to strengthen themselves, and as we have seen, these are an important part of their magico-religious preparation for battle. The meat is believed to give strength, and the use of it is almost pharmaceutical, different quantities of meat being prescribed for each foe.[70] In a text recorded by Merker, a Masai leader tells his men, "[This enemy] is strong, and you therefore should first take a meat feast [*Waldmahl*] of twelve days."[71] It must be emphasized that the killing in these feasts is not sacrifice, and the means employed for slaughtering the animals is quite different from that used in sacrificial ritual.[72]

The Dinka have yet a third means whereby warriors eat illicit beef to gain strength. While the Masai eat before battle, the Dinka warrior falls on the cattle he has captured immediately after the successful completion of a raid and apparently eats the meat to recover the strength he has expended in battle.[73] Deng notes that the practice is considered shameful and refers to the animals thus killed as "disgracefully skewered for

66. Howell, "Age-Set System," p. 176; Jackson, p. 146; Evans-Pritchard, "The Nuer: Age-Sets," pp. 245 ff.; and *The Nuer,* p. 26; Merker, p. 60.

67. This has been the opinion of every authority who has commented on the practice. Evans-Pritchard, however, was so disturbed by this apparent breach of sacrificial etiquette that he changed his interpretation of the *nak* camps no fewer than three times. See "The Nuer: Age-Sets," pp. 245–46; *The Nuer,* p. 26; the postscript to Howell's "Age-Set System;" "The Sacrificial Role of Cattle," p. 193; and *Nuer Religion,* p. 264. In his last statement on the subject his contention—based on terribly scanty evidence collected for him at second hand by Lienhardt—was that while the killings in the *nak* camps were clearly not proper sacrifices, still they had "to some extent a sacrificial character" (*Nuer Religion,* p. 265). This opinion is, however, totally untenable in the light of all the other evidence among the Nuer and the comparative case of the Masai.

68. This was the opinion of the first to report the custom, and in my opinion it remains fully justified. See Jackson, p. 146; Seligmans, p. 209. The informant of the Seligmans told them that it was designed to increase the sexual power of the young men, an idea inextricably intertwined with that of "strength," as in our own notion of "virility." Howell, "Age-Set System," p. 178, is inclined to see the meat feast as connected with initiation, being one last ritual to bind the age-set together. Evans-Pritchard, "Sacrificial Role of Cattle," p. 193, tentatively agreed with this opinion, but this would in no way explain the significance of the eating of meat—any type of activity might serve equally well. In fact, Evans-Pritchard seems to have been closest to the truth in his first attempt to deal with the problem, when he said that the *nak* camps had no function other than meat eating ("The Nuer: Age-Sets," pp. 245–46).

69. Merker, p. 61; Hollis, p. 317; Bernardi, "Age System of the Masai," pp. 298–99; Leakey, p. 208; R. W. E. Lewis, p. 73.

70. Merker, p. 92.

71. Ibid., p. 91. "Sie ist stark und ihr werdet deshalb erst ein zwolftägiges Waldmahl."

72. Ibid., pp. 61, 73, 192.

73. Deng, *The Dinka,* p. 76.

meat."[74] Yet it is a normal part of the raiding practice and one of great importance to the warrior. Nuer, Masai, and Dinka differ in the means by which their warriors obtain and consume meat for strengthening food, but they all have the practice in common.

The meat feast is, then, an anomaly. Cattle are killed solely for their meat and without regard for proper sacrificial practice. These animals are taken out of the sacred cycle in which they properly circulate, and they are used by the warriors for their own ends. The practice is sacrilegious, marking the warriors as impure and exposing them to spiritual danger,[75] but it continues because it is necessary to their success and thus to the tribe's survival. In order to carry out their proper, sacred function of procuring cattle in raids, the warriors must first indulge in the sacrilegious eating of meat. For this reason they are ambiguous figures, both sacred and profane, and therefore inferior and subordinate to the priests.[76]

Priests and Warriors in Conflict

This subordination of warriors to priests, which is so necessary in the maintenance of the cattle cycle, is not without its negative consequences. Resentment is aroused, and tensions do exist between the two groups that threaten the harmony of the tribe. Again, the clearest example is the Dinka.

In the Pagong hymn cited above, we caught a glimpse of the way in which the priestly clans exult in their position above the warriors. There are other examples, however—even more striking and painful to the warriors' pride. All the priests' claims—that they are closer to the celestial sovereign, that their clans originated in heaven, that they have more life force than the others, that they alone are entitled to wield the ancestral spears, or to rule—all these have derogatory implications for the warrior clans. A more direct form of disparagement comes in the matter of the clan divinities.

Among the Dinka, each clan is associated with several clan divinities or totemic spirits.[77] Of these deities, the most important and powerful is Ring, whose name literally means "flesh."[78] Ring is said to be possessed by all the priestly clans, which is to say that they are privileged to partici-

74. Ibid. Note that Deng is himself a member of a priestly clan of the Dinka.

75. This is the reason for the ritual precautions that surround the meat feasts and not some vague "perils of initiation" as Howell would have it. In point of fact, all the initiatory rites are open, and the presence of all is welcome. It is difficult to understand, then, why the *nak* camps would be closed if the only danger is from initiation.

76. Is it possible that this is the significance of the fact that among the Dinka the deity *Ring* (literally, "flesh") belongs only to the priests and not to the warriors (Lienhardt, p. 109)? I am inclined to think so. Also note that the diet of the Masai priest is restricted to goat liver, milk, and honey, no beef being permitted (Forde, p. 301).

77. Lienhardt, passim; Stubbs, pp. 245 ff.

78. Lienhardt, p. 143.

pate in his worship, but this is not the case for the warrior clans—a fact that the priests are quick to point out.[79] Sacrifice to him is very special, and only priests may participate in it.[80] It takes place at night, unlike any other offering, and the meat is eaten raw by the priests,[81] while all other meat must be boiled.[82] Moreover, only priests may eat this meat, while in all other sacrifices the meat is shared.[83]

Priests also slander the clan divinities that the warriors do possess. In this light, Lienhardt reported, "I have heard it suggested, by members of important priestly clans, that some of the minor warrior clans have really no clan divinity at all—that they have in fact invented the divinities which they now lay claim to."[84]

This is an extremely provocative statement, which any warrior would find offensive, but his position of inferiority is such that in many cases he might not be able to object. Occasionally, however, the warriors' resentment and strength permit countermeasures. Thus, one warrior clan, Padiangbar, when present in sufficient numbers, claims to have Ring as their clan divinity, and thereby to equal the priests in rank.[85] This kind of conflict—claims, counterclaims, insult, and indignation—is always beneath the surface of normal Dinka society. For the most part the tension is controlled, and the integrated functioning of warriors and priests continues unimpeded, but in one significant instance a dramatic schism and open warfare seems to have been the result.

Most authorities have suspected that the Nuer and Dinka were originally one people,[86] and the tribes themselves hold this opinion,[87] but it is only recently that the nature of the relation between them has been perceived. The latest research now indicates that the Nuer were originally a warrior clan of the Dinka,[88] which achieved military superiority over the other clans through an improved system of kinship organization[89] and which effectively broke away from the main tribe and began raiding on it.[90] While the two main authorities who have proven this case disagree on the

79. Ibid., pp. 109, 143–44.
80. Ibid., pp. 143–44.
81. Ibid.
82. Ibid., p. 82; Stubbs, p. 249.
83. Lienhardt, pp. 23, 233–34.
84. Ibid., p. 116.
85. Ibid., p. 145.
86. Seligmans, p. 206; Evans-Pritchard, *The Nuer,* p. 3; Howell, *Manual of Nuer Law,* p. 7.
87. This is clear in the myths of origins and in the willingness of Nuer to adopt Dinka and Dinka to adopt Nuer. In fact, neither tribe regards the other as "foreigners," and the Dinka regard the Nuer as one of the Dinka "peoples."
88. Newcomer; and Glickman, cited above, note 5, chapter 2.
89. Newcomer, pp. 7–8; Glickman, p. 586. Both rely heavily on Sahlins, cited above, note 6, Chapter 2.
90. Newcomer, pp. 7–8; Glickman, p. 587.

EAST AFRICA: PRIESTLY CYCLE AND WARRIOR CYCLE

extent to which ecological features contributed to the Nuer "mutation" and schism,[91] this point is not in any way crucial to our discussion.

It is worthy of note, however, that the Nuer were a warrior clan and not a subtribe.[92] Had they been a subtribe, they would have included priests among their numbers, and this was not the case. Perhaps the most striking difference between the Nuer and the Dinka is the importance of the priesthood among the Dinka.[93] And, whereas Dinka priests occupy a clear position of hierarchical supremacy, the Nuer are fiercely egalitarian and such "priests" as they have are considered no better than any other man.[94] They do not hold any special prerogatives, do not even preside at sacrifice,[95] and the functions they do retain are as much juridicial as religious.[96]

Observing this, Lienhardt concluded that the Nuer priesthood was "less developed" than that of the Dinka.[97] But in the light of the most recent scholarship it appears rather that the Nuer system is a conscious reaction against the Dinka hierarchy, with its subordination of warriors to priests. Originally every Nuer was a warrior, and this remains the case.[98] Their systems are the result of a warriors' rebellion against priestly domination. As a result, their interpretation of the cattle cycle is somewhat different from that of the Dinka and Masai, and warrior elements of the cycle play a more prominent role.[99]

In all instances, however, the presence of cattle remains the central feature. Warriors and priests each have a characteristic means of seeking to ensure the wealth and well-being of the tribe, and often the two groups work together in harmony, as is the usual case among the Masai and Dinka. Certain tensions are always present, however, and open hostility or schism can occur, as with the Nuer.

Nonetheless, many cultural and religious forms remain constant within these tribes; cattle sacrifice, cattle raiding, myths of the first sacrifice and first raid, the celestial sovereign, and warrior gods always tend to be present. These features dominate the religious life of the East African Nilotic tribes, and it will be interesting to see if they are found among the Indo-Iranians, to whom we now turn our attention.

91. Glickman, pp. 587-88, 592.
92. This follows from a consideration of the differences between Nuer and Dinka institutions, and from the analysis of Newcomer, pp. 6-9.
93. See above, note 1, this chapter.
94. Evans-Pritchard, *The Nuer*, p. 173.
95. Evans-Pritchard, *Nuer Religion*, pp. 287-89. The officiant at any sacrifice is the *gwan buthni*, the "master of ceremonies," who may be any senior man who is specifically qualified to preside at that specific sacrifice, usually by virtue of his position within the lineage group.
96. Evans-Pritchard, *The Nuer*, chapter 4. The chief function of the leopard-skin priest is now the settlement of homicide disputes.
97. Lienhardt, p. 219.
98. Evans-Pritchard, *The Nuer*, p. 254.
99. The two chief differences are that the myth of the first sacrifice is not found among the Nuer and that the role of priests in sacrificing cattle to the celestial sovereign has been taken over by lineage heads or other qualified men.

IV

THE INDO-IRANIAN PRIESTLY CYCLE

In moving to the Indo-Iranian portion of the study, we find a situation considerably more complex than that encountered in East Africa in terms of the materials available for research. Obviously, there are no first-hand reports by an Evans-Pritchard or a Herskovits to guide us, and, what is more, true primary texts are lacking as well. For the Proto-Indo-Iranian culture ceased to exist more than 3,500 years ago, before the composition of even the earliest written texts. We are thus forced to rely on later texts for evidence, and here there is an overabundance of data, in contrast to the absence of earlier sources. In Iran, the *Gātha*s of Zarathustra, dating to 1000 B.C.,[1] are extremely valuable, as are the great *Yašt*s of the Younger Avesta, and even the Pahlavi texts from the ninth century A.D. contain some material that is quite old in origin. In India the situation is

---

1. I follow those who have been unwilling to accept the traditional dating of Zarathustra to the 6th century B.C. since it is supported by only one citation in texts from the 9th century A.D., which states that Zarathustra lived 258 years before Alexander. The chronology of these texts is most imaginative, and all other evidence argues against the acceptance of this date. See Herman Lommel, "Der medische Name Mazdaka," *Zeitschrift für vergleichende Sprachforschung* 58 (1930):140–42; Christian Bartholomae, "Zarathustra: His Life and Doctrine," in *Indo-Iranian Studies in Honour of Sanjana* (London, 1925), p. 8; Arthur Christensen, "Quelques notices sur les plus anciennes périodes du Zoroastrisme," *Acta Orientalia* 4 (1926):81–92; Roland G. Kent, "The Name Ahuramazda," in *Oriental Studies in Honor of Pavry* (London, 1933), pp. 200–208. Recently, Paul Freidrich, *Proto-Indo-European Syntax* (Butte, Mont., 1975), pp. 44–46, has produced results that make the traditional dating completely untenable. He has shown that the syntax of the *Gāthas* lies much closer to that of Proto-Indo-European (subject-object-verb word order), while that of the Younger Avesta (tending toward subject-verb-object) has shifted considerably. Such a major syntactic change could only have occurred over many centuries and makes the dating of the prophet to around 900–1000 B.C. highly likely, as was urged by the above authors on the strength of other evidence.

similar: the *Rg Veda*, composed some time between the twelfth and six-teenth centuries B.C.,[2] is a veritable storehouse of information, as are the other *Vedas*, the *Brāhmaṇas*, and even such a late source as the *Bṛhaddevata*. Each of these texts has its own peculiar history, point of view, and peculiarities that merit careful inspection. Given the wealth of this material, one might easily despair of ever making a way through the welter of detail.

In this drought or deluge situation, it is important to remain aware of the primary goal, namely, the reconstruction of Indo-Iranian religion, and thus the facts of later Indian and Iranian development are of interest only insofar as they aid in the reconstruction of this earlier stratum. Recon-struction is made possible only through the use of correspondences—one-to-one pairings of items found in both India and Iran. When such a corre-spondence has been adduced, we mark it with an asterisk and regard it as a reconstructed element of Indo-Iranian culture.[3] The use of correspon-dences has usually been confined to linguistic realms—chiefly words and divine names—but more recently it has been powerfully employed for adducing myths and ritual actions as well.[4] In general, I have concentrated my search for corresponding features on the oldest Indian and Iranian materials, but I have never hesitated to go wherever a correspondence may lead, for ultimately the date of a text's composition is no measure of the age of the material it contains.

2. Arthur Berriedale Keith, *The Religion and Philosophy of the Veda and Upanishads* (Cambridge, Mass., 1925), p. 7; Renou, *Vedic India*, p. 10.

3. On the linguistic use of correspondences, see Hoenigswald, pp. 13–14, 119 ff.; Meillet, *Méthode comparative*, pp. 1–2, 22–40.

4. In the broadest sense, analysis of myths through the use of correspondences has been employed by Claude Lévi-Strauss in such works as *The Raw and the Cooked* (New York, 1969) and the other volumes of his *Mythologiques* series. But with regard to Indo-European studies, the most important advances have been made by Georges Dumézil, whose lifetime of research is now culminated in *Mythe et epopée*, 3 vols. (Paris, 1968–73). Dumézil's work has excited great interest, and two journals have devoted special issues to him of late (*Journal of Asian Studies* 34 [1974], and *Nouvelle Ecole* 21–22 [Winter 1972–73]). His theories have been highly controversial, however, and he has sparked sharp antagonism such as that expressed in Thieme, *Mitra and Aryaman;* John Brough, "The Tripartite Ideology of the Indo-Europeans: An Experiment in Method," *Bulletin of the School of Oriental and African Studies* 22 (1959):69–85; and Jan Gonda, "Some Observations on Dumézil's Views of Indo-European Mythology," *Mnemosyne* 13 (1960):1–15. In brief, let me state here that while I do accept Dumézil's view of the I-E and I-I class structure (with the reservations expressed below in note 6, this chapter), I have serious difficulties with his view of their respective pantheons. In particular, I cannot accept the opinions expressed in his *Naissance d'Archanges*, in which he tries to show that Zarathustra retained the old I-I gods under the guise of the Amǝša Spǝntas. The textual evidence adduced is not terribly con-vincing, and such a theory is in total opposition to the spirit of Zarathustra's reform. I do ac-cept the crucial importance of the gods *Mitra, *Varuna, and *Indra *Vṛtraghna, but I do not feel that they can be recovered among the Amǝša Spǝntas: one must look elsewhere to recover their trace. For a good assessment of the failings of Dumézil's treatment of Iranian material, see Gherardo Gnoli, "L'Iran e l'ideologia tripartita," *Studia e Materiali di Storia delle Religioni* 36 (1965):193–210.

THE INDO-IRANIAN PRIESTLY CYCLE

One further consideration has served to limit the scope of the investigation, however. A complete reconstruction of Indo-Iranian religion is not intended. Rather, I have undertaken a study of a major, perhaps even a crucial feature of Indo-Iranian religion—the role of cattle—and this will serve as the organizing focus of the investigation.[5] Ultimately, if my hypothesis is correct, some similarities will emerge between East African religious forms and those of the ancient Indo-Iranians.

One of the first and most striking resemblances between these societies is the clear distinction made in both areas between priestly and warrior classes.[6] Further, there is a corresponding distinction made at the divine level between sovereign gods—the *asuras* (Skt. *ásura-* = Av. *ahura-*)[7]— and warrior gods—the *daivas* (Skt. *devá-* = Av. *daēva-*, OPers. *daiva*).[8] This opposition has been noted by virtually all Indologists and Iranists

5. Thus, some features that are clearly Indo-Iranian, such as the god *Apām *Napāt (Skt. *Apā́m Nápāt* = Av. *Apąm Napāt*), "Descendant of the Waters," and the cult of fire will not figure in this study. On the former, see Dumézil, *Mythe et Epopée*, 3: 21–89; Jaan Puhvel, "Aquam Exstinguere," *Journal of Indo-European Studies* 1 (1973):378–86; and C. Scott Littleton, "Poseidon as a Reflex of the Indo-European 'Source of Waters' God," *Journal of Indo-European Studies* 1 (1973):423–40.

6. Dumézil has consistently argued in favor of a tripartite social order among the Indo-Europeans and the Indo-Iranians. He divides these societies along the lines priests (or sovereigns) and warriors and those concerned with fertility and prosperity (i.e. herdsmen, agriculturalists, merchants, women, etc.). For a concise statement of his views, see *Les dieux des indo-européens* (Paris, 1952), *L'idéologie tri-partie des indo-européens* (Brussels, 1958), or Littleton, *New Comparative Mythology*. Certainly Dumézil is right in making this division, but there are problems with regard to his "third function" that bother me. The category is terribly general, and I am inclined to see it as something of a catch-all, including everyone in society who was not a priest or a warrior. Thus I do not see it as a "function" in the same sense that members of the first two groups were identifiable by a specialized vocation, and I would simply call it the "third class" or better, the "commoners." Priests and warriors do predominate in the mythology and religious ideology (although it may be that the lower class mythology was preserved only in folk traditions that were not recorded), and for this reason they will play the major role in this study.

7. Güntert, *Arische Weltkönig*, p. 102, first noted the correspondence of these terms to Germanic *ansuz (ON *áss*, plural *æsir;* OE *ōs;* OHG *ansi-, ans-* as an element in persons' names), a term designating sovereign gods among the Germans. His argument is accepted by Julius Pokorny, *Indogermanisches etymologisches Wörterbuch* (Bern, 1959), p. 48; Manfred Mayrhofer, *Kurzgefasstes etymologisches Wörterbuch des Altindischen*, 3 vols. (Heidelberg, 1956), 1:65; Jan de Vries, *Altnordisches etymologisches Wörterbuch* (Leiden, 1961), p. 16; Franz Rolf Schröder, "Ase und Gott," *Beiträge zur Geschichte der deutschen Sprache und Literatur* 51 (1927):29–30; and Edgar Polomé, "L'etymologie du terme germanique *ansuz,* 'dieu souverain,' " *Études Germaniques* 8 (1953):36–44, who added the Hittite term *haššuš,* "king," "lord," to the equation. Note the opposing theory of B. Schlerath, "Altindisch *asu-,* awestisch *ahu-* und ähnlich klingende Wörter," in *Pratidānam: Studies Presented to F. B. J. Kuiper* (The Hague, 1968), pp. 142–53. In India, the Asuras gradually sank to the level of demons or antigods, and the transition is already apparent in the 10th book of the *Rg Veda,* although it is not evident in the earlier books and must thus be dated as an India-specific transformation. In Iran, the Ahuras find their chief representative in the highest god, Ahura Mazdā, but it must be noted that the term does still occur in the plural to denote the gods grouped around him (*Y.* 30.9, 31.4). On this, see B. Geiger, pp. 93–99; and R. C. Zaehner, *The Dawn and Twilight of Zoroastrianism* (New York, 1961), pp. 82–83.

8. Derivation from P-I-E *deiwo-* "god," "heavenly one," has been established in Grace Sturtevant Hopkins, *Indo-European *Deiwos and Related Words* (Philadelphia,

who have written on the topic and is generally taken as one of the chief features of the Indo-Iranian religious system.[9] In this chapter I will examine the former group and the elements of the "priestly cycle," namely, the celestial sovereign, his role in giving cattle, and the role of the priest in returning those cattle to him by means of sacrifice. Finally, we shall look at the myth that establishes this sacrificial exchange arrangement and serves as a "charter" for it.[10]

The Celestial Sovereigns

The Indo-European sky god and sovereign *Dieu-s stands out as the one figure who can be identified clearly in most of the Indo-European regions. His name is derived from P-I-E *deiwo- ("sky," "heaven") and appears in Greek as Ζεύς (genitive Διϝός), in Latin as Diūs (locative Iove, vocative Iū-piter), in Germanic as *Teiwaz (ON Týr; OE Tīg, Tīw; OHG Ziu), and in Sanskrit as Dyáus.[11] There is, moreover, a generally unnoticed occurrence of his name in Avestan, Yt. 3.13:

> Aša strikes thousands of thousands, myriads of myriads of the daēvas. Death-bringing Aŋra Mainyu (the "evil spirit"), the lyingest of the daēvas, falls from the far side of heaven (dyaoš).[12]

The word translated "heaven" here is Avestan dyav- (genitive dyaoš),[13]

1932); accepted by Pokorny, pp. 185–86; Mayrhofer, Etym. Wörterbuch, 2: 63–64. In later Zoroastrian texts, daēva- has come to mean "demon," but the fact that it retains the meaning "god" in certain Iranian dialects shows that this was the original I-I sense. See Theodore Nöldeke, "Der weisse Dēv von Mazandaran," Archiv für Religionswissenschaft 18 (1915):597–600; and "Dēva," Zeitschrift für Indologie und Iranistik 2 (1923):318; and Geo Widengren, Die Religionen Irans (Stuttgart, 1965), p. 160. Also, it has been established that Zarathustra himself used the word in the sense of "the old gods" in a somewhat contemptuous tone, but did recognize the status of the daēvas as gods. See E. Benveniste, "Hommes et dieux dans l'Avesta," in Festschrift für Wilhelm Eilers (Wiesbaden, 1967), pp. 144–47; and Ilya Gershevitch, "Die Sonne das Beste," in Mithraic Studies, pp. 79–81.

9. See, inter alia, Abel Bergaigne, La religion védique, 3 vols. (Paris, 1883; repr. 1963), 3: 74 ff., 139 ff.; Jan Gonda, Die Religionen Indiens, 3 vols. (Stuttgart, 1960), 1: 76; Keith, Religion and Philosophy, p. 101; Renou, Vedic India, pp. 93–94; Herman Lommel, Die Religion Zarathustras (Tubingen, 1930), pp. 51–52, 248–49; Widengren, Religionen Irans, p. 20; Zaehner, p. 39; Dumézil, Dieux des Indo-Européens, pp. 7–8, 15–16; Güntert, Arische Weltkönig, p. 116.

10. Using this term in the sense pioneered by Malinowski. See esp. "Myth in Primitive Psychology," Magic, Science, and Religion (Garden City, N.J., 1954), p. 108.

11. Hopkins, pp. 15, 75–79; Pokorny, p. 185.

12. yō janat aēšąm daēvanąm hazaŋrāi hazanrō pairi; baēvarāi baēvanō; pairi paourva.naēmāt patat dyaoš daēvanąm draojištō aŋrō mainyuš pouru.mahrkō.

13. Peter von Bradke, Dyaus Asura (Halle, 1885), p. 83, argued that dyaoš here is a nominative form, but Bartholomae, Arische Forschungen, 3 vols. (Halle, 1882), 1: 67 showed it to be an irregular genitive, similar to the gaoš drafšo of Y. 10.14. Clearly, dyaoš depends on the ablative paurva.naēmāt, "from the far side of . . . ." The phrase is properly translated in Lommel, Yašts, p. 23.

which corresponds exactly to Sanskrit *Dyáus*. This is the sole Avestan occurrence, and here the word that signifies the lofty sky god in so many other Indo-European languages is used only in the sense of the sky, without divine connotation. This is a common fate of sky gods, who because of their separation from man tend to gradually become remote and inactive—*dei otiosi*.[14] In India Dyaus fares little better. Generally he appears as Dyaus pitṛ, "Father Sky," mentioned in a formulaic and cursory way—frequently joined with Pṛthivī matṛ, "Mother Earth." Even when he does appear alone, he rarely plays a role of any importance, being simply characterized as the heavenly father (as in *RV* 4.1.10, 1.164.33). There is nothing to indicate that a god *Dyaus figured actively in the Indo-Iranian pantheon, although such a god seems to have been known. Apparently the great Indo-European god had already moved into the background by the time of Indo-Iranian unity.[15]

But if it is a common fate for the sky god to become otiose, it is also quite common for him to be replaced by other sovereign deities, sometimes "splitting" into two or more figures.[16] This is clearly the case with *Dyaus. In Indian and Iranian texts, a group of six or seven closely associated deities take over the sovereign role (Skt. Ādityās·, Av. Aməša Spəntas),[17] indicating the existence of a similar Indo-Iranian group. The term Aməša Spənta, "Beneficent Immortal," seems to be a late coining in Avestan, and we thus cannot reconstruct the earlier Indo-Iranian name of the group.[18] Also, given that most of the Zoroastrian entities contained in the circle of the Aməša Spəntas are simply personified abstractions brought to prominence by Zarathustra,[19] we are similarly frustrated in any attempt to recover the names of all the members of the original group.

Two members, however, are distinct and stand at the head of the group as a dual deity. The first of these is named *Mitra (Skt. *Mitrá-* = Av. *Miθra-*; OPers. *Miθra-*), while the Indo-Iranian name of the second is less clear. In Sanskrit he is known as *Váruṇa*, which would find its phonetic correspondence in an Iranian *Vouruna*. This *Vouruna is unattested, however, and thus an Indo-Iranian *Varuna cannot be reconstructed with certainty. Given this state of affairs, some have been led to posit a god named *Asura (Skt. *ásura-*, as in *RV* 10.124.3 and elsewhere; Av. *Ahura*

14. See Eliade, *Patterns in Comparative Religion*, pp. 46–50; Pettazzoni, *Dio*, esp. pp. 351, 366–67.

15. As opposed to the thesis of von Bradke, *Dyaus Asura*, who considered Dyaus to have been the greatest god of the I-I and early *Rg Vedic* periods.

16. Widengren, *Hochgottglaube*, p. 77.

17. The best treatment of this correspondence remains that of B. Geiger, preferable to that of Dumézil, *Naissance d'Archanges;* Paul Thieme, "Die vedischen Āditya und die zarathustrischen Aməša Spənta," *Zarathustra* (Darmstadt, 1970), pp. 397–412; or Hermann Oldenberg, *Die Religion des Vedas* (Berlin, 1894), 185–93.

18. B. Geiger, pp. 93–99.

19. Ibid., p. 245.

Mazdā) as *Mitra's companion,[20] but given the overwhelming usage of this term in Sanskrit as a name for a class of deities, a usage also evident in such Gāthic passages as *Y.* 30.9 and 31.4, only very rarely being applied to an individual god whose *asura*-hood is being emphasized for the moment, I am inclined to believe that there was an Indo-Iranian *Varuna, whose Iranian reflex was fully replaced by Ahura Mazdā as a result of Zarathustra's reform.

In any event, the names of these two gods are consistently joined together in a dual dvandva compound (Skt. *Mitrā́várunā-*; Av. *Miθra.ahura;*[21] OPers. **Miça-ahuramazdā,* as attested by Gk. μεσόρομαςδης).[22] The literature of the *Brāhmaṇas* consistently links them together in a relation of complementarity to one another, a state of affairs already attested in *RV* 5.3.1, *AV* 9.3.18, and *AV* 13.1.13.[23] Earlier scholars sought to identify them as night and day,[24] or sun and moon,[25] while more recently they have been seen as contract and true speech,[26] legal sovereignty and magical sovereignty,[27] or—a most suggestive formulation—the progressive and regressive forces of the netherworld.[28]

Of the two gods, *Mitra is the easier to characterize. In both India and Iran his name occurs in the neuter gender as well as in the masculine, Av. *miθram* ("contract," "treaty") and Skt. *mitrám* ("friend," "friendship"). While most scholars have followed Meillet in positing "contract" as the original sense of the neuter, seeing the god as a personification of this social entity,[29] I believe a broader sense is preferable, deriving *Mitra from P-I-E *√*m(e)i-* ("to join together," "bind") with the instrumental suffix *-tro-* giving the sense of "that which joins together" for the neuter,

---

20. Thieme, " 'Aryan' Gods of the Mitanni Treaty," p. 308–309, following von Bradke, *Dyaus Asura.*

21. On the order of this compound, see J. Duchesne-Guillemin, "Ahura Miθra," *Mélanges Franz Cumont* (Brussels, 1936), pp. 683–85.

22. Stig Wikander, "Mithra en vieux-perse," *Orientalia Suecana* 2 (1953):66–68.

23. As stressed by F. B. J. Kuiper, "Review: Paul Thieme, *Mitra and Aryaman,*" *Indo-Iranian Journal* 3 (1959):210–11.

24. Bergaigne, 3: 21.

25. Oldenberg, *Religion des Vedas,* p. 193.

26. Thieme, *Mitra and Aryaman,* pp. 60–67, who sees a complementary relation between the gods as unattested in the earliest sources. He prefers to see them as parallel entities.

27. Georges Dumézil, *Mitra-Varuṇa* (Paris, 1948), esp. pp. 79–85. His formulations have been severely attacked by Thieme, *Mitra and Aryaman,* and Jan Gonda, *The Vedic God Mitra* (Leiden: E. J. Brill, 1972); and "Some Observations," pp. 1–15.

28. F. B. J. Kuiper, "Remarks on the *Avestan Hymn to Mithra,*" *Indo-Iranian Journal* 5 (1961):46.

29. Antoine Meillet, "Le dieu indo-iranien Mitra," *Journal Asiatique* 10 (1907):143–59. Meillet's argument, long accepted by Thieme, Gershevitch, Dumézil, et al., has now been called into question by Gonda, *The Vedic God Mitra;* and "Mitra in India," in *Mithraic Studies,* pp. 48–52.

which could cover friendship, contracts, alliances,[30] love, piety,[31] peace (comparing Russian *mir*),[32] and even so specific a referent as "girdle," "headband," as evidenced by Greek μίτρη. Correspondingly, the masculine **Mitra* could be rendered as "he who joins together [in friendship, harmony, contracts, and so on]."

For the most part, **Mitra* is a benign figure, protecting the man who honors and preserves the bonds he creates but punishing ruthlessly the one who is unfaithful, the **mitra-dhrugh* (Skt. *mitradrúḥ*, nom. *mitradhrúk-* = Av. *miθrō.drug-*), "he who betrays Mitra." In India, Mitra is not a very vivid god, usually being overshadowed by his "big brother," Varuṇa. In the entire *Rg Veda*, there is only one hymn addressed to Mitra by himself (3.59), from which we gain most of our knowledge about him. In contrast to this, the Iranian Miθra is one of the most distinct and picturesque of the Avestan gods, and the longest hymn of the Avesta is addressed to him (*Yt.* 10). Yet we must beware of relying on this *Yašt* too much, for the Iranian Miθra has a long and complex history. It appears that he was banished from the pantheon by Zarathustra[33] and reentered at a later date, perhaps as the result of Achaemenid political considerations.[34] In this later form, for which his *Yašt* is the chief evidence, he acquired numerous characteristics that were originally foreign to his nature. In particular, the Younger Avestan Miθra has a more markedly martial air to him than his Indian counterpart, and in numerous instances he can be seen to have acquired features of the Indo-Iranian warrior god, **Indra.*[35]

In using these sources, our test must be, as always, the existence of clear correspondences between India and Iran. Only those features attested in both areas may be presumed to have been present in the Indo-Iranian

30. Hanns-Peter Schmidt, "Indo-Iranian Mitra: The State of the Central Problem," *Études Mithriaques* (Leiden, 1978):348–93.

31. Wolfgang Lentz, "The 'Social Functions' of the Old Iranian Mithra," *W. B. Henning Memorial Volume* (London, 1970), pp. 245–55.

32. V. N. Toporov, "Parallels to Ancient Indo-Iranian Social and Mythological Concepts," in *Pratidānam*, pp. 108–13.

33. This is the classic view, and there is every reason why it should be maintained. Recently, however, Mary Boyce, "On Mithra's Part in Zoroastrianism," *Bulletin of the School of Oriental and African Studies* 32 (1969):10–34, has tried to argue that Miθra was never banished from the pantheon, but her arguments rest on speculation with little evidence. Along contrary lines, Helmut Humbach, "Der iranische Mithra als Daiva," in *Festgabe für Herman Lommel* (Wiesbaden, 1960), pp. 75–79, contended that Miθra was originally a *daēvic*, warrior god, but has retracted this in "Mithra in the Kuṣāṇa Period," in *Mithraic Studies*, p. 137–38.

34. Thus, Miθra was invoked first by Artaxerxes II but not by any of his predecessors. I. Scheftelowitz, "Die Mithra-Religion der Indoskythen," *Acta Orientalia* 11 (1933):296 and n., suggested that Miθra was rehabilitated when the Achaemenids absorbed the Scyths into their empire.

35. Zaehner, pp. 102–5; Widengren, *Religionen Irans*, p. 14.

period. Several specific features can thus be adduced, in addition to the general picture given above. In the first place *Mitra is sleepless, ever-vigilant in his protection of the law (*RV* 3.59.1 / *Yt.* 10.7).[36] Second, his realm stretches over all of heaven and earth (*RV* 3.59.1, 3, 7 / *Yt.* 10.12, 16, 44), while he himself is situated in the heavens (*RV* 5.63.1, 6.67.6 / *Yt.* 10.49–50). He is a sovereign, described as a "king whose lordship (or sovereignty) is good" in India (*rā́jā sukṣatró*, *RV* 3.59.4), and as "the lord of the country of all the countries" in Iran (*vīspanąm dahyunąm daiŋhupaitīm*, *Yt.* 10.145). He receives a libation sacrifice as his offering (*RV* 3.59.1–2, 5 / *Yt.* 10.4, 6, 16, 77). To those who have observed the law and offer sacrifice to him, he grants protection (*RV* 3.59.2 / *Yt.* 10.54–55), in addition to tangible gifts, which go unspecified in the Vedic hymn,[37] but which are listed as "herds of cattle and men" in Iran (*gə̄uśca vąθwa vīranąmca*, *Yt.* 10.28; see also *Yt.* 10.65).

When we turn to *Varuna, we find considerably more data with which to work than we did in the case of *Mitra. Although certain scholars have refused to accept the descent of Ahura Mazdā and Varuṇa from a common Indo-Iranian predecessor[38]—whose name I take to be *Varuna, although it may well have been something else—the vast majority have been willing to do so. Certainly the correspondences between the two deities are strong and numerous, such as would indicate a genetic relation.

Among the clearest of these is the god's supreme sovereignty: his ruler-ship over men, the world, and even other gods. This is clear throughout the Avesta, as in *Yt.* 1.15, where Ahura Mazdā lists among his names *xšaθryō.təma-* ("most sovereign"). In *RV* 6.67.5, the supreme sovereignty of Mitra and Varuṇa is noted and given a mythical background: "All the gods unanimously and readily, exulting, bestowed sovereignty *(kṣatrám)* on you two."[39] *Varuna's sovereignty is not only supreme—a fact also indicated by the Sanskrit title *samrā́j* ("universal monarch")—it is also good, as is indicated by his epithet *suksatra* (Skt. *sukṣatrá-* = Av. *huxšaθra-*), "he whose sovereignty is good."[40]

*Varuna's chief activity as sovereign was guarding the principle of *Rta (Skt. *r̥tá-* = Av. *aša-*; OPers. *arta-*), just as *Mitra's was establishing and preserving those ties which hold men together. *Rta has often been rendered as "truth,"[41] but the concept includes much more than that. It is

36. B. Geiger, p. 111. The term used would be *asvapna-* (Skt. *ásvapnaj-* = Av. *axᵛafna-*). Note also Miθra's chief epithet in Avestan, *vouru.gaoyaoiti-*, "protector of wide cattle pastures," on which see E. Benveniste, "Mithra aux vastes pâturages," *Journal Asiatique* 248 (1960):421–29. A Vedic reflex, *urú-gavyūti-*, occurs once (*RV* 9.90.4), with reference to Soma.

37. Mitra's favor is simply said to be *sānasí*, "bringing riches (*RV* 3.59.6).

38. Most notably Lommel, *Religion Zarathustras*, pp. 13–14, 101–105.

39. víśve yád vām maṅhánā mándamānāḥ kṣatrám deváso ádadhuḥ sajóṣāḥ /

40. B. Geiger, p. 225–26.

41. See especially, Heinrich Lüders, *Varuṇa*, Vol. 2: *Varuṇa und das R̥ta* (Göttingen, 1951).

THE INDO-IRANIAN PRIESTLY CYCLE

derived from the P-I-E verb *√ar-, "to fit together properly," "dovetail," "be suitable,"[42] and in Indo-Iranian speculation it is elevated to a cosmic scale, encompassing all that is fitting and proper.[43] In India, ṛtá- is usually presented as an impersonal principle (although occasionally personified),[44] while its Iranian counterpart, Aša, is personified as one of Ahura Mazdā's chief lieutenants, but in both instances an intimate relation is established between the sovereign god and this principle of world order.[45] As a token of this, *Varuna is called *ṛtắvan (Skt. ṛtávan- = Av. ašavan-), "possessor of the world order," as both Varuṇa and Ahura Mazdā frequently bear that title (RV 2.28.6, 5.65.2 / Y. 28.6, 48.3), guarding that cosmic order jealously and separating those who observe it from those who do not (RV 10.124.5 / Y. 30.4). The former are rewarded while the latter are sternly punished (RV 7.89.5, 7.60.5 / Y. 30.8, 11). The sovereign's favor usually takes the form of protection (RV 2.28.3, 8.42.3 / Yt. 1.24; Y. 34.7), and in Iran there is a strong eschatological coloring to his gifts,[46] but in both areas he is also believed to bestow concrete wealth in the form of herds (RV 5.41.1, 5.62.9 / Y. 46.2, 51.5; Yt. 1.7). He does not give these animals as *Indra gives them, that is, as booty won in battle, for this is the characteristic of the warrior god, as we shall see in the following chapter. Rather, *Varuna bestows cattle as a sovereign does, directly from the highest heaven (RV 3.56.2 / Y. 62.10).

Most earlier scholars regarded Varuṇa and Ahura Mazdā as sky gods,[47] and adduced much evidence in favor of this view. In their zeal, however, they tended to overvalue the now untenable linguistic equation of Váruṇa and the Greek Οὐρανός and were also inclined to a simplistic naturalistic interpretation of his godhood at the expense of his sovereign nature.[48] But if

42. Pokorny, p. 55–56.
43. Keith, Religion and Philosophy, pp. 83–85; B. Geiger, pp. 164–99.
44. B. Geiger, p. 166, notes that the personification of ṛta- occurs only in books 1 and 10 of the Ṛg Veda, i.e., the most recent stratum.
45. Keith, Religion and Philosophy, pp. 84–85; Zaehner, pp. 45–46. In general, the Zoroastrian "beneficent immortals" (Aməša Spəntas) must be understood as reified aspects of Ahura Mazdā's own personality. Aša is by far the most active of them, but it must be noted that his name in the Gāthas generally occurs in the instrumental case, indicating that he acts only at the bidding of, or as the agent of Ahura Mazdā.
46. Helmut Humbach, Die Gāthās des Zarathustra, 2 vols. (Heidelberg, 1959), 1: 74.
47. Bergaigne, 3: 85–86; Alfred Hillebrandt, Varuṇa als Himmelsgott und Herr über Tag und Nacht (Breslau, 1877); Keith, Religion and Philosophy, p. 102; Lüders, 1: 55; James Darmesteter, "Le dieu suprême dans la mythologie aryenne," Essais Orientaux (Paris, 1883), pp. 105–33; Roth, "Die höchsten Götter," pp. 70–71; Leopold von Schroeder, Arische Religion, 2 vols. (Leipzig, 1914), 1: 322.
48. On the Οὐρανός comparison, see Jakob Wackernagel, "Miszellen zur griechischen Grammatik," Zeitschrift für vergleichende Sprachforschung 29 (1888):129; and Hjalmar Frisk, Griechisches etymologisches Wörterbuch, 2 vols. (Heidelberg, 1973), 2: 446–47. The clearest case of overreliance on this false etymology is that of A. B. Keith, who defended it in "The God Varuṇa," Indian Historical Quarterly 9 (1933):515–20, and "Varuṇa and Ouranos," Indian Culture 3 (1937):421–30. No satisfactory etymology has yet been proposed

they were in error in this regard, the reaction against this view has been too strong, and there is no real cause to reject *Varuna's connection (not identification) with the celestial realm.[49] Numerous passages (*RV* 5.69.4, 8.25.7, 5.62.7 / *Y.* 1.1; *Yt.* 13.2-3; *Vd.* 19.30-32) make it clear that he resided in the highest heavens, from which he watched over the world, bestowing his gifts and chastisements on those who deserved one or the other.

This position allowed him to be all-seeing and thus all-knowing (*RV* 1.25.20, 8.42 / *Y.* 31.13; *Yt.* 1.8),[50] classic characteristics of the sky god, as Pettazzoni has shown.[51] It is this quality of omniscience that gave the god his name in Iran—Ahura Mazdā, "the Knowing Lord"[52]—and we must note that Varuṇa is characterized by a closely related term, *médhira-*, "knowing," "wise" (*RV* 1.25.20), as well as others that point to his wisdom (especially *prácetas*, as in *RV* 1.24.14, where he is called *asura pracetā rájan*, "wise king Asura"). The wisdom with which both gods are credited is not just conventional wisdom, however, but has a sinister side to it, although this has largely been repressed in Iran as a result of the Zarathustrian reform.[53] There are enough traces in the Avesta (such as *Y.* 41.3), however, to see that the ancient *Varuna was a master of magic, *māyā* (Skt. *māyá-* = Av. *hu-māyā-*),[54] and it is by virtue of this magical wisdom and power that he was thought to have created the world (*RV* 8.42.1, 5.85.1 / *Y.* 1.1, 57.2).

In Iran, Ahura Mazdā's creative acts are spelled out clearly and take place in a fixed, canonical order. In the beginning he established six original creations, the last two being the first ox and the first man, who together stand as the culmination of creation.[55] In India Varuṇa also played something of a cosmogonic role, although it is not so well estab-

in place of the old one, although numerous attempts have been made. For a summary, see Mayrhofer, *Etymologisches Wörterbuch*, 3: 151-3.

49. Thus Dandekar, "Asura Varuṇa," p. 178; Gonda, *Religionen Indiens*, 1: 73-74.

50. Note the correspondence of Skt. *viśvávedas-* and Av. *vīspō.viδvah-*, "all- knowing." Jan Gonda, *The Dual Deities in the Religion of the Veda* (Amsterdam, 1974), p. 161.

51. Raffaele Pettazzoni, *The All-Knowing God* (London, 1956). See also his more specific discussion, "Ahura Mazda, the Knowing Lord," in *Indo-Iranian Studies in Honour of Sanjana*, pp. 149-62.

52. F. B. J. Kuiper, "Avestan Mazdā-" *Indo-Iranian Journal* 1 (1957):86-95; and "Ahura Mazdā: 'Lord Wisdom'?" *Indo-Iranian Journal* 18 (1976):25-42; and Humbach, "Ahura Mazda und die Daēvas," pp. 81-94, have conclusively shown this to be the proper interpretation, with Av. *mazdā-* derived from *mṇz-dhā-*, "in whom knowledge is placed."

53. Kuiper, "Notes on the Avestan Hymn to Mithra," pp. 46-53. Note that Varuṇa's darker side has also been glossed over to a certain extent in the *Rg Veda* and appears more clearly in the *Atharva Veda*. On this, see Louis Renou, "Varuṇa dans l'Atharvaveda," *Festgabe für Herman Lommel*, pp. 122-28.

54. The prefix *hu-*, "good," in the Zoroastrian version serves to purify the sovereign god's magical power from any hint of evil.

55. On the six original creations, see Darmesteter, *Zend Avesta*, 1: 36 ff. Sometimes only the last two (ox and man) are mentioned, as a sort of shorthand notation for the whole of creation, as in *Y.* 5.1, 12.7, or even the Gāthic verse, *Y.* 51.7.

lished as in Iran. The chief text here is *RV* 5.85, and for our purposes the most interesting verse is the second:

> He spread the sky over the forests, placed strength in
> horses, and milk in the red cows;
> Varuṇa placed insight in hearts, fire in the waters, the
> sun in the heavens, and *soma* in the press-stone.[56]
> [*RV* 5.85.2]

Here the idea seems to be that Varuṇa has provided the essence of all things and that creation owes its vitality to him. A number of specific creations (here seven) are credited to him, and again cattle figure prominently in the list.

In neither India nor Iran, however, does his creativity take on a concrete, physical aspect. Rather, he seems to have ordered the creation and left the actual construction to someone else—a specific demiurgic figure by the name of *Twarštar (Skt. *Tvášṭr-* = Av. Θwōrǝštar-),[57] the "Shaper," and artisan par excellence. In the *Rg Veda*, he regularly forms all things (*RV* 3.55.19, 10.184.1), including the species of domestic animals (*RV* 10.49.10, 1.84.15).

> Truly outstanding *Tvášṭr* fit together the forms of all live-
> stock. "Bring to us increase of these!"
> (*RV* 1.188.9).[58]

Tvaṣṭr's equivalent in the Avesta is Gǝuš Tašan, the "Shaper of the Ox," who is also called Θwōrǝštar in *Y.* 29.6.[59] There, Ahura Mazda tells the Soul of the Ox (Gǝuš Urvan), "The Shaper (Θwōrǝštar) formed you for the herdsman and the pastoralist."[60]

Among the Iranians, or at least among the Zoroastrian Iranians, the creation of the ox came to be thought of as the demiurge's characteristic act, and therefore his name shifts from Θwōrǝštar to Gǝuš Tašan. In a sense, his activity was only the first step of creation, in which the materials necessary for the complete creation were established. And, as we shall see, all that was needed for the fulfillment of creation was two men and an

---

56. váneṣu vy àntárikṣaṃ tatāna vájam árvatsu páya usríyāsu / hṛtsú krátuṃ váruṇo apsv àgníṃ diví sū́ryam adadhāt sómam ádrau //

57. On this name, see, most importantly, Manu Leumann, "Der Indoiranische Bildnergott Twarštar," *Asiatische Studien / Études Asiatiques* 8 (1954):79–84; also, Gershevitch, *Avestan Hymn to Mithra,* pp. 55–56; Ernst Risch, "Die indogermanischen Verwändten von griechisch σάρκες," *Die Sprache* 7 (1961):93–98; and Manfred Mayrhofer, "Über Kontaminationen der indoiranischen Sippen von ai. *takṣ-, tvakṣ-, *tvarś-,*" *Indo-Iranica: Mélanges présentés à Georg Morgenstierne* (Wiesbaden, 1964), pp. 141–8.

58. tváṣṭā rūpā́ṇi hí prabhúḥ paśū́n víśvān samānajé / téṣāṃ naḥ sphātím á yaja //

59. On the interplay of the two terms Θwōrǝštar and *tašan,* see Mayrhofer, "Über Kontaminationen," esp. pp. 144–45.

60. at zī θwā fšuyantaēcā vāstryāicā θwōrǝštā tatašā.

ox. *Twarštar actually occupies something of an intermediate position between *Varuna, who is responsible for creation in a spiritual sense, and the first men, who complete the drama of creation.[61] With regard to the celestial sovereigns, then, our results show some similarities with and some differences from the East African situation. There one god dominated the pantheon as the sovereign, in a relatively uncomplicated state of affairs. Among the Indo-Iranians, however, numerous different deities may be discerned: an otiose sky god (*Dyaus); a large group of associated deities (the forerunner of the Ādityās and the Aməša Spəntas), headed by two major figures; a legal sovereign (*Mitra) and a magical sovereign (*Varuna); and finally, a separate demiurge (*Twarštar). The multiplicity of figures is almost bewildering, and yet with reference to the two major figures who can rightly be called celestial sovereigns, *Mitra and *Varuna, much can be seen that closely resembles the characteristics of Ngai, Kwoth, or Nhialic: all reside in the heavens, play a role in the creation, and rule over the world, dispensing favors and punishments to man. In turning to the priestly organization, we will again find some dissimilarities between the East Africans and the Indo-Iranians, but also a strong general resemblance.

The Priestly Class

The research of Georges Dumézil and Emile Benveniste over the last forty years has gone to vindicate the vision of such earlier scholars as Sénart and Oldenberg,[62] and it is now generally accepted that the tripartite social system that hardened into the Indian and Iranian systems of social class (Skt. *várṇa-*; Av. *pištra-*) was already well-established among the Indo-Iranians. This system separated priests, warriors, and commoners[63] and ranked them hierarchically in that order. The priests were placed at the head of the social system, above kings,[64] warriors, and all others, and their position seems to have been hereditary.[65]

---

61. It is worth noting that the chief characters in the Indo-European and Indo-Iranian myths are in fact not the gods, but rather the first men whose actions served to establish the world.

62. See esp. Georges Dumézil, "La préhistoire indo-iranienne des castes," *Journal Asiatique* 216 (1930):109–30, which first broke the ground in this field. Emile Benveniste, "Les classes sociales dans la tradition avestique," *Journal Asiatique* 221 (1932):117–34; and "Traditions indo-iraniennes sur les classes sociales," *Journal Asiatique* 230 (1938):529–49. More recently, see also E. Grantovskij, "Indoiranische Kastengliederung bei den Skythen," *Twenty-Fifth International Congress of Orientalists* (Moscow, 1960), pp. 1–21; Emile Sénart, *Caste in India* (London, 1930), pp. 113–19, 124–29; Hermann Oldenberg, "Zur Geschichte des indischen Kastenwesens," *Zeitschrift der deutschen morgenlandischen Gesellschaft* 51 (1897):271–74.

63. Dumézil has tended to refer to this "third function" as "agriculteurs-éleveurs." I prefer the designation "commoners" for the reasons stated above, note 6, this chapter.

64. The problem of kingship is extremely thorny for the Indo-European and Indo-Iranian periods, and several different notions of the king's place in the class system may have been current. For the most part, however, the king seems to have come from the warrior class, while being regarded as a figure who spanned all three classes.

65. Keith, *Religion and Philosophy*, p. 291. Darmesteter, *Zend Avesta*, 1: L.

61

THE INDO-IRANIAN PRIESTLY CYCLE

Numerous different types of priests existed in the Indo-Iranian period, but all of them seem to have shared certain characteristics. For the most part they were itinerant, not fixed to any specific place or deity.⁶⁶ Some of these priestly types can be reconstructed, such as the *kavis (Skt. kaví- = Av. kavi-), who were poets, magicians, and keepers of secrets related to immortality and who in Eastern Iran managed to win a large share of temporal power.⁶⁷ Another was the *atharvan (Skt. átharvan- = Av. aθaurvan-, āθravan-), a priest charged with the tending of the fire.⁶⁸ Others, whose names we cannot determine with certainty, played specific roles in the sacrifice—bearing gifts to the fire, filtering liquids, and so forth.⁶⁹

One priestly type of particular interest to us was the *usig (Skt. uśíj- = Av. usig-), whose role has never been adequately explained.⁷⁰ From the relevant texts, however, we may deduce that he was chiefly concerned with assisting warriors in cattle raiding. In the Rg Veda the uśij does not appear all that frequently (thirty times), and often the references are not specific. Yet, in most instances where a clear activity can be discerned, the uśij is involved in assisting warriors going out to win booty, especially cattle. Thus in five verses he aids warriors to win cattle (RV 2.21.5, 4.1.15, 7.90.4, 10.45.11, 10.46.2); in two he aids Indra to win cattle (1.131.5, 4.16.6); in another he aids Indra in battle in a general sense (3.34.4); and in another he aids the worshiper to gain riches in battle (3.15.3). Thus, in roughly one third of the occurrences the uśij is seen to aid in cattle-raiding activity, and the Avestan evidence that we have supports this conclusion. Usig occurs only once in the Avesta, Y. 44.20: "the karapan and the usig deliver the ox up to furor (aēšəmāi)."⁷¹ While this verse has often been cited to show the relation of the usig to animal sacrifice, no such claim is made here.⁷² Rather, the ox is said to be ren-

66. Keith, Religion and Philosophy, p. 291.
67. Louis Renou, "Quelques termes du Rgveda," Journal Asiatique 241 (1953); Dumézil, Mythe et Epopée, 2: 186–96. In Iran, kavi- is used to denote political leaders rather than religious (as in Y. 46.14, 51.16, 12.7), ultimately becoming the proper name of the Kavian dynasty. That it was originally a priestly title, however, is established by comparison to Gk. Κοίης, the title of the priest in the Mysteries of Samothrace (Mayrhofer, Etymologisches Wörterbuch, 1: 185–86).
68. Following Jarl Charpentier, "Zur alt- und mittelindischen Wortkunde," Monde Oriental 13 (1919):44 ff., and contra Paul Kretschmer, "Weiteres zur Urgeschichte der Inder," Zeitschrift für vergleichende Sprachforschung 55 (1927):80 ff., who saw this as a loan word into Sanskrit from Iran.
69. On these, see Victor Henry's appendix, "Esquisse d'une liturgie indo-eranienne," in W. Caland and V. Henry, L'Agniṣṭoma, 2 vols. (Paris, 1907), 2: 478–79.
70. The most recent attempts, T. Burrow, "Nirvacanani," Annals of Oriental Research 13 (1957):7–9; and Bailey, "Second Stratum of Indo-Iranian Gods," pp. 18–19, have tried to establish etymological bases for a view of the *usig as "Incantator," without notable success.
71. . . . . gạm karapā ušixšcā aēšəmāi dātā . . .
72. This older theory is held by such authorities as Zaehner, p. 84; Lommel, Religion Zarathustras, p. 78; and Widengren, Religionen Irans, p. 28.

dered up to *aēšma*-, which, as we shall see, is the technical term for the state of furor cultivated by the young warriors headed out to battle. Thus, the *usig* does not actually do anything to the ox, but rather he helps the warrior to assume a furious state in which he will be able to win cattle in raids; it is in this sense that he "delivers the ox up to furor."

Undoubtedly the most important type of priest was the **zhautar* (Skt. *hótr̥* = Av. *zaotar*-), the "pourer" who offered libations, whose very name is derived from the verb "to pour."[73] The ritual of the **zhautar* has been preserved for us to a greater extent than that of any other priestly group, since the *Rg Veda* is the manual of the *hotr̥* priest and Zarathustra himself was a *zaotar* (*Y.* 33.6).[74]

These different types of priests do not seem to have been set apart from one another by devotion to differing gods but by the employment of differing ritual techniques and concerns. They all seem to have been generalists, capable of performing sacrifice to any of the deities, although personal preferences must have played some part.[75] Thus, while there are differences in emphasis among the family *maṇḍalas* of the *Rg Veda* (Books 2-7 each contain the hymns of one family of *hotr̥* priests), each one tends to have an eclectic nature, containing hymns to numerous gods.[76] Similarly, a Zoroastrian priest is expected to perform sacrifice to all the deities of the pantheon and to recite each god's appropriate *Yašt*.[77]

Ultimately, sacrifice is the chief business of the priestly class. It plays a crucial role in the religion of all the Indo-European tribes[78] and is at the heart of the cultus in India and Iran.[79] The well-being of the entire com-

73. < I-I **√zhau*- < P-I-E **√gh'eu*-, "to pour," from which are also derived Greek χέ(ϝ)ω; Latin *fundō*; Gothic *giutan* (Modern German *giessen*); and Armenian *joyl;* all of which mean "to pour." See Pokorny, pp. 447-48; Emile Benveniste, *Le vocabulaire des institutions indo-européennes*, 2 vols. (Paris, 1969), 2: 216-24.

74. On Zarathustra's priesthood, see Herman Lommel, "War Zarathustra ein Bauer?," *Zeitschrift für vergleichende Sprachforschung* 58 (1930):248-65; Kurt Rudolph, "Zarathustra—Priester und Prophet," *Numen* 8 (1961):81-116; and Mary Boyce, "Zoroaster the Priest," *Bulletin of the School of Oriental and African Studies* 33 (1970):22-38.

75. For an excellent study of the subtle differences between the various *Rg Vedic* families, see V. G. Rahurkar, *The Seers of the Rgveda* (Poona, 1964).

76. The most striking divergences from the general eclectic nature of the family maṇḍalas are to be found in the book of the Viśvāmitras (3), which contains no hymns to Varuṇa or Mitra-Varuṇa, and that of the Vasiṣṭhas (7), which contains proportionately many more hymns to these gods (13) than any other book. I shall deal with the figures of Viśvāmitra and Vasiṣṭha more thoroughly in Chapter 6.

77. Darmesteter, *Zend Avesta*, 1: 5.

78. See especially the excellent article by E. Mayrhofer-Passler, "Haustieropfer bei den Indoiraniern und den anderen indo-germanischen Völkern," *Archiv Orientalni* 21 (1953):182-205; and the classic treatment of J. Vendryes, "Les correspondences de vocabulaire entre l'indo-iranien et l'italo-celtique," *Mémoires de la Société Linguistique de Paris* 20 (1918):265-85.

79. This has been recognized by virtually all authors to write on either culture. For particularly sensitive interpretations, see Bergaigne, 1: 121-31 for India; and Marijan Molé, *Culte, mythe et cosmologie dans l'Iran ancien* (Paris, 1963), pp. 86 ff., and *passim* for Iran.

munity depends on the proper execution of sacrifice, and thus its performance is entrusted only to those who are qualified to carry it out correctly, namely, the priests. A king or a warrior cannot sacrifice for himself but must employ a priest to do so for him.[80] If the priest carries out this duty successfully, the benefits that accrue from it—wealth, well-being, victory, and the like—are delivered to the patron.[81] Naturally the patron is grateful for this service, and he usually rewards his priest liberally. It is worth noting that the payment he delivers generally consists of cattle and other livestock.[82] This fact is significant, for it furnishes one of the major links in the Indo-Iranian cattle cycle. But in order to appreciate that we must first take a closer look at sacrificial practices among the Indo-Iranians.

Sacrifice

To reconstruct the sacrificial practices of the Indo-Iranians is no easy matter, for they were enormously complicated. Details abound, and volumes could be filled with analyses of the specific correspondences between Indian and Iranian rituals. For our purposes, however, a broader and more general view will be sufficient.[83]

In the first place, it is clear that several different forms of sacrifice were practiced. Two important Indo-Iranian terms that survive mark off a major distinction, namely, the distinction between immolation and libation. The first term is *yagna (Skt. yajñá- = Av. yasna- < √yaz-), which has come to mean simply "sacrifice," "worship" in both Sanskrit and Avestan but which originally denoted animal sacrifice of a bloody nature, as Benveniste clearly demonstrated.[84] The second is *zhautrā (Skt. hótrā- = Av. zaoθrā-), a word derived from the verb "to pour" and intimately connected with the title of the *zhautar priest.[85]

Moreover, it seems that there were also at least two different forms of libation sacrifice, depending on the substance offered and on the

80. Keith, *Religion and Philosophy*, p. 289; Humbach, *Gathas*, 1: 59–61.
81. Keith, *Religion and Philosophy*, p. 299; Humbach, *Gathas*, 1: 59–61.
82. On this, see Chapter 6, the section, "Sacrificial Stipends and the Cattle Cycle."
83. Mary Boyce, "Zoroaster the Priest," pp. 22 and 24–25, has pointed to a number of features found in the Indo-Iranian sacrificial cultus, including "a devout belief in the efficacy of sacrificial offerings, and in that of prayers, praises, and invocations accurately repeated with a right intention" (p. 22); veneration of fire and consumption of offerings partly by fire, partly by priests and sacrificer; consecration of sacred bread or cakes; consecration of pure water; crushing of stems of *sauma, mixing of the juice thus extracted with water, the mixture being drunk by priests; strew of grass and twigs; bull's urine used as a purifier; dedication of the sacrifice to any god, but the necessity of having a specific named recipient rather than just the gods in general.
84. Emile Benveniste, "Sur la terminologie iranienne du sacrifice," *Journal Asiatique* 252 (1964):45–58.
85. All these are derived from P-I-E *√gh'eu-, on which see above, note 73, this chapter.

THE INDO-IRANIAN PRIESTLY CYCLE

recipient. Libations of milk or butter seem to have been appropriate for the celestial sovereigns, while an offering of the intoxicating drink *sauma* (Skt. *sóma-* = Av. *haoma-*) was originally proper only for the warrior gods.[86] Accordingly, the *sauma* libation will be dealt with more fully in the next chapter.

For if there is a sense in which the offering of *sauma* and the offering of butter or milk ought to be grouped together as libation sacrifices, there is another sense in which the animal sacrifice and the butter or milk libation are much closer in that they are both an offering of *gau-* (Skt. *gó-* = Av. *gav-*, both of which < P-I-E *$g^w ou$-),[87] a term that could signify either "cattle," "ox," "cow" or "milk," "milk products" in Sanskrit and Avestan.[88] Moreover, the libation of milk or butter is seen as a substitute or a short-hand version of the offering of cattle in many instances, as can be seen from certain ritual expressions. Thus, in India ghee is sometimes called "the essence of cattle,"[89] and in Iran the milk used in sacrifice is called "the living cow" (*gąm jīvyam*).[90]

Considering this and other evidence, some scholars have taken the animal sacrifice to have been a forerunner of libation (and the still later vegetal offerings),[91] but I am forced to disagree with this. Rather, it would seem that both existed side by side from the earliest Indo-European times.[92] Nor can one separate them on the basis of the deities to whom

86. K. R. Potdar, *Sacrifice in the Rg Veda* (Bombay, 1953), pp. 58, 98; Bergaigne, 3: 150; Keith, *Religion and Philosophy,* p. 284.

87. From which are also derived Greek βοῦς; Latin *bōs, bovis;* Old Irish *bó;* Old High German *chuo;* Slavic **govędo;* etc. Pokorny, pp. 482–83; Mayrhofer, *Etymologisches Wörterbuch,* 1: 351.

88. A. A. Macdonell and A. B. Keith, *Vedic Index of Names and Subjects,* 2 vols. (London, 1912; repr. Delhi, 1967), 1: 234; Christian Bartholomae, *Altiranisches Wörterbuch* (Berlin, 1961), pp. 507–508. There is still further subcategorization of libations: **āzhuti* (Skt. *ā́huti-* = Av. *āzŭiti-*) being the libation of butter, and **išdā* (Skt. *íḍā-* = Av. *ižā-*, with **-šd-* > -ḍ- in Sanskrit as in *nīḍá-* "nest" < P-I-E **nī-sd-o-*) being the libation of milk. On these, see Helmut Humbach, "Milchprodukte im zarathustrischen Ritual," *Indogermanische Forschungen* 63 (1957):40–42. A taxonomy of Indo-Iranian libations could be set up as follows:

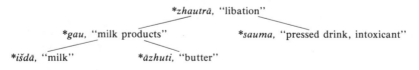

*zhautrā, "libation"

*gau, "milk products"   **sauma,* "pressed drink, intoxicant"

*išdā, "milk"   **āzhuti,* "butter"

89. *SB* 5.3.4.20.
90. *Y.* 3.3.
91. Thus Alfred Hillebrandt, *Vedische Mythologie,* 3 vols. (Breslau, 1929), 2: 26 f.; Sylvain Lévi, *La doctrine du sacrifice dans les Brāhmaṇas* (Paris, 1898), pp. 134–38; Gonda, *Religionen Indiens,* 1: 147.
92. The evidence for libation is well established on linguistic grounds (see note 73, this chapter), and immolation has always been inferred on other grounds, following Vendryes and Mayrhofer-Passler, cited above, note 78, this chapter. Now, however, an I-E root for a verb "to sacrifice" **ad-√bher-* has been reconstructed by Eric Hamp, "Religion

THE INDO-IRANIAN PRIESTLY CYCLE

they are directed, for they seem to have been distinguished primarily according to expense. The more costly animal sacrifice was reserved for the more important occasions, while libation was more common in usage. Only domestic animals might serve as sacrificial victims; horses, cattle, sheep, and goats were most frequently offered.[93] Of these, the horse had special significance and was reserved for royal coronation sacrifices.[94] Of the others, cattle were by far the most important for general use,[95] although the less expensive sheep or goats might be freely substituted.[96] In Iran, however, sheep and goats were always referred to as "beneficent cattle" (Pahl. *gōspand* < . Av. *gav- spǝnta-*).[97] Another term that was similarly used is **pasu* (Skt. *páśu-* = Av. *pasu-*), which means "domestic animals," "livestock," "sacrificial animals,"[98] but which also frequently comes to signify simply "cattle" as the domestic animal and the sacrificial animal par excellence.[99]

In Indo-Iranian times cattle sacrifice was fairly common, as can be seen from such texts as *RV* 2.7.5, 6.16.47, 8.43.11, 10.91.14; *SB* 3.4.1.2; *AB*

and Law from Iguvium," *Journal of Indo-European Studies* 1 (1973):318–23. Also, significant parallels in Greek and Sanskrit terminology and praxis have been noted by Meinrad Scheller, "τρίττοια βόαρχος," *Zeitschrift für vergleichende Sprachforschung* 74 (1956): 233–35; and "Rinder mit vergoldeten Hörnern," *Zeitschrift für vergleichende Sprachforschung* 72 (1955):227–28.

93. Alfred Hillebrandt, "Tiere und Götter im vedischen Ritual," *Schlesische Gesellschaft für väterlandische Cultur* 83 (1905):4–5.

94. See Franz Rolf Schröder, "Ein altirischer Kronungsritus und das indogermanischer Rossopfer," *Zeitschrift für Celtische Philologie* 16 (1927):310–12; Jaan Puhvel, "Vedic Aśvamedha- and Gaulish Iipomiidvos," *Language* 31 (1955):353–54; and "Aspects of Equine Functionality," *Myth and Law Among the Indo-Europeans* (Berkeley, Calif., 1970), pp. 159–72; Oldenberg, *Religion des Veda,* p. 356; Gonda, *Religionen Indiens,* 1: 168. Koppers, "Pferdeopfer und Pferdekult," failed to realize this very special significance of the horse sacrifice and was thus led into making very exaggerated claims for its importance.

95. Oldenberg, *Religion des Veda,* p. 355; Hillebrandt, "Tiere und Götter," p. 5.

96. In India, the well-known system of the five *paśus*—man, horse, cattle, sheep, goat—is, in effect, a list of potential victims ranked in descending order according to expense. Similar conclusions are drawn regarding Roman practices by G. Capdeville, "Substitution de victimes dans les sacrifices d'animaux à Rome," *Mélanges d'Archéologie et d'histoire de l'école française de Rome* 83 (1971):283–323.

97. See Duchesne-Guillemin, "Miettes iraniennes," pp. 98–99.

98. Derived from P-I-E **pek'u-*, from which come also Lat. *pecus,* Goth. *faihu* ("property"), ON *fé,* OHG *fihu.* OPruss *pecku,* etc. Benveniste, *Vocabulaire,* 1: 47–48, has shown the old derivation from the verb "to shear" to be incorrect. His argument that the original sense was "movable wealth," and that "livestock," "cattle" is a secondary development, however, cannot be accepted. His case rests on Lat. *pecūnia,* which he believes preserved the original sense of "wealth," but this is disproven in a most important text from Elias Steinmeyer and Eduard Sievers, *Die althochdeutschen Glossen,* 5 vols. (Zurich, 1968), vol. 3, p. 10, lines 15 ff. This text is a bilingual list of the names of animals in Latin and Old High German: *cauallus-hros, equm-hengist, boues-ohsun, uaccas-choi, porciu-suuinir,* etc. The first term in this list, which serves to introduce all the rest, is *pecunia-fihu* (line 15). *Fihu* always means "domestic animals," "cattle," in OHG. But the Latin term that would normally be expected here is not *pecūnia* but *pecus.* Given that *pecūnia* does appear, it must have had the sense of "livestock," "domestic animals," "cattle" as well as that of "wealth," and Benveniste's argument cannot be sustained.

99. Mayrhofer, *Etymologisches Wörterbuch,* 2: 239–40.

THE INDO-IRANIAN PRIESTLY CYCLE

3.4.6, and so on, in India, and *Y.* 4.1, 7.20, 11.1, 24.1; *Yt.* 5.21, 5.25, and so on, in Iran. In both areas, however, later events caused a decline in its usage, as in Iran Zarathustra vigorously condemned cattle sacrifice (although not animal sacrifice in general),[100] while in India the development of the doctrine of *ahiṃsā*, "noninjury to all living things," inhibited such practices.[101]

Fortunately, we are able to reconstruct the nature of at least one form of Indo-Iranian animal sacrifice by means of a striking correspondence. The Iranian material is supplied by Herodotus, who either observed a non-Zoroastrian Persian sacrifice or received a detailed description from a knowledgeable source.[102] His testimony is invaluable, however, in that the sacrifice described in the Avesta is strongly colored by Zarathustra's rejection of cattle offerings, and it is only in the Western sources that a record of earlier Iranian sacrificial practices has been preserved.[103] Herodotus's account reads as follows:

> And this is the sacrifice of these Persians with regard to the aforesaid gods. They build no altars and kindle no fires when thinking to sacrifice, nor do they indulge in libations, flutes, fillets, or barley. And whichever one of them wishes to sacrifice leads the beast [κτῆνος—an ox or sheep] to an open place clear of dirt, and he calls the god, being wreathed with a tiara chiefly of myrtle. Now

100. The problem of Zarathustra's view on sacrifice is an extremely thorny one. It is clear from a very few texts, most notably *Y.* 32.12 and 14, that he condemned cattle sacrifice, but this is not expressly extended to the sacrifice of any other animals. Moreover, such sacrifices are recommended in the Younger Avesta (e.g. *Vd.* 18.70, *Yt.* 8.58) and continue to the present day (Duchesne-Guillemin, "Miettes iraniennes," pp. 98–99; Mary Boyce, "Ātaš-zōhr and Āb-zōhr," *Journal of the Royal Asiatic Society*, 1966, pp. 105–107), while cattle sacrifice has virtually disappeared. I am thus inclined to believe that the prophet's prohibition applied only to the bovine species.

101. On the development of *ahiṃsā,* see the detailed treatments of Alsdorf; and Hanns-Peter Schmidt, "The Origin of *Ahiṃsā,*" *Mélanges d'indianisme à la mémoire de Louis Renou* (Paris, 1968), pp. 625–55.

102. Benveniste, *Persian Religion,* p. 22.

103. One must, of course, be very careful in using foreign evidence of this sort. Use of the late Mithraic evidence from Europe and Asia Minor led Lommel into serious error in his famous articles, "Mithra und das Stieropfer," *Paideuma* 3 (1949):207–19, and "Die Sonne das Schlechteste?" *Oriens* 15 (1962):360–73, and others such as Nyberg and Zaehner have similarly erred in placing Miθra at the center of an ancient myth or cult of bull sacrifice. This theory is based on reading late and foreign data back into early sources, and no native Indian or Iranian material has ever been produced that shows Miθra as a bull slayer. As Carsten Colpe, "Mithra-Verehrung, Mithras-Kult, und die Existenz iranischer Mysterien," in *Mithraic Studies,* pp. 378–405, has convincingly shown, Mithraism is a separate development and has its origin in Hellenistic Asia Minor (probably in the kingdom of Pontus) and not in Iran. In the case of Herodotus, however, we are dealing with material that is much older than the Mithraic materials, and that can be independently verified by the correspondences in Indian sources. The strength of these correspondences must be the ultimate test and led such a normally skeptical scholar as Keith to accept the authenticity of Herodotus' testimony (*Religion and Philosophy,* p. 386).

THE INDO-IRANIAN PRIESTLY CYCLE

in truth, they do not pray for blessings for the sacrificer himself but pray for good to come to all Persians and to the King, for he [the sacrificer] thinks himself to be among all the Persians. Then, having cut the victim into pieces limb from limb, boiled the flesh, and strewn the softest grass, particularly clover, he then places all the flesh on top of this. When this is arranged, a man—a Magus—standing beside him sings a theogony, as it is not their custom to perform sacrifices without a Magus. Having waited a little while, the sacrificer carries away the flesh, and uses it as he pleases. (1.132)[104]

Striking similarities to the details of this ritual appear in an *Rg Vedic* verse:

According to the ancient custom of the Priyamedhas,
Those who scattered the sacred grass, and who placed
down oblations of food attained the foremost offering.[105]
[*RV* 8.69.18]

It should be noted that Priyamedha is the name of a Vedic seer, one of whose descendants is said to have composed the hymn from which this verse is taken. But his name, I would argue, has a special significance. Literally, it is a *bahuvrīhi* compound that means "he whose food offering (Skt. *medhá-* = Av. *myazda-*)[106] is well-beloved (Skt. *priyá-* = Av. *frya-*)." *Medhá-*, moreover, is the term typically used in India to denote animal sacrifices, as in *aśva-medha*, "horse sacrifice"; *go-medha*, "cattle sacrifice"; *puruṣa-medha*, "human sacrifice"; and even *sarva-medha*, "sacrifice of all [species]." Thus, what is described in this verse is the animal sacrifice "according to ancient custom" (*ánu pratnásyaúkasaḥ*). And we find here two strong correspondences with the sacrifice described by Herodotus: the sacred grass (Skt. *barhíṣ-*; Av. *barəsman-*) is spread out, and the pieces of the victim's body are laid out upon it. Other

---

104. Θυσίη δὲ τοῖσι Πέρσῃσι περὶ τοὺς εἰρημένους θεοὺς ἥδε κατέστηκε· οὔτε βωμοὺς ποιεῦνται οὔτε πῦρ ἀνακαίουσι μέλλοντες θύειν, οὐ σπονδῇ χρέωνται, οὐκὶ αὐλῷ, οὐ στέμμασι, οὐκὶ οὐλῇσι· τῶν δὲ ὡς ἑκάστῳ θύειν θέλῃ, ἐς χῶρον καθαρὸν ἀγαγὼν τὸ κτῆνος καλέει τὸν θεόν, ἐστεφανωμένος τὸν τιάραν μυρσίνῃ μάλιστα. ἑωυτῷ μὲν δὴ τῷ θύοντι ἰδίῃ μούνῳ οὔ οἱ ἐγγίνεται ἀρᾶσθαι ἀγαθά, ὃ δὲ τοῖσι πᾶσι Πέρσῃσι κατεύχεται εὖ γίνεσθαι καὶ τῷ βασιλέι. ἐν γὰρ δὴ τοῖσι ἅπασι Πέρσῃσι καὶ αὐτὸς γίνεται. ἐπεὰν δὲ διαμιστύλας κατὰ μέλεα τὸ ἱρήιον ἐψήσῃ τὰ κρέα, ὑποπάσας ποίην ὡς ἁπαλωτάτην, μάλιστα δὲ τὸ τρίφυλλον, ἐπὶ ταύτης ἔθηκε ὧν πάντα τὰ κρέα. διαθέντος δὲ αὐτοῦ Μάγος ἀνὴρ παρεστεὼς ἐπαείδει θεογονίην, οἵην δὴ ἐκεῖνοι λέγουσι εἶναι τὴν ἐπαοιδήν· ἄνευ γὰρ δὴ Μάγου οὔ σφι νόμος ἐστὶ θυσίας ποιέεσθαι. ἐπισχὼν δὲ ὀλίγον χρόνον ἀποφέρεται ὁ θύσας τὰ κρέα καὶ χρᾶται ὅ τι μιν λόγος αἱρέει.

105. ánu pratnásyaúkasaḥ priyámedhāsa eṣām /
púrvam ánu práyatiṃ vṛktábarhiṣo hitáprayasa aśata //

106. Mayrhofer, *Etymologisches Wörterbuch*, 2: 685; Pokorny, pp. 711–12. See also Louis Renou, "Les éléments védiques dans le sanskrit classique," *Journal Asiatique* 231 (1939):378–79.

THE INDO-IRANIAN PRIESTLY CYCLE

corresponding features, such as the role of the priest, the dismemberment of the animal, and the eating of the meat following the ceremony, can be found in later Indian texts such as the *Brāhmaṇa*s and the *Śrauta Sūtras*.[107]

A definite ideology is at work here, as has been pointed out by Thieme.[108] The strew of sacred grass is a seat for the god, to which he is invited to descend. Once present, he is treated as an honored guest: songs are sung in praise of him, and he is given the finest of food.[109] But Thieme does not go far enough in his analysis, for it must be recognized that the sacrifice is not just the entertaining of a guest but the bestowing of a valued gift upon him, and the gift—as Mauss so brilliantly demonstrated—is no simple matter but a presentation that establishes a relation of reciprocity between giver and receiver, calling forth a countergift in return.[110] This is certainly the case with regard to Indian, Iranian, and Indo-Iranian sacrifice. In nearly every hymn, the offering priest announces the return gift that he desires from the deity. With overwhelming consistency, these requests have a temporal focus—wealth, success, and well-being. One specific request emerges as most characteristic of India and Iran: over and over again the worshiper requests men and cattle as his rewards, either in the form "men and cattle," "men and animals," "cattle and sons," or "two-footed and four-footed beings" (see such verses as *RV* 5.41.17, 3.16.5–6, 5.20.4, 3.1.23 / *Y.* 4.5, 24.10, 62.10; *Yt.* 8.15, 10.28).[111]

In sacrifice, one ideally presents a gift of cattle to the gods, who have descended from the heavens to sit as guests. The presentation of this gift enables the sacrificer to request a return gift from the god, and this hoped-for return gift tends to take the form of numerous men and numerous cattle, that is, an increase in the main forms of a pastoralist's wealth.[112] When we combine this fact with our knowledge that the priest

107. For full descriptions of the classic form of animal sacrifice, see Julius Schwab, *Das altindische Thieropfer* (Erlangen, 1886); or R. N. Dandekar, ed., *Śrautakośa: Encyclopedia of Vedic Sacrificial Ritual*, 2 vols. (Poona, 1962), 2: 770 ff.

108. Paul Thieme, "Vorzarathustrisches bei den Zarathustriern und bei Zarathustra," *Zeitschrift der deutschen morgenlandischen Gesellschaft* 107 (1957):67–77. While one may agree with his general conception, Thieme's rendering of *haomayō gava* as "haoma and barley-milk," pp. 75–76, is simply perverse. See, rather, Karl Hoffmann, "Avestisch haoma yō gauua," *Münchener Studien zur Sprachwissenschaft* 21 (1967):11–20.

109. Keith, *Religion and Philosophy*, p. 278; Thieme, "Vorzarathustrisches," p. 77.

110. Marcel Mauss, *The Gift* (New York, 1967). This is actually a much closer description of Indo-Iranian sacrifice than that found in Mauss and Hubert, *Sacrifice: Its Nature and Function*, which draws most of its material from the later, more speculative *Brāhmaṇa* period. On the exchange nature of early Vedic sacrifice, see Keith, *Religion and Philosophy*, pp. 257–59; Potdar, p. 193. This is in keeping with the general exchange nature of the Indo-European economies. See Emile Benveniste, "Don et échange dans le vocabulaire indo-européen," *Problèmes de linguistique générale* (Paris, 1966), pp. 315–26.

111. See Wackernagel, "Indoiranica: Zum Dualdvandva," and Benveniste, "Sur quelques dvandvas avestiques," two highly important studies.

112. See the articles cited in the preceding note, and such texts as *Y.* 46.2, where Zarathustra attributes his powerlessness to the fact that he has few men and few animals.

was paid in cattle by his patron,[113] we arrive at a picture that very much resembles the one we described in discussing the East African priestly cycle (Figure 4).

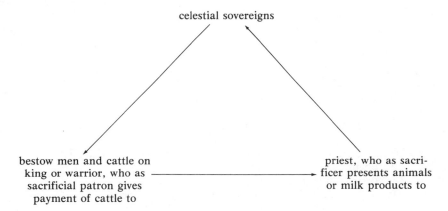

Figure 4. The Indo-Iranian Priestly Cycle

There is, however, a second level of meaning present in the performance of the sacrifice. For while the offering does function for the benefit of the sacrificer in a practical sense as a gift exchange with the gods, it also acts for the benefit of the whole world as a reenactment and recreation of the first sacrifice, the memory of which is preserved in myth. This primordial sacrifice served to create the world, and it is the prototype not only of all sacrifice but also of all creative action. Each sacrifice makes that first offering real again and reestablishes the entire creation.[114] But in order to appreciate this, we must first reconstruct the myth of the first sacrifice.[115]

The Myth of the First Sacrifice

The myth of the first sacrifice is not just an Indo-Iranian myth but an Indo-European myth as well, for independent Indian, Iranian, Germanic, and Roman versions can be located, in addition to Greek, Russian, Jewish, and Chinese versions that seem to be the result of secondary diffusion.[116] While some scholars have tried to argue that the myth is Old

113. See Chapter 6, the section, "Sacrificial Stipends and the Cattle Cycle."
114. The theory here has been stated in general terms by Eliade, *Cosmos and History,* pp. 21–27; and by Adolf E. Jensen, *Myth and Cult Among Primitive Peoples* (Chicago, 1963), pp. 162–90. It has been set out with specific reference to India by Lévi, pp. 11–38; and to Iran by Molé, pp. 86 ff., 126 ff., and passim.
115. Much of the section that follows has been taken from my article, "The Indo-European Myth of Creation," *History of Religions* 15 (1975):121–45, to which some important new materials have been added.
116. On the Greek texts and their possible derivation from Iranian sources, see Albrecht Götze, "Persische Weisheit in griechischem Gewände," *Zeitschrift für Indologie und Iranistik* 2 (1923): 60–98, 167–74; H. H. Schaeder, *Studien zum antiken Synkretismus aus*

Asiatic and not Indo-European in origin,[117] this hypothesis fails to account for the Norse and Roman versions and for the fact that the characters in the myth bear names that are plainly of Indo-European origin. In light of this we must conclude that the myth is of Indo-European origin, and it can be reconstructed with a great deal of accuracy if all the primary versions are considered.[118]

Three classic texts furnish the starting point for our investigation:

> 6. When the gods performed sacrifice with Puruṣa as
> the oblation,
> Spring was its butter, summer its fuel, autumn its
> oblation.
> 7. They consecrated as sacrifice on the sacred grass,
> Puruṣa, born in the beginning.
> With him, the gods, the Sādhyās and the seers sacrificed.
> 8. From that sacrifice, offered completely, the
> curdled butter was collected.
> It made the animals of the air, those of the forest,
> and those of the village.
> 9. From that sacrifice, offered completely, the Ṛg
> and Sāman verses were born,
> The meters were born from that, and the Yajur was born
> from it.
> 10. From it, horses were born and those animals with
> teeth in both jaws;

Iran und Griechenland (Leipzig, 1926), pp. 205–40; and Anders Olerud, *L'idée de macro-cosmos et de microcosmos dans le Timée de Platon* (Uppsala, 1951). Note, however, the objections of J. Duchesne-Guillemin, "Persische Weisheit in griechischem Gewände?," *Harvard Theological Review* 49 (1956):115–22. On the Old Russian version, see Stanislaus Schayer, "A Note on the Old Russian Variant of the Purushasūkta," *Archiv Orientalni* 7 (1935):319–23. On the Jewish version, see Götze, pp. 171–74; and David Winston, "The Iranian Component in the Bible, Apocrypha, and Qumran," *History of Religions* 5 (1966): 196–97. On the Chinese versions and their probable diffusion from India, see Hoang-son Hoang-sy-Quy, "Le mythe indien de l'homme cosmique dans son contexte culturel et dans son évolution," *Revue de l'histoire des religions* 175 (1969):142.

117. Thus Koppers, "Pferdeopfer und Pferdekult," pp. 320–63; Hoang-sy-Quy, p. 143; A. W. Macdonald, "A propos de Prajāpati," *Journal Asiatique* 240 (1953):323–38. Koppers' argument is somewhat complicated. He does take the myth to be of I-E origin, affirming the genetic relation of the I-I and Germanic versions, but he also adds that there was an older, Palaeo-Asiatic, or "Southern" myth underlying the Indo-European one. See esp. his p. 325.

118. On the I-E origin of this myth, see Güntert, *Arische Weltkönig*, pp. 315–43; Aram M. Frenkian, "Puruṣa—Gayōmard—Anthropos," *Revue des Etudes Indo-Européennes* 3 (1943):118–31; and Franz Rolf Schröder, "Germanische Schopfungsmythen," *Germanisch-Romanisch Monatsschrift* 19 (1931):1–26, 81–99. The fullest attempt at reconstruction is that of Güntert, *Arische Weltkönig*, pp. 315–70, who felt that the myth described the dismemberment of a primordial androgyne. In my opinion, this was based on the overvaluation of an incorrect etymology (*Yemo = Zwitter*) and insufficient attention was paid to the texts and the events they describe. While Güntert's attempt was brilliant for its time, it must now be replaced by a sounder reading of the myth in all its variants with fuller attention to details of the mythic narrative.

Truly, cattle were born from it, and goats and sheep
were born from it.
11. When they divided Puruṣa, how many pieces did they
prepare?
What was his mouth? What are his arms, thighs, and
feet called?
12. The priest was his mouth, the warrior was made from
his arms;
His thighs were the commoner, and the untouchable was
born from his feet.
13. The moon was born of his mind; of his eye, the
sun was born;
From his mouth, Indra and fire [Agni]; from his
breath, wind [Vāyu] was born.
14. From his navel there was the atmosphere; from his
head, heaven was rolled together;
From his feet, the earth; from his ear, the directions.
Thus they caused the worlds to be created.
15. Seven-mouthed were the sacrificial enclosures;
thrice seven bundles of wood were made
When the gods, performing sacrifice, bound Puruṣa as
the sacrificial animal.
16. By sacrifice, the gods sacrificed the sacrifice;
these were the earliest obligations.
Indeed, those great ones sought heaven, where the
ancient Sādhyās are gods.[119]

[RV 10.90.6-16]

119. yát púruṣeṇa havíṣā devá yajñám átanvata /
vasantó asyāsīd ájyaṃ grīṣmá idhmáḥ śarád dhavíḥ //
7. táṃ yajñám barhíṣi praúkṣan púruṣaṃ jātám agratáḥ /
téna devá ayajanta sādhyā ŕṣayaś ca yé //
8. tásmād yajñát sarvahútaḥ sámbhṛtam pṛṣadājyám /
paśún tāńś cakre vāyavyàn āraṇyán grāmyáś ca yé //
9. tásmād yajñát sarvahúta ŕcaḥ sámāni jajñire /
chándāṅsi jajñire tásmād yájus tásmād ajāyata //
10. tásmād áśvā ajāyanta yé ké cobhayádataḥ /
gávo ha jajñire tásmāt tásmāj jātá ajāváyaḥ //
11. yát púruṣaṃ vy ádadhuḥ katidhá vy ákalpayan /
múkhaṃ kím asya kaú bāhú ká ūrú pádā ucyete //
12. brāhmaṇò 'sya múkham āsīd bāhú rājanyàḥ kṛtáḥ /
ūrú tád asya yád vaíśyaḥ padbhyáṃ śūdró ajāyata //
13. candrámā mánaso jātáś cákṣoḥ súryo ajāyata /
múkhād índraś cāgníś ca prāṇád vāyúr ajāyata //
14. nábhyā āsīd antárikṣaṃ śīrṣṇó dyaúḥ sám avartata /
padbhyám bhúmir díśaḥ śrótrāt táthā lokāṅ akalpayan //
15. saptásyāsan paridháyas tríḥ saptá samídhaḥ kṛtáḥ /
devá yád yajñáṃ tanvānā ábadhnan púruṣam paśúm //
16. yajñéna yajñám ayajanta devás tāni dhármāṇi prathamány āsan /
té ha nākam mahimánaḥ sacanta yátra púrve sādhyáḥ sánti deváḥ //

In the month of Frawardin, on the day of Ohrmazd [New Year's Day], he [Ahriman] assaulted at noon, and the sky was afraid, as sheep are afraid of wolves. Next he came to the water, arranged below the earth, as it is said [in the Avesta]. Next he bored through the middle of the earth and entered. Then he came to the plants, then he came to the ox and Gayōmart. Next he came up to the fire. Like a fly, he assaulted all creation. . . .

This also is said [in the Avesta]: When the sole-created ox passed away, it fell on its right side; when Gayōmart passed away, [he fell] on his left side. . . .

It is said in the religion: When the sole-created ox passed away, there where it sent forth its marrow, the fifty-five species of grain grew up, and the twelve species of healing plants. . . .

The semen of the ox was borne up to the moon station. There, they purified it, and he [Ohrmazd] created domestic animals of all species [from it]. First [he created] two bovines, one male and one female; then a pair of every species in the earth appeared in the Aryan home over [a space of] eight *hāsar*s, which are equal to three *frasang*s [roughly 10–12 miles]. As it says [in the Avesta]: Because of the value of cattle, they were created twice—once in the [sole-created] ox, and once with the domestic animals of all species. . . .

It is said in the religion: I created men in ten [different] species. The first was that which was radiant and white of eye, namely, Gayōmart, and the ninth from Gayōmart was Gayōmart again. The tenth was the monkey, said to be the least of mankind.

When illness came over Gayōmart, he fell on his left side. From his head, lead became manifest; from his blood, tin; from his marrow, silver; from his legs, iron; from his bones, copper; from his fat, crystal; from his arms, steel; and from his soul's departure, gold, which men now give their souls for, due to its value.

From the left, death entered the body of Gayōmart. [Therefore] death comes over all creatures until the Renovation.

When Gayōmart emitted seed while passing away, they purified that seed in the light of the sun. The fire Nērōsang kept watch over two parts of it, and Spandarmad [the earth] received one part. It was forty years in the earth. (*GBd.*, selections)[120]

---

120. Text from Ervad Tahmuras Dinshaji Anklesaria, ed., *The Bundahishn, being a Facsimile of the TD Manuscript No. 2* (Bombay, 1908).

mäh ī Frawardīn rōz ī Ohrmazd andar dwārēd
nēmrōz, uš asmān ēdōn uš bē tarsēd ciyōn
gōspand az gurg. pas ō āb mad *cē guft kū: azēr ī ēn

THE INDO-IRANIAN PRIESTLY CYCLE

(The text continues, describing the creation of the ten species of mankind from the semen of Gayōmart at length.)

6. Then Gangleri said, "Where did Ýmir dwell, and what did he live on?" [High One said:] "Thereafter, when the frost fell, there was a cow, who was called Auð-humla, and four streams of milk ran from her udders, and she fed Ýmir."

Then Gangleri said, "On what did the cow feed?" High One said, "She licked frost stones which were salty, and the first day on which she licked the stone, by evening there came from the stone a man's hair, the next day a man's head, and on the third day all of the man was there: he was named Buri. He was fair in appearance, tall and mighty. He begat a son, then, who was called Bǫr. That one took himself a wife, who was called Besla, the daughter of the giant Bǫlthorn, and they had

zamīg winarēd estēd. uš pas mayānag ī zamīg suft;
andar āyēd. ō ī urwar mad; pas ō gāw [ud] Gayōmard
mad; pas ō ātaxš abar mad. magas homānag pad harwisp
ud dahišn bē dwārēd.

[page 42, lines 4-10]

ēniz gōwēd kū: ka gāw ēkdād frāz
widard pad dašn dast ōbast. Gayōmard pas ān ka
bē widard pad hōy dast [obast].

[page 46, lines 3-5]

gōwēd pad dēn kū: ka gāw ēkdād bē widard, ānōh
kuš mazg bē frēstēd, jōrdā abāz rust 50 ud 5 sardag ud 12
sardag urwar ī bēšaz.

[page 93, lines 9-11]

šusar [ī] gāw abar ō māh pāyag burd. ānōh bē pālūd hēnd,
gōspand[ān] purrsardag frāz brēhēnēd. nazdist 2 gāw ēk nar ud ēk
mādag, pas az har sardag ī juxt ī andar zamīg 8 hāsar kē 3
frasang homānāg, pad Ērānwēz paydāg būd. ciyōn gōwēd
kū: arzōmandīh [ī] gāw rāy 2 bār dād, ēw bār pad gāw ud
ēw bār abāg gōspand[ān] ī purrsardag.

[page 94, lines 4-9]

pad dēn gōwēd kūm:
mardōmān frāz brēhēnēd 10 sardag, nazdist ān ī rōšn ī
spēd ī dōysar ī ast Gayōmard, tā 10 sardag ciyōn ēk
Gayōmard 9om az Gayōmard abāz būd. 10om kabīg [ī]
mardōmān nidom gōwēd. ka Gayōmard wēmārīh abar mad
pad hōy dast ōbast. az sar srub; az *xōn arzīz; ud az mazg
*asēm; az pāy āhanag; ud az astag rōy; ud az pīh *ābgēnag; ud az
bāzā pōlāwad; az gyān bē šawišn zarr ō paydāgīh āyēd,
kē nūn arzōmandīh rāy mardōmān abāg gyān bē dahēnd.
hōyag margīh pad tan ī Gayōmard andar šawēd, harwisp dāmān tā
frašgird margīh abar mad. ka Gayōmard andar widerišnīh tōxm
bē dād, ān tōxm pad rōšnīh [ī] xwaršēd bē pālūd hēnd.
uš 2 bahr *Nērōsang nigāh dāšt, ud bahr ī Spandarmad padīrēd.
40 sāl andar zamīg bawēd.

[page 100, lines 3-15; page 101, line 1]

74

three sons. One was called Óðinn, the next Vili, and the third Ve, and it is my belief that this Óðinn and his brothers must be the rulers of heaven and earth. We think that he must thus be called, for thus is called that man whom we know to be greatest and most famous, and they may well allow him to be called thus."

7. Then Gangleri said, "What then came about regarding them, and which of them was more powerful?" Then High One said, "The sons of Bǫr killed the giant Ýmir, and when he fell, then so much blood ran from his wounds that with it they drowned all the race of frost giants except one. . . ."

8. Then Gangleri said, "What happened to Bǫr's sons then, if you believe that they are gods?" High One said, "There is not a little of that to tell. They took Ýmir and brought him to Ginnungagap and made the earth of him: of his blood, the sea and waters; of his flesh, the earth was made; and mountains of bones. They made rocks and stones of teeth and jawbones and of the bones which were broken." Then Just-as-High said, "Of the blood which ran freely, they made the sea then, and they made the earth, and fastened it together, laying the sea in a ring around it, and it is thought perilous by most men to cross over it." Then Third said, "And they took up his skull, and made heaven of it, and set it up over the earth with its four corners, and under each corner they set a dwarf. These were called East, West, North, and South." (*Gylfaginning* 6-8)[121]

121. Þá mælti Gangleri: hvar bygði Ýmir? eða við hvat lifði hann? Næst var þat, þá er hrímit draup, at þar varð af kýr, sú er Auðhumla hét enn IV mjólkár runnu or spenum hennar, ok fœddi hon Ými. Þá mælti Gangleri: við hvat fœddist kýrin? Hár segir: hon sleikti hrímsteina, er saltir váru, ok hinn fyrsta dag, er hon sleikti steina, kom or steininum at kveldi manns hár, annan dag manns hǫfuð, þriðja dag var þar allr maðr; sá er nefndr Buri; hann var fagr á litum, mikill ok máttugr; hann gat son þann, er Bǫrr hét. Hann fékk þeirrar kona, er Besla hét, dóttir Bǫlþorns jǫtuns, og fengu þau III sonu: hét einn Óðinn, annar Vili, III Ve; ok þat er mín trúa at sá Óðinn og hans brœðr munu vera stýrandi himins ok jǫrðar; þat aetlum vér, at hann muni svá heita; svá heitir sá maðr, er vér vitum mestan ok ágæztan, ok vel megu þeir hann láta svá heita.

7. Þá mælti Gangleri: hvat varð þá um þeirra sætt? eða hvárir váru rikari? Þá svarar Hár; synir Bǫrs drápu Ými jǫtun; enn er hann féll, þá hljóp svá mikit blóð or sárum hans, at með því drektu þeir allri ætt Hrímþussa nema einn. . . .

8. Þá svarar Gangleri: hvat hǫfðust þá at Bǫrs synir, ef þú trúir, at þeir sé guð? Hár segir: eigi er þar litið af at segja: Þeir tóku Ými, ok fluttu í mitt Ginnunga-gap, ok gjǫrðu af honum jǫrðina; af blóði hans sæinn og vǫtnin, jǫrðin var gjǫr af holdinu, enn bjǫrgin af beinnum; grjót ok urðir gjǫrðu þeir af tǫnnum ok jǫnxlum, ok af þeim beinum, er brotin váru. Þá mælti Jafnhár: af því blóði, er or sárum rann og laust fór, þar af gjǫrðu þeir sjá þann, er þeir gjǫrðu ok festu saman jǫrðina, sik lǫgðu þann sjá í hring utan um hana, ok mun þat flestum manni ófœra þykja, at komast þar yfir. Þá mælti þriði: tóku þeir ok haus hans ok gerðu þar af himin, ok settu hann upp yfir jǫrðina með IV skautum, ok undir hvert horn settu þeir dverg; þeir heita svá: Austri, Vestri, Norðri, Suðri.

The general resemblance among these texts is quite clear. In each a primordial being is killed and dismembered, and from his body the cosmos is fashioned. This may not be quite as evident in the Iranian text as in the other two, for there the basic ideology has been somewhat transformed under the influence of Babylonian or Ṣabian astronomical speculation, in which the seven planetary spheres are identified with specific metals and colors. Thus the seven metals that come from the body of the dying Gayōmart actually represent the seven celestial spheres, and his death thus causes the creation of the entire cosmos.[122] Similarly, the mythologem has been somewhat transformed in the Indian text, for while a man and a bovine appear together in the Iranian and the Norse accounts, it would seem that only a man is present in the Puruṣa hymn. Again, however, this deviation from the apparent pattern is only illusory, for as J. Otrębski has demonstrated, the word púruṣa- must be understood as a compound that combines a word for "man" (Skt. pú-, as in pú-mān and pú-tra-) and a word for "bull" (Skt. vṛṣa-, —-ruṣa- by metathesis).[123] Thus, behind the figure of Puruṣa, the primordial being, lies an older notion of two primordial beings, a man and a bull together. This sort of transformation is only to be expected, for as time went on each group became more distant from its Proto-Indo-European origins and underwent its own idiosyncratic course of development. Each group carried certain common traditions with it, but these traditions were always subject to revision and reinterpretation. Thus, we see that the primordial act of dismemberment is performed by gods in two of these accounts, but in Iran, where a strongly dualistic outlook had entered the religious world view and where cattle sacrifice had come to be condemned, the dismemberment is said to have been performed by the chief of the demonic powers. Thus in Iran the act is no longer called a sacrifice but is seen as the first assault of the powers of evil, and among the Germans—where creation is often understood as the victory of the gods over the frost giants—this creative act is seen as the first such victory. Only in India is its significance as a sacrifice preserved.

One of the most perplexing areas where we might look for correspondences is the names of the victims in these three accounts. According to one text the primordial victim is named Ýmir; in another, Gayōmart; and in the third, Puruṣa. The question must arise: are these figures who are structurally so similar related in any historical way?

The answer to this is certainly yes, and it is here that the Old Norse version best preserves the Proto-Indo-European heritage. Old Norse Ýmir, as Güntert first demonstrated, is derived from Proto-Germanic

122. See Schaeder, pp. 226 n., 228 n. and ff.; Geo Widengren, "The Death of Gayōmart," in Myths and Symbols: Studies in Honor of Mircea Eliade (Chicago, 1969), p. 190.

123. J. Otrębski, "Aind. puruṣaḥ, pumān und Verwandtes," Zeitschrift für vergleichende Sprachforschung 82 (1968):251–58.

yumīyaz, which in turn is derived from P-I-E *yə₂m(i)yó-s* (or *yṃ(mi)yó-s*, as it might be written in a more modern orthography), a term intimately related to P-I-E *yemo-*, "twin."[124] This word corresponds to Latin *gem-inus* and Middle Irish *emon*, which both mean "twin," Lettish *jumis*, "double fruit," and, most importantly for us, Avestan *yəma-*, "twin," and the proper names, Av. *Yima* and Skt. *Yamá*, which mean "twin" as well.[125] Based on this phonological and semantic correspondence, I hypothesize that there was originally a mythic correspondence as well.

Iranian evidence tends to support this hypothesis, for behind the figure of Gayōmart can be perceived the figure of Yima.[126] The way in which this transformation took place is complex. First, it must be recognized that in pre-Zoroastrian Iran, Yima was not merely the king of the golden age but, as Christensen so skillfully demonstrated, was also regarded as the first king, the first mortal, and the first to die.[127] This tradition was rejected by Zarathustra, however, who soundly condemns Yima the one time he mentions him by name (*Y.* 32.8). There is another verse, however, in which the prophet makes an oblique reference to the myth of creation through sacrifice:

> And when these two spirits [the good and the evil]
> first met, they instituted
> Life [*gaya-*] and death, and how life should be
> at the end.[128]
>
> [*Y.* 30.4]

This verse tells of the primordial meeting of two spiritual beings, personages who are explicitly called "twins" (*yəmā*) in the verse immediately preceding this one (*Y.* 30.3). What is more, we are told that their encoun-

---

124. Güntert, *Arische Weltkönig*, p. 337, who argued, however, for a translation of "androgyne" (*Zwitter*) rather than "twin" (*Zwilling*). The "twin" interpretation has now been accepted by most Indo-Europeanists and most Germanicists as well. See Pokorny, p. 505; de Vries, *Altnordisches etymologisches Wörterbuch*, p. 678; and *Altgermanische Religionsgeschichte*, 2 vols. (Berlin, 1957), 2: 364; F. Botzler, "Ymir, Ein Beitrag zu den eddischen Weltschopfungsvorstellungen," *Archiv für Religionswissenschaft* 33 (1936):231; Schröder, "Germanische Schopfungsmythen," p. 7; E. O. G. Turville-Petre, *Myth and Religion of the North* (New York, 1964), p. 278; Otto Höfler, "Abstammungstraditionen," *Reallexikon der germanischen Altertumskunde* (Berlin, 1973), p. 19; Rudolf Much, *Die Germania des Tacitus* (Heidelberg, 1967), p. 51; Koppers, "Pferdeopfer und Pferdekult," pp. 320–21; Puhvel, "Aspects of Equine Functionality," p. 170.

125. Pokorny, p. 505; Mayrhofer, *Etymologisches Wörterbuch*, 3: 8.

126. Arthur Christensen, *Le premier homme et le premier roi dans l'histoire légendaire des Iraniens*, 2 vols. (Uppsala, 1918), 1: 35–37; Schaeder, pp. 212, 216 n. and ff.; Zaehner, p. 136; Güntert, *Arische Weltkönig*, p. 346; Koppers, "Pferdeopfer und Pferdekult," p. 136. See also the controversial work of Sven S. Hartman, *Gayōmart* (Uppsala, 1953), which for all its problems does contain some valuable insights.

127. Christensen, see esp. 2: 45, but all of Vol. 2 is devoted to the figure of Yima.

128. atcā hyat tā həm mainyū jasaětəm paourvīm dazdē /
gaēmcā ajyāitīmcā yaθācā aṇhat apəməm aṇhuš //

THE INDO-IRANIAN PRIESTLY CYCLE

ter resulted in the establishment of death (*ajyāitīm*, lit. "non-life") for the first time. Several eminent Iranists have recognized that in this verse Zarathustra attempted to deal with an earlier myth of creation, which he found objectionable but which he could not ignore completely.[129] Thus he philosophized the myth, changing its characters into abstract entities while retaining the essential mythologem that the first living man died at the creation of the world.

Ironically, however, a remythologization of Zarathustra's version took place in later centuries. In the verse cited above, the Avestan term translated as "life" is *gaya*-. In later portions of the Avesta, it is qualified by the term *marətan*-, "mortal," and from the combination of these words comes the name of the first mortal man, who died at the beginning of the world— *Gaya marətan*.[130] This name comes into the Pahlavi (Middle Persian) of the *Bundahišn* as *Gayōmart*. Thus the development is:

MPers. *Gayōmart* < YAv. *Gaya marətan* < GAv. *gaya* < Old Iranian *Yima* < P-I-E *Yemo*

The *Gāthās* and the *Bundahišn*, however, are theological in nature and contain theological transformations of the tradition. Another Iranian text that preserves heroic elements serves to support our conclusions:

> 30. We sacrifice to the strong kingly *x'arənah* [glorynimbus], created by Mazdā,
> 31. Which belonged to Shining Yima of the Beautiful Herds for the long time when he ruled over the sevenpartite earth of *daēva*s and men, magicians and sorceresses, tyrants, *kavi*s and *karapan*s; [32.] who carried away from the *daēva*s both riches and profit, both abundance and herds, both peace and glory. In his realm, both of the foods that are eaten were inexhaustible, men and animals were immortal, and water and plants did not dry up.
> 33. In his realm there was neither cold nor heat, there was neither old age nor death, nor envy created by the *daēva*s. Formerly there was no untruth, until he began to think the false, lying word.
> 34. Then, having seen him begin to think the false, lying word, the *x'arənah* departed from this one, in the form of a bird. That *x'arənah* which had been sent to him [became] invisible. Shining Yima was joyless before his foes, and he fell down and hid himself upon the earth.

129. Lommel, *Religion Zarathustras*, pp. 136–37; Zaehner, p. 136; Schaeder, p. 211; Hartman, pp. 18–22.
130. E.g., *Yt.* 13.87, 13.145; *Y.* 67.2. Gaya marətan appears with Gōuš Urvan ("Soul of the Ox") in *Visp.* 21.2 and elsewhere.

35. The first *x'arənah* fled from Shining Yima; the *x'arənah* departed from Yima, son of Vīvahvant, in the form of a falcon. Then Miθra, who is protector of wide pastures, keen of hearing, possessed of a thousand powers, seized the *x'arənah*. We sacrifice to Miθra, lord of all lands, whom Ahura Mazdā created greatest in *x'arənah* of the good deities worthy of sacrifice.

36. Then the second *x'arənah* departed from Yima, son of Vīvahvant, in the form of a falcon. Then Θraētaona seized the *x'arənah*, the prince of the house of Aθwya, of the house of the hero, who was the most victorious of victorious men other than Zarathustra.

37. Who struck down Aži Dahāka, the three-mawed, three-skulled, six-orbed, possessed of a thousand powers —the powerful *daēvic* lie, which is evil to the world, which is the most powerful lie Aŋra Mainyu created against the righteous world for the destruction of the world of Aša.

38. Then the third *x'arənah* fled from Shining Yima; the *x'arənah* departed from Yima, son of Vīvahvant, in the form of a falcon. Then the manly-hearted Kərəsāspa seized the *x'arənah*, who was the strongest of powerful men other than Zarathustra for his manly courage.

39. That strong manly courage clave to him. We worship that manly courage, firm of foot, sleepless, wakeful, that does not rest in bed, which clave to Kərəsāspa. (*Yt.* 19.30–39)[131]

131. uγrəm kavaēm x'arənō mazdaδatəm tā anyāiš dāmąn. 31. yat upaŋhacat yim yiməm xšaētəm hvąθwəm darəγəmcit aipi zrvānəm yat xšayata paiti būmīm haptaiθyąm daēvanąm mašyānąmca yāθwąm pairikanąmca sāθrąm kaoyąm karafnąmca. 32. yō uzbarat haca daēvaēibyō uye īštīšca saokāca uye fšaonīca vąθwāca uye θrafasca frasastišca. yeŋhe xšaθrāt x'airyanti astu uye x'arəθa ajyamna amarəšinta pasu.vīra aŋhaošəmne āpa.-urvaire. 33. yeŋhe xšaθrāt nōit aotəm åŋha nōit garəməm nōit zairva åŋha nōit mərəθyiš nōit araskō daēvō.dātō para anādruxtōit para ahmāt yat həm aēm draogəm vācəm aŋhaiθīm cinmāni paiti barat. 34. āat yat həm aēm draogəm vācəm aŋhaiθim cinmāni paiti baraiti vaēnəmnəm ahmat haca x'arənō mərəyahe kəhrpa frašūsat avaēnō x'arənō fraēštō yō yimō xšaētō hvąθwō barasat yimō ašatō dōušmanahyāica hō starətō nidārat upairi ząm. 35. paoirīm x'arənō apanəmata x'arənō yimāt haca xšaētāt šūsat x'arənō yimāt haca vīvaŋhušāt mərəyahe kəhrpa vāraγnahe. aom x'arənō hangōurvayata miθrō yō vouru.gaoyaoitiš yō srut.gāošō hazaŋrā.yaoxštiš. miθrəm vīspanąm dax'yunąm daŋhupaitīm yazamaide. yim fradaθat ahurō mazdå x'arənąuhastəməm mainyavanąm yazatanąm. 36. yat bitīm x'arənō apanəmata x'arənō yimāt haca xšaētāt šūsat x'arənō yimāt haca vīvaŋhušāt mərəyahe kəhrpa vāraγnahe. aom x'arənō hangōurvayata vīsō puθrō āθwyānōiš vīsō sūrayå θraētaonō yat ās mašyanąm vərəθravanąm vərəθrayastəmō anyō zaraθuštrāt. 37. yō janat ažīm dahākəm θrizafanəm θrikamərəδəm xšvaš.ašīm hazaŋra.yaoxštīm ašaojaŋhəm daēvīm drujəm ayəm gaēθavyō drvantəm yąm ašaojastəmąm drujəm fraca kərəntat aŋrō mainyuš avi yąm astvaitīm gaēθąm mahrkāi ašahe gaēθanąm. 38. yat θritīm x'arənō apanəmata x'arənō yimāt haca xšaētāt šūsat x'arənō yimāt haca vīvaŋhušāt mərəyahe kəhrpa vāraγnahe. aom x'arənō hangōurvayata nara.manå kərəsāspō yat ās mašyānąm uγranąm aojištō anyō zaraθuštrāt nairyayāt parō hąm.varətōit. 39. yat dim upaŋhacat yā uγra naire hąm.varətiš nairyąm hąm.varətīm yazamaide. ərəδwō.zangąm ax'afnyąm āsitō.gātūm jaγāurūm yā upaŋhacat kərəsāspəm.

The story here is ostensibly about the flight of Yima's royal glory (x^varǝnah- < P-I-E *swel-n-o-s*, "solar essence").[132] The crux of the matter, however, lies in Iranian and Indo-European notions of kingship. To the Indo-Europeans, the king represented the complete man, containing within his very body the essence of all three social classes—priests, warriors, and commoners.[133] In Iran, these essences were thought to reside in the x^varǝnah, the glorious nimbus that surrounds the king.[134] The myth that is recounted in this text, as Darmesteter first perceived and as Dumézil has since confirmed, tells how Yima fell from his kingship and lost the x^varǝnah, which then separated into three functional portions— Miθra receiving the portion of the priests or sovereigns, Θraētaona receiving the portion of the warriors, and Kǝrǝsāspa receiving the portion of the commoners or herdsmen.[135] It is, in truth, a myth of the dismemberment of Yima and the creation of the social order from him, just as *RV* 10.90.11–12 is a myth of the dismemberment of Puruṣa and the creation of of the tripartite social order from him.[136] The original mythologem has been transformed along royal lines, and an ethical element, the sin of Yima,[137] has been added, but the essential concept is still the same. It is also no accident that the saga of Yima ends with his physical dismemberment by his own brother, Spityura (*Yt.* 19.46)—a point to which we shall return.[138]

132. As demonstrated by Wilhelm Brandenstein, "Arica," Μνήμης Χάριν: *Gedenkschrift Paul Kretschmer* (Vienna, 1956), pp. 53–54, contra H. W. Bailey, *Zoroastrian Problems in the Ninth Century Books* (Oxford, 1971), pp. 1–51.

133. See Benveniste, "Traditions indo-iraniennes sur les classes," pp. 534–35; Georges Dumézil, "Le Rex et les Flamines Maiores," in *La Regalità Sacra* (Leiden, 1959), pp. 408 and 412; and K. A. H. Hidding, "The High God and the King as Symbols of Totality," in *La Regalità Sacra*, p. 57.

134. See John Greppin, "X^{v}arǝnah as a Transfunctional Figure," *Journal of Indo-European Studies* 1 (1973):232–42; and J. Duchesne-Guillemin, "Le X^{v}arǝnah," *Annali dell'Instituto Orientale di Napoli, Sezione Linguistica* 5 (1963):19–31, esp. pp. 25–26.

135. Darmesteter, *Zend Avesta*, 2: 625; Georges Dumézil, *The Destiny of the King* (Chicago, 1973), pp. 38–42. I am inclined to differ with them on a detail of interpretation, however, and feel that Θraētaona is properly the warrior figure in the original version of the list. Kǝrǝsāspa, a rival warrior figure (see Stig Wikander, *Vayu* [Leipzig, 1941], pp. 162–77), seems to have entered for reasons of syncretism in the establishment of the Achaemenid empire, replacing a figure who must originally have represented the third class.

136. One must also note that the Old Russian version, which may be derived from Iranian sources, contains a clear statement to the effect that the three social classes were established from the primordial sacrifice. See Schayer, pp. 320–21.

137. Interestingly enough, the sin of Yima according to the only *Gāthic* mention is that he "made men eat pieces of the ox" (*ahmākǝ̄ng gāuš bagā x'ārǝmnō*, in apposition to *yimascīt*), although in the later sources it is usually simply stated that he lied. Humbach, "Zur altiranische Mythologie," *Zeitschrift der deutschen morgenlandischen Gesellschaft* 107 (1957):366–67, tried to reconcile these two testimonies but without notable success.

138. Note that the story of Yima's defeat and death at the hands of Aži Dahāka (Zohāk in the epic) has largely been assimilated to the Near Eastern "kingship in heaven" theme, as has been demonstrated by C. Scott Littleton, "The 'Kingship in Heaven' Theme," in *Myth and Law Among the Indo-Europeans*, pp. 83–121. In the *Shahnāmeh*, however, it is only Zohāk who kills and dismembers Yima. The figure of Spityura, who appears in the

THE INDO-IRANIAN PRIESTLY CYCLE

In India also, it seems that the figure of Yama lies behind the Puruṣa of the Vedic hymn. Most scholars have agreed that Yama is another first man and first king figure and have noted that he is the first to die, thus establishing the realm of the dead.[139] Several scholars, however, have been willing to go further and equate the traditions of his having freely chosen death, abandoning or transcending his body (see especially *RV* 10.13.4; *AV* 18.3.13), with the sacrifice of Puruṣa described in *RV* 10.90.[140] As Dandekar put it, the Puruṣasūkta is merely a more detailed setting of the Yama mythologem of *RV* 10.13.4, and in the light of the comparison with Ýmir and Yima I am inclined to agree.[141] As we have seen above, the name Puruṣa seems to be a secondary formation replacing some earlier name. That name, I submit, was Yama. The morphological and structural features convince me that this is the same figure encountered in Iran and Scandinavia—*Yemo, "the twin," the first king[142] and first sacrificial victim, from whose body the world was made.

The question now arises: who played the role of the first sacrificer in this primordial drama? In the texts already considered, the first sacrificer was Ahriman, Óðinn and his brothers, and the entire assemblage of Vedic gods. Yet there is reason to believe that all these are late developments in which an originally human figure was either deified or demonized depending on attitudes toward the sacrificial rites. In order to recover the original figure, we must consider yet another version of the myth, in which the Indian Manu figures prominently:

> 14. There was a bull of Manu. An Asura-killing, foe-killing voice had entered into him, and from his snorting and roaring, Asuras and Rakṣasas were continually being ground down. Then the Asuras spoke together: "Alas, this bull does evil to us. How shall we destroy him?" Now Kilāta and Ākuli were the priests of the Asuras.
> 15. They said, "Manu is truly trusting in the gods;

---

earlier Avestan text, cannot be explained as part of the "kingship in heaven" mythologem and must be viewed as the remnant of an earlier mythological tradition.

139. Following Rudolf von Roth, "Die Sage von Dschemschid," *Zeitschrift der deutschen morgenlandischen Gesellschaft* 4 (1850):429. See also Oldenberg, *Religion des Veda,* p. 276; Gonda, *Religionen Indiens,* 1: 183, etc.

140. R. N. Dandekar, "Yama in the Veda," in *B. C. Law Volume,* 2 vols. (Calcutta, 1945), 1: 201–3; Güntert, *Arische Weltkönig,* p. 321; Koppers, "Pferdeopfer und Pferdekult," p. 323.

141. Dandekar, "Yama in the Veda," p. 202.

142. Note, however, that the Norse Ýmir has been transformed from a king to a giant in accordance with two developments within the Germanic realm: (1) the overriding conception of creation as involving victories over the frost giants, and (2) shifts in the Germanic kingship ideology away from the I-E ideal, as indicated by the disappearance of terms based on the P-I-E root *rēg-. On the latter, see Werner Winter, "Some Widespread Indo-European Titles," in *Indo-European and Indo-Europeans,* pp. 50–51.

now we must find out." They went [to him] and said,
"Manu, we must sacrifice for you."
"With what?"
"With this bull!"
"So be it." When it had been sacrificed, the voice
departed.
16. It then entered into the wife of Manu, Manāvī.
When they heard her speaking, then truly the Asuras
and Rakṣasas were continually being crushed. The Asuras
spoke together: "Indeed, our state becomes even worse
here when the human voice speaks." Kilāta and Ākuli
then said, "Manu is truly trusting in the gods: now we
must find out." They went [to him] and said, "Manu, we
must sacrifice for you."
"With what?"
"With this wife!"
"So be it." When she had been sacrificed, the voice
departed.
17. It entered the sacrifice itself and the sacrificial
vessels. Thereupon, they were not able to kill it, and this
Asura-killing voice roars out. For him who truly knows
this, they [the sacrificial instruments] cause that voice to
resound here, and his enemies become very miserable.
(*SB* 4.1.4.13–17)[143]

Certainly this is a late, aetiological text, yet preserved within the aetiology
is an ancient myth. Several points must be noted. First, the sacrificial victim is here Manāvī, Manu's wife, and—to judge from the appearance of
her name—his sister as well.[144] Behind her lies the figure of Yama, "the
twin," who is here taken as a female twin of Manu. Second, the human
victim is joined by a bovine victim, just as the victim in the Iranian and
Norse versions was joined by a bovine, which assures us that such an
animal appeared in the Proto-Indo-European myth.[145]

For the moment, however, we are concerned with the figure of Manu.
Etymologically, Skt. *Mánu-* is derived from P-I-E *manu-*, "man." It

143. manor ha vā ṛṣabha āsa / tasmin asuraghnī sapataghnī vāk praviṣṭāsa tasya ha sma
svasathād ravathād asurarakṣasāni mṛdyamānāni yanti / te hāsurāḥ samūdire pāpaṃ vata
no 'yam ṛṣabhaḥ sacate kathaṃ nv imam dabhnuyāmeti kilātākulī iti hāsurabrahmā vāsatuḥ
// 15. tau hocatuḥ / śraddhādevo vai manur āvam nu vedāveti tau hāgaty ocatur mano
yājayāva tveti kenety anena ṛṣabheṇeti tatheti tasyālabdhasya sā vāg apacakrāma // 16. sā
manor eva jāyāṃ manāvīṃ praviveśa / tasyai ha sma yatra vadantyai śṛṇvanti tato ha
smaivāsurarakṣasāni mṛdyamānāni yanti te hāsurāḥ samūdira ito vai naḥ pāpīyaḥ sacate
bhūyo hi mānuṣī vāg vadīti kilātākulī hai vocatuḥ śraddhādevo vai manur āvaṃ nv eva
vedāveti tau hāgaty ocatur mano yājayāva tveti kenety anayaiva jāyayeti tatheti tasyā 'ālab-
dhāyai sā vāg apacakrāma // 17. sā yajñam eva yajñapātrāṇi praviveśa / tato hainaṃ na
sekatur nirhantum / saiṣāsuraghnī vāg udravadati sa yasya haivam viduṣa etām atra vācam
pratyudvādayanti pāpīyāṃsi haivāsya sapatnā bhavanti //
144. Just as Yama's sister-wife is named Yamī.
145. Güntert, *Arische Weltkönig*, pp. 343–70, tried to separate the myths of the

corresponds to Avestan *Manuš, Proto-Germanic *manwaz (German *Mann*, and so on), and Old Church Slavonic *mozъ*, the first being a proper name and the latter two meaning "man" in general.[146] Within the Indian · texts, this Manu appears consistently as the first sacrificer (*RV* 8.10.2, 10.63.7, 10.70.8, and so on), who is said to have established Agni as the sacrificial fire (5.21.1, 8.23.13), and when men sacrifice, they are said to be acting as Manu did (6.4.1, 1.76.5). In fact, his association with sacrifice is so strong that those who do not sacrifice are called *ámānuṣāḥ*, "non-Manus" (8.70.11, 10.22.8), a word that carries the sense of "inhuman" as well as "unlike Manu."

There is, moreover, a consistent relation of Manu to Yama as first sacrificer to first king,[147] and this relation goes farther than a mere typological pairing. Already the *RV* knew them as brothers, as both are said to be sons of Vīvasvat (9.11.8, 10.58.1, 8.52.1). Later speculation at a time when the myth had been much transformed and was no longer fully understood made them into half-brothers, sharing only a father, and as a result of this many scholars have attempted to explain them as doublets brought together with an artificial aetiology.[148] But the fact is that both Manu and Yama have correspondences in Germanic versions of the myth, and we are thus assured that they are separate Proto-Indo-European figures. Their relation is that of brothers, and it is only the general Vedic avoidance of matronyms that permitted later speculation to make half-brothers of them. I would further argue that the significance of Yama's name, "the twin," is found in his relation to Manu. We have here a virtually universal mythic theme, namely, the twins at the beginning of time, imbued with a typically Indo-European content, namely, the complementarity of priests and kings.

In Iran, the figure of *Manu is well hidden but discernible nonetheless. I have already noted that in the heroic tradition Yima is dismembered by his brother, Spityura, and I would suggest that this Spityura is one transformed version of *Manu, but that there are others as well.

Urmensch and the *Urstier*, but there is nothing in the texts to support such a view, and Schaeder, pp. 212, 216 n., has rightly stressed the close connection between the two figures. Güntert's attempt was necessitated by his theory of *Yemo as androgynous but is untenable on the strength of the evidence.

146. Pokorny, p. 700; Mayrhofer, *Etymologisches Wörterbuch*, 2: 576–77.

147. Christensen, *Premier homme*, 2: 34; Oldenberg, *Religion des Veda*, p. 276; Roth, "Sage von Djemschid," p. 430.

148. The complicated relation between Yama and Manu as it was later seen is set forth in the *Bṛhaddevata* 6.162-7.7 and has been discussed by Maurice Bloomfield, "The Marriage of Saraṇyū," *Journal of the American Oriental Society* 15 (1893):172–88. The only Vedic evidence, however, makes both Yama and Manu sons of Vīvasvat (= Av. *Vīvahvant-* ⟨ I-I *Vívasvant*) and does not mention their mother. Roth, "Sage von Djemschid," p. 430; Christensen, *Premier homme*, 2: 34; Dandekar, "Yama in the Veda," p. 207; Güntert, *Arische Weltkönig*, p. 346, have all tried to understand Manu and Yama as doublets, but in light of the Germanic evidence this cannot be accepted.

As already noted, one of Zarathustra's most important reforms was the condemnation of cattle sacrifice. As a result, a myth that told of the creation of the world out of such a primordial sacrifice was clearly unacceptable. But rather than being completely lost, this myth managed to reemerge in texts composed after Zarathustra's death, somewhat transformed in accordance with the dualistic theology of the time but fully recognizable nonetheless.[149] The *Greater Bundahišn*, which we cited above, is one such text, and there the first sacrifice, the slaying of Gayōmart and his ox, is attributed to Ahriman (< *Aŋra Mainyu*, the "Evil Spirit"). But in a very sophisticated way the act of killing is itself condemned, while the beneficial results of the killing are accepted. Creation is understood in almost ironic terms, as an indication that Ahriman's destructiveness will always be turned to good ends by the superior power of Ohrmazd (< Av. *Ahura Mazdā*).

Insofar as Ahriman is an original conception of Zarathustra,[150] some other figure must have played this part in the pre-Zarathustrian version of the myth. If our evidence from India is to be trusted, we would expect a figure who corresponds to Skt. Manu to play this role. Phonologically, such a figure would be named *Manuš. Yet in all the Iranian texts we possess, no *Manuš appears.[151] There is, however, in both Avestan and Pahlavi texts, a figure who assures us that such a *Manuš did once exist. This is Mānūščīhr (< Av. *Manuš.ciθra*), whose name literally means "seed" or "son of Manuš."[152] In the genealogies, moreover, Mānūščīhr is made an ancestor of Zarathustra (*GBd*. 35.52-53), and it is explicitly stated: "All the Mōpats of Pars [i.e. the high priests of Persia] are traceable to this race of Mānūščīhr" (*GBd*. 35.55). Further, Christensen has conclusively demonstrated that the antecedents of Mānūščīhr in these genealogies are in fact nothing more than reflexes of *Manuš himself, artificially inserted into the lists at the earliest possible point.[153] Thus it would appear that *Manuš was originally regarded as the first priest but was written out of the tradition because he was too closely identified with a myth rejected by Zarathustra. Later he was replaced by four figures: Ahriman, who took his role as first sacrificer; Spityura, who took his role as the brother who dismembered Yima; Mānūščīhr, who took his role as the ancestor of the priestly line; and Zarathustra, who took his role as priest par excellence. All these figures are later Iranian developments,

---

149. Lommel, *Religion Zarathustras*, pp. 136-37; Schaeder, p. 211; Hartmann, pp. 18-22.

150. Darmesteter, *Ormazd et Ahriman*, p. 5.

151. This is not strictly true. *Manuš* does appear in *GBd*. 35.11 and the corresponding *Bund*. 33.4, but E. M. West, the editor of the latter text, attributes this to scribal error.

152. A. Christensen, "Reste von Manu-Legenden in der iranischen Sagenwelt," in *Festschrift Friedrich Carl Andreas* (Leipzig, 1916), p. 66.

153. Ibid., pp. 64-65.

transformations of an older tradition. For our purposes we have established that *Manu played these roles in the Indo-Iranian version of the myth, and if we can establish a Germanic correspondence it will appear that he is an Indo-European figure as well.

Does such a correspondence exist? In order to see this, we will have to consider yet another text, from Tacitus:

> They celebrate in ancient songs (which are their only means of remembrance or recording the past) an earth-born god, Tuisco,[154] and his son Mannus, as the origin of their race, as their founders. They assign three sons to Mannus, and from their names they call those close to the ocean Ingaevones; those in the middle, Herminones; and all the rest, Istaevones. (*Germania*, Ch. 2)[155]

Once again we encounter a character whose name is derived from Proto-Indo-European *Manu*, who is also described as one of the two first men. The name is a purely Germanic form supported by other Germanic evidence, and there is no reason to doubt Tacitus when he tells us that the name was preserved in ancient songs.[156] What is more, this Mannus is closely related to a figure whose name means "twin" (for that is the proper etymology of *Tuisco*),[157] and still further he is responsible for the division of the world into three parts, which are susceptible to interpretation along lines of class and function.[158] They have been historicized, no doubt, but their original nature is still readily apparent beneath the "historical" overlay.

154. This name appears as both *Tuisco* and *Tuisto* in differing manuscripts but this alternance is inconsequential for the etymology suggested below. See Much, p. 51. I am also grateful to Professor Jaan Puhvel of UCLA for having stressed this point to me, and having called my attention to the Old English alternance of *twist* and *twisc*. Private communication, 7/10/74.

155. Celebrant carminibus antiquis (quod unum apud illos memoriae et annalium genus est) Tuisconem deum terra editum, et filium Mannum, originem gentis conditoresque. Manno tres filios assignant, e quorum nominibus proximi Oceano Ingaevones, medii Herminones, ceteri Istaevones vocentur.

156. See Jakob Grimm, *Teutonic Mythology*, 4 vols. (London, 1883), 1: 345; Höfler, "Abstammungstraditionen," p. 19.

157. Güntert, *Arische Weltkönig*, p. 324; Schröder, "Germanische Schopfungsmythen," pp. 8-9; Much, p. 51; Höfler, "Abstammungstraditionen," p. 19.

158. Dumézil, *Destiny of the King*, pp. 12-13, proposes one possible means of interpretation, and a slightly different (but no less trifunctional) theory has been suggested by Much, pp. 53-55; and Jan de Vries, "Sur certains glissements fonctionnels de divinités dans la religion germanique," in *Hommages à Georges Dumézil* (Brussels, 1960), pp. 89-95. The basis for these interpretations is that the names of the groups mentioned are all derived from gods' names: *Ingaevones* ‹ *Yngvi* (= Freyr, the god of the third class); *Herminones* ‹ *Irmin* (= Týr according to Much and de Vries, Óðinn according to Dumézil, but in either case, a god of the first function); *Istaevones* alone is uncertain in etymology but seems to be derived from terms related to the warrior class (e.g. Skt. *işirá-*, "strong, unbridled," an epithet of Indra and the Maruts).

Similar historicizing of the myth took place in Rome, and yet our mythic scenario of the murder of one primordial twin by the other is discernible nonetheless in the story of Romulus and Remus, as told in Livy:[159]

> 6.3. The Alban state thus being ceded to Numitor, a longing arose in Romulus and Remus for establishing a city in the region where they had been exposed and raised. And the population of Albans and of Latins was overflowing, and herdsmen had also approached there, which all gave the hope that they would easily make Alba small and Lavinium small in comparison with the city that was to be founded.
>
> 6.4 But thereupon an ancestral evil interrupted these thoughts, the longing for kingly power, and also a foul rivalry arising therefrom on a mild enough beginning. Since they were twins, respect of age could not make distinction between them, so the gods protecting these places would choose by auguries which one would give his name to the new city, and which one would rule the country that they established. Thus, Romulus took the Palatine, Remus the Aventine as his augural ground for auguries to be taken.
>
> 7.1. It is told that an omen came first to Remus in the form of six vultures, and at the same time that this augury was announced, twice that number appeared to Romulus. Each of the two was saluted as king by his own people, the one claiming kingly power by priority of time, the other by the number of birds.
>
> 7.2. Then they turned from wrangling and angry words to bloodshed, and in the uproar, Remus was struck down. The more common rumor is that Remus leapt mockingly over the new walls of his brother, and therefore was slain by the enraged Romulus, who added, calling loudly with these words: "Thus hereafter to whoever else leaps over my protective walls."
>
> 7.3. Thus the sole power over the realm was Romulus, and the city thus founded was called by the name of its founder. (1.6.3–7.3)[160]

159. I am grateful to Professor Jaan Puhvel for having suggested this correspondence to me. Private communication, 7/10/74. See his treatment, "Remus et Frater," *History of Religions* 15 (1975):146–57.

160. Ita Numitori Albana re permissa Romulum Remumque cupido cepit in iis locis ubi expositi ubique educati erant urbis condendae. Et supererat multitudo Albanorum Latinorumque; ad id pastores quoque accesserant, qui omnes facile spem facerent parvam Albam, parvum Lavinium prae ea urbe quae conderetur fore. 4. Intervenit deinde his cogitationibus avitum malum, regni cupido, atque inde foedum certamen, coortum a satis miti principio. Quoniam gemini essent nec aetatis verecundia discrimen facere posset, ut dii, quorum tutelae ea

86

The difference between the two versions of Remus's death has little to do with our argument, for it seems to be an outgrowth of the polemics of later Roman politics. The first version is intended to criticize Augustus, who was identified with Romulus, and the second to defend him.[161] But in both accounts the essential mythologem is the same: one of the twins is killed so that the city may be founded. And just as the founding of a city is an act of creation (the institution of laws, rituals, and the class structure follows quickly upon the founding of Rome), so the death of Remus may be seen as the sacrifice that establishes creation.

Romulus is a very complex figure in Roman myth, but here he seems to have assumed the role of *Manu, the first sacrificer. His name is a back-formation from the city of Rōma (earlier *Ruma*), and thus bears no resemblance to *Manu,[162] but the name *Remus* does seem to be directly derived from P-I-E *Yemo. The initial *y-* has changed to an *r-* under the influence of *Ruma*, *Rōma*, and *Rōmulus*, but the word is otherwise as we would expect.[163] Given the fact that Remus is explicitly said to be a twin (Livy calls the two *gemini*), and the meaning of *yemo-* as "twin," this derivation seems inescapable. Even the motif of dismemberment has been recovered in other versions of the legend.[164]

An additional factor supports the inclusion of this version under the rubric of myths of the first sacrifice, namely, the role of the she-wolf. According to the legend, Romulus and Remus were nurtured as infants by a she-wolf, who suckled them and cared for them (see Livy, 1.4.6). This she-wolf can be seen to correspond directly to the cow Auðhumla of the Norse myth, who gave milk to Ýmir at the beginning of time. Roman national pride substituted the ferocious she-wolf for the docile cow as a

loca essent, auguriis legerent, qui nomen novae urbi daret, qui conditam imperio regeret, Palatium Romulus, Remus Aventinum ad inaugurandum templa capiunt.

7.1 Priori Remo augurium venisse fertur, sex vultures, iamque nuntiato augurio cum duplex numerus Romulo se ostendisset, utrumque regem sua multitudo consalutaverat: tempore illi praecepto, at hi numero avium regnum trahebant. 2. Inde cum altercatione congressi certamine irarum ad caedem vertuntur; ibi in turba ictus Remus cecedit. Vulgatior fama est ludibrio fratris Remum novos transiluisse muros; inde ab irato Romulo, cum verbis quoque increpitans adiecisset "sic deinde, quicumque alius transiliet moenia mea," interfectum. 3. Ita solus potitus imperio Romulus; condita urbs conditoris nomine appellata.

161. See the excellent treatment in Michael Grant, *Roman Myths* (New York, 1971), pp. 110–13. Sulla was also identified with Romulus before Augustus.

162. Puhvel, "Remus et Frater," has suggested an etymology based on Romulus's divine name, *Quirinus* (< *Co-vīr-inos*). Thus he reconstructs a Proto-Romulus named *Vīr-inos, "man"—a semantic match for *Manu.

163. Note that the formation *yem- has been preserved nowhere in Latin (*iem- would be expected), and the standard word for twin (*geminus*) has also had its first letter transformed. I owe this suggestion to Jaan Puhvel.

164. Puhvel, "Remus et Frater," pp. 154–55.

means of explaining Roman military prowess, but the Indo-Iranian parallels assure us that the bovine figure is the original one.

We must note, however, that neither the she-wolf nor Auðhumla is sacrificed alongside the human victim, as are the bovines of Indo-Iranian myth, and this fact leads us to reconstruct two major variants of the Indo-European myth. In both, the world begins with a pair of twins: *Manu, "man," and *Yemo, "twin." *Yemo is the first king and *Manu is the first priest, and in the course of the myth *Manu kills his brother, thus performing the first sacrifice. As a result of this act, the world is created and *Manu fashions the earth and the heavens as well as the three social classes from his brother's body. Both the Indo-Iranian and the European versions agree thus far, but it is at this point that they diverge. In the Indo-Iranian variant, a male bovine accompanies the twins and is offered alongside *Yemo. From the ox's body the animal and vegetable species are created. In the European version, however, a female bovine appears, who feeds and cares for the twins before the creative act but who is not involved in the sacrifice itself. This variation between the two traditions may be easier to understand when we recall that the Europeans were an agricultural society for whom the chief value of cattle was the milk-giving ability of the cow. The pastoral Indo-Iranians, however, esteemed their animals in a much broader sense and described their productive value in the mythic image of the primordial ox from whose body numerous goods stream forth.[165]

There is yet another European reflex of the myth, however—one that permits the conclusion that the Indo-Iranian version best preserves the Proto-Indo-European myth. This is the concluding portion of the great Irish epic, *Táin Bó Cúalnge*, the "Cattle-Raid of Cooley." As is well known, the main body of the *Táin Bó Cúalnge* concerns the attempt of Medb, Queen of Connacht, to capture the fabled bull, Donn Cúailnge, "Dark [or brown] of Cooley," in order that her possessions might equal those of her husband, Ailill, whose foremost prize is the equally fabled bull, Findbennach Aí, "White-horned of Aí." Ultimately, Medb fails in this endeavor, but the epic does not end with her failure. Rather, another story is appended, almost as a postscript, namely, the story of the final battle between these two bulls. The text is as follows:

> As for the Donn Cúailnge, when he saw the beautiful
> strange land, he bellowed loudly three times. The Find-
> bennach of Aí heard him. Because of the Findbennach
> no male animal between the four fords of all Mag Aí
> dared utter a sound louder than the lowing of a cow. The

---

165. Schrader, *Prehistoric Antiquities,* pp. 284–85; and *Die Indogermanen,* pp. 29–33; Brandenstein, *Erste "indogermanische" Wanderung,* pp. 25–29; Crossland, p. 24; von Bradke, *Über Methode und Ergebnisse,* pp. 190–94.

Findbennach tossed his head violently and came forward to meet the Donn Cúailnge.

Then the men of Ireland asked who should be an eyewitness for the bulls, and they all decided that it should be Bricriu mac Garbada.—A year before these events in the Foray of Cúailnge, Bricriu had come from one province to another begging from Fergus, and Fergus had retained him in his service waiting for his chattels and wealth. And a quarrel arose between him and Fergus as they were playing chess, and Bricriu spoke very insultingly to Fergus. Fergus struck him with his fist and with the chessman that he held in his hand and drove the chessman into his head and broke a bone in his skull. While the men of Ireland were on the hosting of the Táin, Bricriu was all that time being cured in Crúachu, and the day they returned from the hosting was the day Bricriu rose from his sickness.—[And the reason they chose Bricriu in this manner was] because he was no fairer to his friend than to his enemy. So Bricriu was brought to a gap in front of the bulls.

Each of the bulls caught sight of the other, and they pawed the ground and cast the earth over them. They dug up the ground [and threw it] over their shoulders and their withers, and their eyes blazed in their heads like distended balls of fire. Their cheeks and nostrils swelled like smith's bellows in a forge. And each collided with the other with a crashing noise. Each of them began to gore and to pierce and to slay and slaughter the other. Then the Findbennach Aí took advantage of the confusion of the Donn Cúailnge's journeying and wandering and traveling, and thrust his horn into his side and visited his rage on him. Their violent rush took them to where Bricriu stood and the bulls' hooves trampled him a man's length into the ground after they had killed him.

Hence that is called the Tragical Death of Bricriu.

Cormac Cond Longas, the son of Conchobor, saw this happening and he took a spear which filled his grasp and struck three blows on the Donn Cúailnge from his ear to his tail. "No wonderful lasting possession may this chattel be for us," said Cormac, "since he cannot repel a calf of his own age." Donn Cúailnge heard this for he had human understanding and he attacked the Findbennach, and for a long time and space they fought together until night fell on the men of Ireland. And when night fell, all the men of Ireland could do was to listen to their noise and their uproar. That night the bulls traversed the whole of Ireland.

Not long were the men of Ireland there early on the

morrow when they saw the Donn Cúailnge coming past Crúachu from the west with the Findbennach Aí a mangled mass on his antlers and horns. The men of Ireland arose and they knew not which of the bulls was there. "Well now, men," said Fergus, "leave him his triumph. I swear that what has been done concerning the bulls is but little in comparison with what will be done now."

The Donn Cúailnge arrived. He turned his right side to Crúachu and left there a heap of the liver of the Findbennach. Whence the name Crúachna Aé ("Liver-reeks").

He came forward to the brink of Áth Mór, and there he left the loin of the Findbennach. Whence the name Áth Luain ("Loin-ford").

He came eastward into the land of Meath to Áth Troim ("Liver-ford") and there he left the liver of the Findbennach.

He tossed his head fiercely and shook off the Findbennach over Ireland. He threw his thigh as far as Port Lárge ("Port of the Hind Leg"). He threw his rib cage as far as Dublind which is called Áth Clíath ("Ford of the Ribs"). After that he faced towards the north and recognized the land of Cúailnge and came toward it. There there were women and boys and children lamenting the Donn Cúailnge. They saw the forehead of the Donn Cúailnge coming toward them. "A bull's forehead comes to us!" they cried. Hence the name Taul Tairb ("Bull's Brow") ever since.

Then the Donn Cúailnge attacked the women and boys and children of the territory of Cúailnge and inflicted great slaughter on them. After that he turned his back to the hill and his heart broke like a nut in his breast.

So far the account and the story and the end of the Táin.

A blessing on every one who shall faithfully memorize the Táin as it is written here and shall not add any other form to it. (*Táin Bó Cúalnge*, from the *Book of Leinster*, lines 4854–4920)[166]

Although the myth has been recast in epic terms as the titanic struggle of the two finest bulls that ever lived, its cosmogonic nature is evident nonetheless. A man, Bricriu (described as the most even-handed of judges), and a bull, the White-horned of Aí, are killed and dismembered,

---

166. Translation from Cecile O'Rahilly, ed. and trans., *Táin Bó Cúalnge from the Book of Leinster* (Dublin, 1967), pp. 270–72, slightly altered to include glosses of place names from Joseph Dunn, trans., *The Ancient Irish Epic Tale Táin Bó Cúalnge* (London, 1914), pp. 367–68.

and from their bodies the world is constructed. The dismemberment of Bricriu has been transformed somewhat; in part, this motif appears in the story of his quarrel with Fergus, where his head was shattered, and in part it is preserved in the story of his death, where his body becomes one with the earth, embedded there by the mighty bulls' hooves. The dismemberment of Findbennach is more clearly preserved, however, as his liver, loins, thighs, and ribs go to create the features of the Irish landscape. In other versions of the Táin, the body of the Donn Cúailnge serves similarly: "He turned his back to the hill then and his heart broke in his breast, even as a nut breaks, and he belched out his heart like a black stone of dark blood. He went then and died between Ulster and Ui Echach at Druim Tairb. Druim Tairb ('Bull's Back') is the name of that place."[167] On the strength of this evidence, we may thus conclude with certainty that where the Indo-Iranian reflexes differ from the Roman and Germanic, it is the Indo-Iranian that most accurately preserve the Proto-Indo-European cosmogony. That is, in the oldest reconstructible version, a male bovine (ox or bull) accompanied the first men, and this animal served as one of the victims in the first sacrifice alongside the first king.

That Bricriu is a transformed version of the first king is implied by the emphasis placed on him as a fair and righteous judge, although Bricriu is portrayed as a suppliant and retainer to Fergus, the one-time king of Ulster, rather than as a king in his own right. This demotion may be because the story of the bulls' battle was subordinated to the epic, no king from which could be permitted to die in what was essentially a postscript. The royal nature of the victim in this myth, however, may be recovered in a related text, as may the priestly nature of his slayer.

The text in question is one of the prologues to the *Táin Bó Cúalnge*, entitled *De Chophur in da Muccida*, "The Quarrel of the Two Pig-Keepers."[168] There the story is told of two royal swineherds, one in the service of Ochall Ochne, king of the *síd* (faery-hill, supernatural realm) of Connacht, and the other in the service of Bodb, king of the Munster *síd* located on Femen Plain. The two herdsmen were close friends and were equally skilled in magical arts, being able to "form themselves into any shape, like Mongán mac Fiachna."[169] Popular speculation as to which of them had the greatest power, however, led to rivalry between the two friends and ultimately to quarreling. Making use of their magic powers, the herdsmen changed themselves into birds of prey, sea monsters, stags, warriors, phantoms, dragons, and maggots, continuing their competition

---

167. Dunn, p. 368. Note also the detail of Cormac's striking three blows on the back of Donn as mentioned in the text cited above. Might this be a dimly preserved reflex of the P-I-E theme of the victim's division into the three social classes, as attested in *RV* 10.90. 11-12 and elsewhere?

168. Translation in Thomas Kinsella, trans., *The Tain* (London, 1970), pp. 46-50.

169. Kinsella, p. 46.

with every change of form. With each form they took on a new name, but their names always indicated their intimate relation to one another. Sometimes the names are only related by phonetic similarity: Bled ("Whale") and Blod ("Seabeast") when they were sea monsters; Scáth ("Shadow") and Sciath ("Shield") when they were phantoms; Cruinniuc (?) and Tuinniuc (?) when they were maggots. Sometimes the names are related by meaning: Rucht ("Boar's Grunt") and Friuch ("Boar's Bristle") when they were pig-keepers; Ingen ("Talon") and Eitte ("Wing") when they were birds of prey; Rinn ("Swordpoint") and Faebur ("Swordedge") when they were warriors.[170] In each instance the names serve to emphasize the symmetry and inseparability of the two swineherds—one might even go so far as to say their twinship. This same relation carries over into their last incarnation. Having been maggots, both entered into springs where they were drunk by cows and were reborn as the most magnificent bulls of their day: Findbennach ("White-horn") and Donn ("the Dark" or "the Brown").

The two prize bulls are thus seen to be swineherds in reality. They are not simply swineherds, however, but royal swineherds and swineherds possessed of extraordinary magical powers. On the one hand they are thus attached to kings, on the other they resemble priests, and two figures with whom they are connected may be shown to be the Celtic first king and first priest figures. These are Bodb, king of the Munster *síd*, and Manannán mac Lir, father of Mongán mac Fiachna.[171] These two are among the Tuatha Dé Danaan, the ancient Irish gods, most of whom were killed at the catastrophic second battle of Mag Tured.[172] Bodb and Manannán were among the survivors, however, and together they were named joint sovereigns, the former—who was the son of the Dagda, who had been king of the Tuatha Dé—as their king, who led them into the *síde*, apportioned these mounds out and ruled over them within the *síde*, and the latter as their instructor, who lived in the oceans and visited his kinsmen from time to time, giving them gifts of invisibility, immortality, and inexhaustible food.[173] It is thus Bodb who appears as the first king of the present era and Manannán who is first priest. The two swineherds are related to both of them, insofar as one is the servant of Bodb and both have powers reminis-

170. Kinsella, p. 49. According to his note, p. 49, one text gives *Runce* in place of *Friucht,* substituting a phonetic resemblance for a semantic one.

171. The story of Mongán as told in the *Lebor na hUidre* and elsewhere is summarized in: H. d'Arbois de Jubainville, *The Irish Mythological Cycle and Celtic Mythology* (Dublin, 1903), pp. 189–90; and Alwyn and Brinley Rees, *Celtic Heritage* (London, 1961), pp. 221–22.

172. On the second battle of Mag Tured as a reflex of the P-I-E eschatological myth, see now Steven O'Brien, "Indo-European Eschatology: A Model," *Journal of Indo-European Studies* 4 (1976):295–320, following lines laid out by Wikander and Dumézil.

173. On the complementarity of Bodb and Manannán, see Arbois de Jubainville, p. 156; Rees and Rees, p. 139; and Marie-Louise Sjoestedt, *Gods and Heroes of the Celts* (London, 1949), p. 45.

cent of (and perhaps even bestowed by) Manannán and his son Mongán. Moreover, the names the swineherds take as bulls are also reminiscent of the complementary powers of king and priest: Findbennach, "Whitehorn," recalling the radiance of the king,[174] and Donn, "the Dark," recalling the dark, mysterious, druidic powers of the priest.[175] The two figures have sunk to the level of swineherds for reasons that are obscure,[176] but beneath the surface lie the first king and first priest of myth.

This Irish variant of the Proto-Indo-European myth has been much transformed. Relegated to a position as prologue and postscript to an epic tale of battle and adventure, its characters and values are thoroughly subjugated to those of the epic. Its heroes become retainers and servants of epic kings, or alternatively, the bulls sought by those kings as booty. Its central act of sacrifice becomes an epic duel between those noble bulls. For all these transformations, it remains recognizable nonetheless and provides invaluable confirmation of the authenticity of the Indo-Iranian versions of the myth on numerous points.

We are thus brought to the conclusion that the Indo-Iranian myth of creation, like the myth of their Proto-Indo-European ancestors, is a myth characteristic of pastoralists. It tells of the creation of the world through the primordial sacrifice of a man and an ox or a bull, and it establishes a pattern for all future sacrifice and all future creation.[177] This ideology furnished the conceptual base for a sacrifical system that was understood on a more practical level as a gift exchange with the gods—an exchange that regulated the flow of men and cattle through the cosmos. One might sup-

174. This notion of the royal radiance is best seen in the Iranian x*ar∂nah (on which see references listed in the index), but is present in all notions of nimbus, halo, etc. Note also Yima's common epithet xšaēta, "shining."

175. Like the Indian Yamá, Donn ends his mythic career by becoming the lord of the dead (on which, see Kuno Meyer, "Der irische Totengott und die Toteninsel," *Sitzungsberichte der preussischen Akademie der Wissenschaften* (1919), pp. 537–46. On the basis of this correspondence, we can posit a P-I-E ideology in which the first king and first mortal became first of the dead, on which see Bruce Lincoln, "The Lord of the Dead," forthcoming in *History of Religions*, vol. 20 (1980–81).

176. The subordination of this preserved myth to the epic explains why the reflexes of *Manu and *Yemo have sunk to the level of servants or retainers in the service of other kings. What is perplexing is why they should be swineherds. Numerous authors have noted the important connection of pigs to the Otherworld in Celtic myth (Rees and Rees, p. 178; T. F. O'Rahilly, *Early Irish History and Mythology* [Dublin, 1971], pp. 122–23), but I am inclined to see other facts as more relevant. First, pork had replaced beef as the favorite meat in Ireland (O'Rahilly, p. 122), and thus swineherds might be seen as those people most related to the nutritive aspects of the animal world (an intimate relation with swine replacing the intimate relation with cattle in the P-I-E myths). Second, identification as swineherds would specify the figures' lower class origins, it being forbidden for noblemen to own swine (Rees and Rees, p. 391, n. 19).

177. For several uses of this myth in contexts other than sacrifice, see my articles: "Treatment of Hair and Fingernails Among the Indo-Europeans," *History of Religions* 16 (1977):351–62; and "Death and Resurrection in Indo-European Thought," *Journal of Indo-European Studies* 5 (1977):247–64.

pose, although there is no way of proving the supposition, that priests considered the repetition of mythic events the most important element in sacrifice, while kings and warriors focused on the gift exchange. The various correspondences that have supported my reconstruction are listed below in Table 1, and the transformations we have observed are listed in Table 2.

All in all, we are not so far from the thought world of East Africa. The priestly cycle seems to function in much the same way, and a myth of the first sacrifice seems to have had much the same importance. The Indo-Iranian myth appears somewhat more speculative in nature than that of the Nilotes, for it deals with the creation of the cosmos, a topic untouched in the East African myths we have examined. Nonetheless the resemblances are very strong. The East Africans and the Indo-Iranians are both pastoral peoples; both worship celestial sovereigns; both have priestly castes; both perform cattle sacrifice, expecting cattle in return for their gift to the gods; and both emphasize in their myths of beginnings the first sacrifice of cattle. The resemblances are not confined to individual details but are systematic. Further similarities may also be perceived in considering the elements of the warrior cycle.

Table 1 The Indo-European Myth of the First Sacrifice: Correspondences

P-I-E	RV 10.90	SB 1.1.4	GBd.	Yt. 19	Gylf.	Germ.	Livy	Táin	De Chophur
First priest *Manu "man"	Gods	Manu	Ahriman	Spityura	Óðinn and Bǫr's sons	Mannus	Romulus	Donn	Friuch and Rucht
First king *Yemo "twin"	Puruṣa	Manāvi	Gayōmart	Yima	Ýmir	Tuisco	Remus	Bricriu	Friuch
First bovine	Puruṣa	Manu's bull	Sole created ox	Omitted	Auðhumla	Omitted	She-wolf	Findbennacht (and Donn)	Findbennacht and Donn
First sacrifice	Man	Woman and bull	Man and ox	Xᵛarənah	Man	Omitted	Man	Man and bull	Man in the form of a bull
Creation	World Classes Animals Plants	Omitted	Metals Men Animals Plants	Classes	World	Tribes	City	Landscape	Omitted

Table 2 The Indo-European Myth of the First Sacrifice: Transformations

	RV 10.90	SB 1.1.4	GBd.	Yt. 19	Gylf.	Germ.	Livy	Táin	De Chophur
First priest	Deified	Rejected as dupe of demons	Demonized	Historicized	Deified	Historicized	Historicized	Fused with bull	Reduced to magical swineherds
First king	Fused with bovine	Feminized	Philoso-phized	Ethicized	Deroyalized, changed to giant	Deified	Historicized	Reduced to retainer	Reduced to royal swineherd
First bovine	Fused with king	Portrayed as powerful and heroic	Portrayed as suffering and tragic	Omitted	Portrayed as nutritive	Omitted	Portrayed as nutritive and martial	Doubled, made martial	Doubled, made last of a set of transfor-mations
First sacrifice	Deified	Condemned as demonic	Demonized	Historicized, royalized	Changed to victory over giants	Omitted	Portrayed as murder	Changed to battle	Omitted (except by implication)
Creation	Animal's role fuses with king's	Omitted, only tells how power came to be in sacrifice	Portrayed as ironic	Only creation of classes preserved	Animal's role changes	Genealo-gized	Historicized	Set in specific geography	Omitted

V

THE INDO-IRANIAN
WARRIOR CYCLE

Turning to the warrior in Indo-Iranian religion, we again find a strong general resemblance with the East African system, along with numerous specific differences. Among these differences perhaps the most noteworthy is the appearance of a single warrior god, a towering figure whose importance at times rivals that of the celestial sovereigns. In East Africa, as we noted above, there exists a vague group of lesser deities, such as the Nuer Spirits of the Air, who are concerned with raiding and other warrior matters. Among the Indo-Iranians a similar group existed, although we cannot reconstruct their name (Skt. *Marúts*; Av. *Fravašis*),[1] who were martial figures located in the atmospheric region beneath the heavens and were associated with storm phenomena in some ways.[2] Also, the personification of the stormy wind, *Vayu (Skt. *Vāyú-* = Av. *Vayu-*), often cuts a martial figure.[3] But transcending these in importance is the one deity who must be considered the warrior par excellence among the pantheon of the Indo-Iranians, the god *Indra (Skt. *Índra-* = Av. *Indra-*), also known as *Vṛtraghna (Skt. *Vṛtrahán-* = Av. *Vərəθraγna-*).

---

1. Georges Dumézil, "Viṣṇu et les Marut à travers la réforme Zoroastrienne," *Journal Asiatique* 241 (1953):18–24. On these figures, see references in index to Maruts and Fravašis.
2. See Keith, *Religion and Philosophy*, pp. 152–154. It must be emphasized, however, that this natural association is only part of the picture, and a much more satisfying treatment is that of Wikander, *Arische Männerbund*, passim, esp. p. 75, who sees the Maruts as the projection of an age-set troop or warrior band into the realm of the skies.
3. Wikander, *Vayu*, p. 73 et passim. Note also the frequent association of the Indian Vāyu with Indra, as in *RV* 1.135, 4.46, 4.47, 7.91, and so on.

The Warrior God

*Indra's name is best interpreted as "the manly one," being derived from a P-I-E base *əner-, from which also come Gk. ἀνήρ, genitive ἄνδρος, and Hitt. *Inara,*[4] although another etymology has been suggested comparing OCS *jędrъ* "strong," "powerful," and Bulgarian *jĕdar,* "powerful," "bold."[5] In either event the name is a fitting one, the god's aggressiveness, daring, and raw power being his foremost characteristics.

His epithet *Vṛtraghna also emphasizes these same traits. Originally denoting an abstract concept, as shown by Benveniste and Renou, the word is a compound built on two members: a neuter *vṛtra- (Skt. *vṛtrá-* = Av. *vərəθra* =), "resistance," "obstruction," and the verb *√ghan- (Skt. √han- = Av. √gan-), "to strike," "smite," "smash," "kill." The name thus signified "that which overcomes resistance," or, as applied to the god, "the smasher of resistance." He who bears it is the personification of offensive victory.[6]

There has been some dispute over whether *Indra was truly an Indo-Iranian deity or not, the controversy stemming largely from the fact that his name appears in only two Avestan verses, both of which are late (*Vd.* 10.9, 19.43).[7] There are strong reasons for accepting these as authentic Iranian material, however, and not just a borrowing from India as has been suggested. In the first place both of these texts make Indra the leader of the *daēva*s, (< *daiva-), which is precisely his role in India. These *daēva*s, however, were rejected by Zarathustra, who regarded them as the "old, worn-out, sinister gods," unworthy of inclusion in the new religion.[8] In later Iranian literature they appear as demons, as they do in the one book of the Avesta where Indra does appear, the *Vīdēvāt*—the name of which signifies "the law against the *daēva*s" (< Av. *vī- daēvō- dātəm*). It

4. H. Jacobi, "Über Indra," *Zeitschrift für vergleichende Sprachforschung* 31 (1892): 316-19; Jarl Charpentier, "Indra: Ein Versuch der Aufklärung," *Monde Oriental* 25 (1931):1-6 and 26-27; Bailey, "Second Stratum of the Indo-Iranian Gods," pp. 9-10, note 21; and Helmut Humbach, "Der Fugenvokal a in gāthisch-awestischen Komposita," *Münchener Studien zur Sprachwissenschaft* 4 (1954):54.

5. V. Machek, "Name und Herkunft des Gottes Indra," *Archiv Orientalni* 12 (1941): 143-54.

6. E. Benveniste and L. Renou, *Vṛtra et Vṛθragna* (Paris, 1934). Their findings have been contested several times, most notably by A. B. Keith, "Indra and Vṛtra," *Indian Culture* 1 (1935):461-66; Lommel, *Arische Kriegsgott,* pp. 46-68; Gershevitch, *Avestan Hymn to Mithra,* pp. 159-63; and Steven Greenbaum, "Vṛtrahan—Vərəθragna: India and Iran," in *Myth in Indo-European Antiquity* (Berkeley, Calif., 1974), pp. 93-97. None of these, however, have in any way dented the strength of the Benveniste-Renou argument.

7. Benveniste-Renou, pp. 190 ff., see Indra as originally separate from Vṛtrahan, and some scholars, such as R. N. Dandekar, "Vṛtrahā Indra," *Annals of the Bhandarkar Oriental Research Institute* 31 (1950):35-36; and Burrow, "The Proto-Indo-Aryans," pp. 128-29, have contended that Indra was strictly an Indian god, the two Avestan citations being the result of Indian influence on Iran at some later time.

8. See Arthur Christensen, *Essai sur la démonologie iranienne* (Copenhagen, 1941), pp. 3-8, and the literature cited above, note 8, chapter 4.

THE INDO-IRANIAN WARRIOR CYCLE

should also be noted that in these two verses, Indra appears alongside two two other *daēva*s, Saurva (= Skt. *Śarvá-*), an Indo-Iranian reflex of the Proto-Indo-European goddess of death, *Kolvo-, "the Coverer,"[9] and Nāŋhaiθya (= Skt. *Nā́satya-*, although this is always in the dual).

In India both the proper name Indra and the epithet Vṛtrahan- survived, the latter occasionally being applied to other gods as well (for example, Agni in *RV* 1.74.3, or Soma in *RV* 1.91.5). In Iran, however, the names became separated, and Indra was rejected as a demon, while Vərəθraγna, purified of some of his *daēvic* traits—many of which were later absorbed by Miθra[10]—was admitted to the Zoroastrian pantheon as a *yazata* ("one worthy of sacrifice"), a deity of the second order.[11]

The Indo-Iranian warrior god also bore another epithet pointing to his martial strength: *bāghu-aujas (Skt. *bāhvója-* = Av. *bāzuš.aojah-*), "strong of arm."[12] As his name indicates, *Indra was depicted as invincible, possessed of awesome strength, and invariably victorious.

In certain contexts there is an ethical coloring to his combats and a sense in which he is subordinate to the celestial sovereigns. For in these instances the warrior god functions as the punisher of those who betray *Mitra, the *Mitra-draugas (Skt. *mitradrúh-*, *dróghamitra-* = Av. *miθrō.druj-*). This role is explicit in both Vedic and Avestan texts:

> Like the banner of radiant dawn, your insatiable
> weapon must proceed, O Indra!
> Like a stone hurled from the sky, strike with your
> burning strength those who betray Mitra.[13]
> [*RV* 10.89.12]

> (Vərəθraγna) cuts them all into pieces at once. He
> mixes the bones and the hair and the skulls and the
> blood of those who betray Miθra together upon the
> ground. (*Yt.* 10.72)[14]

The Avestan text cited here is more graphic than the Indian, showing the wild rage of the god, who races through the opposing army in the form of a wild boar (*Yt.* 10.70–72). This is but one of his forms, however, and the

9. Hermann Güntert, *Kalypso* (Halle, 1919), p. 141f.

10. Thus, for instance, it is Miθra who carries the warrior's club, the *vagra (Skt. *vájra-* = Av. *vazra-*).

11. Thus Widengren, *Religionen Irans*, p. 18; Zaehner, p. 89.

12. Actually, Vərəθraγna himself is never called *bāzuš.aojah*, nor is Indra. The title occurs only twice in the Avesta, once referring to Miθra (*Yt.* 10.25) and once to Sraoša (*Y.* 57.33). Yet as Vərəθraγna is said to grant strength of arm (*bāzvā aojō*), we may be certain he too bore this title at an earlier period. On the related term *ugra-bāghu (Skt. *ugrábāhu-* = Av. *uγra.bāzu-*), "bold of arm," see Wikander, *Vayu*, pp. 109–16.

13. prá śóśucatyā uṣáso ná ketúr asinvá te vartatām indra hetíḥ /
    áśmeva vidhyá divá á sṛjánás tápiṣṭhena héṣasā dróghamitrān //

14. hakat vīspā aipi.kərəntaiti yō hakat astāsca varəsəsca mastarəγnasca vohunīšca zəmāδa ham.raēθwayeiti miθrō.drująm mašyānąm.

THE INDO-IRANIAN WARRIOR CYCLE

Avestan Vərəθraɣna is able to transform himself into ten different mani-festations, all male and all ferocious—the wind, a bull, a fighting stallion, a camel, a boar, a youth of fifteen years, a falcon, a ram, a fighting buck, and a full-grown man.[15] Similarly, his Indian counterpart takes the form of a youth, an old man, a swan, a cuckoo, a lion, a tiger, an elephant, a bird, and the wind in the *Mahābhārata* (Calcutta Edition, 13.2273 ff.), and in *SB* 12.7.1, he becomes a he-goat, a ram, a bull, a horse, a mule, an ass, an eagle, a wolf, a tiger, and a lion.[16] The specific animals that appear in both cultures—bull, horse, falcon or eagle, ram, youth, man, and wind—are forms that might be assumed by the Indo-Iranian warrior god at will and all carry clear martial associations of vigor and impetu-osity. The ability to transform into a wild beast while in a state of furor is an ancient form of warrior magic and is well attested for both the Indo-Iranians and the Indo-Europeans.[17]

This leads to another point, one that may be somewhat unexpected, for it is at great variance from our usual assumptions about the nature of any deity. For the strength of *Indra is not inherent: he is not mighty by nature, nor does he possess great physical power at all times. Rather, he enters into a state of furor just as human warriors do (see below), becom-ing invincible only at those times when he is in such a state of frenzy. He is, furthermore, ultimately dependent on men for his strength, and it is the purpose of their cultic activity to bring him to this state of increased power. Thus they offer him songs and libations of the intoxicating *sauma (Skt. *sóma-* = Av. *haoma-*), both of which have the effect of invigorating and fortifying him,[18] as can be seen in such texts as *Yt.* 14.5 and 14.57 or *RV* 1.42.6, 2.12.14. Perhaps the ideology is clearest in:

> Indra Vṛtrahan is raised to intoxication and power by men.
> We call him alone in great battles and small; may
> he lead us to prizes won by strength![19]

[*RV* 1.81.1]

The warrior god delights in *sauma more than any other god, for it is necessary to his very being. Without it, he lacks his full strength and

---

15. *Yt.* 14.1-27. For the fullest analysis of these forms, see Jarl Charpentier, *Kleine Beiträge zur indoiranischen Mythologie* (Uppsala, 1911), pp. 25-68.

16. These correspondences were first recognized by B. Geiger, pp. 70-71.

17. On animal transformation in general, see Mircea Eliade, *Shamanism* (Princeton, 1970), pp. 459-60 and passim. With regard to the Indo-Iranians and the Indo-Europeans, see Lommel, *Arische Kriegsgott*, pp. 73-74; Benveniste-Renou, pp. 194-95; and Dumézil, *Destiny of the Warrior* (Chicago, 1970), pp. 139-47.

18. Dandekar, "Vṛtraha Indra," pp. 34-35; Keith, *Religion and Philosophy*, p. 124; Lommel, *Arische Kriegsgott*, pp. 11-12; Helmut Humbach, "Gāthisch und Jungawestisch," *Wiener Zeitschrift für die Kunde des Süd- und Ostasiens* 2 (1958):25-26. See such verses as *RV* 1.16.6, 2.36.5, 3.32.12, 8.4.4.

19. Índro mádāya vāvṛdhe śávase vṛtrahá nṛ́bhiḥ /
tám ín mahátsv ājíṣūtém árbhe havāmahe sá vā́jeṣu prá no 'viṣat //

cannot fulfill his function. As Bergaigne observed, Indra is a god only when in battle,[20] and he is able to pursue battle only when fortified by his favorite drink. While the sacrifice of cattle or butter is appropriate to the sovereigns, the warrior receives the energizing draught of *sauma.[21] With this gift, the sacrificers ensure that their god will be strong and victorious and will come to their aid.

For just as sacrifice to *Mitra and *Varuna established a bond of reciprocity, calling forth a return gift, the sacrifice to *Indra works in similar ways. Given strength, he can give strength in return; given *sauma, he can award victory to his devotees. It is not just that he can give aid in battle or lead the host in their onslaught,[22] but it is often apparent that the warrior god is a reservoir of might, from which those who offer a proper sacrifice can draw strength. It is in this sense that the following passage is to be taken:

> I bear haoma, which saves from defeat; I bear haoma, which overcomes resistance; I bear [haoma], which protects the good; I bear [haoma], which protects the body; I bear haoma, which, when offered, frees from bonds and from the one whose spirit is evil in battle, so that I might overwhelm that army, so that I might strike down that army which races behind me. (Yt. 14.57–58)[23]

This ideology, which is everywhere implicit in the Indra-hymns of the Rg Veda, is directly expressed in such verses as the following:

> Being joyously intoxicated, drink the soma
> strongly, O Indra!
> Strengthen us well in battles, O Conqueror, with
> lofty songs to heaven![24]
>
> [RV 2.11.15]

The god, then, must be strengthened in order to give strength, and the *sauma sacrifice is the proper mechanism for this exchange.[25] There is, however, a rather mechanical nature to this transaction, which when

20. Bergaigne, 2: 170–71.
21. Bergaigne, 3: 150; Potdar, pp. 49, 58, 98–99, and 273; Schlerath, "Opfergaben," p. 134.
22. See, for instance, such verses as RV. 3.34.2, 4.22.9, 6.46.3, 8.3.2, to name but a few examples.
23. haomǝm baire sāiri baoyǝm. haomǝm vǝrǝθrājanǝm baire. nipātārǝm vohu baire. pātārǝm tanuye baire. haomǝm yim nivazaiti nivandāt apayeiti dušmainyaot pǝšana haca. 58. yaθa azǝm aom spāδǝm vanāni yaθa azǝm aom spāδǝm nivanāni yaθa azǝm aom spāδǝm nijanāni yō me paskāt vazaite.
24. mandasānás tṛpát sómam pāhi drahyád indra /
    asmǻn sú pṛtsv ǻ tarutrǻvardhayo dyǻm bṛhádbhir arkaíḥ //
25. See the remark of Keith, Religion and Philosophy, p. 259: "This theory of the sacrifice and its result as an exchange of gifts, of strength for strength, is the fundamental fact of the whole Vedic religion."

THE INDO-IRANIAN WARRIOR CYCLE

carried to its logical conclusion comes into conflict with the ethical nature of the god noted above. In certain contexts it thus appears that rather than scourging the *Mitra-draugas or granting victory to the righteous man who obeys the cosmic law set down by *Varuna, *Indra will aid anyone who sacrifices to him properly. What is more, there are cases in which both sides in the conflict sacrifice to him, in which event he grants his aid on a first-come, first-served basis (RV 4.24.3 ff. / $Yt.$ 14.42–44). This only occurs, of course, when two groups of Aryans are struggling against one another, as the indigenous populations could hardly be expected to know the proper forms of the offering.[26] For while the warrior god has tended to lose most of his ethical coloration by the time of the composition of the Vedic hymns, he does continue to be the consistent champion of the Indo-Iranian invaders against all other peoples.[27]

*Indra grants to them strength and victory, enabling them to win rich booty, which seems to be the main goal of battle. The gain of territory is virtually unmentioned in either the Vedas or the Avesta, while the winning of rich plunder is a constant theme. Wealth won in battle is considered the gift of the god. Frequently, when sacrificers ask for booty, they leave the nature of the loot unspecified, but when they do make specific requests, it is worth noting that they ask for cattle far more frequently than any other form of wealth. Literally scores of times in the Rg $Veda$, cattle are referred to as prize booty,[28] while horses, food, or other forms of wealth are much less frequently mentioned, a situation that prompted an unsympathetic A. B. Keith to remark, "The stress laid by the [Vedic] poets on the possession of cows is almost pathetic."[29]

The importance of winning cattle is reflected in the frequently used term for "battle," Skt. $gáviṣṭi$-, which literally means "desire for cattle,"[30] and the term for a successful prince or war leader, $gopá$-, "lord of cattle."[31] A good many scholars, both Indian and Western, however, have been unwilling to accept this at face value, pointing out that the word for cattle in Sanskrit, $gó$-, is frequently used in allegorical fashion, referring to the rays of the sun or the streams of rain.[32] These scholars regard as

---

26. On an ideological level this was seen as the chief offense of the aboriginal peoples, which justified the Aryans' aggression against them. See, for instance, RV 4.24.5, 5.34.6, or 6.14.3.

27. Indra takes this role so consistently that Dandekar, "Vṛtraha Indra," p. 20, argued that he was originally the human hero who led the Indo-Aryan invasion of India, and who was later raised to divine status.

28. See, e.g., RV 1.11.3, 1.16.9, 1.36.8, 1.48.2, 1.51.3, 1.53.2, 1.62.2, 1.73.5–6, 1.81.7, 1.82.4, 1.83.4, 1.86.3, 1.102.6, 1.111.22, 1.130.3, 1.156.4, 1.169.8, 1.174.4, for just some of the occurrences in the first Maṇḍala alone.

29. Keith, "The Age of the Rigveda," in The $History$ of $India,$ 1: 88.

30. Macdonell and Keith, 1: 223.

31. Ibid., 2: 212.

32. The Indian tradition of allegorical interpretation can be traced at least to Yāska, who in $Nirukta$ 2.6 states that in his time there were two schools of thought on Vṛtra's iden-

nature allegory passages in which Indra is asked to win cattle or to free cows from their pen, rather than taking the request at face value.

In fact, this view, which was once much more prevalent than it is today, is not totally without merit. Indra does mete out not only literal cows but rain-cows and solar-cows as well. As Bergaigne first observed, these three forms of gifts correlate to the three cosmic regions of the Indian world view: the true cows deriving from the earth, rain from the atmosphere, and sun from the heavens.[33] I will not contend that cattle in the Veda always signify "cattle" and nothing more; surely there was often a rich and multivalent symbolism at work. I do, however, maintain that in the majority of occurrences the term "cattle" does signify simply cattle and bears no allegorical or metaphoric significance, and also that the symbolic associations of cattle with rain and sun are primarily an Indian innovation, there being little in the way of Iranian evidence to support a reconstruction of "cattle" as Indo-Iranian metaphoric language. Only the symbolic genius of the Indian Ṛṣis made such a usage possible, and it was by the leap of their speculative thought that a familiar human enterprise, the cattle raid, was viewed in cosmic proportions. In the Iranian material there is no such elevation to the cosmic level. When the god Vərəθraγna grants booty, he grants cattle, as in *Yt.* 14.41: "We sacrifice to Vərəθraγna, created by Ahura. Vərəθraγna covers this house with glory (*x'arənah*), together with riches in cattle."[34] As we shall see, this is in keeping with the reality of the Indo-Iranian warrior's situation, as cattle raiding was his main pursuit. It is, moreover, consonant with a mytho-

---

tity; one of which made him a cloud, the cows freed from his grip thus being rain. Sāyaṇa held to this view in his commentaries, and as a result it has continued to show up in scholarly discussion with a bent toward nature allegory. See, e.g., Spiegel, pp. 194–98; Venkantasubbiah, p. 133. Edward Delavan Perry, "Indra in the Rig-Veda," *Journal of the American Oriental Society* 11 (1891):117–23; and Alfred Hillebrandt, "Indra und Vṛtra," *Zeitschrift der deutschen morgenlandischen Gesellschaft* 50 (1896):665–66. Two scholars have made more sophisticated attempts to integrate nature allegory into their views of the warrior god: Bergaigne, 2: 175–84; and Lommel, *Arische Kriegsgott,* pp. 19–44. Both of these could be freely accepted were it not for Lommel's insistence (pp. 44–45) that the elements of nature allegory found in the Veda mount to the I-I period. Recently several attempts have been made to interpret the "cows" not as allegory but as metaphor for some social or psychic entity. In this vein, see Wolfgang Schmid, "Die Kuh auf der Weide," *Indogermanische Forschungen* 64 (1958):1–12; George B. Cameron, "Zoroaster the Herdsman," *Indo-Iranian Journal* 10 (1968):261–81; Hanns-Peter Schmidt, *Zarathustra's Religion and His Pastoral Imagery* (Leiden, 1975); and "Is Vedic *Dhenā* Related to Avestan *Daēnā?*" in *Monumentum H. S. Nyberg,* Vol. 2 (Leiden, 1975), pp. 165–79; B. L. Ogibenin, "Baltic Evidence and the Indo-Iranian Prayer," *Journal of Indo-European Studies* 2 (1974):23–46. I find none thoroughly convincing and would emphasize that the burden of proof is upon those who contend that "cows" in any given passage does not mean "cows."

33. Bergaigne, 2: 176–77.

34. Vərəθraγnəm ahura.δātəm yazamaide. Vərəθraγnō avi imat nmānəm gaosūrābyō x'arənō pairi.vərənavaiti.

logical "charter" handed down from a very early period, which tells of man's first cattle raid.[35]

The Myth of the First Cattle Raid

Two texts, one from India and one from Iran, furnish the starting point for reconstruction of an ancient Indo-European myth:

> Āptya, knowing the ancestral weapons, and impelled by
>   Indra, did battle.
> Having killed the three-headed, seven-bridled one,
>   Trita drove off the cattle of Tvaṣṭṛ's own son.
> The mighty lord Indra struck down the conceited one
>   who had sought great power.
> Driving forth the cattle of Viśvarūpa, Tvaṣṭṛ's own
>   son, he tore off those three heads.[36]
>
> > > > [RV 10.8.8-9]

> Θraētaona, the prince of the house of Aθwya, of the heroic house, sacrificed to him [Vayu] in four-cornered Varəna on a golden chair, on a golden pillow, on a golden rug. He strewed the sacred twigs from cupped hands, streaming [libations].
>
> He asked, "Grant success to me, O Vayu, whose deeds are the highest, that I might be victorious over Aži Dahāka, the three-mawed, three-skulled, six-orbed, strong daēvic lie of a thousand senses, the evil betrayer of mankind, who is the strongest lie created by Aŋra Mainyu against the material world of Aša. And may I carry off his two women, Savaŋhavāc and Arənavāc, who raised themselves with the most beautiful bodies for the world, who are the most excellent in the world." (Yt. 15.23-24)[37]

---

35. Much of the following section has appeared in my article, "The Indo-European Cattle-Raiding Myth," *History of Religions* 16 (1976):42-65, to which important new materials have been added.

36. sá pítryāṇy áyudhāni vidván índreṣita āptyó abhy àyudhyat /
    triśīrṣáṇaṃ saptáraśmiṃ jaghanván tvāṣṭrásya cin níḥ sasṛje
        tritó gáḥ //
    bhúríd índra udínakṣantam ójó 'vābhinat sátpatir mányamānam /
    tvāṣṭrásya cid viśvárūpasya gónām ācakraṇás tríṇi śīrṣá párā vark //

37. Təm yazata vīsō puθrō aθwyanōiš vīsō sūrayå Θraētaonō upa varənəm
    caθru.gaošəm zaranaēne paiti gātvō zaranaēne paiti fraspaiti
    zaranaēne paiti upastarəne frastarətāt paiti barəsman pərənaēibyō
    paiti γžārayatbyō. 24. aom jaiδyat avat āyaptəm dazdi.mē vayuš yō
    uparō.kairyō yat bavāni aiwi.vanyā ažim dahākəm θrizafanəm
    θrikamərəδəm xšvašašīm hazaŋra.yaoxštīm ašaojaŋhəm daēvim
    drujəm ayəm gaēθavyō drvantəm yəm ašaojastəməm drujəm fraca
    kərəntat aŋrō mainyuš avi yəm astvaitīm gaēθąm mahrkāi ašahe

Both of these texts describe the slaying of a three-headed monster. Moreover, the name of the hero in both is the same, for the Indian Trita Āptya is equivalent to the Avestan Θraētaona Āθwya. Their first names, while not fully identical, are closely related. Θraētaona is a patronym formed from Av. Θrita, which is a perfect match for Skt. Tritá, yielding an Indo-European original *Trito-, which means literally "third," as do the other forms derived from it: Gk. τρίτος; ON þridi; Albanian tretë; Lat. tertius; Welsh trydydd; OHG dritto; and so forth.[38] The second name, *Ātpya, seems simply to be the name of a family of heroes[39] and contrary to the generally accepted opinion has nothing whatever to do with water, as Bartholomae[40] and Wackernagel[41] have convincingly demonstrated.

The only shift, then, that needs to be accounted for is that from I-I *Trita to Avestan Θraētaona, "Son of Θrita." Why should we have this slip in generations? The answer seems to be found in the Iranian ideology of the making of a hero. To judge from certain texts, most particularly Yasna 9, heroism was a product of two generations among the Iranians. It is carried in the semen of the father and transmitted to the son, in whom it develops fully. Should the father wish heroic offspring, he prepares and drinks the intoxicating haoma according to ritual. Once within his body, it descends to the genitals, where it is distilled into semen, and when transmitted to a son, it develops into the xᵛarənah, the radiant nimbus that marks kings and heroes.[42] This complex theory seems to be a specifi-

---

gaēθanąm uta.hē vanta azāni saṇhavāca arənavāca yōi hən kəhrpa sraēšta zazāitəe gaēθyāi tē yōi abdōtəme.
Translation of the final phrase following Karl Hoffmann, "Jungawestisch zazāite," *Münchener Studien zur Sprachwissenschaft* 4 (1954):48-52.

38. Walther Wüst, "Trita und Verwandtes," *Wörter und Sachen* 3 (1940):225-27; Bartholomae, *Altiranisches Wörterbuch,* p. 800; Pokorny, p. 1091; Mayrhofer, *Etymologisches Wörterbuch,* 1: 534-35; Güntert, *Arische Weltkönig,* pp. 30-31; Bergaigne, 2: 327; Georges Dumézil, "Deux traits du monstre tricéphale indo-iranien," *Revue de l'histoire des religions* 120 (1939):5. Two other positions have been proposed, however. First, Kasten Rönnow, *Trita Aptya, eine vedische Gottheit* (Uppsala, 1927), attempted to connect *Tritá* to Gk. Τρίτων, seeing both as water deities. The comparison has been rejected, however, due to the difference in vowel length, as Τρίτων has a long -ī-. See Frisk, 2: 933-34. Second, J. Wackernagel, "Akzenstudien I," *Nachrichten der Göttingen Gesellschaft der Wissenschaften* (1909), pp. 60-61, felt that *Tritá* was an abbreviated form of *tri-tavan(a)-,* "the thrice-strong," and his argument was accepted by Herman Lommel, "Naotara und Spitāma," *Indogermanische Forschungen* 53 (1935):183; and J. Duchesne-Guillemin, "Aw. Θraētaona-," *Indogermanische Forschungen* 54 (1936):205.

39. Hillebrandt, *Vedische Mythologie,* 3: 341-43. This remains the most probable explanation, although not the most widely accepted one.

40. Bartholomae, *Arische Forschungen,* 1: 8-9; and "Arica, I," *Indogermanische Forschungen* 1 (1892):180-82.

41. Wackernagel, "Akzenstudien," p. 61 n.; and note contributed to Hanns Oertel, *The Syntax of Cases in the Narrative and Descriptive Prose of the Brāhmaṇas* (Heidelberg, 1926), p. 328.

42. Thus, in *Yasna* 9, each of the first four men to prepare haoma were blessed with heroic sons: Vīvaṇhant with Yima, Āθwya with Θraētaona, Θrita with Kərəsāspa, and Pourušaspa with Zarathustra. All the fathers prepare haoma, and all the sons bear the xᵛarənah. On the nature of this xᵛarənah and its relation to mystic physiology, see J.

105

cally Iranian piece of speculation; in India one who prepares and drinks *soma* is himself gifted with heroic properties without having to wait a generation.[43] In the original version of the myth, then, *Trito apparently prepared the *sauma*, drinking some himself (as in *R V* 8.12.16, 1.187.1 / *Y.* 9.10), and gained heroic strength from it. The development whereby Avestan Θrita → Θraētaona is a later development, and both Θrita and Θraētaona can be understood as reflexes of an earlier *Trito.[44]

It should be noted that this *Trito was a mythic personage and a great hero but almost certainly not a god. There is no Iranian evidence for divine status,[45] and the majority of the forty-odd places where he occurs in the *Rg Veda* show him to be human—in contact with the gods and aided by them but no god himself (for example, *R V* 2.11.19, 2.34.14, 5.86.1, 8.52.1, 9.34.4, 10.48.2, 10.64.3).[46] Those verses where he does appear as a god (such as *R V* 5.41.4, 8.41.6) are evidence of either independent Indian elevation of the hero or perhaps even the existence of a second Indian Trita.[47] But originally, like *Manu and *Yemo (with whom he is often grouped)[48] *Trito was one of the first men in myth, whose actions helped shape the world and continue to serve as a prototype for human behavior.

Given the Indo-Iranian evidence and other Indo-European correspondences with which we will deal below, numerous scholars have been inclined to treat the Indian Trita as the original figure in the dragon-slaying myth, regarding Indra, who often takes the role of the dragon slayer, as a late intruder in the mythic cycle.[49] In their opinion, in the

---

Duchesne-Guillemin, "Le Xᵛarǝnah," pp. 25 ff.; also G. Gnoli, "Lichtsymbolik in Alt-Iran," *Antaios* 8 (1967):528–49.

43. As in the famous hymn, *R V* 10.119.

44. Spiegel, p. 270, came very close to this formulation without being able to finally pin it down.

45. See Rudolf von Roth, "Die Sage von Feridūn in Indien und Iran," *Zeitschrift der deutschen morgenlandischen Gesellschaft* 2 (1848):220–21, 225. Roth's reporting of the evidence is flawless, but he mistakenly concluded that Trita was originally a god who sank to human status in Iran while retaining his original nature in India.

46. Hillebrandt, *Vedische Mythologie,* 2: 344; Oldenberg, *Religion des Veda,* pp. 143–44. Compare such views as Bergaigne, 2: 328–29, who identified Trita with Apām Napāt; A. A. Macdonell, "Mythological Studies in the Rigveda: The God Trita," *Journal of the Royal Asiatic Society* (1893), pp. 419–96; and Murray Fowler, "Trita Soter," *Journal of the American Oriental Society* 67 (1947):59–60, who saw him as the third form of Agni; Perry, pp. 142–48; and Roth, "Sage von Feridūn," pp. 223–24, who saw him as a storm god; Rönnow, *Trita Aptya,* passim, who saw him as a water god; and L. D. Barnett, "The Genius: A Study in Indo-European Psychology," *Journal of the Royal Asiatic Society* (1929), pp. 740–41, who saw him as the father of the Marúts.

47. Spiegel, pp. 268–69. The appearance of a Trita Vaibhūvasa in *R V* 10.46.3, in contrast to our Trita Āptya, lends credence to this suggestion.

48. See *R V* 10.64.3, 1.163.2–3, 8.52.1 / *Y.* 9.3–13; *Yt.* 19.36.

49. Charpentier, *Kleine Beiträge,* p. 56; Keith, *Religion and Philosophy,* p. 127; Oldenberg, *Religion des Veda,* p. 143; Perry, p. 144; Leopold von Schroeder, *Mysterium und Mimus im Rigveda* (Leipzig, 1908), p. 132; Dandekar, "Vṛtraha Indra," pp. 10–11. In contrast, Lommel, *Arische Kriegsgott,* pp. 57, 59–60 and 69, sees Indra as original and Trita as a late intruder.

earliest versions of the myth Trita alone slew the monster, while in later versions Indra takes this part. Those versions in which both appear together are seen as cases of incomplete dominance composed before Indra had completely overshadowed his predecessor. This theory, however, is not supported by the evidence. Rather than a gradual process of eclipse, there is a consistent relation of assistance and dependence between Indra and Trita. In *RV* 10.8 cited above, Trita is said to be "impelled by Indra" (*índreṣita*) and similarly he is aided by the god in *RV* 10.48.2, 5.86.1 and 2.11.19. Trita, in turn, gives *soma* to Indra (*RV* 9.34.4, 9.86.20) and is said to drink the intoxicating brew alongside him in *RV* 8.12.16. Their relation is an exchange of strength, the typical relation between the warrior and the warrior god. Given this, it seems that both Trita and Indra were originally present in the Indian version of the myth, Trita appearing as the hero who actually slew the monster and Indra as the god who aided him in the exploit.

The Iranian evidence is inconclusive on this point. In the text I have cited, Θraētaona calls on the god Vayu for help, and in other parallel passages he calls on Ardvi Sūra Anāhita (*Yt.* 5.33–34), Drvāspa (*Yt.* 9.13–14), and Aši Vaṇuhī (*Yt.* 17.33–34) for assistance against the tricephal. Clearly the hero was aided by a deity in Iran also, the only question being which one figured in the earliest version of the myth. Given the changes that Zarathustra's reform brought about in the status of *Indra *Vṛtraghna, I am led to hypothesize that this deity originally took the part, and after his demotion at the hands of the prophet other deities filled the vacuum.[50] But we need not rely on hypothesis, for there is another text that affords certainty on this point.

> His [Tigran's] sons were Bab, Tiran, Vahagn: of this latter, the fables tell, "Heaven and earth were in travail, the purple sea was in travail; a red reed had its birth in the seas, from the stems of the reed came forth smoke, from the stems of the reed came forth a flame, and from the flame sprang a young man; this youth had fiery hair, also a beard of flame, and his eyes were suns." All sing of this one, I have heard it with my own ears; they thus recount in song along with cymbals, his battle with the dragon and his victory, and they sing of him in every way as of the heroic deeds of Hercules. (Moses of Chorene: *History of Armenia*, 1.31)[51]

As has long been known, the name *Vahagn* is a loan word into Armenian

---

50. As suggested by Widengren, *Religionen Irans*, p. 18; Zaehner, p. 89; and Dumézil, *Destiny of the Warrior*, pp. 116–17.

51. Translation following the German of M. Lauer, *Des Moses von Chorene Geschichte Gross-Armeniens* (Regensberg, 1869), p. 52.

and is derived from Avestan *Vərəθraγna*.[52] The story of Vahagn's birth from the flaming reed has also been connected with an Indian *itihāsa* tradition telling of the reenergizing of Indra.[53] Thus we are virtually certain that Vahagn is a dependent variant of the Indo-Iranian tradition, and his role as a dragon slayer in this text has frequently aroused scholarly attention.[54] Two other details should be noted, however. First, Vahagn is set in a distinctly human genealogy, being descended of a king and having two human brothers. He is compared with a hero, Hercules, and not with a god.[55] Although his name is derived from that of the warrior god, Vahagn is clearly a mortal. Second, Vahagn is the third child born to Tigran. The other two brothers play no role of any importance and seem to have been added simply to preserve Vahagn's position as third in line.[56] He seems to represent not only the god *Vṛtraghna but also the hero *Trito, "Third." The figures who originally cooperated in the dragon slaying have here fused into one figure, a hero who bears the name of the god.

In the Armenian version the myth is given in a most abbreviated form. As a result, *Trito's enemy has lost much of the specificity he had in the Indian and Iranian versions and is described simply as a "dragon" (Arm. *višap*). But in India and Iran he is said to be a serpent, Avestan *aži-*, Sanskrit *áhi-* (see *RV* 10.48.2), both of which are derived from P-I-E *ṇgʷhi-*, "serpent," of which Latin *anguis*, Lith. *angìs*, Arm. *auj*, Gk. ὄφις, and Middle Irish *esc-ung* (literally "serpent of the waters," that is, "eel") are also reflexes.[57] This serpent is said to be three-headed, Av. *θri-kamərədəm*, Skt. *tri-śīrṣāṇam*. Finally, this three-headed serpent is further marked as a *dāsa-*, an aboriginal inhabitant who is inimical to the Indo-European invaders.[58] The Iranian *Aži Dahāka* displays this trait

52. On Vahagn, see H. Gelzer, "Zur armenischen Götterlehre," *Berichte der Königlich Sächsischen Gesellschaft der Wissenschaften zu Leipzig* 48 (1896):104–109; and Georges Dumézil, "Vahagn," *Revue de l'histoire des religions* 117 (1938):152–70.

53. Dumézil, "Vahagn," pp. 154–63; and *The Destiny of the Warrior*, pp. 123 ff. The text is *Mhb.* 5.9.2 ff.

54. Thus Lommel, *Arische Kriegsgott*, pp. 51–53; Zaehner, p. 103, and others have insisted that since Vahagn was a dragon slayer, the Iranian Vərəθraγna must have played this role also. In anticipation of this line of argument, Benveniste was led to make some ill-founded remarks, deriving Vahagn from Herakles in his deeds and from Vərəθraγna in name alone (*Vṛtra et Vṛθragna*, pp. 75 ff.).

55. There is still further identification of Herakles and *Trito in other sources. Thus, in relating Scythian legends, Herodotus 4.8–10, places Herakles in the role of Feridūn (⟨Θraētaona) in the story of the initiation of his three sons as preserved in the *Shāh-nāmeh*. See Ruben Levy, ed. and trans., *The Epic of the Kings: Shāh-nāmā* (Chicago, 1967), pp. 26–27.

56. For a similar transformation, note that the three-headed monster Geryon is turned into three brothers in Diodorus Siculus 4.17.2. Note also that the hero *Trito is turned into the last of the three Horatii brothers in Titus Livy, 1.25–26.

57. Pokorny, pp. 43–44, with modification of the initial vocalism.

58. On *dāsa-*, see below, p. 135f., and note 5.

THE INDO-IRANIAN WARRIOR CYCLE

in his name, the -ka being a diminutive or pejorative suffix,[59] while Viśvarūpa is described as a dāsá in RV 10.99.6 and 1.158.4–5.

Another element lacking in the Armenian version is one that I take to be crucial, namely, the booty won in the encounter. Moreover, the Indian and Iranian sources leave some ambiguity on this point, for while the Indian story of Trita's victory states that cattle were the plunder,[60] the Iranian version tells how two women previously taken from Yima by Aži Dahāka were recovered by Θraētaona.[61] Some scholars have been led by this data to see both "cattle" and "women" as symbolic terms that refer to natural phenomena, specifically the storm or the seasonal freeing of the waters.[62] The myth is thus interpreted as allegory, *Indra and *Trito being identified with the storm, the serpent with the clouds, and the cows or women with the rain.[63] While the myth may have taken on this allegorical coloration in some variants under the impact of later Indian speculative thought,[64] it is doubtful that this is the original meaning. Rather, the alternation between cows and women can be explained in another fashion.

In order to see this, it is instructive to look at the specific term, Avestan vantā-, used to describe the women won by Θraētaona. Bartholomae, following Darmesteter's line of investigation,[65] glossed this word as "die Geliebte, Frau."[66] But, when one analyzes the term, it is clear that it is

59. See Franklin Edgerton, "The K-suffixes of Indo-Iranian," Journal of the American Oriental Society 31 (1911):133–46. Despite the title, Edgerton takes up almost exclusively Indic materials, but a number of interesting parallels are listed, notably rājaká of RV 8.21.18, "contemptible little king," and kairātaka of AV 10.4.14, "of the Kirātas (contemptuous)." Note also the demon of the Bhagavata Purāṇa, Dhenuka, "contemptible little cow." In Iranian sources, note the string of pejorative adjectives nivayaka nipašnaka apaskaraka apaxraosaka, "fearsome, envious, derisive, abusive" of Yt. 5.95 and the proper name Humayaka (Yt. 5.113).

60. RV 10.48.2, 10.8.8. While other booty does appear in the stories of Indra's various combats, Trita never wins anything other than cattle. Note also the suggestion of Kasten Rönnow, "Viśvarūpa," Bulletin of the School of Oriental and African Studies 6 (1931): 478–80, that the name Viśvárūpa is best understood as "he who presides over the whole animal creation," seeing him as a master of herds.

61. See the analysis of Darmesteter, Zend Avesta, 1: xlvi ff.

62. Macdonell, pp. 467 and passim; Perry, p. 144; Roth, "Sage von Feridūn," pp. 223–24; Schroeder, Mysterium und Mimus, pp. 132 ff.; Widengren, Religionen Irans, pp. 41–42.

63. See Michel Bréal, "Hercule et Cacus," in Mélanges de Mythologie et de Linguistique (Paris, 1882), pp. 1–162; or Leopold von Schroeder, Herakles und Indra (Vienna, 1914), pp. 57–67.

64. In India this myth provided a topic for rich speculative embroidery and was even raised to the status of a cosmogonic account. We must note, however, that this is specifically an Indian development, and does not mount to the I-I period. On these Indian elaborations, see W. Norman Brown, "The Creation Myth of the Rig Veda," Journal of the American Oriental Society 62 (1942):85–98; and "Theories of Creation in the Rg Veda," Journal of the American Oriental Society 85 (1965):23–25; F. B. J. Kuiper, "Basic Concept of Vedic Religion," pp. 109–11.

65. Darmesteter, Zend Avesta, 1: xlvi–xlviii.

66. Bartholomae, Altiranisches Wörterbuch, p. 1355.

nothing more than a feminine form of the past passive participle from the verb $\sqrt{van}$-, "to wish for," "desire," as Bartholomae himself noted.[67] Thus, in reality it means no more than "the female who is desired." Such a term could surely apply equally well to bovines under certain circumstances as to humans.

A similar term is *dhainu (Skt. dhénu- = Av. daénu-), one of the most frequent Indo-Iranian terms for "cow."[68] Yet, as Benveniste has shown, the word means nothing more than "one who lactates, gives milk," being derived from the verb "to give milk," "nourish" (Skt. $\sqrt{dhay}$-).[69] As such, it may be used for the female of any mammal species, homo sapiens included,[70] and in an important verse from the Rg Veda the parallel term dhéna, which is usually rendered as "cows," is used to describe two women who have been captured by the dāsa enemies.[71]

The Iranian version of the myth has been well worked over, as is clear in our text. In general a historicizing tendency is obvious, for the struggle between *Trito and *Ngʷhi has been recast as a dynastic dispute, and the serpentine monster has become a human—albeit three-headed—usurper.[72] It seems highly probable that the ambiguity of such terms as vantā and daēnu allowed for a rationalizing transformation of a myth of a cattle raid to a myth of the recovery of abducted queens.

Such a formulation finds support in the Greco-Roman versions of the myth. These variants and their relation to the Indian Indra-Trita lore were among the first texts to be dealt with by the nineteenth century Indo-Europeanists of the comparative mythology school.[73] Often the texts were abused and nature allegory was hastily imposed on every detail.[74] This cavalier treatment, and Georges Dumézil's striking demonstration that a quite unexpected Roman source (Livy 1.25–26, the story of the Horatii and the Curiatii) contained a different reflex of the myth,[75] combined to relegate the correspondences that had been recognized earlier to the background. The validity of their comparison to Indian and Iranian

67. Ibid.

68. See the numerous citations in Hermann Grassmann, Wörterbuch zum Rigveda (Wiesbaden, 1872; repr. 1964), pp. 695–96; and Bartholomae, Altiranisches Wörterbuch, p. 203.

69. Benveniste, Vocabulaire, 1: 22.

70. Ibid.

71. RV 5.30.9. Widengren, Religionen Irans, pp. 46–47, has called attention to this verse, although for a different purpose.

72. Aži is seen as a Dacian, Turanian, or even an Arab in different eras but is consistently the enemy of native Iranian rule, while Θraētaona is seen as the national Iranian hero par excellence. Note that in the Shāh-nāmeh, two of Zohāk's heads are represented as serpents that sprang from his shoulders, Zohāk being the later Persian reflex of Avestan Aži Dahāka. See Levy, pp. 14–15.

73. See Bŕeal, which first appeared in 1850.

74. Schroeder, Herakles und Indra, pp. 57–67 is a good example of such over-interpretation.

75. Dumézil, Horace et les Curiaces (Paris, 1942), pp. 89–140.

materials, however, has never been soundly challenged.[76] They are important for our argument, for they have preserved unambiguously the fact that in the mythic encounter between a hero and a three-headed serpent, cattle were the prize sought and won.

> And Khrysaor begat the three-headed Geryon,
> Being married to Kallirhoe, the daughter of famed
>   Okeanos.
> Now the force of Herakles killed him
> Beside the shuffling cattle in sea-girt Erytheia
> On that very day when he drove the broad-faced cattle
> To holy Tirynths, having passed over the ford of
>   Okeanos,
> And having killed Orthos and the cow-herd Eurytion
> In the gloomy herdsman's house beyond famed Okeanos.[77]
>   [Hesiod, *Theogony*, lines 287–94]

> In that season when Amphitryon's son bore off
> The young oxen from your stalls, O Erythea,
> He came to the Palatine hill which is unconquered
>   by man
> And himself being weary, he set down his weary cattle
> Where Velabrum overflows its stream and where
> The seaman sails through urban waters.
> But they did not remain safe with Cacus, an unfaithful
> Host: that one defiled Jove with theft.
> Cacus was a native dweller [*incola*], a robber from a
>   dread cave,
> Who uttered sounds through three separate mouths.
> This one, in order that there would not be any
>   sure clues giving signs of the robbery,
> Dragged the cattle backward by the tail into his
>   cave—
> But not without witness by the god. The young
>   oxen betrayed the thief with their sounds,
> And wrath pulled down the rough doors of the thief.
> Cacus lay dead, struck three times by the
>   Maenalian bough,

---

76. This is accepted by even so cautious a scholar as Keith, *Religion and Philosophy*, pp. 127–28.

77. Χρυσάωρ δ'ἔτεκε τρικέφαλον Γηρυονῆα
μιχθεὶς Καλλιρόῃ κούρῃ κλυτοῦ 'Ωκεανοῖο·
τὸν μὲν ἄρ' ἐξενάριξε βίη 'Ηρακληείη
βουσὶ πάρ' εἰλιπόδεσσι περιρρύτῳ εἰν 'Ερυθείῃ,
ἤματι τῷ ὅτε περ βοῦς ἤλασεν εὐρυμετώπους
Τίρυνθ' εἰς ἱερήν, διαβὰς πόρον 'Ωκεανοῖο,
'Ορθόν τε κτείνας καὶ βουκόλον Εὐρυτίωνα
σταθμῷ ἐν ἠερόεντι πέρην κλυτοῦ 'Ωκεανοῖο.

And Alcides spoke thus: "Go you cattle,
Go you cattle of Hercules, the last labor of
    my club!
Twice sought by me, and twice my booty, you
    cattle—
Sanctify the fields and cattle-place with your
    long lowing.
The Forum of noble Rome will be your pasture."[78]

[Propertius, *Elegies*, 4.9.1–20]

Now these are not fully independent versions of the myth, for Propertius and the other Romans who told this story all seem to rely on the Greek sources in large measure.[79] Hesiod is thus our oldest text, and his account, while terse, does contain some valuable information. In order to appreciate this, however, it is crucial to note that contrary to the general opinion since antiquity[80] Hesiod did not take Herakles to be the slayer of Orthos and Eurytion; rather, this role was allotted to Geryon. The matter hinges on the question of who is the subject of line 291. Grammatically, the verb ἤλασεν has only an implied subject, which may refer back to Geryon (mentioned in the accusative in l. 287, and referred to by the pronoun τόν in l. 289) or Herakles (mentioned in adjectival form [βίη 'Ηρακληείη, "Herakleian force"] in l. 289. What is most persuasive, in my opinion, is the presence of the emphatic particle περ in l. 291, giving the sense of "on that very same day" to the phrase ἤματι τῷ ὅτε περ. If I am correct, the

78. Amphitryoniades qua tempestate iuvencos
    egerat a stabulis, o Erythea, tuis,
    venit ad invictos pecorosa Palatia montes,
    et statuit fessos fessus et ipse boves,
    qua Velabra suo stagnabant flumine quaque
    nauta per urbanas velificabat aquas.
    sed non infido manserunt hospite Caco
    incolumes: furto polluit ille Iovem.
    incola Cacus erat, metuendo raptor ab antro,
    per tria partitos qui dabat ora sonos.
    hic, ne certa forent manifestae signa rapinae,
    aversos cauda traxit in antra boves,
    nec sine teste deo: furem sonuere iuvenci,
    furis et implacidas diruit ira fores.
    Maenalio iacuit pulsus tria tempora ramo
    Cacus, et Alcides sic ait: "Ite boves,
    Herculis ite boves, nostrae labor ultime clavae,
    bis mihi quaesitae, bis mea praeda, boves,
    arvaque mugitu sancite Bovaria longo:
    nobile erit Romae pascua vestra Forum."
    79. See Jean Bayet, *Les origines de l'Hercule romain* (Paris, 1926), p. 233; and Grant, p. 41. But note that there is a considerable Roman substratum that cannot be traced to Greek influence. What we may have is a Roman story remodeled along Greek lines, but it is impossible to be certain.
    80. See, for instance, Apollodorus, *Bibliotheka* 2.5.10, who removes all ambiguity from the story and attributes all three slayings to Herakles. His influence is felt by most interpreters of the passage to the present day.

intent of this phrase is to correlate two separate actions that took place on one and the same day. That is to say, first Geryon killed Orthos and Eurytion, making off with their cattle, and *on that very same day* he was killed by Herakles, who took back the animals. Grammatically there is no reason to reject this reading. Moreover, it is more in keeping with the Indo-European background of the myth, for if this interpretation is accepted it will be seen that Herakles is the third opponent to face Geryon, and Geryon is the original cattle thief, having stolen the animals in an earlier encounter, just as Aži Dahāka stole the two women from Yima before Θraētaona recovered them. We see more of these themes of thirdness and prior theft in the Roman accounts, and there it is even possible to perceive that the original name of the hero in this exploit was not Herakles but most probably τρίτος, "Third."[81]

Of course Herakles is an extremely complicated figure in Greek mythology, and I do not claim to derive him and all his deeds from a Proto-Indo-European hero named *Trito. What I am suggesting is that the original hero of the Geryon-slaying episode bore the name "Third" and is derived from the Proto-Indo-European figure. Herakles is a separate figure, who for one reason or another became the most popular hero of the Greek world. The deeds of many other heroes were attributed to him and were organized into a very late and artificial cycle of twelve deeds.[82] *Trito is but one of his components.

The Roman Hercules-Cacus story, which is largely modeled on Herakles-Geryon, has preserved features that point to the original hero's name.[83] The sources that lead to this conclusion are the following:

1. Propertius, 4.9.15 (cited above); Cacus is specified as being smitten with the Maenalian club three times (*tria tempora*).

81. There are some scattered pieces of evidence from the Greek world which also lead to this conclusion, although none of them in itself is convincing. Thus, Herakles was commonly called "Herakles of the three nights" (τριέσπερος), because of the myth that Zeus lay with Alkmene for that length of time to conceive the hero (See Otto Gruppe, "Herakles," *Pauly Wissowa Realenzyklopädie, Supplement 3* [Stuttgart, 1918], pp. 1004 and 1016). In a lost comedy, three Herakleses seem to have engaged a triple Geryon in an eating contest (Stephanus Oswiecimski, "De tribus Herculibus mimicis," *Eos* 44 [1950]:119-22.) And in Lucian's *Dialogues of the Dead* 16.5, there is talk of both a triple (τρίπλουν) Herakles and a third (τρίτον!) Herakles. It is worth noting that all of these pieces of evidence come from comic sources, and it may be that the tradition of Herakles as "Third" was preserved in this type of literature because of the opportunity for punning and farce that it provided. Franz Rolf Schröder, "Indra, Thor und Herakles," *Zeitschrift für deutsche Philologie* 76 (1957):1-41, also argued in favor of seeing Herakles as "Third," although for different reasons than those advanced here.

82. Bernhard Schweitzer, *Herakles* (Tubingen, 1922), p. 146 and passim.

83. Herakles originally signified "Glory of Hera" (*Ἡρακλεϝής) and this gives us two important pieces of information: it is a purely Greek name and cannot be traced into Indo-European antiquity, and Herakles was originally a hero and not a god, as no god in the Greek pantheon has a name formed from the name of another deity. For two views of the origin of this name, see Paul Kretschmer, "Mythische Namen: Herakles," *Glotta* 8 (1916): 121-29; and Walter Potscher, "Der Name des Herakles," *Emerita* 39 (1971):169-84.

113

2. Ovid, *Fasti*, 1.575; The club with which Hercules kills Cacus is said to be three-noded (*trinodis*).

3. Vergil, *Aeneid*, 8.230 ff.; Having found Cacus's cave, Hercules runs around the mountain three times (*ter . . . lustrat*), batters the door three times (*ter . . . temptat*), and rests three times (*ter . . . resedit*) before breaking in.

In each of the three major versions of the Roman myth, the number three comes into play, and in each version it is in a different fashion. Ovid, Vergil, and Propertius are not quoting from each other but each seems intent on introducing this numerical detail into the story. And in each case the detail can be interpreted as expressing the fact that it was the third of some sort of series—blow, node, circumambulation, or rush at the door—that caused the monster's death. Each author, in his own way, preserves the fact that it was the "Third" who killed the three-headed beast.

Numerous other features from the Greco-Roman texts show resemblance to the versions we have already treated. The hero's enemy is a tricephal (τρικέφαλος; *tria partitos . . . ora*), and his serpentine nature can be discerned in Geryon's genealogy, for his paternal grandmother was Medusa, the serpent-haired Gorgon (*Theogony*, l. 280–81). Cacus, like Aži Dahāka and Viśvarūpa, is identified as a non-Indo-European aborigine (*incola*), hostile to Greek and Roman alike.[84] Moreover, we are told that Cacus first stole the cattle that rightfully belonged to Hercules; the latter's acts were only justified revenge, a situation corresponding to that of the Iranian and Greek versions, in which a non-Indo-European is the original aggressor.

A split is evident, however, between the Indo-Iranian versions of the myth and the Greco-Roman ones with regard to the roles of a warrior god and the libation ritual. To the Indo-Iranians, the help of *Indra *Vṛtraghna was indispensable in securing victory for *Trito, and the hero was careful to pour a *sauma libation before the battle, strengthening the god in order that he might in turn strengthen him. Yet in the Greco-Roman versions, the hero acts alone and needs no help from a divine figure.[85] This seems to be a common feature of European versions of the myth, for a Germanic version likewise seems to preserve no god.

This version is found in a relief on the golden horn of Gallehus, dating from the fifth century A.D. (see Figure 5). Here a three-headed man carrying an axe or a hammer in his right hand leads a horned animal (a goat?) with his left. At his side, three serpents lie dead.

84. Bayet, pp. 208–14. Note also the intriguing argument of H. J. Rose, "Chthonian Cattle," *Numen* 1 (1954):213–27, who sees in the Herakles-Geryon myth and related variants a myth told by the non-Indo-Europeans to account for the I-E's possession of cattle. In all likelihood this was a double-edged myth, told by both sides in the conflict to their own advantage.

85. As indicated by his name (see note 83, this chapter), Herakles cannot originally have been seen as a god or demigod.

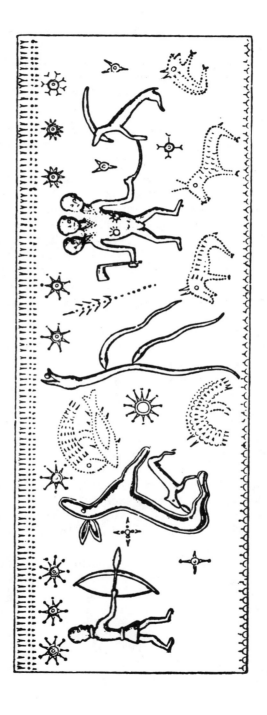

Figure 5. Stamped Relief from the Golden Horn of Gallehus (5th century A.D.)

THE INDO-IRANIAN WARRIOR CYCLE

As always, the interpretation of iconography presents many difficulties. The tricephal with the axe may be the hero *Trito (I lean toward this view), or he may be a doublet of the three serpents. But it is certain that this is an independent German reflex of our myth, containing the themes of triplicity, serpentine enemies, and the taking of livestock by force.

In another Germanic reflex of the myth, a god does appear: Þórr, the warrior god, who most closely approximates the Indo-Iranian *Indra. The story in question is that of his fishing expedition after the Miðgarð serpent. It appears in both the *Younger Edda* of Snorri Sturlason *(Gylfaginning* 48) and the *Elder Edda,* as follows:

> The Protector [Þórr] said he wished to row the waves,
> If the stubborn giant would give him bait.
>
> [Hymir:] "Go back to the herd, if you have such a mind—
> Breaker of giants [there] seek your bait!
> I expect you'll find
> Ox droppings are easy to get."
>
> The boy quickly turned to the woods,
> Where an all-black ox stood before him.
> The slayer of giants broke the high field
> Of the two horns [the head] off from the bull.
>
> [Hymir:] "Methinks thy work much worse,
> Keel-wielder, than when you're sitting still."
>
> The lord of goats (Þórr) bade the kindred of apes
> To sail the ship still further out,
> But the giant told him
> He little wished to row any longer.
>
> Most fiercy Hymir at once drew up
> Two whales on his hook,
> While back in the stern, Óðinn's kin,
> The Protector, with craft made ready his line.
>
> He baited his hook—the rock of men,
> The serpent slayer—with that ox's head.
> She (the Miðgarð serpent) gaped against the hook—she
>   who hates the gods,
> Who encircles all lands from below.
>
> Brave Þórr drew boldly
> Up on board the serpent, gleaming with venom.
> With his hammer he smote the gruesome head
> Of the wolf's kin.

The monster was dashed and the stony field whistled—
The whole ancient earth moved
When that fish sank down in the sea.[86]

[*Hymiskviða* 17-24]

Numerous resemblances to our reconstructed prototype may be recognized. The warrior god and a companion, after eating huge quantities of meat together (*Hymiskviða* 13-14), battle a serpent over the possession of cattle. Unlike the Indo-Iranian versions we have considered, however, it is the god who bears the brunt of the battle, and the companion has been transformed into a giant whom, in the broader context of the poem, Þórr is striving to outwit. Snorri's version provides a detail in which the Proto-Indo-European state of affairs is more perfectly, if less obviously, preserved. There it is told that Þórr visited Hymir "disguised as a youth" (*svá*

86. Véorr kvaz vilja   á vág róa,
     ef ballr jǫtunn   beitor gæfi.

     "Hverfðu til hjarðar,   ef þú hug trúir,
     brjótr berg-Dana,   beitor sœkja!
     18. Þess vænti ek,   at þér myni
     ǫgn af oxa   auðfeng vera."

     Sveinn sýsliga   sveif til skógar,
     þar er uxi stóð,   alsvartr, fyrir.
     19. Braut af þjóri   þurs ráðbani
     hátún ofan   horna tveggja.

     "Verk þikkja þín   verri myklo,
     kjóla valdi,   enn þú kyrr sitir."

     20. Bað hlunngota   hafra dróttinn
     áttrunn apa   útarr fœra;
     enn sá jǫtunn   sína talði
     litla fýsi   at róa lengra.

     21. Dró mœrr Hymir,   móðugr, hvali
     einn á ǫngli   up senn tvá;
     enn aptr í skut   Óðni sifjaðr,
     Véorr, við vélar   vað gorði sér.

     22. Egndi á ǫngul,   sá er ǫldom bergr,
     orms einbani,   uxa hǫfði;
     gein við ǫngli,   sú er goð fjá,
     umgjǫrð neðan   allra landa.

     23. Dró djarfliga   dáðrakkr þórr
     orm eitrfán   upp at borði;
     hamri kníði   háfjall skarar,
     ofljótt, ofan   úlfs hnitbróður.

     24. Hreingálkn hlumðo,   enn hǫlkn þuto,
     fór in forna   fold ǫll saman.
     Søkþiz síðan   sá fiskr í mar.

sem ungr drengr), a fact hinted at in the description of the god as a "boy" (*sveinn*) in the poem cited above. He thus appears simultaneously as a god and a mortal, having fused these originally separate roles. It is thus in the form of the hero that he confronts the serpent, while secretly imbued with the god's strength.

Other aspects of this story are also clearly derived from the Proto-Indo-European myth. Cattle are at the center of the encounter, for it is the ox's head over which god and serpent fight. This strikingly original adaptation of a pastoral people's cattle to a nautical people's bait also preserves the themes of the serpent's initial victory, for it is only after the monster has seized the bait that Þórr attempts to recover it and to slay him in the process. (Neither Snorri nor the *Hymiskviða*, however, tells whether the bait was retrieved, this detail of the myth being of no interest to them.)

The serpentine nature of the enemy is established by the second element of its name, *Miðgarðs-ormr*, which is cognate to OHG *worm*, Goth. *waurms*, OE *wyrm*, all of which mean "serpent" or "dragon" as well as "worm," being derived from P-I-E **wr̥mi-*, from the verb **√wer-*, "to twist," "turn."[87] The first element of that name, a genitive of *Miðgarðr*, implies its role as outsider, "of [surrounding] the world of men (Miðgarð)," the serpent being regularly portrayed as living in the waters that encircle this world, as in *Gylfaginning* 34 and 47 or *Hymiskviða* 22. In order to reach this beast, Þórr and Hymir have to row far beyond normal fishing waters, and Snorri relates how Hymir twice tried to stop Þórr from venturing out so far (*Gylfaginning* 48); we should also note that Hymir dwells at the ends of the earth according to Hymiskviða 5. All that is missing is the multicephalic nature of the serpent, which is strikingly presented in a pictorial version of the myth, a rune stone from Altuna in Sweden (Figure 6), the lower part of which shows Þórr fishing with an ox-head for bait, having hooked a four-headed (!) serpent, which he is pulling into his ship. As in *Gylfaginning* 48, Þórr's exertion is so great that he has driven his feet through the bottom of the ship, and in his right hand he holds the hammer, ready to administer the coup de grace.

Yet another reflex of the myth affords confirmation of all the points I have already made and also permits reconstruction of the name of the Proto-Indo-European god who assisted *Trito. This is a Hittite version, a text said to be the speech of the priest of the storm god of Nerik at the Purulli festival:

> When the storm god and the serpent Illuyanka came
> to blows in the city of Kiškilušša, the serpent Illuyanka
> defeated the storm god, and the storm god called out to
> all the gods; "Come to my aid."
> Inara prepared a festival. She arranged all grandly: a

---

87. De Vries, *Altnordisches etymologisches Wörterbuch,* p. 420; Pokorny, p. 1152.

Figure 6. Rune stone from Altuna, Uppland, Sweden (probably dating to the late pagan period)

vat of wine, a vat of *marnuwan*, a vat of *walhi*. She filled the vats full to overflowing.

Now Inara went to the city Zigaratta and she encountered a man, Hupašiya. Inara said, "Look, Hupašiya, I say such and such—you must hold yourself apart for me." Then Hupašiya said to Inara, "Hail! I will sleep with you. I will come to you. I will do as you desire." And he slept with her.

Inara led Hupašiya away and hid him. Inara adorned herself, and she beckoned the serpent Illuyanka out of its cave. "Look, I am celebrating a festival. Come for the food and drink."

The serpent Illuyanka came up with its children, and they ate and drank. They drank all the vats and became drunk. Then they could no longer go down into the cave.

Hupašiya came and bound the serpent Illuyanka with a rope. The storm god came and killed the serpent Illuyanka there, and the gods were beside him. (*KBo* III 7, recto, lines 9 ff. and *KUB* XVII 5, lines 4 ff.)[88]

88. Text from Emmanuel Laroche, *Textes mythologiques hittites en transcription* (Paris: C. Klincksieck, 1965) 1:6–7:

KBo III 7, Recto, 1. 9. ma-a-an ᵈIM-aš ᵐᵘʸil-lu-ya-an-ka-aš-ša
I-NA ᵘʳᵘKi-iš-ki-lu-uš-ša ar-ga-ti-[i]-e-er
nu-za ᵐᵘʸil-lu-ya-an-ka-aš ᵈIM-an tar-ah-ta
ᵈIM-aš-ta-aš-ša Dᵐᵉʸ-na-aš hu-u-ma-a[n-du]-uš
mu-ú-ga-it an-da-ma 'PA'-ti-i-ya-[x-x-]x-te-en
nu-za ᵈI-na-ra-aš EZEN-an   i-e-et
nu hu-u-ma-an me-ek-ki ha-an-da-it
GEŠTIN-aš DUG pal-hi mar-nu-wa-an-da-aš DUG pal-hi
[wa-]al-hi-ya-aš DUG pal-hi [nu DU]G pal-ha-aš
an-[da]-an i-ya-a-da   i-[e-et]
nu ᵈ[I-na-ra-aš I-NA ᵘʳᵘZ]i?-ig-ga-ra-at-ta pa-it
nu ᵐHu-u-pa-ši-ya-an LÚ.ULÙ.LU ú-e-mi-it
UM-MA ᵈI-na-ar ᵐHu-u-pa-ši-ya ka-a-ša-wa
ki-i-ya ki-i-ya ut-tar i-ya-mi
nu-wa-mu-uš-ša-an zi-iq-qa har-ap-hu-ut
UM-MA ᵐHu-pa-ši-ya A-NA ᵈI-na-ar
ma-a-wa kat-ti-ti še-eš-m[i n]u-wa ú-wa-mi
kar-di-aš-ta-aš i-ya-mi [n]a?-[aš] ka[t-t]i-ši še-eš-ta
nu ᵈI-na-ra-aš ᵐHu-u-p[a-ši-ya-an p]é-e-hu-te-et
KUB XVII 5, l. 4. na-an mu-ú-un-na-it ᵈI-na-ra-aš-ša-az
ú-nu-ut-ta-at na-aš-ta ᵐᵘʸil-lu-ya-an-ka-[an]
ha-an-te-eš-na-az ša-ra-a kal-li-iš-ta
ka-a-ša-wa EZEN-an i-ya-mi
nu-wa a-da-an-na a-ku-wa-an-na e-hu
na-aš-ta ᵐᵘʸil-lu-ya-an-ka-aš QA-DU [DUMUᵐᵉʸ-ŠU]
ša-ra-a ú-e-er nu-za e-te-er e-ku-e[r]
na-aš-ta DUG pal-ha-an hu-u-ma-an-da-an e-k[u-er]
ne-za ni-in-ke-e-er
ne nam-ma ha-at-te-eš-na-aš kat-ta-an-t[a]
nu-u-ma-a-an pa-a-an-zi ᵐHu-u-pa-ši-ya-aš-ša ú-it
nu ᵐᵘʸil-lu-ya-an-ka-an iš-hi-ma-an-ta
ka-le-e-le-e-et
ᵈIM-aš ú-it nu-kán ᵐᵘʸil-lu-y[a-an-ka-an]
ku-en-ta Dᵐᵉʸ-ša kat-ti-iš-ši e-še-er

This text has been the topic of frequent debate, some claiming that it represents a Hittite reflex of the Proto-Indo-European raiding myth, and others contesting those claims.[89] Certainly, many features are suggestive of the Proto-Indo-European myth: the cooperation of a deity and a mortal; the conflict with a serpentine enemy (Illuyanka's name is prefaced with the determinative sign *muš*, meaning "serpent"); the use of intoxicants to overcome this enemy (although here they figure as a means of decreasing the monster's ability to resist rather than a means of increasing the hero's strength); and the alternation of victories, the serpent having first defeated the storm god before being overcome by Inara, Hupašiya, and the storm god, who is ultimately the third to face Illuyanka and as Third (< *Trito) actually kills her. Even the triplicity of the serpent has been preserved, as in the Germanic versions, in iconographic form. Thus, a relief from Malatya (Figure 7) shows a hero and a god confronting a monstrous serpent, the head of which is not visible because of damage to the stone, but the body of which is defined by three massive identical coils.

Opposition to the relation of this myth to the other Indo-European materials considered here has largely centered on the figure of Inara and her dealings with Hupašiya. For while her name is phonologically identical to *Índra* (< P-I-E *Ə̃ner-), if it is truly identical it ought to mean "the manly," a name hardly fitting for a goddess, particularly one as highly sexed as Inara appears to be in this text. This point seems to have given the Hittites themselves some pause, for in certain prayers they make reference to two forms of the deity Inara (there abbreviated by the sumerogram ᵈ*KAL*, "the manly god"): "Inara the effeminate (ᵈ*KAL lu-li-mi-(e)š*)" and "Inara the manly (ᵈ*KAL in-na-ra-u-wa-an-za*)."[90]

It is thus obvious that some sort of transformation has taken place whereby a Proto-Indo-European god has become a Hittite goddess, although some traces of his original gender remain. The question arises:

89. In the past the Indo-European origin of the myth has been championed by Paul Kretschmer, "Weiteres zur Urgeschichte der Inder," pp. 78–79; and "Indra und der hethitische Gott Inaraš," *Kleinasiatische Forschungen* 1 (1927):297–303; accepted by Giuseppe Furlani, *La Religione degli Hittiti* (Bologna, 1936), p. 42; Friedrich Hrozny, "Hethiter und Inder," *Zeitschrift für Assyriologie* 38 (1928):184–85; Jean Pryzluski, "Inara et Indra," *Revue Hittite et Asianique* 5 (1940):142–46; and Walter Porzig, "Illujankas und Typhon," *Kleinasiatische Forschungen* 3 (1930):379–86. In general, their arguments seem more convincing than the objections raised by Ferdinand Sommer, *Die Ahhijavā Urkunden* (Munich, 1932), pp. 22–24, 382; and *Ahhijavāfrage und Sprachwissenschaft* (Munich, 1934), p. 49 n.; Albrecht Götze, *Kulturgeschichte des alten Orient, II, 1.3 Kleinasien* (Munich, 1933), p. 131 n.; Johannes Friedrich, "Das erste Auftreten der Indogermanen," in *Germanen und Indogermanen: Festschrift für Herman Hirt* (Heidelberg, 1936), p. 223 n.; Emmanuel LaRoche, *Recherches sur les noms des dieux hittites* (Paris, 1947), pp. 82–83; and *Recueil d'onomastique hittite* (Paris, 1951), p. 95, although Kretschmer's interpretation of *Illuyanka* as "serpent (*anka-*) of the swamp (*illui,* singular locative)" probably ought to be abandoned.

90. Edgar Howard Sturtevant, "A Hittite Tablet in the Yale Babylonian Collection," *Transactions of the American Philological Society* 58 (1927):5–31.

Figure 7. Relief from Malatya, Anatolia (13th or 14th century B.C.)

what could have motivated such a transformation? In my opinion, the most likely explanation is the association of this myth with the Purulli festival, which in the opinion of most Hittitologists was a New Year's Festival.[91] Such ceremonies in the ancient Near East regularly involve a *hieros gamos,* a sacred marriage of king and goddess, whereby the king receives life and strength for himself and his realm through sexual union with the deity.[92] It is thus no longer a god who is thought to confer strength upon the hero, but a goddess, and Inara changes sex accordingly.

On the basis of all the evidence I have presented, we can reconstruct a myth in which an Indo-European hero by the name of *Trito, "Third," suffered at the hands of a monstrous figure, a three-headed serpent explicitly identified with the aboriginals of the area in which the myth was told. In the first encounter, this serpent stole some cattle belonging to the hero or to someone closely related to him. In a second meeting when the hero was aided by the warrior god *Ꜣner-, "the manly," and fortified by an intoxicating drink, *Trito defeated the monster and recovered the cattle. The elements that have led to this reconstruction are laid out in Tables 3 and 4.

The Warrior Band

In order to understand this myth, it is necessary to put it in its social and ritual setting. As the myth of *Manu and *Yemo relates to sacrifice, the function of the priest, and the nature of the king, so this myth of *Trito tells of a cattle raid, the proper activity of the warrior. We must therefore examine carefully the religious aspects of the Indo-Iranian warrior life. Warriors were marked off as a separate class, and possessed their own initiations, rituals, skills, pursuits, and ideology—indeed, an entire *Weltanschauung* all their own.

The seminal work on this topic is, of course, Stig Wikander's *Der arische Männerbund,*[93] in which he demonstrated the existence of highly specialized warrior bands dating back at least to the Indo-Iranian period.

91. See H. Otten, "Ein Text zum Neujahrsfest aus Bogazköy," *Orientalistische Literaturzeitung* 51 (1956):101–5; Volkert Hass, *Der Kult von Nerik* (Rome, 1970), pp. 43–44 and 48–49.

92. On the sacred marriage in the ancient Near East, see Helmer Ringgren, *Religions of the Ancient Near East* (Philadelphia, 1973), pp. 4, 30, 151; and Samuel Noah Kramer, *The Sacred Marriage Rite* (Bloomington, Ind., 1969), pp. 49–66, *inter alia.*

93. Cited above, note 1, chapter 1. Similar groups have been noted among the other branches of the Indo-European family. On the Germans, see Lily Weiser, *Altgermanische Junglingsweihen und Männerbunde* (Baden, 1927); and Otto Höfler, *Kultische Geheimbünde der Germanen* (Frankfurt, 1934). On the Greeks, H. Jeanmaire, *Couroi et Courètes* (Lille, 1939); and M. P. Nilsson, *Opuscula Selecta* (Lund, 1952), 3:827–49. On the Romans, Gerhard Binder, *Die Aussetzung des Königskindes Kyros und Romulus* (Meisenheim, 1964). Other important works on the Indo-Iranians are A. Alföldi, "Königsweihe und Männerbund bei dem Achämeniden," *Archives suisses des traditions populaires* 47 (1951):11–17; and Karl Jettmar, "Traditionen der Steppenkulturen bei indo-iranischen Bergvölkern," *Jahrbuch des Südasien-Instituts der Universität Heidelberg* (1966):18–23, esp. p. 20.

Table 3 The Indo-European Myth of the First Cattle Raid: Correspondences

P-I-E	RV 10.8	Yt. 15	Moses	Hesiod	Livy	Gallehus	Hymiskviða	KBo III 7
Hero *Trito	Trita	Θraētaona	Vahagn	Herakles	Hercules	Man with axe	Hymir	Hupašiya
Deity *Ǝner-	Indra	Vayu, et al.	(Vahagn)	Omitted	Omitted	Omitted	Þórr	Inara
Enemy	Viśvarūpa	Aži Dahāka	Dragon	Geryon	Cacus	Three serpents	Midgard serpent	Illuyanka
Three heads	tri-śīrṣaṇam	θri-kamarəδəm	Omitted	τρι-κέφαλος	tria partitos . . . ora	Three serpents	Four heads in iconography only	Three coils in iconography
Serpent *Ngʷhi	Ahi	Aži	Omitted	Medusa's grandson	Omitted	Serpents	Miðgarðs-ormr	muš
Aborigine	Dāsa	Dahāka	Omitted	Omitted	Incola	Omitted	Placed at ends of earth	Omitted
First encounter	Omitted	Stole women and realm from Yima	Omitted	Stole cattle from Orthos and Eurytion	Stole cattle from Hercules	Omitted	Serpent grabs ox head bait	Defeat of storm god
Ritual	Soma	Haoma	Omitted	Omitted	Omitted	Omitted	Eat meat	Wine, Walhi, Marnuwan
Booty	Cattle	Women and realm	Omitted	Cattle	Cattle	Horned animal	Ox head	Omitted

Table 4 The Indo-European Myth of the First Cattle Raid: Transformations

	RV 10.8	Yt. 15	Moses	Hesiod	Livy	Gallehus	Hymiskviða	KBo III 7
Hero	Clear	Historicized, shifts generation	Fused with deity	Absorbed by dominant Greek hero	Borrowed from Greek	Becomes tricephal	Changed to giant	Clear
God	Clear	Others substituted when dropped from pantheon	Fused with hero	Omitted	Omitted	Omitted	Clear; disguised as mortal	Becomes goddess
Enemy	Clear	Historicized	Loses specificity	Serpent nature shifts generation	Serpent nature lost	Becomes three serpents	Clear	Clear
First encounter	Omitted	Historicized	Omitted	Clear	Clear	Omitted	Becomes taking of bait	Clear
Ritual	Clear	Clear	Omitted	Omitted	Omitted	Omitted	Becomes hospitality	Becomes means to intoxicate enemy
Booty	Clear	Historicized, rationalized	Omitted	Clear	Clear	Species shifts	Becomes fishbait	Omitted

THE INDO-IRANIAN WARRIOR CYCLE

Certain aspects of these bands remain unclear to us—for instance, whether they were organized as age-sets, secret societies, or along wholly different lines[94]—yet the fact of their existence is indisputable.

Several different names have been adduced for these bands, and two of them are particularly important. The first is *Marya (Skt. *márya-* = Av. *mairya-*; see *R V* 5.59.5, 8.43.25 / *Y.* 9.21; *Yt.* 10.2), "young men."[95] The title is not as simple as it seems, however, for it calls into play a cluster of concepts associated with youth, and for the Indo-Europeans youth carried connotations of being "filled with life force."[96] The young were regarded as the ablest and fittest of men, filled with energy and power, and it was this unbounded vigor that suited them so well for battle.

Second, the troops of warriors were known as *Vṛka, "wolves" (Skt. *vṛka-* = Av. *vəhrka-* < P-I-E *$wḷk^wo$-, as do Lith. *vìlkas*, OCS *vlьkъ*, Toch. B. *walkwe*, Goth. *wulfs*; Gk. λύκος, and Lat. *lupus* < *luk^wo-, a simple variant of the same word).[97] This is seen in such passages as the following:

And if a hostile mortal, a wolf eager for booty, should
   cause us harm, we who are blameless,
Turn him away from our path, O Bṛhaspati! Create a
   good path for us for this, our feast for the gods.[98]
                                                              [*RV* 2.23.7]

May I subdue the enmity of all enemies, of the Daēvas
and of men, of sorcerers and of witches, of rulers, Kavis
and Karapans, of the young warriors [Mairya-] who have
two paws and of heretics, of wolves who have two paws
and who have four paws, of the insidious, flying horde
that advances along a broad front. (*Y.* 9.18)[99]

---

94. Wikander himself wavers on this point, *Arische Männerbund*, pp. 72 and 75, although he seems to lean toward seeing them as secret societies or cultic organizations most of the time. The insistence of such texts as *RV* 5.59.6, 5.60.5 on the fact that the Maruts are all the same age would point to age-set organization.

95. On this term, see Wikander, *Arische Männerbund*, pp. 9–42. His view has been accepted by Mayrhofer, *Etymologisches Wörterbuch*, 2: 569–70. One should also note that the word *maryannu* is found throughout the ancient Near East to signify a group of "chariot warriors" or ruling nobles of I-I origin. The wide diffusion of this I-I term in the period 1700–1550 B.C. attests the great daring, success, and influence of these warrior bands. See R. T. O'Callaghan, "New Light on the Maryannu as 'Chariot-Warriors,' " *Jahrbuch für Kleinasiatische Forschung* 1 (1951):309–24.

96. E. Benveniste, "Expression indo-européenne de l'éternité," *Bulletin de la société de linguistique de Paris* 38 (1937):103–12; Georges Dumézil, "Jeunesse, éternité, aube," *Annales d'histoire économique et sociale* 10 (1938):289–301.

97. Mayrhofer, *Etymologisches Wörterbuch*, 3: 240–41; Pokorny, pp. 1178–79.

98. utá vā yó no marcáyād ánāgaso 'rātīvā mártaḥ sānukó vṛkaḥ /
bṛhaspate ápa tám vartayā pathắḥ sugám no asyaí devávītaye kṛdhi //

99. nī tat yaθa taurvayeni vīspanąm tbaēšavataṃ tbaēšǎ daēvanąm mašyānąmca yaθwąm pairikanąmca sāθrąm kaoyąm karafnąmca mairyanąmca bizangranąm ašəmaoyanąmca bizangranąm vəhrkanąmca caθwarə.zangranąm haēnayằsca pərəθu.ainikayằ davaąiθyằ pataĕθyằ.

In both instances it is clear that it is not a literal wolf that is under discussion but a human. In *RV* 2.23.7, *vŕka-* is set in apposition to *márta-*,
"a mortal," "a man," while in *Y.* 9.18, one variety of wolf is specified as
bizangra-, "two-footed," "biped," or "having two paws."[100] Often the
term carries a pejorative connotation and must have been used thus by the
opponents of the *Männerbunde*,[101] but such was not its original usage, as
is attested by the proper name Dasyave Vṛka, "wolf to the barbarian
[*dásyu-*]" in *RV* 8.51.2, 8.56.1-2. The ideology of man as wolf, the fiercest
and most cunning of predators, is well attested in Baltic, Slavic,
Germanic, Greek, Roman, and Anatolian sources, and thus must ascend
to the Proto-Indo-European period.[102] At that time, and for millennia
thereafter, the ability to magically or ritually transform oneself into a
ravening predator, possibly by the donning of a wolf's skin or a wolf's-
head helmet, was valued as the highest accomplishment of the warrior's
art, at once terrifying and glorious, as is seen in Homer's chilling description of the Myrmidons arming for battle:

100. The syntax here is somewhat difficult. I can see no sense in punctuating
mairyanąmca bizangranąm, ašəmaoγanąmca bizangranąm, vəhrkanąmca caθwarə.zan-
granąm, for that would only be to state the obvious: men have two feet and wolves have four,
a fact which would not be worthy of mention. Rather, I prefer to punctuate mairyanąmca
bizangranąm, ašəmaoγanąmca, bizangranąm vəhrkanąmca caθwarə.zangranąm. The wolf
is thus subcategorized in its two varieties, animal and human, while the first use of
bizangranąm as a modifier of *mairya* serves to identify the *mairya* with the *bizangranąm*
vəhrka.
101. This is particularly true in Iran, where Zarathustra vigorously opposed the
warriors, as we shall see in the following chapter. The pejorative associations attached to the
Männerbunde after Zarathustra color all the texts that have come down to us but were not
necessarily present before the prophet's reform.
102. On the Indo-Iranian usage, see Wikander, *Arische Männerbunde*, pp. 64-65;
Geo Widengren, "Stand und Aufgaben der iranischen Religionsgeschichte," *Numen* 1
(1954):65. For the "wolves" among the Germans, Höfler, *Kultische Geheimbünde*, pp.
55-65, 170-71 (who also touches on Balto-Slavic evidence; best to ignore the thoroughly con-
fused Richard R. Ridley, "Wolf and Werwolf in Baltic and Slavic Tradition," *Journal of
Indo-European Studies* 4 [1976]:321-31); Wilhelm Grimm, "Die mythische Bedeutung des
Wolfes," *Zeitschrift für deutsches Altertumswissenschaft* 12 (1865):203-28; Mary R.
Gerstein, "Germanic *Warg*: The Outlaw as Werwolf," in G. J. Larson, ed., *Myth in Indo-
European Antiquity* (Berkeley, Calif., 1974), pp. 131-56. Among the Greeks, Louis Gernet,
"Dolon le loup," in *Mélanges Franz Cumont*, pp. 189-208; Wilhelm Kroll, "Etwas vom
Werwolf," *Wiener Studien* 55 (1937):168-72; Bruce Lincoln, "Homeric λύσσα, 'Wolfish
Rage,' " *Indogermanische Forschungen* 80 (1975):98-105. On the Romans: Binder, pp. 46
ff., 78-95; Joachim Gruber, "Zur Etymologie von Lat. *lupercus*," *Glotta* 39 (1961):273-76.
On the Thraco-Phrygians: Mircea Eliade, *Zalmoxis: The Vanishing God* (Chicago, 1972),
pp. 1-20. On the Anatolians: Paul Kretschmer, "Der Name der Lykier und andere
kleinasiatische Völkernamen," *Kleinasiatische Forschungen* 3 (1930):14-17; Arthur
Ungnad, "Luwisch = Lykisch," *Zeitschrift für Assyriologie* 35 (1924):1-8; V. V. Ivanov,
"L'organisation sociale des tribus indo-européens d'aprés les données linguistiques," *Cahiers
d'histoire mondiale* 5 (1960):794. More general studies that contain much valuable data
(although often open to question on theoretical grounds) have been attempted by Robert
Eisler, *Man into Wolf* (London, n.d.), see esp. pp. 132-37 and 140-45; Richard von Kienle,
"Tier Völkernamen bei indogermanischen Stämmen," *Wörter und Sachen* 14 (1932):32-39;
and Jean Pryzluski, "Les confréries de loups-garous dans les sociétés indo-européennes,"
Revue de l'histoire des religions 121 (1940):128-45.

And Akhilles, ranging through all the huts arrayed
The Myrmidons with armor. And they were like wolves,
Devourers of raw flesh, unspeakable determination in
their breasts,
Who having slaughtered a great horned deer in the hills,
Rend it, and all their cheeks are red with blood
And in a herd they go to a spring whose water runs dark
To lap the black water with their slender tongues
At the surface, belching the bloody gore, the spirit
In their breasts unquaking, and their bellies glutted.[103]
[*Iliad* 16.155-63]

The assimilation of oneself to the state of a wild beast is not simply a masquerade or a colorful metaphor. The man who thinks himself a wolf is transformed by this belief and becomes formidable in battle as a result. Indo-European warriors cultivated this state of furor or rage to a high art.[104] The Indo-Iranians knew it by many technical terms,[105] the most important of which was *aisma* (Skt. *iṣmín-*, "possessing **iṣma-*"; Av. *aēšma-*), a word derived from the P-I-E verb $*\sqrt{eis}$- "to storm," "move rapidly," "assault,"[106] and cognate with two other Indo-European terms for this state of furor, Greek οἶ(σ)μα and Latin *ira*.[107] In Sanskrit, *iṣmín-* is used only of the Maruts, the divine models of the storming warrior,[108] yet these broader Indo-European correspondences show us that it was a term more general in its usage, originally applied to human warriors for the most part, while the Indian usage is a case of semantic narrowing.

103. Μυρμιδόνας δ'ἄρ' ἐποιχόμενος θώρηξεν Ἀχιλλεὺς
πάντας ἀνὰ κλισίας σὺν τεύχεσιν· οἱ δὲ λύκοι ὣς
ὠμοφάγοι, τοῖσίν τε περὶ φρεσὶν ἄσπετος ἀλκή,
οἵ τ' ἔλαφον κεραὸν μέγαν οὔρεσι δῃώσαντες
δάπτουσιν· πᾶσιν δὲ παρήϊον αἵματι φοινόν.
καί τ' ἀγεληδὸν ἴασιν ἀπὸ κρήνης μελανύδρου
λάψοντες γλώσσῃσιν ἀραιῇσιν μέλαν ὕδωρ
ἄκρον, ἐρευγόμενοι φόνον αἵματος· ἐν δέ τε θυμὸς
στήθεσιν ἄτρομός ἐστι, περιστένεται δέ τε γαστήρ.
104. See Dumézil, *Horace et les Curiaces*, pp. 11-26. Note, however, that he is incorrect in regarding μένος as the Greek equivalent term, for this indicates a more general type of energy. The proper term for the rage of the warrior in Greek is λύσσα (< Gk. λύκος, "wolf"), on which see my "Homeric λύσσα: 'Wolfish Rage,' " pp. 98-105.
105. Thus, e.g., *kratu-*, according to Kasten Rönnow, "Ved. *kratu-*," *Monde Oriental* 26 (1932):1-90; and *manyu-*, according to Gonda, *Religionen Indiens*, 1: 33-34. Neither of these terms carry a warrior meaning in Avestan, and two explanations are possible. Either they were elevated to a spiritual level by Zarathustra in Iran, or in India they took over the function of the older **aišma* as it narrowed its usage.
106. Pokorny, pp. 299-300.
107. First suggested by Adalbert Bezzenberger, "Homerische Etymologien," *Beiträge zur Kunde der indogermanische Sprachen* 4 (1878):334; and accepted by Pokorny, pp. 299-300; Frisk, 2: 362; and A. Walde and J. B. Hofmann, *Lateinisches etymologisches Wörterbuch* (Heidelberg, 1938), pp. 717-18. On the ideology of **aišma*, see Wikander, *Arische Männerbund*, pp. 57-60; and Lommel, *Religion Zarathustras*, pp. 78-79.
108. Grassmann, p. 229.

To the earlier Indo-Iranians, *aišma was the turbulent, power-filled, over-whelming force that comes over a great warrior in battle, similar to that of the Old Norse *berserkr,* literally one "who wears the bear's shirt."[109]

Such abilities were not easily gained, and it is clear that the prospective warrior must have spent some years in training to develop these skills. Moreover, one did not assume the status of a warrior without some form of initiation; it is a status charged with magico-religious power and must be entered accordingly.[110] In some instances initiation took the form of a mock combat, in which the novice had to face a dummy constructed to resemble a fearsome three-headed monster. We find this in the story of Feridūn's (< Av. Θraētaona) testing of his three sons, and although it is not directly attested in India, the presence of this initiatory scenario among other Indo-European peoples assures us of its existence in the Indo-European period.[111] This trial clearly derives from the *Trito myth, as Dumézil rightly observed,[112] and here we discover part of that myth's significance. It serves as an aetiology and a model for the initiation of the young warrior, who himself becomes *Trito in the combat at the beginning of time. The three-headed adversary represents the *Dāsa enemies he will face and whom his ancestors have faced before him. In his encounter with the dummy, he learns that while frightening in appearance, his adversary truly is powerless.

Upon completing his initiation, the young warrior is given the characteristic emblems that marked the warrior band: a mace, *vagra (Skt. vájra- = Av. vazra-), the favorite weapon of the warrior god, [113] and a belt or girdle, which signified his loyalty to the band.[114] Other emblems belonged to the troop at large, and the most important of them was a banner or battle standard, *drapsa (Skt. drapsá- = Av. drafša-), carried into the fray.[115] These emblems marked the band off as a special group, consecrated by initiation and bound to the warrior god and to their comrades.

109. The bear was also popular in warrior magic, especially among the Germans, but the wolf seems to have been far more important for the Indo-Iranians and the Indo-Europeans in general. Note particularly the fact that wolves prey upon domestic livestock, while bears do not.

110. Georges Dumézil, *Mythes et dieux des Germains* (Paris, 1939), pp. 92–106. On warrior initiation in a broader context, see Eliade, *Rites and Symbols of Initiation,* pp. 81–87.

111. See Levy, *Epic of the Kings,* pp. 26–27. The initiatory combat with a tripart dummy is also attested among the Germans in the account of the "combat" between Þórr's servant Þjalfi and the stone image of the giant Hrungnir found in *Skaldskaparmal* 59.

112. Dumézil, *Mythes et dieux des Germains,* pp. 92–106.

113. In India, the *vajra* almost always belongs to Indra, while in Iran it has fallen to either Miθra (*Yt.* 10.132 and 6.5) or his close assistant Sraoša (*Vd.* 18.30 and 36).

114. On the presentation of the belt or girdle as a crucial part of initiation, see J. Duchesne-Guillemin, "L'initiation Mazdéenne," in *Initiation* (Leiden, 1965), p. 13; Mrs. Sinclair Stevenson, *The Rites of the Twice-Born* (London, 1920), p. 27. For interpretation, see Geo Widengren, "Le symbolisme de la ceinture," *Iranica Antiqua* 8 (1968):133–55.

115. See Wikander, *Arische Männerbund,* pp. 60, 63–64; A. Sadashiv Dange, " 'Ketu' or the War Banner in the Rg Veda," *Journal of Indian History* 42 (1964):377–79; and "Aspects of War from the Rg Veda," *Journal of Indian History* 44 (1966):127–28, 131–32.

In a certain sense initiation was also a ritual death and rebirth[116] and served to introduce the novice to his celestial counterparts, the warriors of the dead. The original name of these heavenly troops cannot be recovered, as the Indian and Iranian terminologies differ, but the structural resemblance of the Maruts and the Fravašis is clear nonetheless.[117] The Maruts are probably closer to the Indo-Iranian conception, as the Fravašis have undergone some transformations along theological lines,[118] but in both cases we have spirits of the dead[119] who are decidedly martial in nature,[120] brightly clad in armor (*RV* 2.34.2, 5.54.11 / *Yt.* 13.35), carrying aggressive weapons (*RV* 1.88.2-3, 5.54.11 / *Yt.* 13.37, 13.45), organized in a troop or regiment (*RV* 5.55.2, 6.66.11 / *Yt.* 13.37), and granting victory in battle (*RV* 7.56.19 / *Yt.* 13.24 and 34). Their resemblance to the earthly *Männerbunde* is striking, and the Indian Maruts are even called *márya-* (*RV* 5.59.3 and 5, 5.61.4, 7.56.1 and 14). Both groups display the emblems of the warriors, the club (*RV* 8.7.22 and 23), the belt (*RV* 5.54.12 / *Yt.* 13.29), and the banner (*Yt.* 13.27).

It must be noted, however, that these groups are not composed of all the spirits of the dead but only the warriors among those spirits. They are thus a subset within the broader group of the dead and are characterized in India as the *márya-* of heaven (*RV* 3.34.13, 5.59.6) or the *márya-* of Rudra (*RV* 1.64.2, 7.56.1).[121] The Rudrās in India are this broader group of all the dead.[122] There is a solidarity between the earthly and the heavenly warriors, and together their strength secures the well-being of the total

116. See Eliade, *Rites and Symbols of Initiation,* passim.
117. Dumézil, "Visnu et les Marut," pp. 18-24.
118. See the discussion of Lommel, *Religion Zarathustras,* pp. 151-63, for these Iran-specific developments.
119. For the Fravašis, this is clear and universally accepted. The Maruts, however, pose a more difficult case, although the view of them as spirits of the dead has been advanced by various scholars, among them R. N. Dandekar, "Rudra in the Veda," *Journal of the University of Bombay* 1 (1953):119-21; Güntert, *Arische Weltkönig,* pp. 196-98; Hillebrandt, *Vedische Mythologie,* 2: 285-90; and von Schroeder, *Mysterium und Mimus,* pp. 120-25.
120. See Lommel, *Religion Zarathustras,* pp. 159-61; Zaehner, p. 269; Widengren, *Religionen Irans,* pp. 22-23 for Iran; Dandekar, "Rudra in the Veda," pp. 120-21; Güntert, *Arische Weltkönig,* p. 197; Hillebrandt, *Vedische Mythologie,* 2: 277, 285-90; and Henri Grégoire et al., *Asklépios, Apollon Smintheus et Rudra* (Brussels, 1949), pp. 158-59 for India.
121. Note that Rudra is—at least in part—an Indo-Iranian god, as one of his important by-names, *Śarvá-*, finds a correspondence in the Avestan demon *Saurva,* named alongside Indra and Nåŋhaiθya (= Skt. *Någatya-*) in *Vd.* 10.9 and 19.43, thus permitting reconstruction of an I-I form **Sarva,* which derives from the P-I-E name of the goddess of death, **Kolvo-,* "the coverer," as shown by Güntert, *Kalypso,* pp. 141-42.
122. For Rudra and the Rudrās as the leader and the spirits of the dead, see Leopold von Schroeder, "Bemerkungen zu Oldenbergs Religion des Veda," *Wiener Zeitschrift für die Kunde des Morgenlands* 9 (1895):233-53; Ernst Arbman, *Rudra* (Uppsala, 1922), passim; Jarl Charpentier, "Über Rudra-Śiva," *Wiener Zeitschrift für die Kunde des Morgenlands* 23 (1909):151-79; and Dandekar, "Rudra in the Veda," pp. 94-148, although the argument of the latter is somewhat more complicated than the others. Herman Lommel, *Les anciens aryens* (Paris, 1942), pp. 150-54, 173-82, and 203-5, steadfastly maintained that while the Maruts and the Rudrās were closely related, they were separate nonetheless. I would agree

society. One of the acts of the dead warriors is the bringing of rain (*RV*
5.53.1-10 / *Yt.* 13.14 and 43), and their rushing about in the sky has
brought them into association with the wind, but the naturalistic side
of their character has often been overvalued by scholars.[123] It is but one
part of their complex nature, and by contrast their martial aspects
predominate.

Some of the ritual practices of the terrestrial warriors have been dealt
with already in the discussion of the warrior god and the offerings of
sauma to him. It must now be pointed out, however, that this intoxicating drink was not only poured as a libation but was drunk by the warriors themselves.[124] *Sauma* was a pressed drink, the name of which is
derived from the verb *√su-* (Skt. *√su-* = Av. *√hu-*) "to press," and it is
an Indo-Iranian innovation, having replaced the older Indo-European
intoxicant and fortifier *medhu*, a honey drink.[125] Like *medhu*, however,
it is surrounded with an elaborate mythology in which it was first obtained
for men from the heavenly realms by virtue of a daring theft.[126] And like
the *medhu*, it is believed to be the very elixir of life force. It renders the
gods immortal, and on a less exalted plane it brings health, vigor, and
well-being to men.[127] It is particularly important to two groups, poets and
warriors, giving inspiration to the former and a surge of strength and
power to the latter.[128] Warriors seem to have drunk great quantities of it
before combat, and in both Indian and Iranian texts the drink is continually asked to grant strength and victory (*RV* 9.8.8, 9.45.6 / *Y.*
9:16-20, 9.27-29). *Sauma* was known by the epithet *durauša* (Skt.
duróṣa- =Av. *dūraoša-*), "that which makes destruction difficult,"[129]

and depict the relation of the two in terms of the Maruts being a subset of the Rudrās, based
on *RV* 1.64.2 and 7.56.1.

123. Thus, e.g., Keith, *Religion and Philosophy*, pp. 152-53. It is, however,
equally incorrect to completely deny their naturalistic side.

124. See Bergaigne, 2: 149-51; Oldenberg, *Religion des Veda*, pp. 176-77; Widengren,
Religionen Irans, p. 29 and n.; Mary Boyce, "Haoma, Priest of the Sacrifice," in *W. B.
Henning Memorial Volume*, p. 64. Note, however, that this is only one of *sauma*'s uses, and
it is also frequently drunk by priests for inspiration. Prakash, *Food and Drinks in Ancient
India*, pp. 22-23, believes it to have been the most important beverage of the Vedic Indians,
although his evidence for this is quite thin.

125. See Schrader, *Prehistoric Antiquities*, p. 321.

126. For differing reconstructions of this mythology, see Adalbert Kuhn, *Die Herabkunft
des Feuers und des Göttertranks* (Guttersloh, 1886); Georges Dumézil, *Le festin d'immmor-
talité* (Paris, 1924); and David M. Knipe, "The Heroic Theft: Myths from Rgveda IV and
the Ancient Near East," *History of Religions* 6 (1967):328-60.

127. Boyce, "Haoma, Priest of the Sacrifice," pp. 62-64; Zaehner, p. 88; Keith,
Religion and Philosophy, p. 168; Herman Lommel, "König Soma," *Numen* 2 (1955):
200-201. See *RV* 8.48.3 and 11; *Y.* 9.16-20, where the gifts of *sauma* (inspiration,
strength, victory, health, long life, etc.) are enumerated.

128. Bergaigne, 3: 150; Dange, "Aspects of War," pp. 133-34; Widengren, *Hochgott-
glaube*, p. 340. Note also that virtually all those who participated in the *haoma* ceremony at
Persepolis were high-ranking military officers. See Raymond A. Bowman, *Aramaic Ritual
Texts from Persepolis* (Chicago, 1970), pp. 15, 34, and 36-37.

129. The compound is certainly to be analyzed as *dur-auša-*, the Avestan *dūra-aoša-*,
"who keeps death far away" being a folk etymology. On this form, see H. W. Bailey, "Dvāra

and its consumption was among the most important ritual strengthening practices of the Indo-Iranian warrior. Drunk with the intoxicating beverage, he believed himself to have become invulnerable, and he became furious, raging like the wild beasts. Certain of the Scyths were even called *Haumavarga*, "*Haoma*-wolves," and the ideology holds for others as well.[130]

The warrior, then, was a young man filled with the force of life; he was also a wolf, a ruthless predator. He was a member of a band into which he had been initiated and whose emblems he bore, and his membership in that band linked him to the warriors of the dead. His training made it possible for him to take on a state of wild, untamed rage, and the ritual use of intoxicants heightened this state of fury. Ultimately we must ask: to what end was all this directed?

It is here that the cattle raid looms up once again, shedding light not only on the immediate question but also on the *Trito myth with which we began. To judge from the hymns of the *Rg Veda*, the cattle raid was of enormous importance. *RV* 3.16, 3.31, 3.53, 4.22, 6.17, and 8.75 are among the many accounts of cattle raids, and the very word *gáviṣṭi-*, "desire for cattle," has become synonymous with "conflict," "battle," of whatever sort.[131] In scores of verses cattle raiding plays an important part.[132] In Iran the cattle raid was no less important, although the textual evidence is not as rich. There are clear examples, however, as in *Vd.* 13.45, where it is said that the dog driving in cattle does just as the warriors do,[133] or *Yt.* 10.85–86, where the cow being carried off by opposing warriors calls out to Miθra to bring her home.[134]

This last detail is extremely significant, for it repeats a theme we encountered in the *Trito myth. The cattle that were obtained in that account were not thought to be stolen simply because *Trito needed or

---

Matīnām," *Bulletin of the School of Oriental and African Studies* 20 (1957):55; Jarl Charpentier, "Aw. *dūraoša*: Ai. *duroṣa-*," *Wiener Zeitschrift für die Kunde des Morgenlands* 27 (1913):235–44; B. Geiger, pp. 77–78; Duchesne-Guillemin, *Les Composées de l'Avesta* (Paris, 1936), pp. 168 and 272; Jakob Wackernagel and Albert Debrunner, *Altindische Grammatik: II/2, Die Nominalsuffixe* (Göttingen, 1954), p. 933; and Helmut Humbach, "Review: Wackernagel-Debrunner, *Altindische Grammatik*, Vol. II/2," *Deutsche Literaturzeitung* 78 (1957):300.

130. See Christian Bartholomae, "Beiträge zur altiranischen Grammatik, V," *Beiträge zur Kunde der indogermanischen Sprache* 13 (1887):70–71; Wikander, *Arische Männerbund*, pp. 64–65.

131. Macdonell and Keith, 1: 233.

132. See *RV* 1.10.6–10, 32.11–12, 62.3, 73.8, 83.4, 93.4, 101.5, 103.5–6, 121.4 and 7, 132.4, 151.6; 2.17.1, 23.18, 34.1; 3.32.16, 34.3, 43.7, 44.5, 47.4; 4.2.15–18, 3.11, 16.6–8, 28.5, 50.2, etc. The examples could easily be multiplied many times over.

133. Most of the Avestan texts that mention cattle raiding soundly condemn it. Thus, *Y.* 12.2; *Vd.* 18.2, 5.37; *Yt.* 10.38, 11.5. But note Strabo 15.3.8, a text that Alföldi, pp. 14–15, has related to the Iranian *Männerbund* tells that the young warriors devote their lives to robbing and herding.

134. On Miθra in this connection, see Benveniste, "Mithra aux vastes pâturages"; and Franz Cumont, "St. George and Mithra the Cattle Thief," *Journal of Roman Studies* 27 (1937):63–71.

wanted them. The dialectic was more complex. These cattle were believed to have been his from the beginning and were stolen from him by the three-headed *Ṇgʷhi who is specified as a non-Indo-European. The raid that *Trito mounted, then, was no theft but the recovery of his proper possessions.

The *Trito myth is the myth of the first cattle raid. As such, it sets a precedent and serves as a model for all future raids. When Indian or Iranian warriors undertook an expedition, they looked to the mythic Trita or Θraētaona as their prototype, and various texts show them identifying themselves with this hero (*RV* 2.11.19, 9.86.20, 2.34.14, 5.86.1; *Yt.* 19.92-96: note also the name of Xerxes's general recorded in Herodotus 7.82, τριτανταίχμης, "Bold [Av. *taxma-*] as Θrita").[135] In his raid *Trito established the proper form for all raiding and the rites that ensure success, namely, invocation of the warrior god, the pouring of libations, and the drinking of intoxicants. Finally, he established that raiding was no theft at all but was fully justified repossession of one's own property. Warring with aborigines for cattle was a noble activity, protected by the warrior god and sanctioned by myth. All the Indo-European peoples seem to have pursued it zealously and with a sense of supreme confidence and self-righteousness.[136] Their acts were based upon a mythic prototype and can be diagrammed in a cyclical pattern (Figure 8)—a warrior cycle—which is familiar from our study of East African materials.

---

135. Güntert, *Arische Weltkönig,* p. 29. For another example of the historicization of this myth, see Otto Höfler, "Siegfried, Arminius, und die Symbolik," in *Festschrift für Franz Rolf Schröder* (Heidelberg, 1959), pp. 11-121.

136. On cattle raiding among the Celts, see G. Dottin, "Les razzias épiques," *Revue Celtique* 40 (1923): 127-34, and Josef Weisweiler, "Vorindogermanische Schichten der irischen Heldensage," *Zeitschrift für celtische Philologie* 24 (1954): 27-28; among the Greeks, Norman O. Brown, *Hermes the Thief* (New York, 1947), pp. 3-7, and Peter Walcot, "Cattle Raiding, Heroic Tradition, and Ritual: The Greek Evidence," *History of Religions* 18 (1979): 326-51; among the Germans, Höfler, *Kultische Geheimbünde,* pp. 121-26, 257-69.

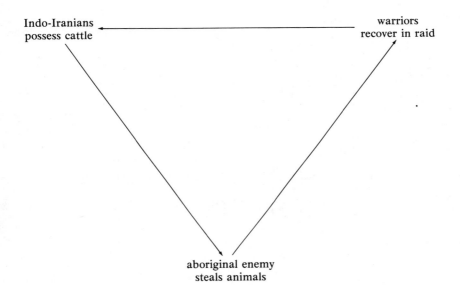

Figure 8. The Indo-Iranian Warrior Cycle

VI

INDO-IRANIANS:
CONFLICT OF PRIESTS
AND WARRIORS

The Nature of Indo-Iranian Society

The investigation thus far has occasionally pointed to some of the signal features of Indo-Iranian social organization, although the main focus has been on the mythic and the religious. Yet we must recognize that these myths do serve, at least in part, as something of a social charter, and their interpretation yields valuable information about the nature of society. Thus what I have dubbed the "myth of the first sacrifice" described the difference between kings and priests, while the "myth of the first cattle raid" set the warrior off as a separate class and described the difference between Indo-European and aboriginal.

Up to this point any observations of a sociological nature have been sporadic and not organized in any systematic fashion. Much work has been done in the past along these lines, however, and there is now a good deal of agreement that the Indo-Iranians were organized along well-defined class lines.[1] This is evident in the correspondence between the first three terms of the Indian and Iranian class systems (Skt. *varṇa-*; Av. *pištra-*). The Indian *brāhmaṇa-* corresponds to the Iranian *zaotar-* in that both designate the class of priests; Indian *kṣatriya-* to Iranian *raθaēštar-*, both designating the class of warriors; and Indian *vaiśya-* to Iranian *vāstrō.fšuyant-*, both designating the class of commoners primarily devoted to pastoral pursuits.[2]

In numerous writings Dumézil has referred to this system of social

---

1. See the works cited in notes 62–65, chapter 4.
2. Benveniste, "Les classes sociales dans la tradition avestique," p. 117.

organization as "tripartite" and has demonstrated the hierarchical nature of the class structure. He often refers to the sets of sovereigns (or priests),[3] warriors, and commoners as the first, second, and third respectively. His argument is persuasive, yet it does not by any means exhaust the topic. There is another way of describing these classes and their various inter-relationships that will perhaps shed still more light on the subject.

The system does not appear simply as a linear ranking of three terms in a hierarchical order but is somewhat more complex in principle. Other terms must be included, and when this is done the system of organization is shown to be a repeated process of binary opposition, as depicted in Figure 9.[4]

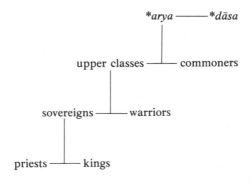

Figure 9. The Organization of Indo-Iranian Society

The first major division here is that between *arya (Skt. aryá-, árya- = Av. airya-, OPers. ariya-) and *dāsa (Skt. dāsá- = Av. daha-ka-, dahā-ka), countryman and foreigner, friend and foe.[5] The aboriginal was perceived as standing outside the proper Indo-Iranian society, hostile to that society and ungoverned by its rules. His existence was recognized,

3. In an article entitled "Religion indo-européenne: Examen de quelques critiques récents," *Revue de l'histoire des religions* 152 (1957):15–16, Dumézil contended that there was no I-E solution to the problem of kingship and that the priest alone was the proper representative of the first function. Yet analysis of the myth of *Manu and *Yemo leads me to include the king within the sovereign class. Certainly the institution of kingship was present for the Indo-Europeans, as witness the well attested word for "king": P-I-E *rēg'-, with Skt. rāj-, Lat. rēx, OIr. rí (genitive ríg), Gallic -rix as reflexes. See Pokorny, pp. 854 ff.; Benveniste, *Vocabulaire*, 2: 9–16.

4. On this sort of system, see, of course, Claude Lévi-Strauss, *The Savage Mind* (Chicago, 1966), p. 217 and passim.

5. Whatever interpretation may be offered for the meaning of *arya, it is of primary importance that it be set in opposition to *dāsa. Of the various possibilities that have been suggested, two seem to me particularly worthy of consideration. The first is that offered by Paul Thieme, *Der Fremdling im Rigveda* (Leipzig, 1938), who derived *arya from Vedic arí-, which he took to mean originally "foreigner," given its alternate senses of "friend" and "foe" in Vedic usage. *Arya thus meant "he who is protecting of foreigners, i.e., a

however, in that he posed a problem to be dealt with, a force to be over-come.[6] As he was not truly a part of Indo-Iranian society, however, no further description of him or his society was thought to be necessary.

The society of the *arya themselves, however, was a topic of great interest and subject to considerably more subcategorization. The next major division to be recognized was that between the upper classes and the commoners. Those in the upper classes had special prerogatives, special duties, and special prestige, while those in the lower class had none of these but supplied the labor that supported the others. No doubt these commoners made up the bulk of the population, but they were something of an undifferentiated mass, a residual category, and the texts that have come down to us (written primarily by and for members of the upper classes) do not tell us much about the specific nature of the lower class. That it was already defined only as that of "commoners" in Proto-Indo-European times, and not in more specific terms, is evident from the text that shows the closest correspondence to Indo-Iranian social ideology, namely, Caesar's account of Celtic social organization in Gaul of the first century B.C., which also gives valuable information on the nature of the two upper classes.

> In all of Gaul there are two classes of men who are in any
> rank and honor at all, for the masses [*plebes*, the com-

---

hospitable one," in his opinion. For my part, I would not go so far in reading a meliorative sense into the term and would suggest "he who comes into contact with foreigners, i.e. a wanderer, an invader." *Dāsa* might then be interpreted as suggested by Vittore Pisani, *Crestomazia Indeuropea* (Turin, 1949), p. 113, as reflecting P-I-E *dṃso-, "dweller," derived from the verb *√dṃ-, "to dwell," as are Skt. *dāmyati,* Gk. δαμάω, and Lat. *domō.* The contrast is thus one between invader and native, with the latter term assuming a distinctly pejorative connotation, as has been argued by J. C. Tavadia, *Indo-Iranian Studies,* 2 vols. (Santiniketan, 1950–52), 1: 2–3.

Alternatively, one might derive *arya* from a verbal base √ar-, "to get," "obtain," as has been suggested by H. W. Bailey, "Iranian Arya- and Daha-," *Transactions of the Philological Society* (1959), pp. 71–94. This analysis implies a view of the *arya* as "the possessor," "holder of property," something that would contrast neatly with Bailey's interpretation of *dasa* (with short -a-) as "servant," "subservient one," as suggested by Middle Parthian *dāhīft* "servitude," New Persian *dāh,* "servant," Buddhist Sogdian δ'yh, "serving girl," and Gk. δοῦλος, Mycenaean *doero-,* "slave" (pp. 107–15). Bailey does go beyond this interpretation, however, proposing a specialized sense for √ar- as "to beget," rather than just "to get," with a consequent reinterpretation of *arya* as the "well-born one," but this is entirely unnecessary and ill-founded, as has been pointed out by Leonard R. Palmer, "Arya-: A Homological Sketch," *Antiquitates Indogermanicae: Gedenkschrift für Hermann Güntert* (Innsbruck, 1974), pp. 11–19 (who in turn errs by interpreting the possessions that characterize the *arya* exclusively in terms of land).

Note also on this question, Georges Dumézil, "Le nom des 'Arya,' " *Revue de l'histoire des religions* 124 (1941):36–59; and "Ari, Aryaman à propos de Paul Thieme, 'ari, Fremder' (ZDMG 117)," *Journal Asiatique* 246 (1958):67–84; Benveniste, *Vocabulaire,* 1: 369–73; Franz Specht, "Zur Bedeutung des Ariernamen," *Zeitschrift für vergleichende Sprachforschung* 68 (1943):42–52.

6. Ultimately the Indians incorporated their Dravidian enemies into the social system as the fourth class, the *śūdras* or "untouchables."

moners] are held almost in the place of servants, dare nothing by themselves, and are not admitted into public deliberations. The majority of them, pressed down by debt, large taxes, or the injustice of those more powerful, give themselves up in servitude to the nobles, who exercise over them the same rights as lords over servants. But of these two [noble] classes, one is the Druids [*druidum*], the other, the knights [*equitum*]. [The Druids] take part in all sacred things, manage the public and private sacrifices, and interpret the holy things. A large number of youths flock to them for instruction, and they are in great honor among them. They decide almost all controversies, public and private. . . .

The Druids habitually are absent from war, do not pay taxes along with the rest, and have freedom from military service and immunity in all things. Excited by such great rewards, many enter instruction, by their own free will or sent by parents and relations. There they are said to learn a great number of verses by heart, and some spend twenty years in instruction. They do not consider it right to commit these [verses] to writing, but with almost all other things, public and private, they make use of Greek letters. . . .

The other class is the knights. When there is need and a war breaks out—which before the arrival of Caesar was wont to happen almost yearly, since either they themselves inflicted injuries or they would redress those [injuries] perpetrated [against them]—all [the knights] take part in the war. (*De Bello Gallico* 6.13-15)[7]

7. In omni Gallia eorum hominum, qui aliquo sunt numero atque honore, genera sunt duo. Nam plebes paene servorum habetur loco, quae nihil audet per se, nullo adhibetur consilio. Plerique, cum aut aere alieno aut magnitudine tributorum aut iniuria potentiorum premuntur, sese in servitutem dicant nobilibus, quibus in hos eadem omnia sunt iura, quae dominis in servos. Sed de his duobus generibus alterum est druidum, alterum equitum. Illi rebus divinis intersunt, sacrificia publica ac privata procurant, religiones interpretantur: ad eos magnus adulescentium numerus disciplinae causa concurrit, magnoque hi sunt apud eos honore. Nam fere de omnibus controversiis publicis privatisque constituunt, . . .

14. Druides a bello abesse consuerunt neque tributa una cum reliquis pendunt, militiae vacationem omniumque rerum habent immunitatem. Tantis excitati praemiis et sua sponte multi in disciplinam conveniunt et a parentibus propinquisque mittuntur. Magnum ibi numerum versuum ediscere dicuntur. Itaque annos non nulli vicenos in disciplina permanent. Neque fas esse existimant ea litteris mandare, cum in reliquis fere rebus, publicis privatisque rationibus, Graecis litteris utantur. . . .

15. Alterum genus est equitum. Hi, cum est usus atque aliquod

INDO-IRANIANS: CONFLICT OF PRIESTS AND WARRIORS

Here we see a situation much like that found among the Indo-Iranians: a class of commoners (*plebes*) without distinction or authority, set far below two superior classes, one of warriors (*equites*) and one of priests (*druides*), both of whom possess rank and power. Moreover, the ultimate sovereignty of the priests is established, for it is they who "decide almost all controversies, public and private."[8] Their authority, then, which rests on their close connection with all things sacred, extends also into the temporal realm, while that of the warriors remains limited to things martial.

Indian and Iranian texts show a similar distinction between the two upper classes, although some differences from the Celtic pattern are apparent. Thus, instead of a simple division between a class of warriors and a class of priests, the Indo-Iranians posited a more complex entity, a class of sovereigns, in place of the latter grouping. Despite this divergence in detail, however, it is clear that both systems of organization and classification derived from the same Proto-Indo-European pattern.[9] In the Indo-Iranian scheme of things, as in the Celtic, a clear distinction is drawn between the two upper classes. While the power of each was certainly great, the power of the first class—sovereigns or priests, respectively—was paramount, and what is more, the nature of power found in the two classes was quite different. On the one hand, the power of the warrior class depended on physical strength and had to be continually proven in battle. On the other hand, the power of the first class inhered in speech rather than in arms and found its expression in prayer, judgments, and commands.

The Indo-Iranian sovereign class was further subdivided, and the twin forms of authority fused in the Druids as described by Caesar (sacral and temporal) were apportioned to priests and kings respectively.[10] The king

---

bellum incidit (quod fere ante Caesaris adventum quotannis accidere solebat, uti aut ipsi iniurias inferrent aut illatas propulsarent); omnes in bello versantur.

8. omnibus controversiis publicis privatisque constituunt.

9. The discussion of Caesar's account in Jan Gonda, *Triads in the Veda* (Amsterdam, 1976), pp. 171–72, and indeed his lengthy discussion of Indo-Iranian and Indo-European social organization (pp. 125–77), seems to me to miss the fundamental principle of reconstructive research. Where evidence from one branch of the Indo-European family shows the slightest divergence from that of another, he is prepared to conclude that this rebuts claims for their common origin. In truth such divergence is always present, as an inevitable result of the independent development of the differing branches. The crucial question is not whether such divergence exists, but whether it can adequately be explained and traced back to a common hypothetical prototype that would permit such independent developments.

10. See Ananda Coomaraswamy, *Spiritual Authority and Temporal Power in the Indian Theory of Government* (New Haven, 1942), and Eugen Wilhelm, "Königthum und Priesterthum im alten Eran," *Zeitschrift der deutschen morgenländischen Gesellschaft* 40 (1886): 102–10. For the fullest treatment of the ideology of kingship in either India or Iran, see Jan Gonda, "Ancient Indian Kingship from the Religious Point of View," *Numen* 3 (1956): 36–71, 122–55; 4 (1957): 24–58, 127–64.

was thus responsible for the preservation of the proper order in this world, and the priest for the maintenance and observation of proper relations between this world and that which lies beyond. To put it differently, the priest perceived the proper world order, while the king established it at the priest's direction.

Consistent throughout this social pattern is a principle of binary opposition that differentiates a group of higher and a group of lower status. *Arya are seen as more worthy than *dāsa; the upper classes than the commoners; sovereigns than warriors; and priests than kings. In every instance, the group of higher status is subject to further categorization and differentiation (priests could also be further subcategorized if necessary). *Arya are broken down into upper classes and commoners; upper classes into sovereigns and warriors; sovereigns into priests and kings. Each binary pair shares a common allegiance to a more general grouping but a clear opposition exists between its own two members, with a definite hierarchical relation established between these two members.

To be sure, this is a view of Indo-Iranian social theory and not of Indo-Iranian society. For social theory is only a part of the picture, and to complete it we must also be aware of social reality. Here things were somewhat more complex. Lower classes do not always submit gladly to their subordinate position and may often contest the matter. Tensions and conflicts existed, and traces of this can be seen in myth and legend.

The myths examined thus far have not shed any light on this side of the picture. In the *Manu-*Yemo myth, kings are properly subordinated to priests, and in the *Trito-*Ngʷhi myth, *arya properly triumph over *dāsa. These are both very old Indo-European myths, and both present an ideal state of affairs. That in reality aborigines often opposed the Indo-European invaders or that kings often rode roughshod over priests are not matters of concern. The myths describe the way things ought to be, not the way they are.

There are, however, other stories that take up the theme of the tensions that actually existed in society. Dumézil has treated one such myth, which tells of the conflict between the upper classes and the commoners.[11] This, too, is an Indo-European myth, with Norse, Roman, and Indian reflexes, and it describes the struggle of the lower class to gain some of the privileges of the sovereigns and warriors. The myth ends with something of a compromise solution, in which the proper hierarchical order is restored but the commoners or their representatives are admitted to new privileges within society.[12]

11. This is the myth that has as its Germanic reflex the conflict of Æsir and Vanir gods; Roman, the war of Romans and Sabines; Indian, the struggle of the Aśvins for full admission to the sacrifice as told in Mhb. 3.123-25. See Georges Dumézil, *Les dieux des Germains* (Paris, 1959), pp. 3 ff.

12. See also, Georges Dumézil, *L'héritage indo-européen à Rome* (Paris, 1949), pp. 139 ff.

INDO-IRANIANS: CONFLICT OF PRIESTS AND WARRIORS

Another myth, one of strictly Indo-Iranian provenance,[13] deals with another tension in society, that between priests and warriors. It is of particular interest to us, for their conflict centers on the issue of possession of cattle.

The Myth of the Bovine's Lament

While there are apparently no other Indo-European reflexes of this myth, it must have been fairly popular among the Indo-Iranians for numerous versions are found in their literatures.[14] The Indian epic tradition contains several different versions,[15] and the *Rg Veda* has one.[16] In Iran, in addition to the hymn of Zarathustra presented below, there are two others in the Younger Avesta[17] and folkloric remnants from Ossetic and Georgian sources.[18] Moreover, there is a very important Pahlavi text in which the ox's tormentor is Sritō (< *Trito), the warrior par excellence.[19] The most complete and intrinsically interesting texts, however, are the *Gāthic* hymn usually referred to as "The Plaint of the Ox,"[20] and the story of the conflict between Vasiṣṭha and Viśvāmitra as told in the *Rāmāyana*. Other sources add little in the way of material that is useful for reconstruction, and it will be sufficient for us to consider these two texts in some detail.

    1. The soul of the ox lamented to you [plural]:
       "For whom did you shape me? Who created me?
    Furor, raiding, cruelty, audacity, and strength
       oppress me.

    13. This, of course, is a provisional statement. Numerous parallels have been suggested from other I-E areas, among them: a passage from the Slavic book of Enoch, chapter 58 (J. Duchesne-Guillemin, "On the Complaint of the Ox-Soul," *Journal of Indo-European Studies* 1 [1973]:103 n.); Chapter 31 of the *Laxðaela Saga* (Georges Dumézil, "A propos de la plainte de l'âme du boeuf [Yasna 29]," *Bulletin de l'Académie royal de Belgique, Classe des Lettres* 51 [1965]:50–51); and *KUB* XXIX 1 (Ivanov, p. 800). But none of these texts is so striking in its details or in its resemblance to the Indo-Iranian texts that it must be considered a reflex of some Proto-Indo-European original. I find none of the suggested comparisons compelling, and I understand the myth as strictly of Indo-Iranian origin.

    14. A more detailed version of this reconstruction appears in Bruce Lincoln, "The Myth of the 'Bovine's Lament,' " *Journal of Indo-European Studies* 3 (1975):337–62.

    15. Dumézil, "A propos de la plainte," p. 44 n., has called attention to the story of Surabhī (*Mhb.* 3.9), of Arjuna and Jamadagni's cow (*Padma Pūraṇa* 6.268), and the Buddhist story of Godatta Thera, in addition to other stories that we will treat below.

    16. *RV* 8.101.15–16.

    17. *Yt.* 10.84–87 and 15.1. The former has been treated by Duchesne-Guillemin, "On the Complaint of the Ox-Soul," pp. 103–104; the latter by Wikander, *Vayu*, p. 20; and Tavadia, *Indo-Iranian Studies*, 2: 31–33.

    18. See Dumézil, "A propos de la plainte," pp. 37–43.

    19. *Dēnkart* (Sanjana) 7.2.62–66 and *Zāt Spram* 12.7–25.

    20. Meillet, *Trois conférences sur les Gāthas*, pp. 43–52, argued that *Y*. 29 was not complete but was a collection of fragments from some older text. His view has not been widely accepted and has been rebutted by Herman Lommel, "Yasna 29: die Klage des Rindes," *Zeitschrift für Indologie und Iranistik* 10 (1935):96–115; and Tavadia, *Indo-Iranian Studies*, 2: 27–75, among others.

There is no other herdsman for me than you. You
proclaimed for me good herding."
2. Then the Creator of the Ox asked Aša, "What
judge have you for the ox,
That the rulers may give him pastures together
with cattle-caring zeal?
Whom do you appoint lord to him, who will
restrain the furor of the followers of the lie?"
3. Aša answered this one: "There is no helper
without enmity to the ox.
None of them can comprehend [how] those who are
high proceed against the lowly.
Of beings, the strongest is the one at whose call
you must come with help.
4. Mazdā, who best remembers proclamations
should have known what was done
By gods and by men [in the past], and should know
that which will be done [in the future].
He, Ahura, is decisive. It should then be for us
as he desires."
5. Then with outstretched hands we two are praying
to Ahura.
My soul and that of the pregnant cow, we two press
Mazdā with requests:
"[Let there] not [be] ruin for the right-living, nor
for the herdsman among the followers of the lie."
6. Then spoke Ahura Mazdā himself, knowing the
prayers by his wisdom:
"Not one lord is known, nor a judge, according to
Aša,
Yet the creator shaped you for the herdsman and the
pastoralist."
7. Ahura, who is of the same will as Aša, created
this formula of libation
And lordly Mazdā by his command created milk of the
cow for those who long for food.
"Whom do you have with Vohu Manah who might take care of
the two of us for men?"
8. "This [man] here is known to me, who alone hears
our teachings—
Zarathustra Spitāma, who wishes, O Mazdā, to proclaim our
thoughts
And those of Aša. I would bestow sweetness of speech
upon him."
9. And then the soul of the ox cried, "Must I let
myself fall to a carer without property,[21]

21. *An-aēša-* implies "without power" as well as "without property." See Bartholomae,
Altiranisches Wörterbuch, p. 32.

To the word of a man without strength? I wish a
powerful lord for me:
Whenever could this one be? Who can give him help
that has hands?"
10. Grant strength and rulership to these, Ahura,
by Aša
and by Vohu Manah, who gives good dwellings and
peace.
Even I, O Mazdā, have known you as the first effect-
er of this.
11. Where are Aša and Vohu Manah and Xšaθra? Now
you welcome me,
Along with man, O Mazdā, to knowledge of the great
gift.[22]
Now, Ahura, there is help for us, and likewise gifts
by us for you.[23]

[*Y.* 29, "The Plaint of the Ox"]

22. *Maga-* is an extremely difficult and hotly debated term. I am persuaded that
the comparison to Skt. *maghá-* must yield the meaning "gift," but the argument of Helmut
Humbach, "Gast und Gabe bei Zarathustra," *Münchener Studien zur Sprachwissenschaft* 2
(1952):11–20, that this is the sacrificial gift, cannot be accepted in light of Schlerath's observation in his review of Humbach's translation of the *Gāthas*, that in Skt., *maghá-* applies
only to the gift given by a god to men, never that of men to a god (*Orientalistische
Literaturzeitung* [1962], p. 579). Thus, in this stanza we have a sacrificial gift exchange, the
rātay- being the gifts (or "services") offered by men, and the *maga-* being the god's return
gift. It is clear that *maga-* is a technical term for Zarathustra, and when used in conjunction
with the adjective *maz-*, "great," as here and in *Y.* 46.14, I am inclined to see eschatological
significance, the "great gift" being the reward that awaits the righteous.
    23. xšmaibyā gə̄uš urvā gərəždā kahmāi mā θwarōždūm kə̄ mā tašat
        ā mā aēšəmō hazascā rəmō (ā)hišāya dərəšcā təvišcā
        nōit mōi vāstā xšmat anyō aθā mōi sąstā vohū vāstryā
    2. adā tašā gə̄uš pərəsat ašəm kaθā tōi gavōi ratuš
        hyat hīm dātā xšayantō hadā vāstrā gaodāyō θwaxšō
        kə̄m hōi uštā ahurəm yə̄ drəgvō.dəbīš aēšəməm vādāyōit
    3. ahmāi ašā nōit sarəjā advaēšō gavōi paitī.mravat
        avaēšąm nōit vīduyē yā šavaitē ādrə̄ng ərəšvą̄ŋhō
        hātąm hvō aojištō yahmāi zavə̄ng jimā kərədušā
    4. mazdą̄ sax'ārə̄ mairištō yā zī vāvərəzōi pairī.ciθīt
        daēvāišcā mašyāišcā yācā varəšaitē aipī.ciθīt
        hvō vīcirō ahurō aθā nə̄ aŋhat yaθā hvō vasat
    5. at vā ustānāiš ahvā zastāiš frīnəmnā ahurāi.ā
        mə̄ urvā gə̄ušcā azyą̊ hyat mazdąm dvaidī frasābyō
        nōit ərəžəjyōi frajyāitiš nōit fšuyentē drəgvasū pairī
    6. at ə̄ vaocat ahurō mazdā vīdvą̊ vafūš vyānayā
        nōit aēvā ahū vistō naēdā ratuš ašātcit hacā
        at zī θwā fšuyantaēcā vāstryāicā θwōrəštā tatašā
    7. tə̄m āzūtōiš ahurō mąθrəm tašat ašā hazaošō
        mazdą̄ gavōi xšvīdəmcā hvō urušaēibyō spəntō sāsnayā
        kastē vohū manaŋhā yə̄ ī dāyāt ə̄əavā marətaēibyō
    8. aēm mōi idā vistō yə̄ nə̄ aēvō sāsną̊ gūšatā
        zaraθuštrō spitāmō hvō nə̄ mazdā vaštī ašāicā
        carəkərəθrā srāvayeŋhē hyat hōi hudəmə̄m dyāi vaxəδrahyā
    9. atcā gə̄uš urvā raostā yə̄ anaēšəm xšąnmə̄nē rādəm

143

The long and complicated story of Vasiṣṭha and Viśvāmitra begins when Viśvāmitra, a king, having led his warriors about the land, comes to the grove of Vasiṣṭha, a priest and hermit (1.50). He pays homage to the sage (1.51.1), and the two converse (1.51). Vasiṣṭha then decides to give a banquet for Viśvāmitra and his men, and this is prepared by Śabalā, his wish-cow, a wondrous animal who is able to create all manner of things from her body (1.52.1–6). Amazed by this performance, Viśvāmitra speaks to Vasiṣṭha as follows:

> "I am honored by you who are worthy of honor, O
>   Priest, and received with great hospitality.
> Listen—I will pronounce this speech, O you who
>   are skilled in speech.
> May Śabalā be given to me for 100,000 cows! O
>   Worthy, she is a jewel, indeed, and jewel-
>   bearing[24] is the lord of earth.
> Therefore, O twice-born, give this Śabalā to me;
>   she is mine according to *dharma*."[25]
>   [*Rām.* 1.52.8–9]

But Vasiṣṭha refuses:

> "Neither for 100,000 nor for ten million cows
> Nor for heaps of silver, O King, will I give
>   Śabalā.
> I am not capable of abandoning her from my
>   presence, O conqueror of foes.
> As glory dwells with those who have a soul, so
>   Śabalā dwells with me for ever more.
> Libations to the gods and offerings to ancestors,
>   my very subsistence,
> The Agnihotra, Bali, and Homa sacrifices all depend
>   on this [cow].

---

vācim nərəš asūrahyā yōm ā vasəmī īšā.xšaθrīm
kadā yavā hvō aŋhat yō hōi dadat zastavat avō
10. yūžəm aēibyo ahurā aogō dātā aša xšaθrəmcā
avat vohū manaŋhā yā hušəitīš rāmąmcā dāt
azəmcīt ahyā mazdā θwąm māŋhī paourvīm vaēdəm
11. kudā ašəm vohucā mano xšaθrəmcā at mā mašā
yūžōm mazdā frāxšnəne mazōi magāi.ā paitī.zānatā
ahurā nū nå avarō əhmā rātōiš yūšmāvatąm.
24. There is an intentional ambiguity here. *Ratnahārin-* can mean either "jewel-bearing" or "jewel-stealing." Viśvāmitra means to use the word in the former sense, of course, but the audience, who knew the story well, would catch this second level of meaning.
25. pūjito 'ham tvayā brahman pūjārheṇa susatkṛtaḥ /
śrūyatām abhidāsyāmi vākyam vākyaviśārada //
gavāṃ śatasahasreṇa dīyatāṃ śabalā mama /
ratnaṃ hi bhagavan netad ratnahārī ca pārthivaḥ /
tasmān me śabalāṃ dehi mamaiṣā dharmato dvija //

> Consecration and ritual exclamation, and knowledge
> of various sorts
> All depend on her, O royal seer, there is no doubt.
> This one, in truth, is all of my possessions, and
> always causes me satisfaction.
> For many reasons, King, I cannot give Śabalā
> to you."[26]

[1.52.11–15]

Viśvāmitra then increases his offer—40,000 elephants, 11,000 horses, all manner of golden implements, and a million cows, all for Śabalā—but still Vasiṣṭha refuses:

> "O King, in no way will I give you Śabalā.
> Indeed she is to me a jewel, indeed she is to me
> a prize;
> Indeed she is all I own, indeed she is my life.
> Indeed she is the new and full moon offerings, and
> sacrifices in which sacrificial fees are received.
> Indeed, she alone is mine, O King, and also many rites.
> All my rites are rooted in her, O King, there is no
> doubt.
> No matter how much you chatter, I will not give my
> desire-yielding cow."[27]

[1.52.21–24]

At this point, Viśvāmitra moves to exercise his force:

> When the hermit Vasiṣṭha would not give up the
> wish-cow,
> Viśvāmitra dragged off his Śabalā, O Rāma.[28]
> But Śabalā, O Rāma, being led off by the great-
> souled king,

26. nāhaṃ śatasahasreṇa nāpi koṭiśatair gavām /
rājan dāsyāmi śabalāṃ rāśibhī rajatasya vā //
na parityāgam arheyaṃ matsakāśād ariṃdama /
śaśvatī śabalā mahyaṃ kīrtir ātmavato yathā //
asyāṃ havyaṃ ca kavyaṃ ca prāṇayātrā tathaiva ca /
āyattam agnihotraṃ ca balir homas tathaiva ca //
svāhākāravaṣaṭkārau vidyāś ca vividhās tathā /
āyattam atra rājarṣe sarvam etan na saṃśayaḥ /
sarvasvam etat satyena mama tuṣṭikarī sadā /
kāraṇair bahubhī rājan na dāsye śabalāṃ tava //
27. na dāsyāmīti śabalāṃ prāha rājan kathaṃcana //
etad eva hi me ratnam etad eva hi me dhanam /
etad eva hi sarvasvam etad eva hi jīvitam //
darśaś ca pūrṇamāsaś ca yajñāś caivāptadakṣiṇaḥ /
etad eva hi me rājan vividhāś ca kriyās tathā //
adomūlāḥ kriyāḥ sarvā mama rājan na saṃśayaḥ /
bahunā kiṃ pralāpena na dāsye kāmadohinīm //
28. This story is addressed directly to Rāma, whose name is occasionally inserted in the vocative case in order to fill out the meter of a line.

> Unhappy, weeping, and pained by sorrow, reflected
> thus:
> "Why am I abandoned by the good and great-souled
> Vasiṣṭha?
> Why am I, who am most unhappy, shamed and afflicted
> by the king's soldiers?
> What evil have I done to that great seer and sage
> That the righteous one abandons me, I who am blame-
> less and have served and revered him?"[29]
>
> > [1.53.1–4]

Śabalā then shakes free from her captors and runs to Vasiṣṭha in order to speak with him.

> And Śabalā, crying and lamenting, spoke thus,
> Standing in the presence of Vasiṣṭha and roaring like
> a thunder cloud or kettle drum:
> "Good sir, why am I abandoned by you, O priest's son,
> Whereby the king's soldiers lead me off from your
> presence?"[30]
>
> > [1.53.7–8]

And Vasiṣṭha answers:

> "I do not abandon you, O Śabalā, nor have you done
> evil to me.
> This king whose power is great, drunk with that power,
> carries you off by force.
> Indeed, there is not a comparable force for me; but
> today the king is distinguished.
> He is a powerful king and warrior, truly a lord of
> the earth.
> [His retinue] is filled with quick race chariots,
> many carts and horses,
> Elephants and banners. Thus, he is more powerful."
> Thus addressed by Vasiṣṭha, she humbly replied,
> Being knowledgeable in speech, she made this speech
> to the priest and seer, he whose splendor was
> boundless:

29. kāmadhenuṃ vasiṣṭho 'pi yadā na tyajate muniḥ /
    tadāsya śabalāṃ rāma viśvāmitro 'nvakarṣata //
    nīyamānā tu śabalā rāma rājñā mahātmanā /
    duḥkhitā cintayāmāsa rudantī śokakarśitā //
    parityaktā vasiṣṭhena kim ahaṃ sumahātmanā /
    yāhaṃ rājabhṛtair dīnā 'hriyeyaṃ bhṛśaduḥkhitā //
    kiṃ mayāpakṛtaṃ tasya maharṣer bhāvitātmanaḥ /
    yan mām anāgasaṃ bhaktām iṣṭāṃ tyajati dhārmikaḥ //
30. śabalā sā rudantī ca krośantī cedam abravīt /
    vasiṣṭhasyāgrataḥ sthitvā meghadundubhirāviṇī //
    bhagavan kiṃ parityaktā tvayāhaṃ brahmaṇaḥ suta /
    yasmād rājabhṛta māṃ hi nayante tvatsakāśataḥ //

INDO-IRANIANS: CONFLICT OF PRIESTS AND WARRIORS

"They say that the warrior's [power] is not power;
   that of the priest is more powerful.
O priest, the priestly power derived from heaven is
   more powerful than that of the warrior.
You have immeasureable power; he is not more powerful
   than you.
Viśvāmitra is great in strength, [but] your glory
   is unequaled.
Command me, as I am possessed of your priestly power,
   you whose splendor is great!
I will destroy the arrogant power of that evil-minded
   one."[31]

[1.53.10-16]

Vasiṣṭha orders Śabalā to create an army, which she does, and the soldiers
who issue from her destroy the army of Viśvāmitra. Viśvāmitra himself,
however, destroys these soldiers, and Śabalā creates more, who are in turn
destroyed by Viśvāmitra. Finally, a third set of cow-created soldiers proves
successful, and at this point the hundred sons of Viśvāmitra decide to
intervene:

Seeing the army destroyed by great-souled Vasiṣṭha,
The hundred children of Viśvāmitra, equipped with
   weapons of various sorts
Rushed upon enraged Vasiṣṭha, the best of those who
   mutter prayers.
Merely by making the sound "hum," the great seer burnt
   all of them up.[32]

[1.54.5-6]

With this, Viśvāmitra despairs and recognizes his defeat. Having protected one son, he appoints him to the kingship and enters the forest to

31. na tvāṃ tyajāmi śabale nāpi me 'pakṛtaṃ tvayā /
    eṣa tvāṃ nayate rājā balān matto mahābalaḥ //
    na hi tulyaṃ balaṃ mahyaṃ rājā tv adya viśeṣataḥ /
    balī rājā kṣatriyaś ca pṛthivyāḥ patir eva ca //
    hayamakṣauhiṇī pūrṇā savājirathasaṃkulā /
    hastidhvajasamākīrṇā tenāsau balavattaraḥ //
    evam uktā vasiṣṭhena pratyuvāca vinītavat /
    vacanaṃ vacanajñā sā brahmarṣim amitaprabham //
    na balaṃ kṣatriyasyāhur brāhmaṇo balavattaraḥ /
    brahman brahmabalaṃ divyaṃ kṣatrāt tu balavattaram //
    aprameyabalaṃ tubhyaṃ na tvayā balavattaraḥ /
    viśvāmitro mahāvīryas tejas tava durāsadam //
    niyuṅkṣva māṃ mahātejas tvad brahmabalasaṃbhṛtāṃ
    tasya darpaṃ balaṃ yat tan nāśayāmi durātmanaḥ
32. dṛṣṭvā niṣūditaṃ sainyaṃ vasiṣṭhena mahātmanā /
    viśvāmitrasutānāṃ tu śataṃ nānāvidhāyudham //
    abhyadhāvat susaṃkruddhaṃ vasiṣṭhaṃ japatāṃ varam /
    huṃ kāreṇaiva tān sarvān nirdadāha mahān ṛṣiḥ //

INDO-IRANIANS: CONFLICT OF PRIESTS AND WARRIORS

become a hermit and practice austerities. His ascetic sufferings succeed in attracting the attention of the god Śiva, who offers him a wish, and Viśvāmitra asks for all manner of divine weapons. Having received them, he returns to Vasiṣṭha's grove, which he attacks and burns. Vasiṣṭha, however, is not frightened and addresses his adversary in a menacing fashion:

> "Since you have brought about ruin for this long-
> prospering hermitage—
> Since you are evil in conduct, foolish one, therefore
> you will not continue to exist."[33]
>
> [1.54.27]

Viśvāmitra panics at this warning and throws down his weapon, begging Vasiṣṭha, "Stand, stand!", but the priest replies:

> "I'm standing, O member of the warrior class; show [me]
> what power [you have].
> I will destroy the arrogance of your sword, O Gadhi's
> son.
> Where is your warrior's power and where is the great
> power of the priest?
> Behold my divine priestly power, O contemptible
> warrior!
> The most fiery and fearful weapon of Gadhi's son
> Is extinguished by the priestly staff as a burst of
> fire is by water."[34]
>
> [1.55.3-5]

With that, Viśvāmitra becomes enraged and takes up the battle again, hurling all the superhuman weapons he possesses at his enemy, who renders them all ineffective with his priestly staff. Finally, the king takes up the most fearsome weapon in his arsenal, the Brahma weapon, and the whole world trembles with fright, but this too is swallowed up by Vasiṣṭha's priestly staff, whereupon Vasiṣṭha and the staff flare up, filled with energy absorbed from that weapon.

> Thereupon, the troop of hermits praised Vasiṣṭha,
> best of those who mutter prayers;

---

33. aśramaṃ cirasaṃvṛddhaṃ yad vināśitavān asi /
   durācāro 'si yan mūḍha tasmāt tvam na bhaviṣyasi //
34. kṣatrabandho sthito 'smy eṣa yad balaṃ tad vidarśaya /
   nāśayāmy eṣa te darpaṃ śastrasya tava gādhija //
   kva ca te kṣatriyabalaṃ kva ca brahmabalaṃ mahat /
   paśya brahmabalaṃ divyaṃ mama kṣatriyapāṃsana //
   tasyāstraṃ gādhiputrasya ghoram āgneyam uttaman /
   brahmadaṇḍena tacchāntam agner vega ivāmbhasā //

INDO-IRANIANS: CONFLICT OF PRIESTS AND WARRIORS

> "Unfailing is your power, O priest; withhold this
> splendor by [your] splendor.
> Viśvāmitra, whose austerities are great, is held back
> by you, O priest.
> Settle down, most excellent of those who mutter prayers;
> may the worlds be freed from anxiety!"[35]
>
> [1.55.20-21]

Thus addressed, Vasiṣṭha calms down, and the battle comes to an end. In defeat, Viśvāmitra heaves a great sigh and announces:

> "Fie upon the power that is the warrior's power! The
> power of the priest's splendor is [truly] power!
> By that one priestly staff, all my weapons are destroyed.
> Thus, having perceived this, I—my mind and senses
> being clear—
> Will undertake great austerities, which truly are pro-
> ductive of priestly station."[36]
>
> [1.55.23-24]

The *Rāmāyana* story of their rivalry continues, telling of Viśvāmitra's long and ultimately successful efforts to win priestly rank and of his repeated encounters with Vasiṣṭha. Apparently the story of the two sages' enmity was a favorite one, and may even have had some historic basis,[37] yet it is this specific incident alone which is of interest to us, for it is here that we find strong correspondences to the Avestan "Plaint of the Ox."[38]

Actually, the correspondences that can be noted in these two versions

35. tato 'stuvan munigaṇā vasiṣṭhaṃ japatām varam /
amoghaṃ te balaṃ brahmaṇs tejo dhāraya tejasā //
nigṛhītas tvayā brahman viśvāmitro mahātapaḥ /
prasīda japatām śreṣṭha lokāḥ santu gatavyathāḥ //

36. dhig balaṃ kṣatriyabalaṃ brahmatejobalaṃ balam /
ekena brahmadaṇḍena sarvāstrāni hatāni me //
tad etat samavekṣyāham prasannendriyamānasaḥ /
tapo mahat samāsthāsye yad vai brahmatvakārakam //

37. In the *Rg Veda,* certain verses in the hymns 3.33 and 53; 7.18, 33 and 104 make clear that there was rivalry between the historic Vasiṣṭha and Viśvāmitra as to who would serve as Purohita ("chamberlain") to king Sudās, and this rivalry led to the famous Battle of the Ten Kings, in which Sudās—with Vasiṣṭha's help—overthrew a coalition assembled by Viśvāmitra. In the Vedic tradition Viśvāmitra is always a priest, while in the epic he is always a warrior and king. On the interpretation of the Vedic texts, see Rudolph von Roth, *Zur Literatur und Geschichte des Weda* (Stuttgart, 1846), pp. 87-141; E. W. Hopkins, "Problematic Passages in the Rig-Veda," *Journal of the American Oriental Society* 15 (1895):260-66; Rahurkar, pp. 22-25, 120-22; and Herman Lommel, "Vasiṣṭha und Viśvāmitra," *Oriens* 18/19 (1967):200-207, who also treats many of the later sources (pp. 207-27). We are only interested in this one text, however, where the issue of warrior-priest conflict is so clearly marked. A study of all the traditions involving Vasiṣṭha and Viśvāmitra would be a major undertaking and lies outside the bounds of the present study.

38. The same incident is described in *Mahābhārata* 1.165, but as the *Rāmāyana* text is longer and more detailed it has been chosen for study, although the two are quite close in all respects.

INDO-IRANIANS: CONFLICT OF PRIESTS AND WARRIORS

are not as strong as those in the myths treated in Chapters 4 and 5. Here the names of the principal characters cannot be recovered, and we do not have other Indo-European reflexes to help us. Yet the details of the myth resemble each other so closely that it is possible to reconstruct the original narrative line from which these two texts ultimately derived. The striking figure of the bovine lamenting its fate gives us a starting point for comparison, but the similarities go far beyond this simple motif.

In the first place, it must be recognized that the bovine's complaint is a very specific one: it is being carried off by warriors in a cattle raid. The Indian version makes this explicit. Viśvāmitra is repeatedly and emphatically called a king (rājan-) and a warrior (kṣatriya-),[39] and he drags the cow off expressly by force (1.53.1). She complains of being "shamed and afflicted by the king's soldiers" (1.53.3)[40] and asks of her master, "For what reason do the king's soldiers lead me off from your presence?" (1.53.8).[41]

The Iranian example is similar, for while it is often alleged that the ox and cow are being led off for sacrifice,[42] there is no evidence whatsoever in the text to indicate this. Rather, the issue is cruelty in connection with warriors' raids.[43] All the key terms point in this direction. In verse 1, the ox laments: "Furor (aēšma-), raiding (hazah-), cruelty (rəma-), audacity (dərəš-), and strength (təviš-) oppress me," and all these words refer to the Männerbunde and their raiding practices.[44] Aēšma, as we have seen, is the technical term for the state of furor that the warriors cultivated for battle. Hazah is formed from the Avestan verb √haz-, "to seize" and is always used in the context of forcible seizure.[45] Ultimately it is derived from P-I-E* √segh'-, which must be understood as "to secure by force," most often used in a martial sense.[46] In the Zoroastrian confession of faith, two means of illicit seizure of cattle are mentioned: theft (tāya-) and raiding (hazah-).

---

39. He is called rājan- in 1.52.6, 11, 15, 21, 23, 24; 53.2, 3, 8, 10, 11, 19; and 54.14; kṣatriya- in 1.53.11, 14; and 55.4; rājarṣi- in 1.52.6, 14; and 54.19; kṣatrabandhu- in 1.55.3; pārthiva- in 1.52.9; and mahīpati- in 1.52.10. In 1.54.11, it is specified that he is subject to kṣatradharma-, that which is fitting for members of the warrior class.

40. yāhaṃ rājabhṛtairdīnā hriyeyaṃ bhṛśaduḥkhitā.

41. yasmād rājabhṛtā mām hi nayante tvatsakāśataḥ.

42. Thus, Humbach, Gāthas, 1: 80; Tavadia, Indo-Iranian Studies, 2: 38; Lommel, Religion Zarathustras, pp. 177–79; and Gāthas, pp. 32–34; Zaehner, p. 35; etc.

43. As noted by Duchesne-Guillemin, "On the Complaint of the Ox-Soul," p. 104: Dumézil, "A propos de la plainte," p. 35–36.

44. A more detailed treatment of these terms is found in Lincoln, "The Myth of the 'Bovine's Lament,' " pp. 341–50.

45. Tavadia, Indo-Iranian Studies, 2: 40–41.

46. Comparing Skt. sáhas-, "power," "victory," "strength"; Middle Irish seg, "strength"; Goth. sigis, ON sigr, "victory"; and the verbal forms, Skt. √sah-, "to conquer"; OHG sigirōn, "to be victorious"; Gk. ἔχω "to have," "possess." The last term usually means "to maintain in one's possession," but in the aorist can mean "to steal." See Pokorny, p. 888; Frisk, 1: 602–4.

> I choose the good, lordly Devotion. Let this be for me. I
> renounce the theft and the raiding of the ox, and I re-
> nounce the oppression and destruction of Mazdā-
> worshiping houses. (Y.12.2)[47]

Rǝma (or rāma-) occurs only two other times in the Avesta, but in both of
these it is directly associated with aēšma- and with those who are hostile to
cattle. Thus, for instance:

> Those nonherdsmen among the herdsmen, who by their
> own tongues
> Increase furor (aēšma-) and cruelty (rāma) with an
> evil will,
> Who have prevailed not by their good deeds, but by
> their evil deed—
> They have established the daēvas, which is [to say]
> the religion of the followers of the lie![48]

> [Y.49.4]

Dǝraš is a hapax legomenon but is etymologically related to English
"dare" and other terms.[49] It is particularly related to the daring of the
warrior, and when such daring is combined with the support of a deity it is
of enormous help in battle. When, however, such support is not present, it
is mere audacity and brings about destruction for him who possesses it.[50]
Finally, the ox complains of tǝviš, a neuter cognate of Skt. táviṣi-
(feminine), "strength" (= Av. tǝvišī-), which is most frequently used of
Indra, although it is also used of the Maruts, and even the food and
drink that give warriors their strength.[51] In point of fact, tǝviš comes from
a verbal root meaning "to swell," and seems to denote the warrior's swell-
ing with energy after having eaten heartily and drunk of intoxicating
brews.[52]

The Creator of the Ox fully understands the ox's plea when he asks Aša
for a lord "that should restrain the furor of the followers of the lie" (Y.
29.2). The version of this myth from the Yašt to Miθra is even clearer:

47. spǝṇtạm ārmaitīm vaṇuhīm vǝrǝnē. hā mōi astū. us gǝuš stuyē tāyāatcā
hazaṇhatcā. us mazdayasnanạm vīsạm zyānayaēcā vīvāpatcā.
48. yōi duš.xraθwā aēšǝmǝm varǝdǝn rāmǝmcā
x·āiš hizubīš fšuyasū afšuyaṇtō
yāešạm nōit hvarštāiš vạs dužvaršta
tōi daēvāṇg dạn yā drǝgvatō daēnā
49. ⟨ P-I-E *√dhers-, comparing OPers. √darš-, Skt. √dhṛṣ-, Goth. ga-dars, Lith.
drįsti, Gk. θάρσος (noun form), etc. See Pokorny, p. 259.
50. This is particularly clear from the Old Persian and Homeric usages of the related
terms in those languages. See Lincoln, "The Myth of the 'Bovine's Lament,' " pp. 345–8.
51. Used in conjunction with Indra: RV 1.51.7, 56.4; 3.32.3; 4.16.14; 5.31.10,
32.2 and 8, etc.; with the Maruts: 1.39.2 and 4; 5.55.2; with food and drink: 1.187.1 / Y.
51.7. On the last usage, see Herman Lommel, "Himmlische und irdische Nahrung,"
Zeitschrift der deutschen morgenlandischen Gesellschaft 105 (1955):163–65.
52. See Pokorny, pp. 1080–81.

> [The cow], being robbed of her freedom and carried
> away as booty, calls for help with outstretched hands,
> longing for the cattle herd: "When will the manly
> Miθra, who is protector of wide pastures, driving from
> the rear, bring us to the cattle herd? When will he lead us
> back again to the path of Right (Aša), we who are being
> carried off to the dwelling of the Lie?" (*Yt.* 10.86)[53]

This text lacks an element, however, that was clear in the two texts previously cited. In these, the bovine finds protection in a priest, for so Vasiṣṭha is repeatedly called,[54] and so Zarathustra understood himself according to *Y.* 33.6.[55] In a fascinating way, both texts contrast the power of the priest and the power of the warrior. While the warrior's power lies in his arms and his ability to bear weapons (note the ox's mistaken preference for help "that has hands" in *Y.* 29.9), the power of the priest lies in his mouth or in his speech.[56] Thus, in the crucial verse of *Y.* 29, v. 8, Zarathustra is chosen to be the protector of cattle because he alone wishes to proclaim the teachings of Ahura Mazdā and the other divine powers. Further, when Spənta Mainyu wishes to equip him for the struggle, he does so by bestowing "sweetness of speech" on him. Similarly, Vasiṣṭha is repeatedly called the "choice" or "best of those who mutter prayers,"[57] and when he destroys the sons of Viśvāmitra, he accomplishes this merely by making the mystic sound "*huṃ*" (1.54.5).

Another feature that marks the priest in both accounts is his intimate connection with the celestial sovereigns. Zarathustra is chosen as the only man who hears the teachings of the benificent gods (*Y.* 29.8), and he speaks directly to Ahura Mazdā in the last two verses, acting on behalf of the entire community of those who care for the ox, receiving help from Mazdā (29.11c) and offering gifts in return (29.11c).[58] Moreover, Zarathustra is seen throughout the *Gāthas* as the prophet of Ahura Mazdā, who has received revelation from him and deals directly with the Wise Lord.[59]

---

53. yā varəta azimna bāδa ustānazastō zbayeiti avaiŋhe gavaiθīm paitišmarəmna: kaδa.nō arša gavaiθīm apayāt paskāt vazəmnō miθrō yō vouru.gaoyaoitiš kaδa.nō fraour-vaēsayāiti ašahe paiti pantąm drujō vaēsmənda azəmnąm.

54. He is called *brahman-* in 1.52.8; 53.14; 55.20 and 21; *brahmarṣi-* in 1.53.9 and 13; *brahmaṇaḥ suta-* in 1.53.8 and 55.13. The Vasiṣṭha family always supplies the *brahman* priest for the sacrifice, as they are the *brahmans* par excellence. See *TS* 3.5.2.1; *Jaiminīya Upaniṣad* 3.15.1; Rahurkar, p. 114.

55. See the literature cited above, note 74, chapter 4.

56. One is reminded of *RV* 10.90.12, where the priest is said to be formed from Puruṣa's mouth and the warrior from his arms.

57. *japatām vara-*: 1.54.6, 26; and 55.20; *japatām sreṣṭha-*: 1.55.13 and 21.

58. These two stanzas are usually assigned to Zarathustra, as in Lommel, *Gathas*, p. 40; J. Duchesne-Guillemin, *Hymns of Zarathustra* (Boston, 1963), p. 60; although Humbach, *Gathas*, 2:13, assigns them to the cow along with v. 9.

59. See, for instance, *Y.* 44.1, 44.8, 46.2, 50.6, etc. In all of these, the relation is that of a less powerful friend who asks a more powerful friend for help or instruction.

INDO-IRANIANS: CONFLICT OF PRIESTS AND WARRIORS

The connection of Vasiṣṭha with Mitra and Varuṇa is even closer,[60] for according to *RV* 7.33.10–11, the seer is their own son.[61] Varuṇa made him a seer (*RV* 7.88.4) and spoke with him directly (as in *RV* 7.87.4), and Vasiṣṭha visits with him in the god's thousand-doored palace (7.88.5). A greater proportion of hymns from the seventh book of the *Rg Veda,* composed by the Vasiṣṭha family, is directed to Mitra, Varuṇa, or both than is the case for any of the other family books.[62] Interestingly enough, the Viśvāmitra book has the fewest hymns addressed to Mitra or Varuṇa,[63] and a very high proportion addressed to Indra, while the Vasiṣṭha hymns contain relatively few references to this god.[64] The main theme, then, is this conflict of powers—the warrior's might opposed to that of the priest,[65] the one being centered in strength of arms, the other in sacred speech ultimately derived from the celestial sovereign. But if the opposition is clear, the outcome is not. In both the Indian and the Iranian versions, there is a period in which the warrior holds sway (*Y.* 29.1–7 / *Rām.*

60. On the relation of Vasiṣṭha to Varuṇa and its importance in the later history of Indian religions, see R. N. Dandekar, "Varuṇa, Vasiṣṭha and Bhakti," *Wijisekera Felicitation Volume* (Calcutta, 1970), pp. 77–82.

61. Actually a double paternity is given Vasiṣṭha. He is at once the son of Mitra-Varuṇa by the nymph Urvaśī and of the seer Agastya. But, as Geldner demonstrated, the divine parentage was meant to be taken as authentic, while the human one was simply a convenient way of assigning him to a *gotra*- or family. (K. Geldner and R. Pischel, *Vedische Studien,* 3 vols. [Stuttgart, 1897], 2: 138.)

62. Sixteen percent of the Vasiṣṭha hymns are directed to these gods in one form or another (17/104: 7 to Mitra-Varuṇa, 4 to Varuṇa, 4 to Indra-Varuṇa, and 2 to the Ādityās). The figures for the other families are: Atris, 14% (12/87); Bharadvājas, 4% (3/75); Vāmadevas, 3.5% (2/58); Gṛtsamadas, 2% (1/43); and Viśvāmitras, 1.5% (1/62).

63. See the figures in the preceding note. It is also worth noting that the one hymn of the Viśvāmitras addressed to Mitra and/or Varuṇa is, in fact, the only hymn in the entire *Rg Veda* addressed to Mitra alone. Varuṇa receives no hymns at all, something that occurs in no other family book, and he is seldom even mentioned. While an argument *ex silentio* is always risky, it would appear that the Viśvāmitras harbored some hostility to Varuṇa for one reason or another.

64. The figures here are: Bharadvājas, 48% (36/75); Viśvāmitras, 42% (26/62); Vāmadevas, 40% (22/58); Gṛtsamadas, 30% (13/43); Vasiṣṭhas, 22% (23/104); Atris, 14% (12/87). Thus the two families with the most hymns addressed to the celestial sovereigns are also those with the least addressed to the warrior god (Vasiṣṭhas and Atris), and conversely those with the most addressed to the warrior god have the fewest to the celestial sovereigns (Viśvāmitras, Bharadvājas, Vāmadevas, and Gṛtsamadas). Hillebrandt, *Vedische Mythologie,* 3: 316–17, noted other cultic differences that seemed to separate the Vasiṣṭhas and Viśvāmitras, namely that while the latter always associated the Maruts closely with Indra and with the Vṛtra battle, the former never did. The Vasiṣṭhas also tended to group Indra with the Vasus, gods of prosperity rather than with the Rudrās, and in general their accounts of Indra are quite impoverished. Also, in place of the soma offering they tended to prefer sūra. In the light of all this, it is possible that real cultic differences helped to bring about the historic conflict of the two families and informed the legends that later grew up around them.

65. J. Muir, one of the first to deal with the Indian texts at length, treated the story of Vasiṣṭha and Viśvāmitra under the heading, "Early Contests Between the Brahmans and the Kshattriyas," *Original Sanskrit Texts,* Vol. 1 (London, 1872), pp. 317–426. Others who shared this view were Maurice Bloomfield, "Contributions to the Interpretation of the Veda," *Journal of the American Oriental Society* 16 (1896), pp. 41–42; and G. S. Ghurye, *Caste and Race in India* (Bombay, 1969), p. 67.

1.53.1–8; 53.19–54.1; 54.19–24) and a period of hesitation or doubt, during which it is feared that the priest's power will be insufficient for the struggle (*Y.* 29.9 / *Rām.* 1.53.9–12, 55.14–15).[66] In both instances the priest does prove victorious, and in the Indian account there is a ringing affirmation of this from the lips of the defeated warrior (1.55.23–24).[67]

Another theme in this myth is of particular interest to us. The priest and the warrior do not come into conflict over abstract principles or some general search for power. Rather, they fight over the possession of cattle— a miraculous wish-cow in India, and the representative soul of the ox and pregnant cow in Iran.[68] As the analysis in Chapters 4 and 5 demonstrates, both warriors and priests had legitimate claims to the possession of cattle, warriors because they procured the animals in raids and priests because the animals are important for sacrifice. In a sense the myth of the bovine's lament poses the problem: who is the proper owner of cattle and for what purpose are cattle intended?

The answer is an unequivocal one: the purpose of cattle is to provide the materials for libation sacrifice. Vasiṣṭha, in refusing Viśvāmitra's initial offer, tells him that his cow is necessary for libations *(havyaṃ)* to the gods; offerings to ancestors; the Agnihotra, Bali, and Homa sacrifices; consecration, and ritual exclamation (1.52.13–14). Later he adds that the new and full moon sacrifices, and in fact all the rites, are rooted in her (1.52.23–24). Without the cow, ritual cannot proceed. Similarly, in *Y.* 29.7 it is stated that Ahura Mazdā himself created the "formula of libation" (*āzūtōiš . . . mąθrəm*)[69] as the purpose of the cow.[70] Now the names of these various sacrifices (Skt. *havya-*, *-hotra-*, and *homa-*; Av. *ā-zūtay-*) all come from the P-I-E verb *$\sqrt{gh'eu}$-*, "to pour,"[71] and can thus indicate

---

66. Dumézil, "A propos de la plainte," p. 47, also noted this hesitation, although he interpreted it differently.

67. In the Iranian version the victory is foreseen rather than experienced, but the tone of the final verse is such that the ultimate victory of Zarathustra could hardly be doubted.

68. Lommel, "Die Klage des Rindes," pp. 102–103; and *Gāthas*, pp. 34–35, saw the Soul of the Ox as a precosmogonic figure, but such an interpretation is unnecessary and leads to numerous difficulties.

69. On *āzūtay-* as the libation of butter, see F. C. Andreas and J. Wackernagel, "Die erste, zweite und fünfte Ghātha des Zurathustro," *Nachrichten der Göttingen Gesellschaft der Wissenschaften* (1931), p. 322; Humbach, "Milchprodukte im zarathustrischen Ritual," pp. 50–51; and Schlerath, "Opfergaben," p. 131. The assertions by Zaehner, p. 35; and Boyce, "Zoroaster the Priest," p. 32 and n., that this is the solid fat of an animal victim fly in the face of the etymology.

70. Within the context of the Gāthic hymn cattle are seen to have a somewhat broader purpose, as it is stated in v. 6 that they were shaped for the herdsman and the pastoralist— that is, the members of the third social class. This, however, does not find any correspondence in the Indian text and may be attributed to the political exigencies of Zarathustra's reform and not to I-I origin. This topic is too broad to treat at length, but it is my view that Zarathustra, a priest, made common cause with the members of the third class to oppose the warriors, as argued in the brilliant article of Kaj Barr, "Avestan *drəgu-*, *driγu-*," *Studia Orientalia Ioanni Pedersen* (Copenhagen, 1943), pp. 21–40.

71. See above, note 73, chapter 4.

only a liquid offering, be it of butter or of milk. This sort of rite would be the proper domain of the *zhautar priest, the ritual "pourer." The question is answered: cattle are ultimately destined for the priest, to be used for the ritual return of their products to the gods.

That this was not an entirely satisfactory arrangement from the point of view of the warriors is clear, not only from this myth but also from Zarathustra's numerous denunciations of the warriors' aggression against his cattle[72] and from the hymns of the *Atharva Veda* cursing the warrior who dares to steal or eat the priests' cow (*AV* 5.18 and 19).[73]

The Eating of Meat

This last specification is a provocative one, since it seems to indicate that one of the warriors' motives in raids was the procurement of meat. It coincides, moreover, with an important stanza from the *Rg Veda* in connection with the feud of Vasiṣṭha and Viśvāmitra. This verse appears in the hymn in which Vasiṣṭha denounces Viśvāmitra for the wrongs he has done him[74] and reads:

> O Indra and Soma, may glowing heat scald that evil
> one whose prayer is evil, like a cauldron on
> a fire.
> May you give unceasing enmity to that demonic,
> fearful-eyed, raw-meat-eating enemy of the
> priest.[75]
>
> [*RV* 7.104.2]

And, lest there be any doubt that this meat has been obtained in raids, verse 10 of the same hymn specifies:

> He who wishes to destroy the essence of our nourishment, O Agni,
> of our horses, of our cattle, of our bodies—
> That deceitful thief, perpetrating theft—may he
> go to a state of poverty, may he be humbled,
> him and his children![76]
>
> [*RV* 7.104.10]

72. See, *inter alia*, Y. 50.1-3, 33.3-6, 49.4, and 32.10-12.

73. Note that the warriors here are denounced as *aghnyád-*, "those who eat the cow that ought not to be killed."

74. On this hymn and its relation to the story of the feud between Vasiṣṭha and Viśvāmitra, see Geldner's introduction to the hymn *Der Rigveda*, 2: 273; Rahurkar, p. 126; and Lommel, "Vasiṣṭha und Viśvāmitra," pp. 206-207.

75. índrāsomā sám agháśaṃsam abhy àghāṃ tápur yayastu carúr
  agnivāṃ iva /
  brahmadvíṣe kravyáde ghorácakṣase dvéṣo dhattam anavāyáṃ
  kimīdíne //

76. yó no rásam dípsati pitvó agne yó áśvānāṃ yó gávāṃ yás
  tanūnām /
  ripú stená steyakṛ́d dabhrám etu ní ṣá hīyatāṃ tanvà tánā ca //

This same practice is suggested in Iran by the characterization of the warriors as xrvīšyant-, which literally means "desiring raw meat" (Av. xru- = Skt. kráviṣ-),[77] as in Yt. 10.8 and 36, 13.33, 15.49, 19.54, and Y. 9.30.

> Strike your weapon, O Golden Haoma, for the followers
> of Aša who wish to destroy the body of the bandit, who
> has become powerful and furious, desiring raw meat.[78]
>
> [Y. 9.30]

The purpose of eating this meat is, as the passage implies, to obtain strength from it. Food in general was frequently regarded as "strengthening" by the Indians and Iranians,[79] and SB 11.7.1.3 points out that meat is the best kind of food.[80] Medical texts specify that meat should be eaten for strength,[81] and in Iran there is the direct statement that the usig (the priest who helps the warriors in cattle raiding) delivers the ox up to furor (aēšma-), which is to say he converts the ox to beef, which is eaten for strength (see above, pp. 61f.). This, according to Zarathustra, was also the primordial sin of Yima:

> Of these evildoers, Yima, son of Vīvahvant, is well-
> known,
> Who, wishing to sharpen [his] men, made our [people] eat
> pieces of the ox.[82]
>
> [Y. 32.8]

All this is, however, strictly forbidden in the normal course of events. An old Indo-Iranian term for cattle is *aghn(i)ya- (Skt. ághn(i)yá-, aghn(i)yá- = Av. agənya-), which, as Ludwig Alsdorf has shown, means

---

77. This term, which is derived from P-I-E *kr(e)u- (Skt. kráviṣ-; Av. xru-; Gk. κρέας; Lat. cruor, crūdus; Middle Irish crú; Lith. kraūjas; AS hrēaw; English raw—see Pokorny, pp. 621–22), specifically denotes raw, bloody flesh, in contrast to *memso- (Skt. māṅsá-; Armenian mis; Goth. mimz; Old Prussian mensā; Tocharian B misa—Pokorny, p. 725), which simply denotes "flesh" in general.

78. paiti gaδahe vīvarəzdavatō xrvīšyatō zazarənō kəhrpəm nāšəmnāi ašaone, haoma zāire, vadarə jaiδi.

79. See Lommel, "Himmlische und irdische Nahrung," pp. 162–65; Jan Gonda, "Zur Frage nach dem Ursprung und Wesen des indischen Dramas," Acta Orientalia 19 (1943): 395–98. On meat eating, note also Ilya Gershevitch, "More Meat in Iranian," in Studies in Greek, Italic, and Indo-European Linguistics offered to Leonard R. Palmer (Innsbruck, 1976), pp. 63–64.

80. Cited by P. V. Kane, History of Dharmaśāstra, 5 vols. (Poona, 1941), 2: 773.

81. Thus the Caraka Saṃhita recommends beef for pregnant women to strengthen the foetus, and Anuśāsana 116.8 prescribes meat as the most nourishing food for those who are sick, wounded, weak, or given to too much sexual activity.

82. aēšam aēnaŋhąm vīvaŋhušō srāvī yimascīt yə mašyə̄ng cixšnušō ahmākə̄ng gāuš bagā x°arəmnō.
Cixšnušō has been translated as "wishing to sharpen"; contra Bartholomae, Altiranisches Wörterbuch, pp. 557–58. It is a singular nominative formed on the desiderative past middle participle of a verb *√xšnu- (= Skt. √kṣnu-), attested in Avestan by the form hu.xšnuta- in Yt. 10.24 and 39, derived from P-I-E *√ks-n-eu-, on which see Pokorny, p. 585.

"that which is not to be killed outside of sacrifice."[83] The specification "outside of sacrifice" is important, for killing in a sacrificial context is not understood as killing. Instead of destroying the animal, it elevates it into the realm of the sacred, and verbs signifying "to kill" are never used within the ritual.[84] This is not merely euphemism but the expression of the conviction that sacrifice is something other than killing, something other than the mere procurement of meat. The *Mānava Dharmaśāstra* is firm on this point:

"The eating of meat is for sacrifice"—this law
is known to come from the gods;
But otherwise this practice is said by law to be
of the demons.[85]

[*Mānava Dharmaśāstra* 5.31]

And again:

A priest may never eat cattle[86] unconsecrated by
sacred formulae,
But he may eat those consecrated by formulae while
standing in the eternal law.[87]

[5.36]

The Self-Existent himself created cattle for the
sake of sacrifice.
The sacrifice of this one is for the welfare of
all; therefore, in sacrifice slaughter is
not slaughter.[88]

[5.39]

"In the offering of honey and milk, in sacrifice
and in the act of worship to the fathers,
Here only cattle are to be killed, and not elsewhere,"
Manu proclaimed.[89]

[5.41]

---

83. Alsdorf, pp. 65–68. See also Wilhelm Schulze, *Kleine Schriften* (Göttingen, 1933), p. 207; and Larry DeVries, "*āpo aghn(i)yāḥ*," paper delivered to Midwest Regional Chapter of the American Oriental Society, 1975. Unconvincing are Bailey, "Dvārā Matinām," pp. 44–49 and Vittore Pisani, "Sanskrit *aghnyā,* griech. *aphneios,*" in *Studies in Greek, Italic, and Indo-European Linguistics offered to Leonard R. Palmer,* pp. 283–84.
84. Alsdorf, pp. 67–68. See also Hanns Oertel, *Euphemism in der vedischen Prosa* (Munich, 1942), pp. 7–13.
85. yajñāya jagdhir māṅsasyety eṣa daivo vidhiḥ smṛtiḥ /
ato 'nyathā pravṛttis tu rākṣaso vidhir ucyate //
86. The term rendered "cattle" here is Skt. *paśú-,* on which see note 98, chapter 4.
87. asaṃskṛtān paśūn mantrair nāyād vipraḥ kadācana /
mantrais tu saṃskṛtān ayāc chāśvataṃ vidhimāsthitaḥ //
88. yajñārthaṃ paśavaḥ sṛṣṭāḥ svayam eva svayambhuvā /
yajño 'sya bhūtyai sarvasya tasmāy yajñe badho 'badhaḥ //
89. madhuparke ca yajñe ca pitṛdaivatakarmaṇi /
atraiva paśavo hiṃsyā nānyātrety abravīn manuḥ //

INDO-IRANIANS: CONFLICT OF PRIESTS AND WARRIORS

The text goes on to propose a theory of *ahiṃsā*, noninjury to all animals (43–56), but this is clearly a later stratum, as it is not marked off by the term *iti*, the Sanskrit "unquote," which indicates a teaching that has been received from tradition.[90] Moreover, the earlier teaching finds a correspondence in Iran and therefore must be traced to the Indo-Iranian period:

> The cow calls to the priest who should sacrifice but does not:[91] "May you become childless and dogged by ill-fame, you who do not distribute me when I am cooked, but fatten me for your wife or your son or for your own belly!" (*Y.* 11.1)[92]

It is not that meat eating is forbidden; the priest ought to sacrifice and the meat should be cooked and distributed—this is the practice to the present day among orthodox Irani families.[93] But one should not retain the meat for oneself alone, nor should one kill an animal for the sake of its meat. Only the meat of an animal killed in a ritual context may be eaten, and this practice too has been preserved.[94]

The Indo-Iranian ideology of meat eating, at least as far as we can tell, does not seem to have been terribly different from that of the East African tribes: cattle ought not to be killed outside of sacrifice, but eating the meat of a sacrificial victim is perfectly all right—in fact, under these circumstances, meat is the best of foods. The ability of meat to give strength and vitality is so great, however, that warriors are tempted to eat it illicitly,[95] sometimes going so far as to steal cattle from priests in defiance of all rules of decency.

90. See Alsdorf's analysis, pp. 16–21. I am in agreement with him on all points except his opinion that vv. 5–25 of *Manu*, Book 5 represent the first stage of the dietary laws. Rather, I see these verses as a collection of disparate traditional rules that are laid out before the statement of the general principle, vv. 27–44. To my mind there is nothing that indicates historical priority. Thus I see his stages I and II as contemporaneous, but we are both in agreement that his stage III (vv. 44–55, the teaching of *ahiṃsá-*) is considerably later in origin. Alsdorf has also demonstrated that the *Āpastambha, Vasiṣṭha,* and *Kātyāyana Dharma Sūtra*s all taught that beef can be eaten only when taken from a sacrificial victim (pp. 57–61).

91. On this term, *zaotārəm,* see Karl F. Geldner, "Zaotā," in *Indo-Iranian Studies in Honour of Sanjana,* pp. 277–80.

92. gāuš zaotārəm zavaiti. uta buyå afrazaintiš uta dəuš.sravå hacimnō yō mąm x`āstąm nōit baxšahe. āat mąm tūm fšaonayehe nāiryå vā puθrahe vā haoyå vā maršuyå.

93. Boyce, "Ātaš-zōhr and Āb-zōhr," pp. 103–104.

94. Boyce, "Zoroaster the Priest," p. 31 n.; and "Mihragan Among the Irani Zoroastrians," in *Mithraic Studies,* p. 108.

95. Note the fascinating parallel among the Pythagoreans, where warriors and athletes refused the normative vegetarianism and insisted on eating meat, especially beef. See Marcel Detienne, "La cuisine de Pythagore," *Archives de Sociologie des Religions* 29 (1970):141–63, esp. pp. 145–47.

Sacrificial Stipends and the Cattle Cycle

This is not, however, simply a matter of decency or etiquette. Rather, it is a disruption of the normal cosmic order. The correct relation of warrior to priest is that of inferiority and submission, as we have seen, and in transactions involving cattle this is expressed by the donation of cattle to the priest by the warrior in return for his having performed sacrifice on the latter's behalf. The Indians knew this donation or stipend as *dakṣiṇā-*, the Iranians as *mizda-* (Avestan)[96] or *ašōdād* (Pahlavi).[97] It is not just a matter of a fee or payment for services rendered but is a crucial part of the cosmic flow of wealth, particularly of cattle, as has been recognized by Gonda, Heesterman, and others.[98] The standard stipend in India and in Iran is cattle,[99] although other animals may occasionally be substituted; horses, for example, are appropriate for a royal offering.[100] But for the most part cattle are given to the priest by the warrior and open up a heavenly source of more cattle as a result. This is evident in a hymn such as the following:

> All the gods aid him who delivers a bull to the
> priests.
> Having given a bull to the priests, he makes the
> mind broader.

96. Herman Lommel, "Zarathustras Priesterlohn," in *Studia Indologica: Festschift für Willibald Kirfel* (Bonn, 1955), p. 189. Actually, *mizda-* is used in this sense only in *Y.* 44, the hymn in which Zarathustra bemoans the payment promised him by a patron but never given. Elsewhere it acquires an eschatological meaning, being the payment that awaits the just at the end of time. Presumably the term was given this radical new sense by Zarathustra himself.

97. Boyce, "Zoroaster the Priest," p. 33 and note. Literally the term would signify "righteous offering."

98. Jan Gonda, "The Etymologies in the Ancient Indian Brāhmanas," *Lingua* 5 (1955):75–76; and "Gifts and Giving in the Rgveda," *Vishvesh-Varanand Indological Journal* 2 (1964):21–29; J. C. Heesterman, "Reflections on the Significance of Dakṣiṇā," *Indo-Iranian Journal* 3 (1959):241–58.

99. For India, see Macdonell and Keith, 1: 336; and such verses as *RV* 5.61.10; 6.27.8; 7.16.7; 8.46.22; or the delightful 4.24.10 in which the priest offers to "sell" Indra for ten cows. In Iran, the crucial text for seeing this is *Vd.* 9.37–38, in which priests are instructed in the proper stipends for various purifications. One purifies a priest for his blessing, the lord of a country for a male camel of the first quality, the lord of a province for a male horse of the first quality, the lord of a village for an ox of the first quality, the lord of a house for a pregnant cow, the wife of the lord of a house for a mature cow, a servant or laborer for a suckling calf, and a young child for the mewling young of any animal. The placing of a camel at the head of the list is a specifically Iranian development, and the horse is usually appropriate for royal occasions. With these exceptions, all the payments mentioned are cattle.

100. For the royal associations of the horse, see the literature cited in note 94, chapter 4. Thus the horse is the proper victim for the Indian coronation sacrifice (*rājasūya*) and for the purification of the highest official named in the Avesta, the lord of a country (*Vd.* 9.37). This provides the answer to a problem that plagued Lommel, "Zarathustras Priesterlohn," p. 190, namely, why the stipend specified in *Y.* 44.18 included ten mares and stallions but no cattle, when cattle were the base of the Iranian economy. The sacrifice must have been commissioned by a king, whose betrayal was thus that much more painful.

159

He sees the growth of cattle in his own cattle stall.
Let there be cattle! Let there be progeny! Let
there also be bodily strength!
Let the gods grant all to the one who is giving
a bull![101]

[AV 9.4.18b-20]

Thus far we have spoken in terms of a priestly cycle and a warrior cycle, which we have not attempted to relate to one another in any way. Each cycle has its own mythic prototype: the *Manu-*Yemo myth establishes the institution of sacrifice as the central feature of the priestly cycle, while the *Trito myth establishes the institution of cattle raiding as the central feature of the warrior cycle. Were it not for the sacrificial stipend, these two cycles would never coalesce; priest and warrior would remain separate; and wealth (that is to say, cattle) could not flow freely through the cosmos and through society. Heesterman speaks of the stipend as establishing or expressing "a generative alliance between the giving and receiving parties,"[102] in which there is "a continuous stream of dakṣiṇā wealth which is dispersed by the sacrificer and then returns to the sacrificer to be renewed again."[103] The notion of cyclicity is everywhere implicit: the priest benefits from the stipend, the gods benefit from the sacrifice, and the warriors benefit from the gods' return gifts.[104] All this follows from the stipend, which is understood in the Indian ritual texts to be the very cornerstone of the sacrifice.[105]

The flow of this cycle can be diagrammed (Figure 10), and the crucial role that the stipend plays in completing the circuit is evident. Yet for the warrior to steal cattle from the priest is to reverse the entire flow of the cosmic circuit, and for him to eat the animals is to remove them from the flow altogether (Figure 11). Such an act is truly a cosmic catastrophe and threatens the well-being of all society and the gods as well. It is this sort of issue which is at stake in the myth of the bovine's lament.[106]

This disruption of the cycle can be understood as, at least in part, a

101. jínvanti víśve táṃ devā́ yó brahmaṇá ṛṣabhám ajuhóti //
brahmaṇébhya ṛṣabhám dattvá várīyaḥ kṛṇute mánaḥ /
púṣṭiṃ só aghnyā́nāṃ své goṣṭhé 'va paśyate //
gávaḥ santu prajā́ḥ santv átho astu tanūbalám /
tát sárvam ánu manyátāṃ devā́ ṛṣabhadāyíne //
102. Heesterman, "Reflections on the Significance of Dakṣiṇā," p. 245.
103. Ibid., p. 248.
104. See Gonda, "Gifts and Giving," pp. 19-20, 26 and note; Keith, Religion and Philosophy, p. 259; Potdar, pp. 170, 192-93; and Betty Heimann, "The Supra-Personal Process of Sacrifice," Rivista degli Studi Orientali 32 (1957):731-39.
105. Gonda, "Etymologies in the Ancient Indian Brāhmaṇas," p. 75. One must note, however, that these texts were composed by priests and it was very much in their own interest to emphasize the importance of the stipends.
106. This applies with certainty only to the stealing of cattle. Eating might be inferred from the evidence of RV 7.104.2 and the use of the terms təviš- and aēšma- in Y. 29.1 but cannot be claimed with certainty for the I-I myth.

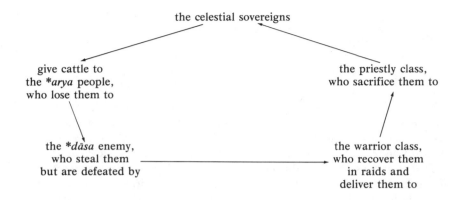

Figure 10. The (Ideal) Indo-Iranian Cattle Cycle

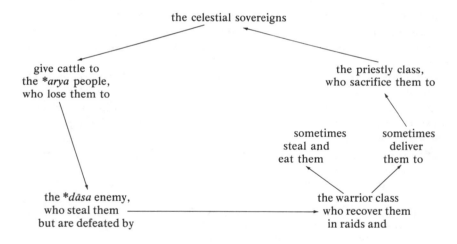

Figure 11. The (Real) Indo-Iranian Cattle Cycle

161

INDO-IRANIANS: CONFLICT OF PRIESTS AND WARRIORS

problem that stems from the failure of myth. At every other step of the cattle cycle, a myth furnishes a sacred precedent for the required action. Thus, priests sacrifice cattle just as (one could almost say, "because") *Manu sacrificed *Yemo's bull. The gods deliver abundant cattle in return for this offering, just as all animals came from the body of the first sacrificial victim. Cattle are stolen from their rightful owners, just as the serpent *Ngʷhi stole the primordial herd, and they are recovered just as *Trito won them back. In all these instances, man's activity in the present is guided by patterns established in the creative time of the beginnings, the creative time of myth. When one sacrifices or raids, one repeats the events that took place at the dawn of time—events through which one's distant ancestors established the proper order of this world.[107]

The myths of *Manu and *Yemo and of *Ngʷhi and *Trito are both ultimately of Indo-European origin. Both were preserved by the Indo-Iranians and played an important part in organizing their society. Together, they *almost* form a pattern for a complete revolution of the so-called cattle cycle. Yet one important step lacks a mythic precedent, namely, the sacrificial stipend. Nowhere is there any indication of an Indo-European or Indo-Iranian myth in which, for example, *Trito gives cattle to *Manu for sacrifice. Yet in order to complete the cycle, this is precisely the action that is required.

That the payment of the stipend was the generally accepted practice is abundantly clear.[108] But as it lacks a mythic precedent, it remained the weak link in the cattle cycle. Dispute could always arise over payment of the stipend and thus over the proper relation of warrior and priest. As neither side could appeal to a definitive myth, the argument could never be settled conclusively and might always arise anew. It is this situation that gives birth to the myth of the bovine's lament—a myth of specifically Indo-Iranian provenance and thus much later in time than the other myths we have discussed. Moreover, it is somewhat different in type from the others, being more descriptive than prescriptive. Rather than establishing the eternal norms as do the myths of the first sacrifice and the first cattle raid, this myth describes a problem that exists in this world—something that ought not to be but is.

In India, attempts were made to rectify this problem by way of mythic invention. In later versions of the cattle-raiding myth, such as that in which Indra and Vala[109] play the main parts, priestly figures such as the

107. For the finest statement of the role of myth and repetition, see Eliade, *Cosmos and History*, pp. 27–34 and passim.
108. Lommel, "Zarathustras Priesterlohn," p. 195; Humbach, *Gāthas*, 1: 59–61; Keith, *Religion and Philosophy*, p. 299.
109. Güntert, *Arische Weltkönig*, pp. 21–22, saw *Valá* as a reflex of *Vṛtrá*, both being derived from the P-I-E verb *√wel-*, "to cover," "enclose." J. A. B. van Buitenen has suggested to me another means of deriving *Valá* from *Vṛtrá* within the Indian context alone: *Valá* < *Vaḍá* < *Vṛtrá* (Private communication, 5/24/75). In any event, the mythic

INDO-IRANIANS: CONFLICT OF PRIESTS AND WARRIORS

Aṅgirasās are included. They sing praises to Indra before the battle in order to fortify him for combat, and following his victory he distributes cattle to them.[110] In Iran no such accommodation was made, and the split between warrior and priest seems to have worsened rather than mended. For contrary to the usually held opinion, the struggle in which Zarathustra was involved was not one of settled agriculturalist against nomad[111] or one in which tribal or cultic rivalries were at stake.[112] Rather, as Barr's research has shown, this was a class struggle in which warriors were pitted against priests and in which the priests under Zarathustra's leadership sought the support of the class of commoners.[113] His polemic against the warriors emphasizes all their misdeeds: *haoma* intoxication,[114] furor and violence,[115] stealing of cattle,[116] eating of meat[117] to produce furor,[118] and lastly, refusal to pay the sacrificial stipends they had promised.[119] Some of these are acts that were perfectly proper for warriors in the ancient Indo-European and Indo-Iranian traditions. But the last two, the eating of meat for furor and the failure to pay the proper stipends, were in violation of the basic principles that held society together. The conflict set in motion by these excesses brought an end to the old Indo-Iranian system in Iran, while in India change came in a slower and more gradual way.

---

resemblances are so strong and the linguistic resemblances so suggestive that they must be seen as being genetically related.

110. See J. C. Heesterman, "Vala and Gomatī," *Bulletin of the Deccan College Research Institute* 19 (1958):320-29; Hanns-Peter Schmidt, *Bṛhaspati und Indra* (Wiesbaden, 1968), pp. 139-213; and Doris Srinivasan, "The Myth of the Panis in the Rig Veda," *Journal of the American Oriental Society* 93 (1973):53-54.

111. Held by, *inter alia,* Bartholomae, "Zarathustra: His Life and Doctrine," pp. 12-13; Christensen, "Quelques notices sur les plus anciénnes périodes," p. 84; and Zaehner, p. 34.

112. The theory of Gertrud Hermes, "Zur Soziologie der Lehre Zarathustras," *Anthropos* 33 (1938):181-94, 424-44, esp. pp. 188-89, that Zarathustra's opponents represented the pre-Indo-European elements of the population cannot be accepted, because of their adherence to the *daēva*s, who are clearly I-E. Similarly, the theory of Nyberg, which he advanced in his *Die Religionen des alten Iran* (Leipzig, 1938), whereby the prophet's opponents are viewed as a "Mithra-Community," is founded on terribly slight evidence and has not gained wide acceptance.

113. Barr, cited in note 70, this chapter. The linguistic side of his argument has been accepted by Benveniste, "La prière Ahuna Vairya," *Indo-Iranian Journal* 1 (1957):83-84; and Lommel, "Awestisch Drigu, Vāstra und Verwandtes," *Pratidānam,* pp. 127-29, although it is not clear that either one fully grasped the revolutionary importance of his work.

114. *Y.* 48.10.

115. *Y.* 48.7, 49.4.

116. *Y.* 29.1.

117. *Y.* 32.8.

118. *Y.* 44.20.

119. *Y.* 44.18-19.

VII

CONCLUSIONS

Thus far we have dealt with the East African Nilotes and the Proto-Indo-Iranians separately, and the time has come to bring them together. Throughout the preceding chapters the occasional perception of similarities between the two cultures has been inescapable; for instance, the warriors of both cultures perceive themselves as ferocious beasts in battle. Leopards and lions are the animals usually emulated in East Africa,[1] and wolves played a similar part among the Indo-Iranians.[2]

Yet such similarities are only similarities of detail, any one of which might be misleading. The emulation of predatory animals is a well-known phenomenon among warrior groups of all peoples: Dakota warriors are said to become kit-foxes; Kwakiutl warriors, killer whales; and so forth.[3] In itself, this detail proves nothing. If comparison is to be useful, it must be based on more than a simple matching of specific points. It is not a matter of details but of total systems.

This is not to say that details are irrelevant or of no importance at all. On the contrary, the study of a system is impossible without a study of the details. It is, however, the way in which the details fit together, the over-arching pattern of organization, that is more important than any of the details themselves. This pattern has been the object throughout this study.

If details cannot serve to prove the case, neither are they sufficient to

1. See above, p. 30.
2. See above, pp. 125-27.
3. Clark Wissler, "Societies and Ceremonial Associations in the Oglala Division of the Teton-Dakota," *Anthropological Papers of the American Museum of Natural History* 41 (1921):14-16; Franz Boas, *Kwakiutl Ethnography* (Chicago, 1966), p. 114.

164

disprove it. Thus, the fact that the Nilotic tribes appear to have had only one celestial sovereign[4] while the Indo-Iranians had several[5] is not in itself a significant argument against the comparison of the two religious systems, provided that the Indo-Iranian deities share important characteristics with the single sovereign of the East Africans—creation of the world, maintenance of the cosmic order, location in the above, and giving of goods in return for sacrifice. When we see that this is the case,[6] we can conclude that the two systems are comparable on this point despite the difference in detail.

As analyzed here, the East African religious system is composed of two major elements, which we have dubbed the priestly cycle[7] and the warrior cycle.[8] Each of these cycles can be seen to have all the following: characteristic deities, specialized human representatives, certain specific actions of a ritual nature, and a mythology that establishes the basis for these actions.

In the instance of the priestly cycle, the relevant deity is the celestial sovereign, who established the world and maintains it from on high.[9] His name is Kwoth, "Spirit," Ngai, "Rain," or Nhialic, "In the above," and it is he who made the world as it is.[10] He has created all things, but most importantly he has created cattle, which are his greatest gift to his people.[11]

The human representatives in the priestly cycle are of course the priests. Among the Dinka and Masai, they occupy a position of hierarchical supremacy, although this has largely been lost among the more egalitarian Nuer.[12] Their position is hereditary and carries with it a good amount of temporal power,[13] but their chief function is to organize and preside over rituals, the most important of which is sacrifice.[14]

While simple in practice, the rite of sacrifice carries an extremely subtle and complex ideology. At the most basic level, an ox or an appropriate substitute is immolated as an offering to the celestial sovereign.[15] To this simple act, numerous levels of meaning are added: the victim is, in a sense, a substitute for the life of a man;[16] the division of its meat among those attending serves to reestablish the social order, inasmuch as the parts of the body are allotted along standardized preferential lines;[17] and

4. See above, pp. 16-19.
5. See above, pp. 52-60.
6. See below, pp. 16-17, 54-59.
7. See above, p. 37.
8. See above, p. 38.
9. See above, pp. 16-17.
10. See above, pp. 17-18.
11. See above, pp. 19-23.
12. See above, pp. 41-43.
13. See above, p. 41.
14. See above, pp. 31-33, 40-41.
15. See above, p. 32.
16. See above, p. 33.
17. Ibid.

the killing of the beast is also a sanctification of its meat for eating, as beef, although the favorite food of the Nilotes, may not be eaten unless the animal has been killed in ritual fashion.[18] All these factors enter into the sacrifice, as do two others which seem most important: the sacrifice is a gift exchange with the celestial sovereign whereby new wealth in cattle is obtained,[19] and it is a repetition of an important part of the creation myth.

This section of the myth, which appears in its clearest form among the Masai, tells of the first sacrifice and thus establishes the rite for all time. The first Masai was instructed by Ngai to offer up the first head of cattle, and when he did so, Ngai rewarded him with an enormous outpouring of cattle from the sky.[20] Each Masai who sacrifices repeats this action, becoming again the first Masai and winning new cattle in return.

The warriors also have their own specialized gods, best seen in the Nuer Spirits of the Air and perhaps in the Dinka clan divinities of the warrior clans.[21] They are of lesser stature than the celestial sovereign and function chiefly to aid warriors in battle and to ensure success in cattle raiding.[22] They are located in the sky below the celestial sovereign, rushing about with the winds between heaven and earth as almost literal "storm troopers."[23]

The human representatives of the warrior cycle are obviously the warriors—the group of young men set off by initiation and organized in age-sets[24] who bear responsibility for the tribe's martial affairs. They are given to special practices for increasing their strength or attaining a state of frenzy for battle, most notably the eating of huge quantities of meat,[25] although the drinking of intoxicants is also practiced.[26] In addition, they will don the skins of lions or leopards for battle, considering themselves transformed into these wild beasts.[27]

The chief function of the warriors is cattle raiding, an act that assumes a ritual nature.[28] Raids are always preceded by consultation with priests, reading of omens, and obtaining of charms.[29] Prayers and magical rites will be performed for success in raiding, as the well-being of the entire tribe depends on the continual obtaining of cattle from other peoples. But again, the chief way in which the practice is ritualized is through the repetition of an important segment of the creation myth.

18. See above, pp. 43–44.
19. See above, p. 33.
20. See above, pp. 20–21, 33.
21. See above, pp. 30–31.
22. Ibid.
23. I owe the use of this term to Professor J. A. B. van Buitenen, who used it with regard to the Maruts.
24. See above, pp. 24–27.
25. See above, pp. 44–46.
26. See above, p. 30.
27. Ibid.
28. See above, pp. 27–31.
29. See above, pp. 29, 39–40.

CONCLUSIONS

Thus the myth tells of how the first Dinka stole the first calf from the first Nuer, and how the Nuer took it back by force, or alternatively how the first Masai obtained cattle from Ngai at the first Dorobo's expense.[30] All the tribes involved interpret these myths in their own favor and take them as an eternal sanction for their raiding activities. Cattle were originally theirs at the beginning of time, they argue, and should continue to be theirs. Any other tribe that possesses cattle has obtained them by illegal means, in their opinion, and they can rightly be taken back by force.[31] The warrior who goes out raiding repeats the deeds of his primordial ancestor and becomes contemporaneous with the time of the beginnings. Moreover, he acts at the creator's command.[32] His quest is a sacred one, crucial to his tribe's survival, and it has been divinely sanctioned since the beginning of time.

One final point must be noted in the East African situation: there is clear evidence of friction between priests and warriors, brought about by the warriors' occasional contestation or defiance of the usual hierarchical supremacy of the priests.[33] Among the Dinka the priests have managed to preserve their position,[34] and among the Masai the situation seems to be fairly stable, but the Nuer appear to have originally been a warrior clan of the Dinka who split off and organized a new tribe free from the domination of priests and characterized by a ferocious egalitarianism of warriors.[35]

The chief characteristics of the East African religious system could be organized in an outline fashion as follows:

PRIESTLY CYCLE
A. Deity: celestial sovereign
  1. Located in the above
  2. Responsible for creation
  3. Responsible for the maintenance of world order
B. Representatives: priests
  1. Preside over ritual
  2. Hierarchically superior to warriors
  3. Hereditary position
C. Ritual: sacrifice
  1. Cattle preferred as victim
  2. Substitute victims acceptable

30. See above, pp. 20-22.
31. See above, p. 23.
32. Ibid.
33. See above, pp. 41-43, 46-48.
34. See above, pp. 46-47.
35. See above, pp. 47-48.

    3. Victim given to celestial sovereign in exchange
       for return of more cattle
    4. Meat eaten only as the result of sacrifice
D. Myth: first sacrifice
    1. Tells of first man's first offering
    2. Establishes model or charter for all offerings thereafter

WARRIOR CYCLE

A. Deity: warrior gods
    1. Located in the atmosphere
    2. Martial in nature
    3. Aid warriors in raiding
B. Representatives: warriors
    1. Chief function is cattle raiding
    2. Hierarchically inferior to priests
    3. Set off by initiation
    4. Organized in age-sets
    5. Given to strengthening practices for state of furor
      (a) Eating of meat for strength
      (b) Use of intoxicants
    6. Emulate predatory beasts
C. Ritual: cattle raid
    1. Obtain stock from traditional enemy
    2. Assisted by priests with charms, omens, and the like
    3. Idealized as heroic endeavor
D. Myth: first raid
    1. Tells of first man's first exploit
    2. Establishes model or charter for all raids
    3. Gives justification for aggression against traditional enemy

EVIDENCE OF CONFLICT BETWEEN
PRIESTS AND WARRIORS

A. Warriors uneasy at subordination to priests
B. Meat eating often a major issue

    Turning to the Indo-Iranians, we see much of the same configuration, starting with the division into priestly cycle and warrior cycle. Further, we find the same possibility of subcategorization within each cycle by deity, human representative, ritual, and myth. Within these categories, much differs from the East African system by way of detail, but the broad strokes are remarkably similar.

    With regard to the deities characteristic of the priestly cycle, we find not one but many celestial sovereigns, a whole group of reigning deities named

*Asuras,[36] who were responsible for the creation of the world and the maintenance of the world order. Among these was an otiose sky god, *Dyaus, whose name remained but whose active role in the Indo-Iranian period was minimal.[37] He was largely replaced by a dual deity, *Mitra-*Varuna, located in the high heavens and regarded as sovereign deities, *Mitra being particularly concerned with establishing and preserving the ties that join men together[38] and *Varuna with magic and cosmic law, most particularly the subtle principle of *ṛta, the cosmic order.[39] Along with these great gods there existed a set of lesser divinities, six or seven in number (Skt. Ādityās; Av. Aməša Spəntas), including *Mitra and *Varuna, but whose individual names in most cases cannot be recovered.[40] Finally there was a demiurge, *Twarštar, who effected the physical process of creation and among whose creations cattle occupied an important place.[41]

The human representatives of the priestly cycle among the Indo-Iranians could be grouped as a single class (Skt. brāhmaṇa-; Av. zaotar-), and as such occupied the highest rank of the class system.[42] They were, however, specialized, and several different types of priest are known to us —the *zhautar or libation pourer,[43] the *kavi or magical singer concerned with the powers of life and immortality,[44] the *usig or specialist in assisting cattle raids,[45] the *atharvan who had charge of the sacred fire,[46] and the numerous bearers and assistants in the performance of the sacrificial ritual.[47] Ultimately, however, almost all these were concerned with the ritual, and their chief function on earth was the proper performance of sacrifice, the link that connected man with the gods.[48]

Sacrifice took several forms, most importantly *yagna or immolation of animal victims, which were ideally cattle for most occasions,[49] but the substitution of other victims was allowed, including the horse for royal offerings.[50] *Zhautrā or libation was another important form of sacrifice, and milk-products could be offered,[51] or the intoxicating *sauma, this

36. See above, p. 51 and note 7.
37. See above, pp. 52–53.
38. See above, pp. 54–56.
39. See above, pp. 56–59.
40. See above, p. 53.
41. See above, pp. 59–60.
42. See above, p. 60.
43. See above, p. 62.
44. See above, p. 61.
45. See above, pp. 61–62.
46. See above, p. 61.
47. Ibid.
48. See above, pp. 62–63.
49. See above, pp. 63–65.
50. See above, p. 65.
51. See above, pp. 63–64.

being a rite specifically directed to the warrior gods.[52] As in East Africa, many different levels of meaning were present in the sacrifice—the feeding and entertaining of the gods, the presentation of a gift, and the sanctifying of meat, which could only be eaten as a result of sacrifice.[53] With regard to the sacrifices of the priestly cycle, however, the sacrifice can be seen as a very specialized sort of gift exchange. That which is presented is always (ideally) either cattle or cattle products, and one word, *gau, denotes them both.[54] A standard request is usually made in return for this gift, a request for men and cattle.[55]

This request seems to imply an earlier stage of the sacrifice, in which a man and a head of cattle were offered in return for an increase of men and cattle. Such a rite does not occur among the Indo-Iranians, but judging from archaeological evidence it may have been a part of their Proto-Indo-European ancestors' practice.[56] Moreover, an Indo-European myth that was preserved among the Indo-Iranians tells of the first sacrifice, in which the first priest, *Manu, sacrificed the first king, *Yemo, along with the first bovine and created the world from their bodies.[57] This myth set the pattern for all sacrifice to follow, telling how the repetition of this primordial offering serves to recreate the world and bring forth the riches of creation each successive time.

Turning to the warrior cycle, we note that it too has its own specialized deities. But whereas the warrior gods of the Nilotic tribes were of considerably less importance than the celestial sovereign, at least one of the Indo-Iranian gods need take second place to none. This was *Indra, also known as *Vṛtraghna, the Smasher of Resistance, chief aid of men in battle.[58] Another god of the warriors was *Vayu, the personification of the wind, who took on a distinctly martial cast in certain circumstances.[59] In addition to these two gods, there was a whole set of lesser deities organized in a troop of warriors dashing madly through the skies (Skt. Maruts; Av. Fravašis),[60] closely associated with the storm and with the spirits of the dead (Skt. Rudrās; Av. Fravašis).[61]

Moving from the divine level to the human, we note the existence of distinct bands of young men (*marya) organized in warrior troops.[62] But while their existence is clear, the texts do not always allow us a complete

52. See above, pp. 99–100.
53. See above, pp. 68, 156–57.
54. See above, p. 64.
55. See above, p. 68.
56. Gimbutas, "Proto-Indo-European Culture," p. 170.
57. See above, pp. 69–95, esp. p. 87.
58. See above, pp. 97–101.
59. See above, p. 96.
60. See above, p. 129.
61. See above, pp. 129–30.
62. See above, p. 125.

CONCLUSIONS

view of their activities. They did fit within the warrior class (Skt. *kṣatriya;* Av. *raθaēštar*), which ranked below that of the priests.[63] They were set off by an initiation in which they encountered a mock monster,[64] and they cultivated a state of furor (**aišma*),[65] drinking the intoxicant **sauma* and eating meat to attain great strength.[66] While in their state of rage, they thought of themselves as wolves (**vṛka*) and took on the nature of these ferocious predators.[67] But the way in which they most resembled wolves was the danger that they posed to cattle herds, for their chief raison d'être was the practice of cattle raiding.[68]

In their raids they identified themselves as Indo-Iranian heroes (**arya*), preying on the aboriginal enemies they encountered (**dāsa*).[69] They were assisted by a special priest (the **usig*), who was primarily concerned with aiding warriors in cattle raids.[70] The raid took on a markedly ritual aspect, for certain rites had to be performed in order to ensure its success. Most importantly, the aid of the warrior god had to be secured, and in order to do this a special type of sacrifice was performed. Libations of **sauma* were poured and the god's praises were sung in order to give him strength, so that he might give strength to the warriors in return.[71] If this were done properly, victory was assured.

This ritual of cattle raiding also found its support in the precedent of myth, for a very old and important myth told of the first such raid. According to that story, the hero **Trito, with the help of **Indra **Vṛtraghna, slew a three-headed serpent, **Ngʷhi, and took his cattle from him. Actually, these were not rightfully his cattle to begin with, as **Ngʷhi had himself stolen them in an earlier encounter.[72] The myth tells how the taking of cattle from aborigines by Indo-Europeans is justified, for these cattle came into the native's possession only by stealth. Cattle raiding merely redresses this earlier wrong. The Indo-European or Indo-Iranian warrior who performed such a raid acted as the first warrior did and found his model in the events of mythic time.

Finally, as in East Africa, there is evidence of tension and conflict between priests and warriors, and there is even a myth to this effect in which a bovine laments to a priest his ill-treatment at the hands of warriors.[73] In some instances warriors stole cattle from priests,[74] and their eating of raw

---

63. See above, pp. 60, 138–39.
64. See above, p. 128.
65. See above, pp. 127–28.
66. See above, pp. 130–31, 154–55.
67. See above, pp. 125–127.
68. See above, pp. 131–32.
69. See above, pp. 131–32, 135–36.
70. See above, pp. 61–62.
71. See above, pp. 99–100.
72. See above, pp. 103–22, esp. p. 122.
73. See above, pp. 140–54.
74. See above, p. 154.

meat that had not come from a sacrificial victim also led to friction,[75] with the result in Iran of what amounted to class war along priest-warrior lines.[76]

Setting out these characteristics of the Indo-Iranian system, we find a picture strikingly similar to that obtained from the analysis of East Africa.

PRIESTLY CYCLE

A. Deities: celestial sovereigns
  1. Otiose sky god
  2. A dual deity
    (a) Sovereigns
    (b) Masters of the world order
    (c) Located in the above
  3. A set of minor deities
  4. A demiurge
B. Representatives: priests
  1. Most of whom preside over ritual
    (a) Pourer of libations
    (b) Tender of fire
    (c) Other attendants
  2. Other specialists
    (a) Magician of life force
    (b) Assister of cattle raids
  3. Hierarchically highest class
C. Ritual: sacrifice
  1. Immolation
    (a) Cattle are preferred victims
    (b) Substitute victims acceptable
    (c) Horse preferred for royal sacrifice
  2. Libation
    (a) Of milk-products (milk and butter)
    (b) Of intoxicants
  3. Offerings given to celestial sovereigns in exchange for return of men and cattle
  4. Meat eaten only as result of sacrifice
D. Myth: first sacrifice
  1. First priest sacrifices first king and first bovine
  2. World created as a result
  3. Establishes model for all future sacrifice

WARRIOR CYCLE

A. Deity: warrior gods
  1. Warrior god

75. See above, p. 155.
76. See above, p. 162.

    2. Wind personified
    3. Lesser spirits in troop
      (a) Linked to storm
      (b) Subset of the broader group of the spirits of the dead
  B. Representatives: warriors
    1. Chief function cattle raiding
    2. Hierarchically inferior to priests
    3. Bands of young warriors
      (a) Set off by initiation
    4. Given to state of furor
    5. Use of strengthening practices
      (a) Intoxicants
      (b) Meat eating
    6. Emulate wild beasts
  C. Ritual: cattle raid
    1. Obtain stock from traditional enemy
    2. Assisted by special priest
    3. Requires invocation and strengthening of warrior god
    4. Idealized as heroic endeavor
  D. Myth: first raid
    1. Tells of first warrior's exploit against a three-headed serpentine monster, the prototype of all aboriginals
    2. Establishes a model for all raids
    3. Gives justification for all raids against traditional enemy

EVIDENCE OF CONFLICT BETWEEN PRIESTS AND WARRIORS

  A. Myth telling of such a conflict
  B. Warriors' raids on priests a major issue
  C. Warriors' meat eating also an issue

Point by point, there are many similarities between these two lists. However, one consistent difference is that, although in East Africa there is one celestial sovereign, one priestly group, one form of sacrifice, and one set of warrior gods, the Indo-Iranians had a multiplicity of representatives for each of these categories. Whether this is because of some difference whereby the Nilotes strove for clarity and the Indo-Iranians for elaboration in their symbolic formulations, or whether it is because we have primary sources for the Indo-Iranians that span thousands of years but for the Nilotes only seventy years or so of reporting by outsiders is not clear. All we can do is note the difference, not explain it.

What is more significant than the point-by-point resemblances, however, is the overarching similarity between the two systems. Both bind priest and celestial sovereign together through a sacrifice that involves a

CONCLUSIONS

gift exchange of cattle chartered by a primordial myth. Both set the warrior in opposition to traditional enemies in cattle raiding, supported by warrior gods and sanctioned by myth. Both strive to integrate these two separate cycles into a broader cycle by forcing the warriors to yield up cattle to the priests for sacrifice,[77] but both run into difficulty on this point, as warriors are not always anxious to give up their hard-won wealth.[78]

All in all, the similarities become overwhelming when considered in a systematic fashion. But how are we to explain such strong resemblances between two such separate peoples? Clearly, appeals to common origin, historical contact, or cultural diffusion cannot be accepted.[79] As indicated at the outset, the most likely solution lies in the fact that the ecological base of both cultures is the possession of cattle.[80]

Certainly this may seem simplistic at first, and yet we have seen the tremendous importance of the role that cattle play in the religions of these cattle-keeping peoples. Cattle figure prominently in their myths, their rites, their gifts to the gods, and their requests of them. Cattle are a constant concern in the daily life of the Nilotes and the Indo-Iranians, and religion is no exception to this.

Still, this does not answer the question of why such similar religious systems are found in the two cultures. That cattle would be important in the religion of cattle keepers is obvious. But it does not account for the dichotomy of priests and warriors, sovereign gods and warrior gods, conflicts over the rules regarding the eating of meat, and the other similarities perceived in this study.

In order to deal with this question, it is necessary to recognize the truly generative role of ecology with regard to culture and religion. It is not enough simply to state that culture is based in ecology. One must go further and put it more strongly: the given features of ecology serve to mold or shape culture, which in turn serves to mold or shape religion. This can be seen in the case at hand.

Given the practice of cattle keeping as a starting point, two features seem to follow almost automatically, namely, cattle raiding and cattle sacrifice. The first is born of the natural desire to increase one's own stock of the most prized and valuable commodity. The second is born of the equally natural desire to share one's goods with whatever deities there may be out of gratitude, desire for blessings, desire to feed and maintain the deities, or other such motives.

The existence of these two separate modes of action, both of which have cattle as their focus, leads eventually to the development of specialists who

77. See above, pp. 33–34, 158–61.
78. See above, pp. 37–39, 43–46, 161–62.
79. See above, pp. 3–6.
80. See above, p. 6 ff.

174

make it their business to perform either raiding or sacrifice as well as possible. These are the warriors and priests, who develop subtleties of practice within their respective areas of concern and pass their knowledge on to the generations that follow. As the two groups refine their specialties to an ever greater degree, they become more separated from one another and tend to harden into classes.

Devoted to different activities, each class tends to develop separate modes of valued conduct. The warrior cultivates strength, bravery, loyalty to comrades, and so forth; the priest cultivates his ties to the sacred and his knowledge of correct ritual procedure. Ultimately two completely different *Weltanschauungen* evolve.

The relation of these two classes to the world of the sacred poses a curious problem. There is a sense in which the priest is closer to the sacred, and this leads to a hierarchical superiority, as Dumont has argued in the case of India.[81] But in another sense neither group is truly separate from the sacred; they merely perceive and deal with it in different ways. The priest's relation in sacrifice is clear, but the warrior also feels the need of the support of some transcendent power in his life and thus resorts to a class of deities more appropriate to his endeavors, namely, the warrior gods, who seem to be shaped in his own image.

Moreover, both groups feel the need of a sacred precedent for their actions and have recourse to myth. These myths deal not so much with the gods but with the deeds of the first men at the time of the beginnings, when the world was set in order and the creative power of the divine realm was much more in evidence than it is now. Myths came to be formulated that told of the first sacrifice and the first cattle raid, which set the pattern for all sacrifice and all raiding to follow. As priests and warriors pursued their individual tasks, they felt themselves to be repeating these exemplary events of the creative mythic time and thus reestablishing their contact with the sacred.

The fact of cattle, then, gives rise to the practices of sacrifice and cattle raiding. These, in turn, generate classes of specialists—priests and warriors—who in turn establish their own sets of deities and myths. The process might be charted, as in Figure 12.

If this analysis is correct, the result is two systems that are in large measure separate: a priestly system or cycle and a warrior system or cycle. They are related in that the members of both groups belong to one tribe or group and in that they are concerned with the well-being of that group, specifically with regard to cattle. Yet there are tensions between the two and serious differences between their outlooks on certain issues. Two of these differences are the disposition of cattle resources, namely, should they be kept for their productive value or should they be sacrificed, and

81. Louis Dumont, *Homo Hierarchus* (Chicago, 1970).

175

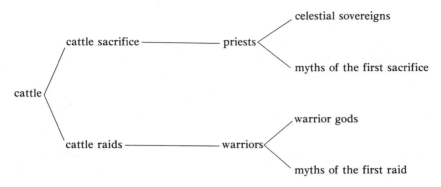

Figure 12. The Genesis of Cattle-Keepers' Religion

the rules relating to the eating of meat, namely, should beef be eaten for its strength-giving value or only in a ritual context. On these and other issues conflict is always likely to break out.

In some instances accommodation can be made between priests and warriors. This may be done by establishing a clear and universally accepted hierarchy, or myths that defuse potentially volatile areas, or both.[82] The first technique was employed with success by the Dinka and Masai,[83] and both were employed by the Indians.[84] When either strategy is successfully adopted, the priestly cycle and the warrior cycle can be brought together to form a complete unit—a cattle cycle that governs the flow of cattle (the society's most prized resource) through the entire world, human and divine.

In some instances, however, the tensions between priests and warriors are exacerbated to the point where rapprochement is no longer possible. The result of this is schism, as among the Nuer,[85] or class war, as among the Iranians.[86] In large measure such developments may rightly be seen as social, political, and economic, deriving from an intense struggle between competing classes for the control not merely of valued goods but of the very means of production, namely, cattle. With regard to these points a Marxist analysis has much to offer.[87]

82. See above, pp. 41–42, 46–47, 161–62.
83. See above, pp. 41–42.
84. See above, pp. 60, 161–62.
85. See above, pp. 47–48.
86. See above, p. 162.
87. An attempt at such an analysis of herding practices in India has been made by Walter Ruben, "Arische Hirten und vorarische Bauern im alten Indien," in *Das Verhältnis von Bodenbauern und Viehzüchtern in historischer Sicht* (Berlin, 1968), pp. 48–61, but his approach is less sophisticated than one might hope for. Certainly, more work needs to be done along these lines.

CONCLUSIONS

It must be noted, however, that there is an important religious dimension to this struggle, in that priests and warriors alike cast their claims to the disputed herds in a religious form. Both groups cite myths that justify their possession of cattle; both maintain that they need the animals for ritual purposes. A simple view of religion as the "opiate of the people" does not do justice to the complexity of the situation, for while religion is undoubtedly used by the ruling priestly class to justify its position and holdings, it is equally used by the subordinate warrior class to challenge priestly supremacy. Religion thus is not simply a means whereby one class suppresses another but is also a means of encouraging and sanctioning opposition to the existing order. Religion is thus a sword that cuts both ways —a tool of oppression and of rebellion, an instrument of class struggle open to use by either side.

One must also not be too quick to impute narrow self-interest as the sole motivation of both priests and warriors. Both groups claim to be concerned for the broader well-being of their people at large, and such claims ought not be dismissed too lightly, for both groups seem sincere in their belief that their myths and their practices show how the general welfare may best be secured, that is, how ever more cattle may be obtained. The struggle is thus not just a question of competing interests, although this element is undeniably present, but on a broader scale it is a question of competing ideologies, world views, and myths. Two separate religious outlooks exist, both of which equally have their origin in a society based on the herding of cattle, and the reconciliation of these outlooks is not always an easy matter.

As indicated at the outset, this study intended to raise the problem of the relationship between culture and religion: given similar cultures, do resemblances appear between religions as well?[88] In the course of the investigation, numerous questions of detail pertinent to East African ethnology, Indo-European linguistics, and other allied fields have been examined. On all these specific points there is always the possibility of error, and it is to be expected that certain of the arguments will be subject to debate and may even be proven incorrect. Yet, as maintained throughout the study, the case does not rest on any one of these details but rather on the totality of the religious systems being discussed.

I have tried to show that the basic structures of the religious life and the religious imagination of two widely separate peoples exhibit similarities that are overwhelming in their scope. Not only are there similar myths, deities, rituals, and so forth, but the religious systems taken as a whole show the most impressive similarities of all. And in both examples we have examined, cattle play a role of central importance in the religious life of these cattle-keeping peoples.

88. See above, p. 12.

CONCLUSIONS

Recourse has often been made to the ecological fact of cattle keeping to explain the similarities that have appeared between the religion of the East Africans and that of the Indo-Iranians. Certainly no theory of common origin or historical diffusion can account for the resemblances we have observed.[89] Rather, they seem to stem from the fact that both groups were cattle keepers—similar cultures, similar religions.

In this one example of cattle-keeping pastoralists, we have seen that culture does shape religion and is itself shaped by the givens of ecology. It might be said that man's everyday concerns are not separate from his religious concerns and the way in which he lives his life has an enormous influence on the ways in which he perceives and deals with the sacred. It is not enough for him to herd cattle or plant yams or hunt buffalo, but he continually seeks to imbue the necessary activities of his daily life with a significance and a meaning that transcend his earthly existence. It is not simply that cattle herders project cattle herding onto the sacred, although that is in part true; more importantly, however, they strive to draw the sacred into their world of cattle herding.

In principle, the same might be supposed to be true of all peoples, whatever their ecological situation, but such an audacious claim lies beyond the scope of the present study. Other cultural systems will have to be examined and their evidence carefully weighed.[90] For the moment, we have at hand the one example and the suggestion of a broader theory.

89. See above, pp. 3-6.
90. An interesting beginning would be the comparison of the religious system of another group of semi-settled cattle-keeping pastoralists to the results of the present study. Along these lines, see Cristiano Grottanelli, "Per un Mitico Giacobbe Domestico, Pastore e Mago," in *Magia: Studi di Storia delle Religioni in Memoria de Raffaela Garossi* (Rome, 1976), pp. 127-45, who compares Nuer mythic materials to those of patriarchal Israel, noting that where the two diverge, it is due to the increased importance of agriculture in the latter society.

APPENDIX
On the Use of Archaeology in the Reconstruction of Indo-Iranian Religion

On several occasions valued colleagues, most notably Kees Bolle and Edgar Polomé, have suggested to me that my conclusions regarding the Indo-Iranian side of my research might be strengthened by the use of archaeological evidence. While the suggestion is an interesting one, I have been hesitant to include such evidence in the body of this book on two accounts. The first is my lack of training in archaeology and my consequent fear that I cannot adequately assess the evidence that is available. The second is that I am in general agreement with Rüdiger Schmitt in insisting that the study of the Proto-Indo-European and Proto-Indo-Iranian peoples is first and foremost a linguistic discipline, to which archaeology can add relatively little.[1]

The basis for this contention is, of course, the great uncertainty in locating a group of people whom we can identify with the Proto-Indo-Europeans or Proto-Indo-Iranians. Both of these groups are nothing more than hypothetical constructs, strongly posited on the basis of systematic linguistic comparison. Thus, on the strength of numerous shared grammatical structures and lexical items, often of great complexity and subtlety, we believe that the Indic and Iranian languages descended from a common parent language, and, by extension, that the speakers of Indic and Iranian descended from the speakers of that parent language. It is the speakers of this parent language whom we posit as the Proto-Indo-Iranians. Further, as systematic comparison reveals the same type of

1. Rüdiger Schmitt, "Proto-Indo-European Culture and Archaeology: Some Critical Remarks," *Journal of Indo-European Studies* 2 (1974):279–87.

180

grammatical and lexical correspondences between the Indo-Iranian languages and other such groups (Germanic, Celtic, Italic, Greek, Balto-Slavic, Anatolian, and so forth), we posit a more distant ancestor language, which we call Proto-Indo-European, the hypothetical speakers of which we posit as the Proto-Indo-Europeans.

Our knowledge of these hypothetical cultures, Proto-Indo-Iranian and Proto-Indo-European, is based almost entirely on analysis of their reconstructed lexicons.[2] Thus, in order to understand their kinship system we study their terminology for kinship relations;[3] in order to understand their arboreal world we study their names for trees;[4] in order to understand their political institutions we study their words for king,[5] council,[6] law,[7] and so forth. From this method, dubbed linguistic paleontology by Pictet more than a hundred years ago,[8] a picture of the Proto-Indo-Iranian and Proto-Indo-European worlds gradually emerges.

Now, were we able to conclusively identify a Proto-Indo-European or Proto-Indo-Iranian homeland, archaeological evidence would become tremendously useful, serving to correct and amplify the picture gained from linguistic paleontology at innumerable crucial points. More importantly, we could move from talking about a hypothetical culture known only by inference (albeit strong inference) to talking about a real culture known by material evidence.

The problem, of course, is how such a conclusive identification might be made. If documents written in the Proto-Indo-European or Proto-Indo-Iranian languages were to be uncovered, they would certainly clinch the argument, but such documents have never been found, and given the probability that both cultures lacked a system of writing, it is unlikely that they ever will be found. In the absence of this type of evidence the method of addressing the problem adopted by most reputable archaeologists[9] is to accept the picture of Proto-Indo-European culture gained from linguistic paleontology and then compare that picture with cultures known from archaeological evidence. When a nearly perfect match is found, that is,

2. The three great lexicons are Pokorny, organized alphabetically; Buck, organized by subject but dealing primarily with linguistic analyses; and Otto Schrader, *Reallexikon der indogermanischen Altertumskunde*, 2 vols., 2d ed. revised by A. Nehring (Strassburg, 1917-23), organized by subject and presenting more culturally based analyses.

3. See Benveniste, *Le vocabulaire des institutions indoeuropéennes*, 1: 203-76; Paul Friedrich, "Proto-Indo-European Kinship," *Ethnology* 5 (1966):1-36; and Robert S. P. Beekes, "Uncle and Nephew," *Journal of Indo-European Studies* 4 (1976):43-65.

4. Paul Friedrich, *Proto-Indo-European Trees* (Chicago, 1970).

5. Benveniste, *Le vocabulaire des institutions indo-européennes*, 2: 9-15; Jan Gonda, "Semantisches zu idg. *rēg'*-, 'König' und zur Wurzel *reg'*-, '(sich aus)strecken,' " *Zeitschrift für vergleichende Sprachforschung* 73 (1955):151-66.

6. Ivanov, "L'organisation sociale des tribus indo-européens," pp. 792-99.

7. Benveniste, *Le vocabulaire des institutions indo-européennes*, 2: 97-176.

8. Adolfe Pictet, *Les origines indo-européennes* (Paris, 1877).

9. This excludes those attempts to argue from the spurious evidence of physical anthropology, as in the badly racist works of, e.g., Karl Penka or Gustaf Kosinna.

when the material remains of a given culture conform most closely to the total Proto-Indo-European lexicon as reconstructed by linguistics, then it may be claimed that this culture was that of the Proto-Indo-Europeans.

The application of this method, however, has produced varying results. Some have argued that the Linear Ware culture was that of the Proto-Indo-Europeans; others, the Corded Ware culture, the Funnel Beaker culture, the Battle Axe culture, the Cucuteni-Tripolje culture, or the Kurgan culture, and the Proto-Indo-European homeland has variously been placed in Scandinavia, on the Baltic shore, in the Balkans, and in the Russian steppes between the Volga and the Don.[10]

In order to judge between these competing hypotheses, two tests are possible. The first of these is the degree to which they can account for what is known of the chronology of the appearance of the descendant Indo-European families, that is, the appearance of the Indo-Aryans in India around 1500 B.C., the waves of invasion into Greece around 1600–1000 B.C., into Anatolia around 2000 B.C., and so forth.[11] The second and the more important in many ways is the degree to which they conform to the picture of the Proto-Indo-European world already gained from linguistic paleontology.

The result of this second test is that archaeology can offer nothing new to the study of Proto-Indo-European civilization. For any candidate culture advanced by archaeologists as the Proto-Indo-European culture, only two types of evidence can be offered: evidence that conforms to the evidence offered by linguists, which will be tautological (although helpful as support and external validation), or evidence that differs from the linguistic evidence, which will then call into question whether the candidate ought not be rejected in favor of another that better fits the linguistic evidence.

Of those candidates which have been advanced, there now seems to be the broadest support for identifying the Kurgan culture of southern Russia with that of the Proto-Indo-Europeans, as argued by Marija Gimbutas,[12] and I am inclined to accept this conclusion given the close correspondence of the material evidence with the linguistic evidence. It is to be regretted, however, that the weak point in Gimbutas's argument is her attempt to account for the migration of the Indo-Iranian peoples from

10. A convenient survey of these and other theories may be found in Mallory, "A Short History of the Indo-European Problem."

11. Of these three areas, the dates for the entry of Indo-Europeans into Greece is the most controversial. On this, see the papers collected in R. A. Crossland and Ann Birchall, eds., *Bronze Age Migrations in the Aegean* (Park Ridge, N.J., 1974).

12. See esp., Marijas Gimbutas, "The Indo-Europeans: Archaeological Problems"; "Proto-Indo-European Culture"; "An Archaeologist's View of PIE in 1975," *Journal of Indo-European Studies* 2 (1974):289–308; and J. P. Mallory, "The Chronology of the Early Kurgan Tradition," *Journal of Indo-European Studies* 4 (1976):257–94; and 5 (1977): 339–68.

the Proto-Indo-European homeland into India, Iran, and the ancient Near East (the last as evidenced by the Indo-Iranian ruling stratum among the Kassites and the Mitanni). Gimbutas's real strength lies in her painstaking attention to the waves of Indo-European migration into Europe, developed in numerous books and articles,[13] in contrast to which she has only devoted a single article to the Indo-Iranian migrations, an apologetic response to Heine-Geldern's criticism,[14] which was itself extremely feeble.[15] If there is thus considerable difficulty in identifying the Proto-Indo-European community, the location of the Proto-Indo-Iranian center is equally uncertain, and there is also considerable debate as to the route that the Indo-Iranian groups followed in their migrations— specifically on whether they moved via the Caucasus[16] or east of the Caspian Sea.[17]

Given these difficulties, it is my opinion that we ought be extremely cautious in making use of archaeological data. At best it may offer confirmation of points already arrived at through other means (linguistics, mythic reconstruction, and so on), but such confirmation is only tentative. With these reservations, then, I would point to the following as a few areas in which archaeology might lend support to the arguments adduced above in Chapters 4–6.

First, with regard to the Proto-Indo-Europeans, if Gimbutas is correct, one can see the fundamental importance of the herds for the Proto-Indo-European economy, especially cattle and horses.[18] The performance of animal sacrifice and occasional human sacrifice is also attested.[19] Particularly noteworthy is that in the Kurgan area only one implement was discovered, which in Gimbutas's opinion might possibly have been a

13. Marija Gimbutas, *Bronze Age Cultures of Central and Eastern Europe* (The Hague, 1965): "Old Europe c. 7000–3500 B.C.: The Earliest European Civilization Before the Infiltration of the Indo-European Peoples," *Journal of Indo-European Studies* 1 (1973):1–20; "The Beginning of the Bronze Age in Europe and the Indo-Europeans: 3500–2500," *Journal of Indo-European Studies* 1 (1973):163–214; *The Gods and Goddesses of Old Europe* (Berkeley, Calif., 1974); "The First Wave of Eurasian Steppe Pastoralists into Copper Age Europe," *Journal of Indo-European Studies* 5 (1977):277–338.

14. Marija Gimbutas, "Comments on Indo-Iranians and Tokharians: A Response to R. Heine-Geldern."

15. Robert Heine-Geldern, "Comments on Gimbutas' 'The Indo-Europeans: Archaeological Problems.' "

16. Bosch-Gimpera, "The Migration Route of the Indo-Aryans"; Jettmar, "Zur Wanderungsgeschichte der Iranier"; Heine-Geldern, "Comments on Gimbutas' 'The Indo-Europeans: Archaeological Problems.' "

17. Ghirshman, *Iran*, p. 63; T. Cuyler Young, "The Iranian Migration into the Zagros," *Iran* 5 (1967):11–34; Jettmar, "Die Steppenkulturen und die Iranier des Plateaus," pp. 68 and 88. Most recently on the question of Indo-Iranian migrations, note M. M. Winn, "Thoughts on the Question of Indo-European Movements in Anatolia and Iran," *Journal of Indo-European Studies* 2 (1974):130–36.

18. Gimbutas, "Proto-Indo-European Culture," pp. 157 and 190; and "An Archaeologist's View of PIE," p. 295.

19. Gimbutas, "Proto-Indo-European Culture," p. 170.

plowshare, while there was no other trace of agricultural tools.[20] In contrast to this, weaponry was highly developed: swords, spears, clubs, arrows, and so on, all of which were buried with their owners on occasion, testified to a strong military stratum within the population and a distinctive warrior ideology.[21] From differences in the wealth of various burials class divisions may be inferred for Proto-Indo-European society, with the warriors definitely constituting one of the upper classes, although all wealthy burials were not of warriors.[22]

Given the present state of our knowledge there is almost nothing that may be said about the Proto-Indo-Iranians on the strength of archaeology. While some scholars have seen them as centered at Balkh or elsewhere,[23] this has hardly been substantiated, nor can we pin them down as a separately located community within the Proto-Indo-European homeland. We can, however, point to the evidence of the Indo-Aryan, Iranian, and other branches of the Indo-Iranian grouping, each of which left archaeological traces as they entered the lands in which they would ultimately settle. In general, continuity of the Proto-Indo-European cultural pattern is evident: the importance of domestic animals (particularly cattle and horses), the relative absence of agriculture, highly developed weaponry, and the division of society into classes, as evidenced by the differing wealth of individual burial sites.[24]

There is yet another way in which archaeological evidence provides some measure of confirmation for my argument. I have argued above for the crucial importance of cattle raiding to the Indo-European and Indo-Iranian warrior class. Yet such an argument only makes sense if the people with whom they came in contact and against whom they conducted their aggression were people who also possessed cattle in sufficient quantities to make raiding profitable. Thus it is of the greatest interest when we discover abundant cattle in Pre-Indo-Iranian India and Iran. Cattle were already domesticated in this area from the fifth millennium B.C.[25] and were extremely important in the economy of the Indus Valley civilization[26] and

20. Gimbutas, "Proto-Indo-European Culture," p. 161; and "An Archaeologist's View of PIE," p. 295.

21. Gimbutas, "An Archaeologist's View of PIE," p. 296.

22. Gimbutas, "Proto-Indo-European Culture," p. 168.

23. Dandekar, "Antecedents and Early Beginnings of the Vedic Period," pp. 39–40; Herzfeld, p. 7.

24. For summaries of the archaeological evidence on the Indo-Iranians as they entered India and Iran, see, *inter alia*, Ghirshman, *Iran*, pp. 60–75; and "Invasions des nomades sur le plateau iranien aux premiers siècles du Ier millénaire avant J. C.," in *Dark Ages and Nomads c. 1000 B.C.* (Istanbul, 1964), pp. 3–8; Piggott, *Prehistoric India*, pp. 244–89; Bridget and Raymond Allchin, pp. 144–56; Walter A. Fairservis, Jr., *The Roots of Ancient India*, 2d ed. (Chicago, 1975), pp. 345–77.

25. Robert H. Dyson, Jr., "Archaeology and the Domestication of Animals in the Old World," *American Anthropologist* 55 (1953):661–73.

26. See Piggott, *Prehistoric India*, pp. 121, 155–56, 176–77; Bridget and Raymond Allchin, pp. 132, 258–59; Fairservis, pp. 179, 184. For a view of what the religious status of

184

in the economy of the Iranian plateau,[27] cattle bones being the most numerous of any animal bones in those sites where such data have been assessed.[28] Moreover, to judge from the weaponry that has survived, it is clear that the indigenous peoples of India and Iran were militarily inferior to the Indo-Iranians, unlike the Sumerians, Babylonians, and Assyrians, who also possessed cattle in great numbers but who were sufficiently well organized and armed to block the bulk of the Indo-Iranian peoples from moving westward, with the exception of such groups as the Kassites, Mitanni, and occasional unidentified *maryannu*. It thus seems plausible, if by no means certain, that the Indo-Iranian invasions were motivated by *gaviṣṭi,* "desire for cattle," which led to warfare in which the Indo-Iranian warriors were successful along a north to south axis but were blocked in their westward expansion by the empires of the ancient Near East.

---

cattle might have been in India before the arrival of the Indo-Aryans, based on archaeological findings in the Deccan, see F. R. Allchin, *Neolithic Cattle Keepers of South India: A Study of the Deccan Ashmounds* (Cambridge, 1963).

27. Ghirshman, *Iran,* pp. 29 and 31; Jean-Louis Huot, *Persia* (London, 1965), p. 81; C. C. Lamberg-Karlovsky, "The Earliest Communities of Iran," *Iranian Studies* 2 (1969):6.

28. J. Boessneck, "Tierknochenfunde vom Zendan-i Suleiman (7 Jahrhundert v. Christus)," *Archaeologische Mitteilungen aus Iran* 6 (1973):96; J. Boessneck and R. Krauss, "Die Tierwelt um Bastam/Nordwest Azerbaidjan," *Archaeologische Mitteilungen aus Iran* 6 (1973):124, 127; R. B. S. Sewell and B. S. Guha, "Zoological Remains," in *Mohenjo-Daro and the Indus Civilization,* Vol. 2 (London, 1931), 654; B. Prashad, *Animal Remains from Harappa* (= *Memoirs of the Archaeological Survey of India* 51 [1936]):43–44.

BIBLIOGRAPHY

Alföldi, Andreas. "Königsweihe und Männerbund bei dem Achämeniden." *Archives suisses des traditions populaires* 47 (1951):11-17.

Allchin, Bridget, and Allchin, Raymond. *The Birth of Indian Civilization.* Baltimore, Md.: Penguin, 1968.

Allchin, F. R. *Neolithic Cattle Keepers of South India: A Study of the Deccan Ashmounds.* Cambridge: Cambridge University Press, 1963.

Alsdorf, Ludwig. *Beiträge zur Geschichte von Vegetarismus und Rinderverehrung in Indien.* Wiesbaden: Akademie der Wissenschaften und der Literatur in Mainz, 1961.

Andreas, F. C., and Wackernagel, Jakob. "Die erste, zweite und fünfte Ghātha des Zurathustrō." *Nachrichten der Göttingen Gesellschaft der Wissenschaften* (1931):304-29.

Anklesaria, Behramgare Tahmuras, ed. and transl. *Zand-Ākāsīh: Iranian or Greater Bundahišn.* Bombay: Rahnumae Mazdayasnan Sabha, 1956.

Anklesaria, Ervad Tahmuras Dinshaji, ed. *The Bundahišn, Being a Facsimile of the TD Manuscript No. 2.* Bombay: British India Press, 1908.

Arbman, Ernst. *Rudra: Untersuchungen zum altindische Glauben und Kultus.* Uppsala: A. B. Akademiska, 1922.

Arbois de Jubainville, H. d'. *The Irish Mythological Cycle and Celtic Mythology,* translated by R. I. Best. Dublin: Hodges, Figgis, 1903.

BIBLIOGRAPHY

Aufrecht, Theodor, ed. *Die Hymnen des Rigveda.* 2 vols. Bonn: Adolph Marcus, 1877.

Bailey, Harold W. "Dvārā Matīnām." *Bulletin of the School of Oriental and African Studies* 20 (1957):41-59.

————. *Zoroastrian Problems in the Ninth Century Books.* 2d ed. Oxford: Clarendon Press, 1971.

————. "The second stratum of the Indo-Iranian gods." In *Mithraic Studies,* pp. 1-20, Edited by John R. Hinnells. Manchester: University of Manchester Press, 1975.

Barnett, L. D. "The Genius: A Study in Indo-European Psychology." *Journal of the Royal Asiatic Society* (1929):731-48.

Barr, Kaj. "Avestan drəgu-, driγu-." In *Studia Orientalia Ioanni Pedersen,* pp. 21-40. Copenhagen: E. Munksgaard, 1943.

Bartholomae, Christian. *Arische Forschungen.* 3 vols. Halle: Max Niemeyer, 1882.

————. "Beiträge zur Kenntniss der Gāthas, I." *Zeitschrift für vergleichende Sprachforschung* 28 (1887):1-54.

————. "Beiträge zur altiranischen Grammatik, V." *Beiträge zur Kunde der indogermanische Sprachen* 13 (1887):54-93.

————. "Arica, I." *Indogermanische Forschungen* 1 (1892):178-94.

————. *Altiranisches Wörterbuch.* Berlin: Walter de Gruyter, 1904.

————. "Zarathustra: His Life and Doctrine." In *Indo-Iranian Studies in Honour of Sanjana,* pp. 1-16, edited by A. V. Williams Jackson. London: Trench, Trübner and Co., 1925.

Bayet, Jean. *Les origines de l'Hercule romain.* Paris: E. de Boccard, 1926.

Bedri, Ibrahim Effendi. "Notes on Dinka Religious Beliefs in Their Hereditary Chiefs and Rainmakers." *Sudan Notes and Records* 22 (1939):125-31.

————. "More Notes on the Padang Dinka." *Sudan Notes and Records* 29 (1948):40-57.

Beekes, Robert S. P. "Uncle and Nephew." *Journal of Indo-European Studies* 4 (1976):43-65.

Beidelman, T. O. "The Baraguyu." *Tanganyika Notes and Records* 54 (1960):245-78.

————. "Beer Drinking and Cattle Theft in Ukaguru: Intertribal Relations in a Tanganyika Chiefdom." *American Anthropologist* 63 (1961):534-49.

————. "Some Baraguyu Cattle Songs." *Journal of African Languages* 4 (1965):1-18.

Benveniste, Emile. *The Persian Religion According to the Chief Greek Texts.* Paris: Paul Geuthner, 1929.

————. "Les classes sociales dans la tradition avestique." *Journal Asiatique* 221 (1932):117-34.

BIBLIOGRAPHY

————. "Sur quelques *dvandvas* avestiques." *Bulletin of the School of Oriental and African Studies* 8 (1935–37):405–409.

————. "Traditions indo-iraniennes sur les classes sociales." *Journal Asiatique* 230 (1938):529–49.

————. "Expression indo-européenne de l'éternité." *Bulletin de la société de linguistique de Paris* 38 (1938):103–12.

————. "La prière Ahuna Vairya." *Indo-Iranian Journal* 1 (1957):76–85.

————. "Mithra aux vastes pâturages." *Journal Asiatique* 248 (1960):421–29.

————. "Sur la terminologie iranienne du sacrifice." *Journal Asiatique* 252 (1964):45–58.

————. *Problèmes de linguistique générale.* Paris: Gallimard, 1966.

————. "Hommes et dieux dans l'Avesta." In *Festschrift für Wilhelm Eilers,* pp. 144–47, edited by Gernot Wiessner. Wiesbaden: Otto Harrassowitz, 1967.

————. *Le vocabulaire des institutions indo-européennes.* 2 vols. Paris: Minuit, 1969.

————. "Le terme iranien *mazdayasna.*" *Bulletin of the School of Oriental and African Studies* 33 (1970):5–9.

Benveniste, Emile, and Renou, Louis. *Vṛtra et Vṛθragna.* Paris: Imprimerie Nationale, 1934.

Bergaigne, Abel. *La Religion védique.* 3 vols. Paris: Honoré Champion, 1963.

Bernardi, B. "The Age System of the Nilo-Hamitic Peoples: A Critical Evaluation." *Africa* 22 (1952):316–32.

————. "The Age System of the Masai." *Annali Lateranensi* 18 (1955): 257–318.

Bezzenberger, Adalbert. "Homerische Etymologien." *Beiträge zur Kunde der indogermanische Sprachen* 4 (1878):313–59.

Binder, Gerhard. *Die Aussetzung des Königskindes Kyros und Romulus.* Meisenheim: Anton Hall, 1964.

Bloomfield, Maurice. "The Marriage of Saraṇyū." *Journal of the American Oriental Society* 15 (1893):172–88.

————. "Contributions to the Interpretation of the Veda." *Journal of the American Oriental Society* 16 (1896):24–42.

Boas, Franz. *Kwakiutl Ethnography.* Chicago: University of Chicago Press, 1966.

Boessneck, J. "Tierknochenfunde vom Zendan-i Suleiman (7 Jahrhundert v. Christus)." *Archaeologische Mitteilungen aus Iran* 6 (1973):95–111.

Boessneck, J., and Krauss, R. "Die Tierwelt um Bastam/Nordwest Azerbaidjan." *Archaeologische Mitteilungen aus Iran* 6 (1973):113–33.

Bosch-Gimpera, Pedro. *Les Indo-Européens: Problèmes Archéologiques.* Paris: Payot, 1961.

188

BIBLIOGRAPHY

————. "The Migration Route of the Indo-Aryans." *Journal of Indo-European Studies* 1 (1973):513-17.

Botzler, Franz. "Ymir: Ein Beitrag zu den eddischen Weltschopfungsvorstellungen." *Archiv für Religionswissenschaft* 33 (1936):230-45.

Bowman, Raymond A. *Aramaic Ritual Texts from Persepolis.* Chicago: University of Chicago Press, 1970.

Boyce, Mary. "Ātaš-zōhr and Āb-zōhr." *Journal of the Royal Asiatic Society* (1966):100-18.

————. "On Mithra's Part in Zoroastrianism." *Bulletin of the School of Oriental and African Studies* 32 (1969):10-34.

————. "Zoroaster the Priest." *Bulletin of the School of Oriental and African Studies* 33 (1970):22-38.

————. "Haoma, Priest of the Sacrifice." In *W. B. Henning Memorial Volume,* pp. 62-80, edited by Mary Boyce and Ilya Gershevitch. London: Lund, Humphries, 1970.

————. "Mihragān Among the Irani Zoroastrians." In *Mithraic Studies,* pp. 106-18, edited by John R. Hinnells. Manchester: University of Manchester Press, 1975.

Bradke, Peter von. *Dyaus Asura, Ahura Mazda und die Asuras.* Halle: Max Niemeyer, 1885.

————. *Über Methode und Ergebnisse der arischen Alterthumswissenschaft.* Giessen: J. Ricker, 1890.

Brandenstein, Wilhelm. *Die erste "indogermanische" Wanderung.* Vienna: Gerold, 1936.

————. "Arica." In Μνήμης Χάριν: *Gedenkschrift Paul Kretschmer,* pp. 52-60, edited by Hans Kronasser. Vienna: Verlag der Wiener Sprachgesellschaft, 1956.

Bréal, Michel. *Mélanges de Mythologie et de Linguistique.* Paris: Hachette, 1882.

Brough, John. "The Tripartite Ideology of the Indo-Europeans: An Experiment in Method." *Bulletin of the School of Oriental and African Studies* 22 (1959):69-85.

Brown, Norman O. *Hermes the Thief.* New York: Vintage, 1947.

Brown, W. Norman. "The Creation Myth of the Rig Veda." *Journal of the American Oriental Society* 62 (1942):85-98.

————. "Theories of Creation in the Rg Veda." *Journal of the American Oriental Society* 85 (1965):23-34.

Buck, Carl Darling. *A Dictionary of Selected Synonyms in the Principal Indo-European Languages.* Chicago: University of Chicago Press, 1949.

Bugeau, François. "Les Wakikouyous et la guerre." *Annali Lateranensi* 7 (1943):183-226.

Bühler, Georg, ed. and trans. *The Laws of Manu.* Oxford: Clarendon Press, 1886.

189

BIBLIOGRAPHY

Burrow, T. "Nirvacanani." *Annals of Oriental Research* 13 (1957):4-13.
_____. "The Proto-Indoaryans." *Journal of the Royal Asiatic Society* (1973):123-40.
Caland, William, and Henry, Victor. *L'Agniṣṭoma.* 2 vols. Paris: E. LeRoux, 1907.
Cameron, George B. "Zoroaster the Herdsman." *Indo-Iranian Journal* 10 (1968): 261-81.
Cameron, George C. *History of Early Iran.* Chicago: University of Chicago Press, 1936.
Capdeville, G. "Substitution de victimes dans les sacrifices d'animaux à Rome." *Mélanges d'archéologie et d'histoire de l'école française de Rome* 83 (1971):283-323.
Carnoy, Albert J. *Les Indo-Européens.* Brussels: Vromant, 1921.
Charpentier, Jarl. "Uber Rudra-Śiva." *Wiener Zeitschrift für die Kunde des Morgenlandes* 23 (1909):151-79.
_____. *Kleine Beiträge zur indoiranischen Mythologie.* Uppsala: Akademische Buchdruckerei, 1911.
_____. "Av. *dūraoša*-; Ai. *duroṣa*-." *Wiener Zeitschrift für die Kunde des Morgenlandes* 27 (1913):235-44.
_____. "Zur alt- und mittelindischen Wortkunde." *Monde Oriental* 13 (1919):1-54.
_____. "Indra: Ein Versuch der Aufklärung." *Monde Oriental* 25 (1931):1-28.
Childe, V. Gordon. *The Aryans: A Study of Indo-European Origins.* New York: Alfred Knopf, 1926.
Christensen, Arthur. "Reste von Manu-Legenden in der iranischen Sagenwelt." In *Festschrift Friedrich Carl Andreas,* pp. 63-69. Leipzig: Otto Harrassowitz, 1916.
_____. *Le premier homme et le premier roi dans l'histoire légendaire des iraniens.* 2 vols. Uppsala: Archives d'études orientales, 1918-34.
_____. "Quelques notices sur les plus anciennes périodes du Zoroastrisme." *Acta Orientalia* 4 (1926):81-115.
_____. "Die Iranier." In *Kulturgeschichte des alten Orients,* pp. 203-309. Munich: C. H. Beck, 1933.
_____. *Essai sur la démonologie iranienne.* Copenhagen: E. Munksgaard, 1941.
Colpe, Carsten. "Mithra-Verehrung, Mithras-Kult, und die Existenz iranischer Mysterien." In *Mithraic Studies,* pp. 378-405, edited by John R. Hinnells. Manchester: University of Manchester Press, 1975.
Coomaraswamy, Ananda. *Spiritual Authority and Temporal Power in the Indian Theory of Government.* New Haven, Conn.: American Oriental Society, 1942.

190

BIBLIOGRAPHY

Coriat, Paul. "Gwek, the Witch-Doctor and the Pyramid of Dengkur." *Sudan Notes and Records* 22 (1939): 221–37.

Crazzolara, J. P. "Die Gar-Zeremonie bei den Nuer." *Africa* 5 (1932): 28–39.

———. "Die Bedeutung des Rindes bei den Nuer." *Africa* 7 (1934): 300–20.

———. *Zur Gesellschaft und Religion der Nueer.* Vienna: Missionsdruckerei St. Gabriel, 1953.

Crossland, R. A. "Indo-European Origins." *Past and Present* 12 (1957): 16–46.

Crossland, R. A., and Birchall, Ann. *Bronze Age Migrations in the Aegean.* Park Ridge, N.J.: Noyes, 1974.

Cumont, Franz. "St. George and Mithra the Cattle Thief." *Journal of Roman Studies* 27 (1937):63–71.

Dandekar, R. N. "Asura Varuṇa." *Annals of the Bhandarkar Oriental Research Institute* 21 (1940): 157–91.

———. "Yama in the Veda." In *B.C. Law Volume,* Vol. I, pp. 194–209, edited by D. R. Bhandarkar. Calcutta: Bhandarkar Oriental Series, 1945.

———. "The Antecedents and the Early Beginnings of the Vedic Period." *Proceedings of the Indian History Conference* 10 (1947):24–66.

———. "Vṛtrahā Indra." *Annals of the Bhandarkar Oriental Research Institute* 31 (1950):1–55.

———. "Rudra in the Veda." *Journal of the University of Bombay* 1 (1953):94–148.

———. "Varuṇa, Vasiṣṭha and Bhakti." In *Wijisekera Felicitation Volume,* pp. 77–82. Calcutta: Bhandarkar Oriental Series, 1970.

Dandekar, R. N., ed. *Śrautakośa: Encyclopedia of Vedic Sacrificial Ritual.* 2 vols. Poona: Vaidika Samsodhana, 1962.

Dange, Sadashiv A. " 'Ketu' or the War Banner in the Rg Veda." *Journal of Indian History* 42 (1964):377–79.

———. "Aspects of War from the Rg Veda." *Journal of Indian History* 44 (1966):125–38.

Darmesteter, James. *Ormazd et Ahriman.* Paris: F. Vieweg, 1877.

———. *Essais Orientaux.* Paris: F. Vieweg, 1883.

Darmesteter, James, trans. *Le Zend Avesta.* 3 vols. Paris: Maissonneuve, 1892; repr. 1960.

Deng, Francis Mading. *Tradition and Modernization: A Challenge for Law Among the Dinka of the Sudan.* New Haven, Conn.: Yale University Press, 1971.

———. *The Dinka of the Sudan.* New York: Holt, Rinehart and Winston, 1972.

BIBLIOGRAPHY

_____. *The Dinka and Their Songs.* Oxford: Clarendon Press, 1973.

_____. *Africans of Two Worlds: The Dinka in Afro-Arab Sudan.* New Haven, Conn.: Yale University Press, 1978.

Detienne, Marcel. "La cuisine de Pythagore." *Archives de Sociologie des Religions* 29 (1970): 141-63.

Devoto, Giacomo. *Origini Indeuropee.* Florence: Sansoni, 1962.

DeVries, Larry. *"apo aghn(i)yaḥ."* Paper presented to the Midwest Regional Chapter of the American Oriental Society, 1975.

Diakonoff, I. M. "Die Arier im vorderen Orient: Ende eines Mythos." *Orientalia* 41 (1972):91-121.

Dottin, G. "Les razzias épiques," *Revue Celtique* 40 (1923):127-34.

Driver, Harold E. *The Contribution of A. L. Kroeber to Culture Area Theory and Practice.* Baltimore, Md.: Waverly, 1962.

Duchesne-Guillemin, Jacques. *Les Composées de l'Avesta.* Paris: E. Droz, 1936.

_____. "Ahura Miθra." In *Mélanges Franz Cumont,* pp. 683-85. Brussels: Secrétariat de l'Institut de Philologie et d'histoire Orientales et Slaves, 1936.

_____. "Aw. Θraētaona-." *Indogermanische Forschungen* 54 (1936): 205.

_____. "Persische Weisheit in griechischem Gewande?" *Harvard Theological Review* 49 (1956):115-22.

_____. "Miettes iraniennes." In *Hommages à Georges Dumézil,* pp. 96-103. Brussels: Collection Latomus, 1960.

_____. *The Hymns of Zarathustra.* Boston: Beacon Press, 1963.

_____. "Le Xᵛarənah." *Annali dell'Istituto Orientale di Napoli, Sezione Linguistica* 5 (1963):19-31.

_____. "L'initiation mazdéenne." In *Initiation,* pp. 112-18, edited by C. J. Bleeker. Leiden: E. J. Brill, 1965.

_____. "Autres miettes." In *Iranian Studies presented to Kaj Barr,* pp. 73-74, edited by J. P. Asmussen. Copenhagen: E. Munksgaard, 1966.

_____. "On the Complaint of the Ox-Soul." *Journal of Indo-European Studies* 1 (1973):101-104.

Dumézil, Georges. *Le festin d'immortalité.* Paris: Paul Geuthner, 1924.

_____. "La préhistoire indo-iranienne des castes." *Journal Asiatique* 216 (1930):109-30.

_____. "Vahagn." *Revue de l'histoire des religions* 117 (1938):152-70.

_____. "Jeunesse, éternité, aube." *Annales d'histoire économique et sociale* 10 (1938):289-301.

_____. *Mythes et dieux des Germains.* Paris: E. Leroux, 1939.

_____. "Deux traits du monstre tricéphale indo-iranien." *Revue de l'histoire des religions* 120 (1939):5-20.

192

BIBLIOGRAPHY

_____. "Le nom des 'Arya'." *Revue de l'histoire des religions* 124 (1941):36–59.

_____. *Horace et les Curiaces.* Paris: Gallimard, 1942.

_____. *Naissance d'Archanges.* Paris: Gallimard, 1945.

_____. *Mitra-Varuṇa.* Paris: Gallimard, 1948.

_____. *L'héritage indo-européen à Rome.* Paris: Gallimard, 1949.

_____. "A propos de Vərəθraγna." In *Mélanges H. Gregoire,* pp. 223–26. Brussels: Secrétariat de l'Institut de Philologie et d'histoire Orientales et Slaves, 1949.

_____. *Les dieux des indo-européens.* Paris: Presses Universitaires de France, 1952.

_____. "Viṣṇu et les Marut à travers la réforme Zoroastrienne." *Journal Asiatique* 241 (1953):1–25.

_____. "Religion indo-européenne: Examen de quelques critiques récents." *Revue de l'histoire des religions* 152 (1957): 8–30.

_____. "Ari, Aryman à propos de Paul Thieme, 'ari, Fremder,' (ZDMG 117)." *Journal Asiatique* 246 (1958):67–84.

_____. *L'idéologie tri-partie des indo-européens.* Brussels: Collection Latomus, 1958.

_____. *Les dieux des Germains.* Paris: Presses Universitaires de France, 1959.

_____. "Le Rex et les Flamines Maiores." In *La Regalità Sacra* pp. 407–17. Leiden: E. J. Brill, 1959.

_____. "A propos de la plainte de l'âme du boeuf (Yasna 29)." *Bulletin de l'Académie royale de Belgique, Classes des Lettres* 51 (1965):23–51.

_____. *Mythe et épopée.* 3 vols. Paris: Gallimard, 1968–73.

_____. *The Destiny of the Warrior.* Chicago: University of Chicago Press, 1970.

_____. *The Destiny of the King.* Chicago: University of Chicago Press, 1971.

Dumont, Louis. *Homo Hierarchicus.* Chicago: University of Chicago Press, 1970.

Dunn, Joseph, trans. *The Ancient Irish Epic Tale Táin Bó Cúalnge.* London, 1914.

Dyson, Robert H., Jr. "Archaeology and the Domestication of Animals in the Old World," *American Anthropologist* 55 (1953):661–73.

Edgerton, Franklin. "The K-suffixes of Indo-Iranian." *Journal of the American Oriental Society* 31 (1911):94–150, 296–342.

Eggeling, Julius, trans. *Śatapatha Brāhmaṇa.* 5 vols. Oxford: Clarendon Press, 1894.

Ehret, Christopher. *Southern Nilotic History.* Evanston, Ill.: Northwestern University Press, 1971.

BIBLIOGRAPHY

Eisler, Robert. *Man into Wolf*. London: Spring Books, n.d.
Eliade, Mircea. *Cosmos and History: The Myth of the Eternal Return*. New York: Harper and Row, 1954.
_____. *Rites and Symbols of Initiation*. New York: Harper and Row, 1958.
_____. *Myths, Dreams, and Mysteries*. New York: Harper and Row, 1960.
_____. *Patterns in Comparative Religion*. New York: Meridian, 1963.
_____. *The Quest*. Chicago: University of Chicago Press, 1969.
_____. *Shamanism: Archaic Techniques of Ecstasy*. Princeton: Princeton University Press, 1970.
_____. "Spirit, Light, and Seed." *History of Religions* 11 (1971):1-30.
_____. *Zalmoxis: The Vanishing God*. Chicago: University of Chicago Press, 1972.
Evans-Pritchard, E. E. "The Nuer: Age-Sets." *Sudan Notes and Records* 19 (1936):233-70.
_____. *The Nuer*. Oxford: Oxford University Press, 1940.
_____. "Some Forms and Features of Nuer Sacrifice." *Africa* 21 (1951): 112-21.
_____. *Kinship and Marriage Among the Nuer*. Oxford: Clarendon Press, 1951.
_____. "The Sacrificial Role of Cattle Among the Nuer." *Africa* 23 (1953): 181-98.
_____. "Nuer Spear Symbolism." *Anthropological Quarterly* 26 (1953): 1-19.
_____. *Nuer Religion*. Oxford: Clarendon Press, 1956.
Fairservis, Walter A., Jr. *The Roots of Ancient India*, 2d ed. Chicago: University of Chicago Press, 1975.
Fergusson, V. H. "The Nuong Nuer." *Sudan Notes and Records* 4 (1921): 146-56.
Fokken, H. "Gottesanschauungen und religiose Überlieferungen der Masai." *Archiv für Anthropologie* 43 (1917):237-52.
Fontenrose, Joseph. *Python*. Berkeley, Calif.: University of California Press, 1959.
Forde, Daryll. *Habitat, Economy, and Society*. London: Methuen, 1946.
Fosbrooke, H. A. "An Administrative Survey of the Masai Social System." *Tanganyika Notes and Records* 26 (1948):1-50.
Fowler, Murray. "Trita Soter." *Journal of the American Oriental Society* 67 (1947):59-60.
Fox, D. Storrs. "Further Notes on the Masai of Kenya Colony." *Journal of the Royal Anthropological Institute* 60 (1930):447-65.
Frenkian, Aram M. "Puruṣa—Gayōmard—Anthropos." *Revue des Etudes Indo-Européennes* 3 (1943):118-31.
Friedrich, Johannes, "Das erste Auftreten der Indogermanen." In *Germanen und Indogermanen: Festschrift für Herman*

194

BIBLIOGRAPHY

              Hirt, pp. 215–24, edited by Helmut Arntz. Heidelberg: Carl Winter, 1936.

Friedrich, Paul. "Proto-Indo-European Kinship," *Ethnology* 5 (1966): 1–36.

————. *Proto-Indo-European Trees*. Chicago: University of Chicago Press, 1970.

————. *Proto-Indo-European Syntax*. Butte, Mont.: Journal of Indo-European Studies Monograph Series, 1975.

Frisk, Hjalmar. *Griechisches etymologisches Wörterbuch*. 2 vols. Heidelberg: Carl Winter, 1973.

Frobenius, Leo. *Leo Frobenius: An Anthology*. Wiesbaden: Franz Steiner, 1973.

Frye, Richard N. *The Heritage of Persia*. Cleveland, Ohio: World, 1963.

Furlani, Giuseppe. *La Religione degli Hittiti*. Bologna: Nicola Zanichelli, 1936.

Geiger, Bernhard. *Die Aməša Spəntas: Ihr Wesen und ihre ursprungliche Bedeutung*. Vienna: Alfred Holder, 1916.

Geiger, Wilhelm. *Civilization of the Eastern Iranians in Ancient Times*. 2 vols. London: Henry Frowde, 1885.

Geldner, Karl Friedrich. "Zaotā." In *Indo-Iranian Studies in Honour of Sanjana*, pp. 277–81, edited by A. V. Williams Jackson. London: Trench, Trübner and Co., 1925.

————, ed. *Avesta*, 3 vols. Stuttgart: W. Kohlhammer, 1896.

————, trans. *Der Rigveda*. 4 vols. Cambridge, Mass.: Harvard University Press, 1951.

————. See also: Pischel, Richard, and Geldner, Karl Friedrich.

Gelzer, H. "Zur armenischen Götterlehre." *Berichte der königlich sächsischen Gesellschaft der Wissenschaften zu Leipzig, Philosophisch-Historisch Classe* 48 (1896):99–148.

Gernet, Louis. "Dolon le loup." In *Mélanges Franz Cumont*, pp. 189–208. Brussels: Secrétariat de l'Institut de Philologie et d'Histoire Orientales et Slaves, 1936.

Gershevitch, Ilya, ed. and trans. *The Avestan Hymn to Mithra*. Cambridge: The University Press, 1959.

————. "Die Sonne das Beste." In *Mithraic Studies*, pp. 68–89, edited by John R. Hinnells. Manchester: University of Manchester Press, 1975.

————. "More Meat in Iranian." In *Studies in Greek, Italic, and Indo-European Linguistics offered to Leonard R. Palmer*, pp. 63-64. Innsbruck: Innsbrucker Beiträge zur Sprachwissenschaft, 1976.

Gerstein, Mary R. "Germanic *Warg*: The Outlaw as Werwolf." In *Myth in Indo-European Antiquity*, pp. 131–56, edited by G. J. Larson. Berkeley, Calif.: University of California Press, 1974.

BIBLIOGRAPHY

Ghirshman, R. *Iran*. Baltimore, Md.: Penguin, 1954.

_____. "Invasions des nomades sur le plateau iranien aux premiers siècles du Ier millénaire avant J. C." In *Dark Ages and Nomads c. 1000* B.C., pp. 3-8, edited by Machteld J. Mellink. Istanbul: Nederlands Historisch-Archaeologisch Institut, 1964.

Ghurye, G. S. *Caste and Race in India*. Bombay: Popular Prakashan, 1969.

Giles, P. "The Aryans." In *The Cambridge History of India*, Vol. I, pp. 58-68. Cambridge: The University Press, 1929.

Gimbutas, Marija. "The Indo-Europeans: Archaeological Problems." *American Anthropologist* 65 (1963): 815-36.

_____. "Comments on Indo-Iranians and Tokharians: A Response to R. Heine-Geldern." *American Anthropologist* 66 (1964): 893-98.

_____. *Bronze Age Cultures of Central and Eastern Europe*. The Hague: Mouton, 1965.

_____. "Proto-Indo-European Culture: The Kurgan Culture During the Fifth, Fourth, and Third Millennia B.C." In *Indo-European and Indo-Europeans*, pp. 155-98, edited by Henry Hoenigswald. Philadelphia: University of Pennsylvania Press, 1970.

_____. "Old Europe c. 7000-3500 B.C.: The Earliest European Civilization Before the Infiltration of the Indo-European Peoples." *Journal of Indo-European Studies* 1 (1973): 1-20.

_____. "The Beginning of the Bronze Age in Europe and the Indo-Europeans: 3500-2500." *Journal of Indo-European Studies* 1 (1973):163-214.

_____. *The Gods and Goddesses of Old Europe*. Berkeley, Calif.: University of California Press, 1974.

_____. "An Archaeologist's View of PIE in 1975." *Journal of Indo-European Studies* 2 (1974):289-308.

_____. "The First Wave of Eurasian Steppe Pastoralists into Copper Age Europe," *Journal of Indo-European Studies* 5 (1977):277-338.

Glickman, Maurice. "The Nuer and the Dinka: A Further Note." *Man* 7 (1972):586-94.

Gnoli, Gherardo. "L'Iran e l'ideología tripartita." *Studi e Materiali di Storia delle religioni* 36 (1965):193-210.

_____. "Lichtsymbolik in Alt-Iran," *Kairos* 8 (1967):528-49.

Goldschmidt, Walter. *Kambuga's Cattle*. Berkeley, Calif.: University of California Press, 1969.

Gonda, Jan. "Zur Frage nach dem Ursprung und Wesen des indischen Dramas." *Acta Orientalia* 19 (1943):329-453.

BIBLIOGRAPHY

————. "The Etymologies in the Ancient Indian Brāhmaṇas." *Lingua* 5 (1955):61–86.

————. "Semantisches zu idg. *rēg'*-, 'König' und zur Wurzel *reg'*-, '(sich aus)strecken.'" *Zeitschrift für vergleichende Sprachforschung* 73 (1955):151–66.

————. "Ancient Indian Kingship from the Religious Point of View," *Numen* 3 (1956):36–71, 122–55; 4 (1957):24–58, 127–64.

————. *Die Religionen Indiens.* 3 vols. Stuttgart: W. Kohlhammer, 1960.

————. "Some Observations on Dumézil's Views of Indo-European Mythology." *Mnemosyne* 13 (1960):1–15.

————. "Gifts and Giving in the Rgveda." *Vishvesh-Varanand Indological Journal* 2 (1964):9–30.

————. "Review: *Studi Linguistici in Onore di Vittore Pisani.*" *Linguistics* 90 (1972):88–97.

————. *The Vedic God Mitra.* Leiden: E. J. Brill, 1972.

————. *The Dual Deities in the Religion of the Veda.* Amsterdam: North Holland, 1974.

————. "Mitra in India." In *Mithraic Studies,* pp. 68–69, edited by John R. Hinnells. Manchester: University of Manchester Press, 1975.

————. *Triads in the Veda.* Amsterdam: North Holland, 1976.

Goodenough, Ward H. "The Evolution of Pastoralism and Indo-European Origins." In *Indo-European and Indo-Europeans,* pp. 253–66, edited by Henry Hoenigswald. Philadelphia: University of Pennsylvania Press, 1970.

Götze, Albrecht. "Persische Weisheit in griechischem Gewande: Ein Beitrag zur Geschichte der Mikrokosmos-Idee." *Zeitschrift für Indologie und Iranistik* 2 (1923):60–98, 167–74.

————. *Kulturgeschichte des alten Orient, II, 1.3 Kleinasien.* Munich: C. H. Beck, 1933.

Gourlay, K. A. "The Ox and Identification." *Man* 7 (1972):244–74.

Graebner, Fritz. *Das Weltbild der Primitiven.* Munich: Ernst Reinhardt, 1924.

Grant, Michael. *Roman Myths.* New York: Charles Scribners, 1971.

Grantovskij, E. "Indoiranische Kastengliederung bei den Skythen." *Twenty-Fifth International Congress of Orientalists,* pp. 1–21. Moscow: Oriental Literature Publishing House, 1960.

Grassman, Hermann. *Wörterbuch zum Rigveda.* Wiesbaden: Otto Harrassowitz, 1872; repr. 1964.

Greenbaum, Steven E. "Vṛtrahan—Vərəthragna: India and Iran." In *Myth in Indo-European Antiquity,* pp. 93–97, edited by Gerald Larson. Berkeley, Calif.: University of California Press, 1974.

BIBLIOGRAPHY

Greenberg, Joseph. *Studies in African Linguistic Classification.* New Haven, Conn.: Compass, 1955.

Grégoire, Henri, Goossens, R., and Mathieu, M. *Asklépios, Apollon Smintheus et Rudra.* Brussels: Académie Royale de Belgique, 1949.

Greppin, John. "Xʸarənah as a Transfunctional Figure." *Journal of Indo-European Studies* 1 (1973):232-42.

Grimm, Jacob. *Teutonic Mythology.* 4 vols. London: George Bell, 1883.

Grimm, Wilhelm. "Die mythische Bedeutung des Wolfes." *Zeitschrift für deutsche Altertumswissenschaft* 12 (1865):203-28.

Grottanelli, Cristiano. "Per un Mitico Giacobbe Domestico, Pastore e Mago." In *Magia: Studi di Storia delle Religioni in Memoria di Raffaela Garossi,* pp. 127-45, edited by Paolo Xella. Rome: Bulzoni, 1976.

Gruber, Joachim. "Zur Etymologie von Lat. *lupercus.*" *Glotta* 39 (1961): 273-76.

Gulliver, P. H. *The Family Herds: A Study of Two Pastoral Tribes in East Africa, the Jie and Turkana.* London: Routledge and Kegan Paul, 1955.

Güntert, Hermann. *Kalypso.* Halle: Max Niemeyer, 1919.

——. *Der arische Weltkönig und Heiland.* Halle: Max Niemeyer, 1923.

Haas, Volkert. *Der Kult von Nerik: Ein Beitrag zur hethitischen Religionsgeschichte.* Rome: Päpstliches Bibelinstitut, 1970.

Hamp, Eric. "Religion and Law from Iguvium." *Journal of Indo-European Studies* 1 (1973):318-23.

Hartman, Sven S. *Gayōmart.* Uppsala: Almquist and Wiksells, 1953.

Heesterman, J. C. "Vala and Gomatī." *Bulletin of the Deccan College Research Institute* 19 (1958):320-29.

——. "Reflections on the Significance of Dakṣiṇā." *Indo-Iranian Journal* 3 (1959):241-58.

Heimann, Betty. "The Supra-Personal Process of Sacrifice." *Rivista degli Studi Orientali* 32 (1957):731-39.

Heine-Geldern, Robert. "The Coming of the Aryans and the End of the Harappa Civilization." *Man* 56 (1956):136-40.

——. "Comments on Gimbutas' 'The Indo-Europeans: Archaeological Problems.'" *American Anthropologist* 66 (1964): 889-93.

Hencken, Hugh. "Indo-European Language and Archaeology." *Memoirs of the American Anthropological Association* 84 (1955):1-68.

Hermes, Gertrud. "Zur Soziologie der Lehre Zarathustras." *Anthropos* 33 (1938):181-94, 424-44.

Herskovits, Melville J. "The Cattle Complex in East Africa." *American Anthropologist* 28 (1926):230-72, 361-88, 494-529, 633-64.

BIBLIOGRAPHY

Herzfeld, Ernst E. *Archaeological History of Iran.* London: Oxford University Press, 1935.

Hidding, K. A. H. "The High God and the King as Symbols of Totality." In *La Regalità Sacra,* pp. 54-62. Leiden: E. J. Brill, 1959.

Hillebrandt, Alfred. *Varuṇa und Mitra.* Breslau: G. P. Aderholz, 1877.

————. *Varuṇa als Himmelsgott und Herr über Tag und Nacht.* Breslau: Robert Nischkowsky, 1877.

————. "Indra und Vṛtra." *Zeitschrift der deutschen morgenlandischen Gesellschaft* 50 (1896):665-66.

————. "Tiere und Götter im vedischen Ritual." *Schlesische Gesellschaft für vaterländische Cultur* 83 (1905):1-12.

————. "Bemerkungen zur vedischen Mythologie." *Zeitschrift für Indologie und Iranistik* 4 (1926):207-22.

————. *Vedische Mythologie.* 3 vols. Breslau: M. and H. Marcus, 1929.

Hirt, Herman. *Indogermanica.* Halle: Max Niemeyer, 1940.

Hoang-sy-Quy, Hoang-son. "Le mythe indien de l'homme cosmique dans son contexte culturel et dans son évolution." *Revue de l'histoire des religions* 175 (1969):133-54.

Hoenigswald, Henry M. *Language Change and Linguistic Reconstruction.* Chicago: University of Chicago Press, 1960.

Hoffmann, Karl. "Jungawestisch *zazāite.*" *Münchener Studien zur Sprachwissenschaft* 4 (1954):45-52.

————. "Avestisch *haomo yō gauua.*" *Münchener Studien zur Sprachwissenschaft* 21 (1967):11-20.

Höfler, Otto. *Kultische Geheimbünde der Germanen.* Frankfurt: Moritz Diesterweg, 1934.

————. "Siegfried, Arminius, und die Symbolik." In *Festschrift für Franz Rolf Schröder,* pp. 11-121, edited by W. Rasch. Heidelberg: Carl Winter, 1959.

————. "Abstammungstraditionen." In *Reallexikon der germanischen Altertumskunde,* Vol. I, pp. 18-29, edited by Herbert Jankuhn. Berlin: W. de Gruyter, 1973.

Hollis, A. C. *The Masai: Their Language and Folklore.* Oxford: Clarendon Press, 1905.

Hopkins, E. W. "Problematic Passages in the Rig-Veda." *Journal of the American Oriental Society* 15 (1895):260-66.

Hopkins, Grace Sturtevant. *Indo-European *Deiwos and Related Words.* Philadelphia: Linguistic Society of America, 1932.

Howell, P. P. "The Age-Set System and the Institution of *Nak* Among the Nuer." *Sudan Notes and Records* 29 (1948):173-82.

————. "Notes on the Ngork Dinka of Western Khordofan." *Sudan Notes and Records* 32 (1951):59-107, 123-89.

————. *A Manual of Nuer Law.* London: Oxford University Press, 1954.

BIBLIOGRAPHY

Hrozný, Friedrich. "Hethiter und Inder." *Zeitschrift für Assyriologie* 38 (1928):184-85.

Hultkrantz, Ake. "An Ecological Approach to Religion." *Ethnos* 31 (1966):131-50.

_____. "Ecology of Religions: Its Scope and Methodology." *Review of Ethnology* 4 (1974):1-12.

Humbach, Helmut. "Gast und Gabe bei Zarathustra." *Münchener Studien zur Sprachwissenschaft* 2 (1952):1-30.

_____. "Der Fugenvokal ā in gāthisch-awestischen Komposita." *Münchener Studien zur Sprachwissenschaft* 4 (1954): 53-71.

_____. "Zur altiranische Mythologie." *Zeitschrift der deutschen morgenlandischen Gesellschaft* 107 (1957):362-71.

_____. "Ahura Mazdā und die Daēvas." *Wiener Zeitschrift für die Kunde des Süd- und Ostasiens* 1 (1957):81-94.

_____. "Milchprodukte im zarathustrischen Ritual." *Indogermanische Forschungen* 63 (1957):40-54.

_____. "Review: Wackernagel and Debrunner, *Altindische Grammatik, II/2, Die Nominalsuffixe.*" *Deutsche Literaturzeitung* 78 (1957):298-301.

_____. "Gāthisch und Jungawestisch." *Wiener Zeitschrift für die Kunde des Süd- und Ostasiens* 2 (1958):22-32.

_____. "Der iranische Mithra als Daiva." In *Festgabe für Herman Lommel,* pp. 75-79, edited by Bernfried Schlerath. Wiesbaden: Otto Harrassowitz, 1960.

_____. "Mithra in the Kuṣāṇa period." In *Mithraic Studies,* pp. 135-41, edited by John R. Hinnells. Manchester: University of Manchester Press, 1975.

Humbach, Helmut, ed. and trans. *Die Gāthas des Zarathustra.* 2 vols. Heidelberg: Carl Winter, 1959.

Huntingford, G. W. B. "Some Aspects of Nandi Stock Raising." *Journal of the East Africa and Uganda Natural History Society* 50 (1933):250-62.

Huot, Jean-Louis. *Persia.* London: Frederick Muller, 1965.

Ivanov, V. V. "L'organisation sociale des tribus indo-européens d'après les données linguistiques." *Cahiers d'histoire mondiale* 5 (1960):789-800.

Ivanov, Vyatcheslav, and Toporov, Vladimir. "Le mythe indoeuropéen du dieu de l'orage poursuivant le serpent: Reconstruction du schéma." In *Échanges et Communications: Mélanges offerts à Claude Lévi-Strauss,* pp. 1180-1206. The Hague: Mouton, 1968.

Jackson, H. C. "The Nuer of the Upper Nile Province." *Sudan Notes and Records* 6 (1923):59-107, 123-89.

BIBLIOGRAPHY

Jacobi, H. "Über Indra." *Zeitschrift für vergleichende Sprachforschung* 31 (1892):316-19.

Jacobs, Alan H. "A Bibliography of the Masai." *African Studies* 8 (1965):40-60.

Jakobson, Roman. "The Slavic God Veles and His Indo-European Cognates." In *Studi Linguistici in Onore di Vittore Pisani*, pp. 579-99. Brescia: Paideia, 1969.

James, L. "The Kenya Masai: A Nomadic People Under Modern Administration." *Africa* 12 (1939):49-73.

Jeanmaire, H. *Couroi et Courètes*. Lille: Bibliothèque Universitaire, 1939.

Jensen, Adolf E. *Myth and Cult Among Primitive Peoples*. Chicago: University of Chicago Press, 1963.

Jettmar, Karl. "Zur Wanderungsgeschichte der Iranier." In *Die Wiener Schule der Völkerkunde* pp. 327-48, edited by J. Haekel. Vienna: F. Berger, 1956.

_____. "Traditionen der Steppenkulturen bei indo-iranischen Bergvölkern." *Jahrbuch des Südasien-Instituts der Universität Heidelberg* (1966), pp. 18-23.

_____. "Die Steppenkulturen und die Iranier des Plateaus." *Iranica Antiqua* 9 (1972):65-93.

Joshi, Hem Chandra. *Recherches sur les conceptions économiques et politiques aux Indes anciennes*. Paris: Jouve, 1928.

Kammenhuber, Annelies. *Die Arier im vorderen Orient*. Heidelberg: Carl Winter, 1968.

Kane, Pandurang Vaman. *History of Dharmaśāstra*. 5 vols. Poona: Bhandarkar Oriental Research Institute, 1941.

Keith, Arthur Berriedale. "The Early History of the Indo-Iranians." In *Commemorative Essays Presented to Sir R. G. Bhandarkar*, pp. 81-92. Poona: Bhandarkar Oriental Research Institute, 1917.

_____. *The Religion and Philosophy of the Veda and Upanishads*. Cambridge, Mass.: Harvard University Press, 1925.

_____. "The Age of the Rigveda." In *The Cambridge History of India*, Vol. I, pp. 77-113. Cambridge: The University Press, 1926.

_____. "Mitanni, India, and Iran." In *Dr. Modi Memorial Volume*, pp. 81-94. Bombay: Fort Press, 1930.

_____. "The God Varuna." *Indian Historical Quarterly* 9 (1933): 515-20.

_____. "Indra and Vṛtra." *Indian Culture* 1 (1935):461-66.

_____. "The Home of the Indo-Europeans." *Indian Historical Quarterly* 13 (1937):1-30.

_____. "Varuṇa and Ouranos." *Indian Culture* 3 (1937):421-30.

BIBLIOGRAPHY

Kent, Roland G. "Cattle Tending and Agriculture in the Avesta." *Journal of the American Oriental Society* 39 (1919): 329–33.

————. "The Name Ahuramazdā." In *Oriental Studies in Honor of Pavry*, pp. 200–208, edited by J. D. C. Pavry. London: Oxford University Press, 1933.

————. *Old Persian*. New Haven, Conn.: Yale University Press, 1953.

Kienle, Richard von. "Tier Völkernamen bei indogermanischen Stämmen." *Wörter und Sachen* 14 (1932):25–67.

Kinsella, Thomas, trans. *The Tain*. London: Oxford University Press, 1970.

Kirfel, Willibald. "Der Aśvamedha und der Puruṣamedha." In *Festschrift für Walther Schubring*, pp. 38–50. Hamburg: de Gruyter, 1951.

Knipe, David M. "The Heroic Theft: Myths from Ṛgveda IV and the Ancient Near East." *History of Religions* 6 (1967): 328–60.

Koppers, Wilhelm. "Die Religion der Indogermanen in ihren kulturhistorischen Beziehungen." *Anthropos* 24 (1929): 1073–89.

————. "Pferdeopfer und Pferdekult der Indogermanen." *Wiener Beiträge zur Kulturkunde und Linguistik* 4 (1936): 279–411.

Kosambi, D. D. *Ancient India*. New York: Pantheon, 1965.

Kramer, Samuel Noah. *The Sacred Marriage Rite*. Bloomington: Indiana University Press, 1969.

Kretschmer, Paul. "Mythische Namen: Herakles." *Glotta* 8 (1916): 121–29.

————. "Varuṇa und die Urgeschichte der Inder." *Wiener Zeitschrift für die Kunde des Morgenlandes* 33 (1926):1–23.

————. "Weiteres zur Urgeschichte der Inder." *Zeitschrift für vergleichende Sprachforschung* 55 (1927):75–103.

————. "Indra und der hethitische Gott Inaras." *Kleinasiatische Forschungen* 1 (1927):297–317.

————. "Der Name der Lykier und andere kleinasiatische Völkernamen." *Kleinasiatische Forschungen* 3 (1930):1–17.

Kroll, Wilhelm. "Etwas vom Werwolf." *Wiener Studien* 55 (1937): 168–72.

Kuhn, Adalbert. "Sprachvergleichung und Urgeschichte der indogermanischen Völker." *Zeitschrift für vergleichende Sprachforschung* 4 (1855):81–124.

————. *Die Herabkunft des Feuers und des Göttertranks*. Gütersloh: C. Bertelsman, 1886.

Kuiper, F. B. J. "Avestan Mazdā-." *Indo-Iranian Journal* 1 (1957):86–95.

BIBLIOGRAPHY

_____. "Review: Paul Thieme, *Mitra and Aryaman.*" *Indo-Iranian Journal* 3 (1959):207-12.

_____. The Ancient Aryan Verbal Contests." *Indo-Iranian Journal* 4 (1960):217-81.

_____. "Remarks on the *Avestan Hymn to Mithra.*" *Indo-Iranian Journal* 5 (1961):36-60.

_____. "Some Observations on Dumézil's Theory." *Numen* 8 (1961): 34-45.

_____. "The Bliss of Aša." *Indo-Iranian Journal* 8 (1964):96-129.

_____. "The Basic Concept of Vedic Religion." *History of Religions* 15 (1975):107-20.

_____. "Ahura Mazdā: 'Lord Wisdom'?" *Indo-Iranian Journal* 18 (1976):25-42.

Lamberg-Karlovsky, C. C. "The Earliest Communities of Iran." *Iranian Studies* 2 (1969):2-7.

Landsberger, B., and Wilson, J. V. K. "The Fifth Tablet of Enuma Eliš." *Journal of Near Eastern Studies* 20 (1961): 154-79.

LaRoche, Emmanuel. *Recherches sur les noms des dieux hittites.* Paris: Maisonneuve, 1947.

_____. *Recueil d'onomastique hittite.* Paris: C. Klincksíeck, 1951.

_____. *Textes mythologiques hittites en transcription,* 2 vols. Paris: C. Klincksíeck, 1965-68.

Lauer, M., trans. *Des Moses von Chorene Geschichte Gross-Armeniens.* Regensburg: Joseph Manz, 1869.

Lawren, William L. "Masai and Kikuyu: A Historical Analysis of Culture Transmission." *Journal of African History* 9 (1968):571-83.

Lazzeroni, Romano. "Per una definizione dell'unità indo-iranica." *Studi e Saggi Linguistici* 8 (1968):131-59.

Leakey, Louis S. B. "Some Notes on the Masai of Kenya Colony." *Journal of the Royal Anthropological Institute* 60 (1930):185-209.

Lentz, Wolfgang. "The 'Social Functions' of the Old Iranian Mithra." In *W. B. Henning Memorial Volume,* pp. 245-55, edited by Mary Boyce and Ilya Gershevitch. London: Lund, Humphries, 1970.

Leumann, Manu. "Der Indoiranisch Bildnergott Twarštar." *Asiatische Studien / Études Asiatiques* 8 (1954):79-84.

Lévi, Sylvain. *La doctrine du sacrifice dans les Brāhmaṇas.* Paris: E. Leroux, 1898.

Lévi-Strauss, Claude. *The Savage Mind.* Chicago: University of Chicago Press, 1966.

_____. *The Raw and the Cooked.* New York: Harper and Row, 1969.

BIBLIOGRAPHY

Levy, Reuben, ed. and trans. *The Epic of the Kings: Shāh-nāmā*. Chicago: University of Chicago Press, 1967.

Lewis, B. A. "Nuer Spokesmen: A Note on the Institution of the *Ruic*." *Sudan Notes and Records*, 32 (1951):77–84.

Lewis, R. W. E. "The Maasai Traditional Way of Life." In *Nairobi: City and Region*, pp. 67–78, edited by W. T. W. Morgan. London: Oxford University Press, 1967.

Lienhardt, Godfrey. *Divinity and Experience: The Religion of the Dinka*. Oxford: Clarendon Press, 1961.

Lincoln, Bruce. "The Indo-European Myth of Creation." *History of Religions* 15 (1975):121–45.

_____. "Indo-Iranian **gautra-*." *Journal of Indo-European Studies* 3 (1975):161–71.

_____. "Homeric λύσσα: 'Wolfish Rage.'" *Indogermanische Forschungen* 80 (1975):98–105.

_____. "The Myth of the 'Bovine's Lament.'" *Journal of Indo-European Studies* 3 (1975):337–62.

_____. "The Indo-European Cattle-Raiding Myth." *History of Religions* 16 (1976):42–65.

_____. "Treatment of Hair and Fingernails Among the Indo-Europeans." *History of Religions* 16 (1977):351–62.

_____. "Death and Resurrection in Indo-European Thought." *Journal of Indo-European Studies* 5 (1977):247–64.

_____. "The Lord of the Dead," *History of Religions* 20 (1980–81): forthcoming.

Littleton, C. Scott. "The 'Kingship in Heaven' Theme." In *Myth and Law Among the Indo-Europeans*, pp. 83–121, edited by Jaan Puhvel. Berkeley, Calif.: University of California Press, 1973.

_____. *The New Comparative Mythology: An Anthropological Assessment of the Theories of Georges Dumézil*. Berkeley, Calif.: University of California Press, 1973.

_____. "Poseidon as a Reflex of the Indo-European 'Source of Waters' God." *Journal of Indo-European Studies* 1 (1973): 423–40.

_____. "Georges Dumézil and the Rebirth of the Genetic Model." In *Myth in Indo-European Antiquity*, pp. 169–80, edited by Gerald James Larson. Berkeley, Calif.: University of California Press, 1974.

Loisleur, Auguste, ed. *Lois de Manou*. Paris: Levrault, 1830.

Lommel, Herman, trans. *Die Yašts des Awesta*. Göttingen: Vandenhoeck and Ruprecht, 1927.

_____. *Die Religion Zarathustras nach dem Awesta dargestellt*. Tubingen: J. C. B. Mohr, 1930.

BIBLIOGRAPHY

_____. "War Zarathustra ein Bauer?" *Zeitschrift für vergleichende Sprachforschung* 58 (1930):248-65.

_____. "Der medische Name Mazdaka." *Zeitschrift für vergleichende Sprachforschung* 58 (1930):140-42.

_____. "Yasna 29: die Klage des Rindes." *Zeitschrift für Indologie und Iranistik* 10 (1935):96-115.

_____. "Naotara und Spitāma." *Indogermanische Forschungen* 53 (1935):165-86.

_____. *Der arische Kriegsgott.* Frankfurt: V. Klostermann, 1939.

_____. *Les anciens aryens.* Paris: Gallimard, 1942.

_____. "Mithra und das Stieropfer." *Paideuma* 3 (1949):207-19.

_____. "Zarathustras Priesterlohn." In *Studia Indologica: Festschrift für Willibald Kirfel,* pp. 187-96. Bonn: Orientalistischen Seminars der Universität Bonn, 1955.

_____. "Himmlische und irdische Nahrung." *Zeitschrift der deutschen morgenlandischen Gesellschaft* 105 (1955):158-65.

_____. "König Soma." *Numen* 2 (1955):196-205.

_____. "Die Sonne das Schlechteste?" *Oriens* 15 (1962):360-73.

_____. "Vasiṣṭha und Viśvāmitra." *Oriens* 18/19 (1967):200-27.

_____. "Awestisch Drigu, Vāstra und Verwandtes." In *Pratidānam: Indian, Iranian, and Indo-European Studies Presented to F. B. J. Kuiper,* pp. 127-35, edited by J. C. Heesterman. The Hague: Mouton, 1968.

_____, trans. *Die Gāthas des Zarathustra.* Basel: Schwabe, 1971.

Long, Charles H. *Alpha: The Myths of Creation.* New York: George Braziller, 1963.

Lüders, Heinrich. *Varuṇa.* 2 vols. Göttingen: Vandenhoeck and Ruprecht, 1951.

Macdonald, A. W. "A propos de Prajāpati." *Journal Asiatique* 240 (1953):323-38.

Macdonell, A. A. "Mythological Studies in the Rigveda: The God Trita." *Journal of the Royal Asiatic Society* (1893): 419-96.

Macdonell, A. A., and Keith, A. B. *Vedic Index of Names and Subjects.* 2 vols. London: John Murray, 1912; repr. Delhi: Motilal Banarsidas, 1967.

Machek, V. "Name und Herkunft des Gottes Indra." *Archiv Orientalni* 12 (1941):143-54.

Malinowski, Bronislaw. *Magic, Science, and Religion and Other Essays.* Garden City, N. J.: Doubleday, 1954.

Mallory, James. "A Short History of the Indo-European Problem." *Journal of Indo-European Studies* 1 (1973):21-65.

_____. "The Chronology of the Early Kurgan Tradition." *Journal*

BIBLIOGRAPHY

of *Indo-European Studies* 4 (1976):257-94; and 5 (1977):339-68.

Maquet, Jacques. *Civilizations of Black Africa.* London: Oxford University Press, 1972.

Mauss, Marcel. *The Gift: Forms and Functions of Exchange in Archaic Societies.* New York: W. W. Norton, 1967.

Mauss, Marcel, and Hubert, Henri. *Sacrifice: Its Nature and Function.* Chicago: University of Chicago Press, 1964.

Mayrhofer, Manfred. *Kurzgefasstes etymologisches Wörterbuch des Altindischen.* 3 vols. Heidelberg: Carl Winter, 1956-76.

_____. "Über Kontaminationen der indoiranischen Sippen von ai. *takṣ-, tvakṣ-, *tvarś-.*" In *Indo-Iranica: Mélanges présentés à Georg Morgenstierne,* pp. 141-48. Wiesbaden: Otto Harrassowitz, 1964.

_____. *Die Indo-Arier im alten Vorderasien.* Wiesbaden: Otto Harrassowitz, 1966.

_____. "Die vorderasiatischen Arier." *Asiatische Studien / Études Asiatiques* 23 (1969):139-54.

Mayrhofer-Passler, E. "Haustieropfer bei den Indoiraniern und den anderen indogermanischen Völkern." *Archiv Orientalni* 21 (1953):182-205.

Meillet, Antoine. "Le dieu indo-iranien Mitra." *Journal Asiatique* 10 (1907):143-59.

_____. *Trois conférences sur les Gātha de l'Avesta.* Paris: Paul Geuthner, 1925.

_____. *Introduction à l'étude comparative des langues indo-européennes.* University, Ala.: University of Alabama Press, 1964.

_____. *La méthode comparative en linguistique historique.* Paris: Honoré Champion, 1966.

Merker, M. *Die Masai: Ethnographische Monographie eines ostafrikanischen Semitenvolkes.* Berlin: Dietrich Reimer, 1904.

Meyer, Kuno. "Der irische Totengott und die Toteninsel." *Sitzungsberichte der preussischen Akademie der Wissenschaften* (1919):537-46.

Middleton, John. *The Kikuyu and Kamba of Kenya.* London: International African Institute, 1953.

Middleton, John, and Tait, David, eds. *Tribes Without Rulers.* London: Routledge and Kegan Paul, 1958.

Molé, Marijan. *Culte, mythe et cosmologie dans l'Iran ancien.* Paris: Presses Universitaires de France, 1963.

Morgenstierne, George. "Indo-European K' in Kafiri." *Norsk Tidsskrift for Sprogvidenskamp* 13 (1945):225-38.

BIBLIOGRAPHY

Much, Rudolf, ed. *Die Germania des Tacitus*. Heidelberg: Carl Winter, 1967.

Muir, J. *Original Sanskrit Texts*, Vol. I. London: Trübner, 1872.

Murdock, George P. *Africa: Its Peoples and Their Culture History*. New York: McGraw Hill, 1959.

Newcomer, Peter J. "The Nuer are Dinka: An Essay on Origins and Environmental Determinism." *Man* 7 (1972):5-11.

Nilsson, Martin Persson. *Opuscula Selecta*, 3 vols. Lund: C. W. K. Gleerup, 1952.

Nöldecke, Theodor. "Der weisse Dēv von Mazāndaran." *Archiv für Religionswissenschaft* 18 (1915):597-600.

_____. "Dēva." *Zeitschrift für Indologie und Iranistik* 2 (1923):318.

Nunn, N. "A Dinka Sacrifice." *Sudan Notes and Records* 31 (1950): 141-42.

Nyberg, Henrik Samuel. *Die Religionen des alten Iran*. Leipzig: J. C. Hinrichs, 1938.

O'Brien, Steven. "Indo-European Eschatology: A Model." *Journal of Indo-European Studies* 4 (1976):295-320.

O'Callaghan, R. T. "New Light on the Maryannu as 'Chariot-Warriors.' " *Jahrbuch für kleinasiatische Forschung* 1 (1951):309-24.

Odede, Walter. "Luo Customs with Regard to Animals (with Particular References to Cattle)." *Journal of the East Africa and Uganda Natural History Society* 72 (1942):127-35.

Oertel, Hanns. *The Syntax of Cases in the Narrative and Descriptive Prose of the Brāhmaṇas*. Heidelberg: Carl Winter, 1926.

_____. *Euphemism in der vedischen Prosa*. Munich: Bayerischen Akademie der Wissenschaften, 1942.

Ogibenin, B. L. "Baltic Evidence and the Indo-Iranian Prayer." *Journal of Indo-European Studies* 2 (1974):23-46.

Oldenberg, Hermann. *Die Religion des Veda*. Berlin: W. Hertz, 1894.

_____. "Zu Mythologie und Cultus des Veda." *Zeitschrift der deutschen morgenlandischen Gesellschaft* 49 (1895): 172-79.

_____. "Zur Geschichte des indischen Kastenwesens." *Zeitschrift der deutschen morgenlandischen Gesellschaft* 51 (1897): 267-90.

Olerud, Anders. *L'idée de macrocosmos et de microcosmos dans le Timée de Platon*. Uppsala: Almquist and Wiksells, 1951.

O'Rahilly, Cecile, ed. and trans. *Táin Bó Cúalnge from the Book of Leinster*. Dublin: Dublin Institute for Advanced Studies, 1967.

BIBLIOGRAPHY

O'Rahilly, T. F. *Early Irish History and Mythology.* Dublin: Dublin Institute for Advanced Studies, 1971.

Osten, H. H. van der. *Die Welt der Perser.* Stuttgart: Gustav Klimt, 1956.

O'Sullivan, Hugh. "Dinka Laws and Customs." *Journal of the Royal Anthropological Institute* 40 (1910):171–91.

Oswiecimski, Stephanus. "Ad Litteras Romanas Symbolae Duae." *Eos* 44 (1950):111–22.

Otrębski, J. "Aind. *puruṣaḥ, pūman* und Verwandtes." *Zeitschrift für vergleichende Sprachforschung* 82 (1968):251–58.

Otten, Heinrich. "Ein Text zum Neujahrsfest aus Bogazköy." *Orientalistiche Literaturzeitung* 51 (1956):101–5.

Oxenstierne, Eric Graf. *Die Goldhörner von Gallehus.* Published by the author, 1956.

Palmer, Leonard R. *"Arya-*: A Homological Sketch." In *Antiquitates Indogermanicae: Gedenkschrift für Hermann Güntert* (Innsbruck: Innsbrucker Beiträge zur Sprachwissenschaft, 1976), pp. 11–19.

Perry, Edward Delavan. "Indra in the Rig-Veda." *Journal of the American Oriental Society* 11 (1891):117–208.

Petersson, Herbert. "Einige Bemerkungen zu den Götternamen Mitra und Varuna." In *Studier tellegnade Esaias Tegner,* pp. 223–34. Lund: C. W. K. Gleerup, 1918.

Pettazzoni, Raffaele. *Dio. Formazione e Sviluppo del Monoteismo nella Storia delle Religioni.* Vol. 1: *L'Essere Celeste nelle Credenze dei Popoli Primitivi.* Rome: Athenaeum, 1922.

———. "Ahura Mazda, the Knowing Lord." In *Indo-Iranian Studies in Honour of Sanjana,* pp. 149–62, edited by A. V. Williams Jackson. London: Trench, Trübner and Co., 1925.

———. *The All-Knowing God.* London: Methuen, 1956.

———. *Essays on the History of Religions.* Leiden: E. J. Brill, 1967.

Pictet, Adolfe. *Les origines indo-européennes.* Paris: Sandoz et Fischbacker, 1877, first published 1859.

Piggott, Stuart. *Prehistoric India to 1000* B.C. Baltimore, Md.: Penguin, 1950.

———. *Ancient Europe.* Chicago: Aldine, 1965.

Pisani, Vittore. *Crestomazia Indeuropea.* Turin: Rosenberg and Seilers, 1949.

———. "Sanskrit *aghnya-*, griech. *aphneios.*" In *Studies in Greek, Italic, and Indo-European Linguistics offered to Leonard R. Palmer,* pp. 283–84. Innsbruck: Innsbrucker Beiträge zur Sprachwissenschaft, 1976.

BIBLIOGRAPHY

Pischel, Richard, and Geldner, Karl Friedrich. *Vedische Studien*. 3 vols. Stuttgart: W. Kohlhammer, 1897.

Pokorny, Julius. *Indogermanisches etymologisches Wörterbuch*. Bern: Francke, 1959.

Polomé, Edgar. "L'étymologie du terme germanique **ansuz*, 'dieu souverain.' " *Études Germaniques* 8 (1953):36-44.

Porzig, Walter. "Illujankas und Typhon." *Kleinasiatische Forschungen* 3 (1930):379-86.

Potdar, K. R. *Sacrifice in the Rg Veda: Its Nature, Origin and Growth*. Bombay: Bharatiya Vidya, 1953.

Potscher, Walter. "Der Name des Herakles." *Emerita* 39 (1971):169-84.

Prakash, Om. *Food and Drinks in Ancient India*. Delhi: Munshi Ram Manohar Lal, 1961.

Prasad, Ganga Upadhyaya, ed. *Śatapatha Brāhmaṇam*. 3 vols. New Delhi: Research Institute of Ancient Scientific Studies, 1967-70.

Prashad, B. *Animal Remains from Harappa* (= *Memoirs of the Archaeological Survey of India* 51 [1936]), pp. 1-64.

Pryzluski, Jean. "Les confréries de loups-garous dans les sociétés indo-européennes." *Revue de l'histoire des religions* 121 (1940):128-45.

––––––. "Inara et Indra." *Revue Hittite et Asianique* 5 (1940):142-46.

Puhvel, Jaan. "Vedic Aśvamedha- and Gaulish Iipomiidvos." *Language* 31 (1955):353-54.

––––––. "The Meaning of Greek Βουκάτιος." *Zeitschrift für vergleichende Sprachforschung* 79 (1964):7-10.

––––––. "Aspects of Equine Functionality." In *Myth and Law Among the Indo-Europeans*, pp. 159-72, edited by Jaan Puhvel. Berkeley, Calif.: University of California Press, 1970.

––––––. "Aquam Exstinguere." *Journal of Indo-European Studies* 1 (1973):379-86.

––––––. "Remus et Frater." *History of Religions* 15 (1975):146-57.

Rahurkar, V. G. *The Seers of the Rgveda*. Poona: University of Poona, 1964.

Ralston, W. R. S. *Russian Folktales*. London: Smith, Elder, 1873.

Rees, Alwyn, and Rees, Brinley. *Celtic Heritage*. London: Thames and Hudson, 1961.

Reitzenstein, Richard, and Schaeder, H. H. *Studien zum antiken Synkretismus aus Iran und Griechenland*. Leipzig: B. G. Teubner, 1926.

Renou, Louis. "Les éléments védiques dans le sanskrit classique." *Journal Asiatique* 231 (1939):321-404.

––––––. "Quelques termes du Rgveda." *Journal Asiatique* 241 (1953): 167-83.

BIBLIOGRAPHY

_____. *Études védiques et pāṇinéennes.* 17 vols. Paris: E. de Boccard, 1955-69.

_____. *Vedic India.* Calcutta: Susil Gupta, 1957.

_____. "Varuṇa dans l'Atharvaveda." In *Festgabe für Herman Lommel,* pp. 122-28, edited by Bernfried Schlerath. Wiesbaden: Otto Harrassowitz, 1960.

Ridley, Richard R. "Wolf and Werwolf in Baltic and Slavic Tradition." *Journal of Indo-European Studies* 4 (1976):321-31.

Rigby, Peter J. *Cattle and Kinship Among the Gogo.* Ithaca, N.Y.: Cornell University Press, 1969.

_____. "The Symbolic Role of Cattle in Gogo Ritual." In *The Translation of Culture: Essays to E. E. Evans-Pritchard,* pp. 257-92, edited by T. O. Beidelman. London: Tavistock, 1971.

Ringgren, Helmer. *Religions of the Ancient Near East.* Philadelphia: Westminster, 1973.

Risch, Ernst. "Die indogermanischen Verwandten von griechisch σάρκες." *Die Sprache* 7 (1961):93-98.

Roe, Frank Gilbert. *The Indian and the Horse.* Norman, Okla.: University of Oklahoma Press, 1955.

Rönnow, Kasten. *Trita Āptya, eine vedische Gottheit.* Uppsala: Appelbert, 1927.

_____. "Zur Erklärung des Pravargya, des Agnicayana und der Sautrāmaṇī." *Monde Oriental* 23 (1929):113-73.

_____. "Viśvārupa." *Bulletin of the School of Oriental and African Studies* 6 (1931):469-80.

_____. "Ved. *kratu-.*" *Monde Oriental* 26 (1932):1-90.

Rose, H. J. "Chthonian Cattle." *Numen* 1 (1954):213-27.

Roth, Rudolph von. *Zur Literatur und Geschichte des Weda.* Stuttgart: A. Liesching, 1846.

_____. "Die Sage von Feridūn in Indien und Iran." *Zeitschrift der deutschen morgenlandischen Gesellschaft* 4 (1850): 216-30.

_____. "Die Sage von Dschemschid," *Zeitschrift der deutschen morgenlandischen Gesellschaft* 4 (1850):417-33.

_____. "Die hochsten Götter der arischen Völker." *Zeitschrift der deutschen morgenlandischen Gesellschaft* 6 (1852): 67-77.

_____. "Wergeld im Veda." *Zeitschrift der deutschen morgenlandischen Gesellschaft* 41 (1881):672-76.

Ruben, Walter. "Arische Hirten und vorarische Bauern im alten Indien." In *Das Verhältnis von Bodenbauern und Viehzüchtern in historischer Sicht,* pp. 48-61. Berlin: Akademie Verlag, 1968.

Rudolph, Kurt. "Zarathustra—Priester und Prophet." *Numen* 8 (1961):81–116.

Sahlins, Marshall D. "The Segmentary Lineage: An Organization of Predatory Expansion." *American Anthropologist* 63 (1961):322–45.

Schaeder, H. H. See Reitzenstein, Richard, and Schaeder, H. H.

Schayer, Stanislas. "A Note on the Old Russian Variant of the Purushasūkta." *Archiv Orientalni* 7 (1935):319–23.

Scheftelowitz, I. "Die Mithra-Religion der Indoskythen." *Acta Orientalia* 11 (1933):293–333.

Scheller, Meinrad. "Rinder mit vergoldeten Hörnern." *Zeitschrift für vergleichende Sprachforschung* 72 (1955):227–28.

_____. "Τρίττοια Βόαρχος." *Zeitschrift für vergleichende Sprachforschung* 74 (1956):233–35.

Scherer, Anton. "Hauptprobleme der indogermanischen Altertumskunde." *Kratylos* 1 (1956):3–21.

Schlerath, Bernfried. "Opfergaben." In *Festgabe für Herman Lommel,* pp. 129–34, edited by Bernfried Schlerath. Wiesbaden: Otto Harrassowitz, 1960.

_____. "Review: Humbach, *Die Gāthas des Zarathustra.*" *Orientalistische Literaturzeitung* (1962):565–88.

_____. "Altindisch *asu-*, awestisch *ahu-* und ähnlich klingende Wörter." In *Pratidānam: Indian, Iranian and Indo-European Studies Presented to F. B. J. Kuiper,* pp. 142–53, edited by J. C. Heesterman. The Hague: Mouton, 1968.

Schmid, Wolfgang. "Die Kuh auf der Weide." *Indogermanische Forschungen* 64 (1958):1–12.

Schmidt, Hanns-Peter. *"Aghnya-."* *Zeitschrift für vergleichende Sprachforschung* 78 (1962):1–46.

_____. *Bṛhaspati und Indra.* Wiesbaden: Otto Harrassowitz, 1968.

_____. "The Origin of *Ahiṃsā.*" In *Mélanges d'indianisme à la mémoire de Louis Renou,* pp. 625–55, edited by Jean Filliozat. Paris: E. de Boccard, 1968.

_____. *Zarathustra's Religion and His Pastoral Imagery.* Leiden: University of Leiden, 1975.

_____. "Is Vedic *dhenā* related to Avestan *daēnā*?" *Monumentum H. S. Nyberg,* Vol. 2, pp. 165–79. Leiden: E. J. Brill, 1975.

_____. "Indo-Iranian Mitra: The State of the Central Problem." In *Études Mithriaques,* pp. 345–93. Leiden: E. J. Brill, 1978.

211

BIBLIOGRAPHY

Schmidt, Wilhelm. *Wege der Kulturen.* St. Augustin bei Bonn: Missionsdruckerei St. Gabriel, 1964.
Schmitt, Rüdiger. "Proto-Indo-European Culture and Archaeology: Some Critical Remarks." *Journal of Indo-European Studies* 2 (1974):279-87.
Schneider, Harold K. "The Subsistence Role of Cattle Among the Pakot." *American Anthropologist* 59 (1957):278-300.
Schrader, Otto. *Prehistoric Antiquities of the Aryan Peoples.* London: Charles Griffin, 1890.
———. *Reallexikon der indogermanischen Altertumskunde,* 2 vols., 2d ed. by A. Nehring. Strassburg: Otto Harrassowitz, 1917-23.
———. *Die Indogermanen.* Leipzig: Quelle and Meuer, 1935.
Schröder, Franz Rolf. "Ein altirischer Kronungsritus und das indogermanischer Rossopfer." *Zeitschrift für Celtische Philologie* 16 (1927):310-12.
———. "Ase und Gott." *Beiträge zur Geschichte der deutschen Sprache und Literatur* 51 (1927):29-30.
———. "Germanische Schopfungsmythen." *Germanisch-Romanisch Monatsschrift* 19 (1931):1-26, 81-99.
———. "Indra, Thor und Herakles." *Zeitschrift für deutsche Philologie* 76 (1957):1-41.
Schroeder, Leopold von. "Indogermanisches Wergeld." In *Festgruss an Rudolf von Roth,* pp. 49-52, edited by Adalbert Kuhn. Stuttgart: W. Kohlhammer, 1893.
———. "Bemerkungen zu Oldenbergs Religion des Veda." *Wiener Zeitschrift für die Kunde des Morgenlandes* 9 (1895): 109-32, 225-53.
———. *Mysterium und Mimus im Rigveda.* Leipzig: H. Haessel, 1908.
———. *Herakles und Indra.* Vienna: Alfred Holder, 1914.
———. *Arische Religion.* 2 vols. Leipzig: H. Haessel, 1914-23.
Schulze, Wilhelm. *Kleine Schriften.* Göttingen: Vandenhoeck and Ruprecht, 1933.
Schwab, Julius. *Das altindische Thieropfer.* Erlangen: A. Deichert, 1886.
Schweitzer, Bernhard. *Herakles.* Tubingen: J. C. B. Mohr, 1922.
Seligman, C. G., and Brenda Z. *Pagan Tribes of the Nilotic Sudan.* London: George Routledge, 1932.
Sénart, Emile. *Caste in India.* London: Methuen, 1930.
Sewell, R. B. S., and Guha, B. S. "Zoological Remains." In *Mohenjo-Daro and the Indus Civilization,* Vol. 2, pp. 649-73, edited by Sir John Marshall. London: Arthur Probsthain, 1931.

212

BIBLIOGRAPHY

Sjoestedt, Marie-Louise. *Gods and Heroes of the Celts*, translated by M. Dillon. London: Methuen, 1949.

Sommer, Ferdinand. *Die Ahhijavā Urkunden*. Munich: Bayerischen Akademie der Wissenschaft, 1932.

_____. *Ahhijavāfrage und Sprachwissenschaft*. Munich: Bayerischen Akademie der Wissenschaft, 1934.

Specht, Franz. "Zur Bedeutung des Ariernamen." *Zeitschrift für vergleichende Sprachforschung* 68 (1943):42–52.

Spiegel, Friedrich. *Arische Periode und ihre Zustände*. Leipzig: W. Friedrich, 1887.

Srinivasan, Doris. "The Myth of the Paṇis in the Rig Veda," *Journal of the American Oriental Society* 93 (1973):44–57.

Steinmeyer, Elias, and Sievers, Eduard. *Die althochdeutschen Glossen*, 5 vols. Zurich: Weidmann, 1968.

Stevenson, Mrs. Sinclair. *The Rites of the Twice-Born*. London: Oxford University Press, 1920.

Steward, Julian Haynes. *Theory of Culture Change*. Urbana, Ill.: University of Illinois Press, 1955.

Stigand, C. H. "Warrior Classes of the Nuer." *Sudan Notes and Records* 1 (1918):116–18.

Stubbs, J. N. "Notes on Beliefs and Customs of the Malwal Dinka of the Bahr el Ghazal Province." *Sudan Notes and Records* 17 (1934):243–54.

Sutton, J. E. G. "The Settlement of East Africa." In *Zamani: A Survey of East African History*, pp. 69–99, edited by B. A. Ogot. Nairobi: East Africa Publishing House, 1968.

Tavadia, J. C. *Indo-Iranian Studies*. 2 vols. Santiniketan: Visva-Bharati, 1950–52.

_____. "Zoroastrian and Pre-Zoroastrian." *Journal of the Bombay Branch of the Royal Asiatic Society* 28 (1953):171–86.

Thieme, Paul. *Der Fremdling im Rigveda*. Leipzig: F. A. Brockhaus, 1938.

_____. "Etymologische Vexierbilder." *Zeitschrift für vergleichende Sprachforschung* 69 (1951):172–78.

_____. *Studien zur indogermanischen Wortkunde und Religionsgeschichte*. Berlin: Akademie Verlag, 1952.

_____. "Vorzarathustrisches bei den Zarathustriern und bei Zarathustra." *Zeitschrift der deutschen morgenlandischen Gesellschaft* 107 (1957):67–104.

_____. *Mitra and Aryaman*. New Haven, Conn.: Yale University Press, 1957.

_____. "The 'Aryan' Gods of the Mitanni Treaties." *Journal of the American Oriental Society* 80 (1960):301–17.

213

_____. "Die vedischen Āditya und die zarathustrischen Aməša Spənta." In *Zarathustra,* pp. 397–412, edited by Bernfried Schlerath. Darmstadt: Wissenschaftliche Buchgesellschaft, 1970.

_____. "The Concept of Mitra in Aryan Belief." In *Mithraic Studies,* pp. 21–39, edited by John R. Hinnells. Manchester: University of Manchester Press, 1975.

Thomas, Elizabeth Marshall. *Warrior Herdsmen.* New York: Alfred Knopf, 1965.

Titherington, G. W. "The Raik Dinka of Bahr el Ghazal Province." *Sudan Notes and Records* 10 (1927):159–209.

Toporov, V. N. "Parallels to Ancient Indo-Iranian Social and Mythological Concepts." In *Pratidānam: Indian, Iranian and Indo-European Studies Presented to F. B. J. Kuiper,* pp. 108–20, edited by J. C. Heesterman. The Hague: Mouton, 1968.

Trager, George L., and Smith, Henry Lee. "A Chronology of Indo-Hittite." *Studies in Linguistics* 8 (1950):61–70.

Turville-Petre, E. O. G. *Myth and Religion of the North.* New York: Holt, Rinehart and Winston, 1964.

Ungnad, Arthur. "Luwisch = Lykisch." *Zeitschrift für Assyriologie* 35 (1924):1–8.

Vendryes, J. "Les correspondances de vocabulaire entre l'indo-iranien et l'italo-celtique." *Mémoires de la Société de linguistique de Paris* 20 (1918):265–85.

Venkantasubbiah, A. "On Indra's Winning of Cows and Waters." *Zeitschrift der deutschen morgenlandischen Gesellschaft* 115 (1965):120–33.

Vries, Jan de. *Altgermanische Religionsgeschichte.* 2 vols. Berlin: W. de Gruyter, 1957.

_____. "Sur certains glissements fonctionnels de divinités dans la religion germanique." In *Hommages à Georges Dumézil,* pp. 83–95. Brussels: Collection Latomus, 1960.

_____. *Altnordisches etymologisches Wörterbuch.* Leiden: E. J. Brill, 1961.

Wackernagel, Jakob. "Miszellen zur griechischen Grammatik." *Zeitschrift für vergleichende Sprachforschung* 29 (1888): 124–52.

_____. "Akzentstudien I." *Nachrichten der Göttingen Gesellschaft der Wissenschaften* (1909):50–63.

_____. "Indoiranica: Zum Dualdvandva." *Zeitschrift für vergleichende Sprachforschung* 43 (1910):295–98.

BIBLIOGRAPHY

Wackernagel, Jakob, and Debrunner, Albert. *Altindische Grammatik, II/2 Die Nominalsuffixe.* Göttingen: Vandenhoeck and Ruprecht, 1954.

Walcot, Peter. "Cattle Raiding, Heroic Tradition, and Ritual: The Greek Evidence." *History of Religions* 18 (1979): 326–51.

Walde, A., and Hofmann, J. B. *Lateinisches etymologisches Wörterbuch.* Heidelberg: Carl Winter, 1938.

Weiser, Lily. *Altgermanische Jünglingsweihen und Männerbünde.* Baden: Konkordia, 1927.

Weisweiler, Josef. "Vorindogermanische Schichten der irischen Heldensage." *Zeitschrift für celtische Philologie* 24 (1954): 10–55, 165–97.

Widengren, Geo. *Hochgottglaube im alten Iran.* Uppsala: Uppsala Universitets Arsskrift, 1938.

———. "Stand und Aufgaben der iranischen Religionsgeschichte." *Numen* 1 (1954):16–83, and 2 (1955):47–134.

———. *Die Religionen Irans.* Stuttgart: W. Kohlhammer, 1965.

———. "Le symbolisme de la ceinture." *Iranica Antiqua* 8 (1968): 133–55.

———. "The Death of Gayōmart." In *Myths and Symbols: Studies in Honor of Mircea Eliade,* pp. 179–94, edited by Joseph M. Kitagawa and Charles H. Long. Chicago: University of Chicago Press, 1969.

Wikander, Stig. *Der arische Männerbund.* Lund: C. W. K. Gleerup, 1938.

———. *Vayu: Texte und Untersuchungen zur Indo-iranischen Religionsgeschichte.* Leipzig: Otto Harrassowitz, 1941.

———. "Mithra en vieux-perse." *Orientalia Suecana* 2 (1953):66–68.

Wilhelm, Eugen. "Königthum und Priesterthum im alten Eran," *Zeitschrift der deutschen morgenlandischen Gesellschaft* 40 (1886):102–10.

Willis, C. A. "The Cult of Deng." *Sudan Notes and Records* 11 (1928): 195–208.

Winn, M. M. "Thoughts on the Question of Indo-European Movements in Anatolia and Iran." *Journal of Indo-European Studies* 2 (1974):117–42.

Winston, David. "The Iranian Component in the Bible, Apocrypha, and Qumran: A Review of the Evidence." *History of Religions* 5 (1966):183–216.

Winter, Walter. "Some Widespread Indo-European Titles." In *Indo-European and Indo-Europeans,* pp. 49–54, edited by Henry Hoenigswald. Philadelphia: University of Pennsylvania Press, 1970.

BIBLIOGRAPHY

Wissler, Clark. "Societies and Ceremonial Associations in the Oglala Division of the Teton-Dakota." *Anthropological Papers of the American Museum of Natural History* 41 (1921):1–100.

Wolff, Fritz. *Avesta, die heiligen Bucher der Parsen.* Berlin: W. de Gruyter, 1924.

Wüst, Walther. "Trita und Verwandtes." *Wörter und Sachen* 3 (1940): 225–27.

Young, T. Cuyler. "The Iranian Migration into the Zagros." *Iran* 5 (1967):11–34.

Zaehner, R. C. *The Dawn and Twilight of Zoroastrianism.* New York: Putnam, 1961.

INDEX VERBORUM

INDEX VERBORUM

J. *Germanic*
  1. Proto-Germanic
     *ansuz, 51n.
     *manwaz, 82
     *teiwaz, 52
     *yumīyaz, 76

  2. Germanic names in Latin transcription
     Herminones, 84 and n.
     Ingaevones, 84 and n.
     Istaevones, 84 and n.
     Mannus, 84 and n.
     Tuisco, 84 and n.
     Tuisto, 84 and n.

  3. Gothic
     faihu, 65n.
     gadars, 150n.
     giutan, 62n.
     mimz, 155n.
     sigis, 149n.
     waurms, 117
     wulfs, 125

  4. Old High German
     ansi-, ans-, 51n.
     choi, 65n.
     chuo, 64n.
     dritto, 104
     fihu, 65n.
     hengist, 65n.
     hros, 65n.
     ohsun, 65n.
     sigirōn, 149n.
     suuinir, 65n.
     worm, 117
     Ziu, 52

  5. New High German
     giessen, 62n.
     Mann, 82

  6. Old English
     hrēaw, 155n.
     ōs, 51n.
     Tīg, 52
     Tīw, 52
     twisc, 84n.
     twist, 84n.
     wyrm, 117

  7. Modern English
     raw, 155n.

  8. Old Norse
     áss, pl. *æsir*, 51n.
     berserkr, 128

fé, 65n.
Irmin, 84n.
Miðgarðr, 117
Miðgarðsormr, 117
ormr, 117
sigr, 149n.
sveinn, 117
þridi, 104
Týr, 52
Ýmir, 75
Yngvi, 84n.

K. *Baltic*
  1. Lithuanian
     angìs, 107
     drįsti, 150n.
     kraũjas, 155n.
     vìlkas, 125

  2. Old Prussian
     mensā, 155n.
     pecku, 65n.

  3. Lettish
     jumis, 76

L. *Slavic*
  1. Proto-Slavic
     *govędo, 64n.

  2. Old Church Slavonic
     jędrъ, 97
     mozъ, 82
     vlъkъ, 125

  3. Russian
     mir, 55

  4. Bulgarian
     jĕdar, 97

M. *Anatolian*
  1. Hittite
     anka-, 120n.
     haššuš, 51n.
     illu-, 120n.
     illuyanka, 120
     Inara-, 97, 120
     innarauwanza, 120
     lulimieš, 120
     muš, 120

     ᵈKAL, 120

N. *Tocharian*
  1. Tocharian B
     misa, 155n.
     walkwe, 125

INDEX VERBORUM

INDEX LOCORUM

INDEX LOCORUM

INDEX OF SUBJECTS

INDEX OF SUBJECTS

Culture: based in ecology, 173; relation to religion, 12, 176-77
Culture area theories, 8
Cumont, Franz, 131n.
Curiatii, 109
Cushites, Southern, 5
Cyclicity, 159

Dacians, in myth, 109n.
Daēvas, 51-52, 125, 150, 162n; as demons, 51n., 77, 97-98
*Daivas, 51-52 and n. See also Warrior Gods
Dagda, 91
Dakota, 163
Dandekar, R. N., 80, 97n., 101n., 129n., 152n.
Daring, 150
Darmesteter, James, 79, 108
*Dāsa, 109, 128, 135-36 and n., 139, 170. See also Aborigines
Dasyave Vṛka (Indic warrior), 126
Dead: lord of, 92n.; spirits of, 129, 169; warriors of, 129-30
Death, goddess of, 98, 129n.
Death, origin of, 72, 76-77, 80
Debt, sacrifice as repayment of, 33
Deities. See specific names and types, e.g., Celestial Sovereigns; Death, goddess of; Demiurge; Warrior Gods
Demiurge, 17, 59-60, 168
Demons, 51n., 97, 156; dismember primordial victim in Iran, 75; prompt Manu's sacrifice, 80-81. See also Asuras, Daēvas; Rakṣasas
Deng, Francis Mading, 24n., 45, 46n.
Detienne, Marcel, 157n.
Deus otiosus, 19, 53, 168
Devas, 51-52 and n.
DeVries, Larry, 156n.
Dhenuka, 108n.
Dindyor (Dinka priestly clans), 42
Dinka, 3n., 6, 13-14, 16, 17, 19, 22, 25-26, 28, 34, 39, 41-43, 44, 45-46, 46-48, 164, 165, 166, 175; clan divinities, 46; class conflict within, 46-48; cunning of and theft by, 22: migration of, 6; priests of, 14, 41-42, 46-48; term selves "slaves of cattle," 16
Dinka (as character in myth), 21-22, 28, 166
Dismemberment, creation by, 75, 79, 89-90
Divination, 29, 40
Dodoth, 13
Dog, 131
Donn Cuailnge, 87-90, 91, 92 and n., 94

Dorobo, 20, 21, 44
Dorobo (as character in myth), 20-21, 166
Dottin, G., 132n.
Dragon-slaying myth, 105
Dravidians, 136n.
Druids, 137-38
Druim Tairb, 90
Drvāspa, 106
Dualism, 11n., 75, 83
Duchesne-Guillemin, Jacques, 8, 54n., 70n., 105n., 128n., 140n., 151n.
Dumézil, Georges, 2n., 12n., 50n., 51n., 53n., 54n., 60, 79, 84n., 91n., 99n., 107n., 109, 125n., 127n., 128, 130n., 134-35, 136n., 139, 140n., 153n.
Dumont, Louis, 174
Dung, cattle, 7, 14
*Dyaus, 53, 60, 168

Eagle, 99
Earth (as deity), 53
Earth spirits (Nuer), 18
East Africa: "Cattle complex" in, 6-8, 13-16; migrations, 5-6; warrior in, 1-3. See also Dinka; Masai; Nilotes; Nuer
Ecology, relation to culture and religion, 10, 173, 176-77
Edgerton, Franklin, 108n.
Egypt, 5
Eisler, Robert, 126n.
Elephant, 20
Eliade, Mircea, xi, 22n., 38n., 69n., 99n., 126n., 128n., 161n.
Elixir, 130
Equites. See Knights
Eschatology, 91n., 142n., 158n.
Ethiopia, 5
Europeans, 4, 87
Eurytion, 110, 111-12, 123
Ēvagdāδ, See Ox, sole created
Evans-Pritchard, E. E., 2, 15, 18, 21, 24n., 27, 29, 32, 33n., 45n.,
*Ǝner, 97, 120, 122, 123

Falcon, 99
Family maṇḍalas of Ṛg Veda, 62
Father Sky, 53
Fees, sacrificial. See Stipend, sacrificial
Fergus, 88, 89
Feridūn, 107n., 128
Findbennach Aí, 87-90, 91, 92, 94
Fire, 61, 82, 98, 105n., 168. See also Agni
First Bovine, 20-22, 59, 72, 73, 75, 77n., 81, 83, 86-87, 89-91, 92, 169
First Cattle Raid, myth of, 20-23, 27-28,

INDEX OF SUBJECTS

Masai (as character in myth), 21-22, 166
Mauss, Marcel, 33*n.*, 68
Mayrhofer, Manfred, 5*n.*, 59*n.*
Mayrhofer-Passler, E., 62*n.*, 64*n.*
Mbatian (Masai *laibon*), 34
Mead, 130
Means of production, cattle as, 6, 10,
174, 175
Meat, 7, 14, 26, 27, 30, 32-33, 43-46,
68, 116, 123, 127, 154-57, 162, 165,
167, 169, 170-71, 175; as best or most
noble food, 14*n.*, 155; division of, 32-
33; eating of, as cause of conflict, 46,
154, 157, 162, 170-71; eating of, as
threat to cosmos, 159; eating of, for
strength, 44-46, 155, 157, 170-71;
eating of, in sacrifice, 32, 156-57, 169
Medb, 87
Medusa, 113, 123
Mɛɛm (Nuer mythic leopard-man), 30*n.*
Meillet, Antoine, 54, 140*n.*
Merker, M., 15, 23, 26, 45
Metals, as representation of planetary
spheres, 75; created from Gayōmart's
body, 72
Meyer, Kuno, 92*n.*
Miðgarð, 117
Miðgarð serpent, 115-16, 117, 123
Mihr Yašt, 55
Milk and milk products, 7, 14, 27, 64
and *n.*, 109, 168
Mitanni, 5, 182, 184
Mitra (Indic), 55, 152
*Mitra (Indo-Iranian), 50*n.*, 53, 54-56,
60, 100, 168; benign figure, 55; creates
social bonds, 54-55; king, 56; location
in heavens, 56; punishes betrayers, 55;
relation to *Varuna, 54; sleepless, 56
Miθra (Iranian), 55, 66*n.*, 78-79, 98,
128*n.*, 131 and *n.*, 151; assumes war-
rior traits, 55, 98 and *n.*; banished
from pantheon, 55; as bull slayer,
66*n.*; receives Yima's x'arənah, 78-79
Mithraism, 66*n.*
*Mitradrauga. *See* Betrayer of *Mitra
Mock combat, as initiatory ordeal, 128
Molé, Marijan, 62*n.*, 69*n.*
Mongán mac Fiachna, 90, 91-92
Monotheism, inaccurate as characteriza-
tion of Nilotic religion, 18
Moral abstractions, personified. *See* Ab-
stractions, moral
Mother Earth, 53
Much, Rudolph, 84*n.*
Muir, J., 152*n.*
Myrmidons, 126-27
Mysteries of Samothrace, 61*n.*
Myth, 3, 7, 36, 44, 161, 174; as allegory,

101-02, 108; as charter, 22-23, 105,
132, 134, 159, 161, 166, 174; as description of problematic conditions,
161; describes elements of cattle cycle,
33, 159, 161; fails to charter sacrificial
stipend, 161; as means to defuse conflict, 175; reenacted in ritual, 34, 69,
128, 132
Mythic ancestors. *See* Ancestors, mythic
Myths: Bovine's Lament, 140-54; conflict
between upper classes and commoners,
139; cosmogony, 19-23, 69-95; dragon
slaying, 107; eschatology, 91*n.*; First
Cattle Raid, 20-22, 34*n.*, 38, 103-24;
First Sacrifice, 21, 33, 37, 69-95;
flood, 74; Kingship in Heaven, 79*n.*,
origin of death, 72, 76-77, 80; schism
of heaven and earth, 17, 19, 20-21;
theft of *sauma, 130

Naiteru-kop (Masai "beginner of the
earth"), 19
Nak ("killing") camps, 27*n.*, 44-45
Nandi, 6, 13
Nāṇhaiθya, 98, 129*n.*
National herd, 34
Nature allegory, in myth, 101-02, 108
Near Eastern mythology, 79*n.*, 122
Nerik (city), 117
Nērōsang, 72
New and full moon sacrifice, 144, 153
Newcomer, Peter J., 14*n.*, 48*n.*
New Year, 72, 122
Ngai, 16, 17, 19, 20-21, 23, 28, 60, 164,
165, 166. *See also* Celestial Sovereigns
*Ng*hi, 107, 109, 123, 132, 139, 161,
170. *See also* Serpent; Tricephal; First
Cattle Raid, myth of
Nhialic, 16, 19, 60, 164. *See also* Celes-
tial Sovereigns
Nilotes, 1-3, 5-6, 6-8, 10, 13-48, 93,
164-67, 172-77; cattle among, 6-8,
14-16, 23, 31, 33-35, 37-38, 43-46,
48; cosmogony, 19-23; deities, 16-19,
30-31, 39, 46-47, 164, 165, 166-67;
migrations, 5-6; myths, 17, 19-23, 33,
37, 38; nature of evidence regarding,
2, 11; priests, 29, 31, 34, 36, 37, 39-
43, 46-48, 164-65, 166-67; prophets,
31, 39; religious system (summarized),
164-67, (compared to that of Indo-
Iranians), 172-77; sacrifice, 17, 21,
31-33, 35, 36, 37, 38, 41, 44, 48, 164-
65, 166-67; warriors, 1-3, 14, 23, 24-
31, 34, 35, 36, 37-38, 41-43, 44-48,
163, 165-67
Nilsson, Martin Perssons, 122*n.*
Nocturnal rituals, 47

238